Multicultural Issues in Counseling

New Approaches to Diversity

• FOURTH EDITION •

edited by

Courtland C. Lee

AMERICAN COUNSELING
ASSOCIATION
5999 Stevenson Avenue
Alexandria, VA 22304
www.counseling.org

Multicultural Issues in Counseling
New Approaches to Diversity
FOURTH EDITION

10 9 8 7 6 5 4 3

American Counseling Association
5999 Stevenson Avenue • Alexandria, VA 22304

Director of Publications • Carolyn C. Baker

Production Manager • Bonny E. Gaston

Editorial Assistant • Catherine A. Brumley

Copy Editor • Beth Ciha

Cover and text design by Bonny E. Gaston.

Library of Congress Cataloging-in-Publication Data

Multicultural issues in counseling : new approaches to diversity / Courtland C. Lee, editor.
—4th ed.
    p. cm.
  Includes bibliographical references and index.
  ISBN 978-1-55620-313-8 (alk. paper)
  1. Cross-cultural counseling—United States.   I. Lee, Courtland C.
BF637.C6M84 2012
158.308—dc23   2012006474

Dedication

To the giants upon whose shoulders I stand!

Table of Contents

• Part I •
Introduction

• Part II •
Direction for Culturally Competent Counseling

• The Experience of Ethnic Groups of Color •

• Part III •

The Counselor as Human Being:
Professional and Personal Issues in Counseling Across Cultures

Acknowledgments

The fourth edition of this book, like the three that preceded it, owes its development to a number of people. As editor I would like to use this space to acknowledge their contributions to the project. I must start by thanking the contributors for the time and creative energy they put into preparing their chapters. As always, their scholarly efforts are intensely admired and greatly appreciated.

I am also deeply indebted to Ana Popovska and Marte Ostvik-DeWilde, who served as my editorial assistants in the development of this book. I am grateful to them for dealing effectively with all of the complex editing issues and administrivia associated with preparing the manuscript for this edition.

This book could not have been completed without the help, guidance, support, and incredible patience of Carolyn Baker, Director of Publications of the American Counseling Association. Her quiet oversight and ongoing encouragement were most welcome. Carolyn's belief in this project helped to keep me motivated and focused throughout the challenging editorial process.

Although he is not a person, a special note of thanks must also go to my black Labrador Retriever Snoopy, who lay at my feet during much of the editing process. Snoopy, you have become a scholar in your own right!

Finally, I acknowledge my wife Vivian. Thank you, Vivian, for your love, support, and understanding. You said it could be done, and you were right!

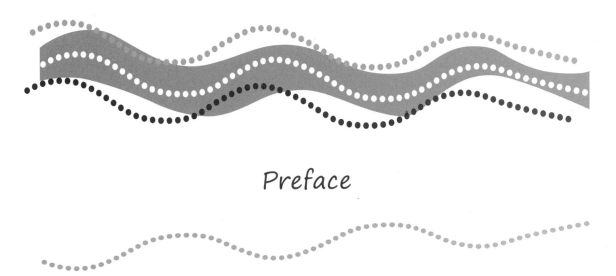

Preface

This book represents the fourth edition of *Multicultural Issues in Counseling: New Approaches to Diversity*. The three previous editions, with their focus on culturally competent counseling practice, have become important books in the counseling profession. They have provided professional counselors with strategies for culturally competent intervention with many client groups. In addition, the three previous editions have been widely adopted as textbooks in counselor training programs.

Developments in the discipline of multicultural counseling have made it necessary to consider publishing a new version of this book. It was decided that in order to stay relevant to counseling practice, the time had come to revisit the content of the book.

This edition attempts to build on the strengths of its three predecessors. It also represents an attempt to incorporate insights gained from listening to those who used one of the three previous books in their counseling studies or practice. Much like the third edition, this fourth edition seeks to broaden the scope of multicultural counseling theory and practice beyond the context of race/ethnicity into other important areas of cultural diversity. In addition to examining race/ethnicity, this edition considers the important issues of sexual orientation, disability, socioeconomic disadvantage, and the world of military service.

Like the previous editions, the purpose of this book is to present culturally competent intervention strategies for professional counselors working with, or preparing to work with, diverse client groups in a variety of settings. It provides practicing counselors and those preparing to enter the profession with direction for culturally competent counseling with clients from a number of diverse backgrounds.

Focus of the Book

This book deals with *multicultural counseling*, defined as the working alliance between counselor and client that takes the personal dynamics of these individuals into consideration alongside the dynamics of both of their cultures. The focus of the book is on providing a broader perspective on diversity as a way to offer direction for multicultural counseling. The book is devoted to multicultural counseling *practice* with selected diverse client groups. It is designed to help counselors apply their awareness of and knowledge about cultural diversity to the development of appropriate skills for use with specific client groups. The ideas presented here developed out of both the professional and personal experiences of the chapter authors, who are scholars from the specific cultural group in question or have intimate knowledge of a particular group. Although this book offers guidance in the practice of multicultural counseling, it is not intended to be a cookbook or a how-to manual. In addition, a concerted attempt has been made to explore the cultural dynamics of the selected groups in as nonstereotypical a fashion as possible. One pervasive theme throughout this book is that not all people of a particular group act or think in the same manner and that although cultural knowledge is important, it is critical to approach each client as a unique individual.

Overview of the Contents

This book is divided into three parts: "Introduction," "Direction for Culturally Competent Counseling," and "The Counselor as Human Being: Professional and Personal Issues in Counseling Across Cultures." The two chapters in "Introduction" lay a conceptual foundation for the rest of the book. After exploring the nature of counseling in a cross-cultural context, Courtland C. Lee and Denise Park discuss important concepts that provide a framework for multicultural counseling competency in Chapter 1, "A Conceptual Framework for Counseling Across Cultures." In Chapter 2, "The Cross-Cultural Encounter: Meeting the Challenge of Culturally Competent Counseling," Courtland C. Lee presents an analysis of encounters between counselors and clients from different cultural backgrounds. He next examines some important issues that should be considered in addressing the challenges of culturally competent counseling and then provides specific guidelines for enhancing the working alliance in a cross-cultural counseling encounter.

In the second part of the book, "Direction for Culturally Competent Counseling," approaches for counseling members of specific cultural groups are presented. This section of the book is composed of 15 chapters, each of which offers ideas and concepts for culturally competent counseling. These chapters include a review of the cultural dynamics of each group and their role in shaping mental health and the social issues and challenges that often affect development. The authors then introduce strategies for addressing these issues and challenges. These counseling practices evolve from an understanding of and appreciation for the unique history and cultural experiences of each group. The authors of these chapters provide the reader with case studies that underscore their ideas on culturally competent counseling.

The first section of Part II focuses on the experiences of ethnic groups of color in the United States. In Chapter 3, "The Spectrum of Counseling American Indians," Tarrell Awe Agahe Portman casts light through the spectrum of counseling on the cultural continuum found among American Indian peoples. After providing a historical overview and review of current population trends among the American Indian population, she provides counseling case studies that emphasize important aspects of American Indian culture. In Chapter 4, "Counseling People of the African Diaspora in the United States," Courtland C. Lee and Kimberly N. Frazier present an overview of the concept of Afrocentricity and its relationship to mental health for people of African descent. This is followed by a discussion of several important issues that must be considered in culturally competent counseling with people of the African diaspora. The authors present case studies of counseling practices with clients of African descent and offer guidelines for culturally competent counseling.

In Chapter 5, "Counseling Asian and Pacific Islander Americans," Song E. Lee and Albert Valencia introduce the majority and minority Asian American and Pacific Islander groups and provide some practical considerations for counseling these populations. Their goal is to ensure that counselors understand the diversity among Asian American and Pacific Islander groups in order to provide culturally competent services to this client group. In Chapter 6, "A Conceptual Approach to Counseling With Latina/o Culture in Mind," Carlos P. Hipolito-Delgado and Jessica M. Diaz highlight the heterogeneity of Latinas/os and provide a basic understanding of this ethnic community by discussing ethnic labels, presenting the demographic profile of Latinas/os, and discussing their experience in the United States. They also explore traditional cultural considerations and present some counseling considerations and interventions for use with this ethnic community. Saara Amri, Sylvia Nassar-McMillan, Sandra Amen-Bryan, and Mary M. Misenhimer explore the issues and challenges of counseling Arab Americans in Chapter 7, "Counseling Arab Americans." The authors of this chapter refer to individuals who trace their roots to those countries in the Middle East. They explore the rich diversity within this culture in terms of religion, family, gender, and sociopolitical history. They also consider some of the ways in which these background issues impact identity development and mental health. Several case studies that illustrate some of this information conclude the chapter.

The second section of Part II continues with an exploration of the experience of multiracial individuals. In Chapter 8, "Counseling the Multiracial Population," Kelley R. Kenney and Mark E. Kenney examine the counseling issues and concerns of multiracial individuals and families. They begin by defining who is included in this client group. The authors then discuss the issues and concerns of interracial couples and multiracial individuals. They present counseling case studies to examine these issues and concerns in greater detail.

The experience of gender and age is explored in the third section of Part II. In Chapter 9, "Issues in Counseling Men," Shawn L. Spurgeon explores the critical, cultural, and clinical issues currently affecting men. He examines theoretical approaches for counseling interventions with men and provides case studies to help the reader understand these approaches. Conversely, in Chapter 10, "Issues in Counseling Women," Kathy M. Evans explores these same issues for women and discusses strategies for counseling women, using case studies that highlight these interventions.

The experience of ageism is examined in Chapter 11, "Combating Ageism: Advocacy for Older Persons." Jane E. Myers and Laura R. Shannonhouse explore demographic changes in the United States with a focus on the aging of the population and within-group factors that predispose some older persons to significant personal and social risk. The traditional professional counseling response to the graying of America is then described. Ageism is then discussed in relation to its personal impact on older individuals. The chapter concludes with a consideration from both macro and micro perspectives of recommended strategies and actions for counselors and a case study that demonstrates the application of these suggestions with an older client.

The sexual minority experience in the United States makes up the fourth section of Part II. In Chapter 12, "Counseling Gay Men," A. Michael Hutchins explores issues associated with counseling this client group. He provides an overview of the dynamics of the cultural context of gay men. Then, through a series of case studies, Hutchins discusses key aspects of homosexual identity development. He focuses not only on the evolution of gay identity for men but the communities in which they live as well. In Chapter 13, "Counseling Lesbian, Bisexual, Queer, Questioning, and Transgender Women," Anneliese A. Singh and Kirstyn Yuk Sim Chun begin by introducing terminology important for counselors to know and use when working with lesbian, bisexual, queer, questioning, and transgender women. They also discuss common counseling concerns, helpful counseling interventions, typical counselor advocacy, and community resources for working with this client group.

The fifth section of Part II of this book considers the experience of people with disabilities. In Chapter 14, "Counseling Individuals With Physical, Cognitive, and Psychiatric Disabilities," Julie F. Smart begins by explaining the importance of including a chapter on disability in a multicultural counseling book. She continues by exploring the three broad categories and models of disability. The chapter concludes with guidelines for counselors working with people with disabilities and a case study.

The experience of deaf culture is explored in the sixth section of Part II. In Chapter 15, "Multicultural Deaf Children and Their Hearing Families: Working With a Constellation of Diversities," Cheryl L. Wu and Nancy C. Grant present important insights into deaf culture. This chapter gives an overview of this culture and then focuses on deaf children born into hearing families, with an emphasis on immigrants, families of color, and deaf children with disabilities. Wu and Grant introduce a social justice situation-framing approach to cultural encounters with culturally diverse deaf children and their families.

The seventh section of Part II considers the experience of socioeconomic disadvantage. In Chapter 16, "Counseling and the Culture of Economic Disadvantage," William Ming Liu and Sherry K. Watt discuss the need to be especially aware of how economic and financial concerns affect the lives of clients. Given the ubiquity of social class issues in U.S. culture, it is almost impossible to escape the salience of money and economics in people's lives. The authors present a rationale for why counselors need to address a client's economic and social class and then present a theory of social class and privilege that will allow counselors to work with clients. They use a case study to illustrate this theoretical approach.

The eighth and final section of Part II represents a unique aspect of this multicultural counseling book: it is an examination of the military experience. Major geopolitical events of the early 21st century (e.g., 9/11, the wars in Iraq and Afghanistan) have dramatically demonstrated that the realities of men and women in military service are vastly different from those of individuals in civilian life. These realities constitute a distinct culture, and the men and women in the service of their country face issues and challenges that are unique to this culture. In Chapter 17, "Counseling Military Clients: Multicultural Competence, Challenges, and Opportunities," Marvin Westwood, David Kuhl, and Duncan Shields describe the prevailing U.S. military culture and the obstacles to help seeking based on the adherence to this culture. The authors introduce a model for overcoming these challenges and discuss its therapeutic implications for working with military clients. They also illustrate how to integrate a multicultural competence approach with military clients in both individual and group counseling contexts.

The third and final part of this book considers aspects of the culturally competent counselor as a professional and, more important, as a human being. In Chapter 18, "Ethical Issues in Multicultural Counseling," Beth A. Durodoye frames important ethical issues and concepts in a multicultural context and examines strategies relevant to ethical practice with culturally diverse client populations.

Courtland C. Lee concludes the book with Chapter 19, "Global Literacy: The Foundation of Culturally Competent Counseling." He introduces the concept of *global literacy,* which comprises the basic information that a person needs to know in order to successfully navigate life in the technologically sophisticated, globally interconnected world of the 21st century. Lee explores the role of global literacy as a foundational aspect of not only developing multicultural counseling competency but promoting a way of life consistent with today's diverse realities.

About the Editor

Courtland C. Lee received his PhD from Michigan State University. He is a professor of counselor education at the University of Maryland, College Park. He is the author, editor, or coeditor of five books on multicultural counseling and two books on counseling and social justice. He is also the author of three books on counseling African American men. In addition, he has published numerous book chapters and articles on counseling across cultures. Dr. Lee is the former editor of the *Journal of Multicultural Counseling and Development* and the *Journal of African American Men.* He has also served on the editorial board of the *International Journal for the Advancement of Counselling* and was a senior associate editor of the *Journal of Counseling & Development.* Dr. Lee is the president of the International Association for Counselling. He is also a Fellow and past-president of the American Counseling Association and a past-president of the Association for Multicultural Counseling and Development. He is also a Fellow of the British Association for Counselling and Psychotherapy, the only American to receive this honor.

About the Contributors

Sandra Amen-Bryan, MA, has a master's in clinical psychology and has worked in the field of mental health for more than 20 years. One of her specialty areas is addressing family and marital issues through a multicultural lens. She recently completed a postgraduate certificate in applied behavior analysis and has turned her focus to the educational needs of children with autism and their families.

Saara Amri is a third-year doctoral student studying counselor education at George Mason University. Ms. Amri is a Muslim Arab American woman. She has worked with the immigrant population, and specifically the Muslim immigrant population, for more than 10 years. She is bilingual in Arabic and English and in her capacity as a mental health therapist currently works primarily with Arabic-speaking survivors of torture and severe trauma.

Kirstyn Yuk Sim Chun, PsyD, received her doctorate in clinical psychology from Indiana University of Pennsylvania in 2003. She is an associate professor and licensed clinical psychologist at Counseling and Psychological Services at California State University, Long Beach (CSULB), where she supervises within the American Psychological Association (APA)–accredited predoctoral internship training program. At CSULB, she is chair of the Lesbian, Gay, Bisexual, and Transgender (LGBT) Task Force and past-chair of the President's Commission on the Status of Women. Dr. Chun served as cochair of the Committee on Racial and Ethnic Diversity of the APA Division 44 Society for the Psychological Study of LGBT Issues, during which time the committee received the President's Award from the Asian American Psychological Association. She is the 2013 Division 44 representative to the National Multicultural Conference and Summit. She publishes and presents on intersections of racial, sexual, and other marginalized identities. Areas of clinical, scholarly, and advocacy interest include LGBT-affirmative counseling, bisexuality, multicultural and social justice issues, women's issues, clinical supervision and training, group therapy, and outreach and consultation.

Jessica M. Diaz is a doctoral candidate in the counselor education program at the University of Maryland studying in the specialty area of multicultural counseling. She has presented on the topic of multicultural counseling at conferences at the national and state levels. She has coauthored chapters in related areas and has tailored her doctoral study to focus on this particular area of study. She has taught courses as an adjunct faculty member at The Johns Hopkins University and Loyola College in multicultural counseling, ethics, human development, helping skills, and counseling theories. Ms. Diaz is involved in a number of research projects focused on urban school education, mentorship, and college going. She has served as president of the Alpha Delta chapter of Chi Sigma Iota and as the Student Representative for the American Counseling Association (ACA) Governing Council and served for 2 years on the ACA Blue Ribbon Panel.

Beth A. Durodoye, EdD, earned her doctorate from the University of Virginia. She is professor and chair of the Department of Leadership, Technology & Human Development at Georgia Southern University. Formerly at the University of Texas at San Antonio where this chapter was written, Dr. Durodoye's research and writing interests speak to the mental health needs of diverse populations in the United States and abroad. Multicultural, social justice, and advocacy themes are reflected in her numerous authored and coauthored publications. She is the former associate editor of *Counseling and Values* journal and currently serves on the editorial board of the *Journal of Counseling & Development.* Dr. Durodoye is a past-president of the Texas Association for Multicultural Counseling and Development.

Kathy M. Evans, PhD, is an associate professor at the University of South Carolina and program coordinator for the Counselor Education program. Dr. Evans's research interests and publications focus on multicultural, career, and feminist issues. She has either authored or edited numerous book chapters and books on multicultural career development, but her most recent publication is a book coauthored with her colleagues from graduate school titled *Introduction to Feminist Therapy: Strategies for Personal and Social Change.* Dr. Evans has been president of the Southern Association for Counselor Education and Supervision and secretary of Chi Sigma Iota Honor Society International. She is currently completing her second term on the editorial board for the *Journal of Counseling & Development* and is cochair of the Association for Counselor Education and Supervision/National Career Development Association Joint Commission for the Preparation of Career Counselors.

Kimberly N. Frazier, PhD, received her doctorate in counselor education from the University of New Orleans. She is a licensed professional counselor, a licensed marriage and family therapist, and a nationally certified counselor. She is an assistant professor of counselor education at Clemson University. Dr. Frazier has published articles on culture-centered counseling with pediatric populations and families, the use of culturally based trauma and crisis counseling with children and families. She has served on the editorial board of the *Journal of Multicultural Counseling and Development* and currently serves as the chair of the Association for Multicultural Counseling and Development Mentoring Program and the Association for Multicultural Counseling and Development Mentoring Program Research Symposium.

Nancy C. Grant founded the Hearing Impaired Program (HIP) Big Brothers/Big Sisters Deaf/Hard of Hearing Program, which grew into the HIP Deaf & Hard of Hearing Youth Project. This program provides multiple services for diverse and multiply disabled San Francisco Bay Area inner-city children, youth, young adults, their families, and communities. She serves as adjunct faculty at Gallaudet University's Department of Counseling and coordinates and teaches in San Francisco State University's Rehabilitation Counseling certificate program focusing on deaf, hard of hearing, and deafened consumers. Ms. Grant is hearing and uses American Sign Language.

Carlos P. Hipolito-Delgado, PhD, received his doctorate in counselor education from the University of Maryland, College Park. He is assistant professor and program coordinator in school counseling at California State University, Long Beach. His research interests include ethnic identity development in Chicana/o and Latina/o students, internalized racism in communities of color, and training to improve multicultural competence. Dr. Hipolito-Delgado is coeditor of a book on multicultural counseling. He has also authored or coauthored articles and book chapters on cultural identity development, internalized racism, empowerment theory in school counseling, and social justice in counseling. Dr. Hipolito-Delgado has presented at numerous conferences nationally and internationally. He currently serves as treasurer for Counselors for Social Justice and as an ad hoc reviewer for the *Journal of Counseling & Development.* He has also served as conference committee chair for the Association for Multicultural Counseling and Development.

A. Michael Hutchins, PhD, received his doctorate in counseling from the University of Idaho. He is a licensed professional counselor in private practice in Tucson, Arizona, and has been an adjunct faculty member in the Department of Educational Psychology at the University of Arizona. He works extensively with men who have histories of sexual abuse and trauma and with adolescent and adult men who are in the process of integrating cultural and sexual identities. He has conducted experiential group workshops nationally and internationally exploring the impact of violence on individuals and communities. He is a past-president of the Association for Specialists in Group Work and of Counselors for Social Justice and is a past-chair of the Association for Lesbian, Gay, Bisexual and Transgender Issues in Counseling. He currently serves on the editorial boards of the *Journal of LGBT Issues in Counseling* and the *Journal for Social Action in Counseling and Psychology.* He has been a member of the City of Tucson Gay, Lesbian, Bisexual and Transgender Commission, on which he chaired the Social Services Committee. He has written in the areas of cross-cultural and experiential group work, counseling and social justice advocacy, trauma, and sexual identity development. Michael is an avid bicyclist.

Kelley R. Kenney, EdD, received her doctorate in counselor education and supervision from George Washington University in Washington, DC. She is a professor in the Department of Counseling and Human Services at Kutztown University in Kutztown, Pennsylvania, and serves as the program coordinator for the Student Affairs in Higher Education (Administration and College Counseling) tracks. Dr. Kenney is a coauthor of the book *Counseling Multiracial Families* and the counseling training videotape *Counseling the Multiracial Population: Couples, Individuals, and Families.* She has authored and coauthored numerous articles and book chapters on counseling the multiracial population and has served as a reviewer for several other books, book chapters, and videos on the multiracial population and other diverse populations. Currently she serves on the editorial board of the *Journal of LGBT Issues in Counseling.* Dr. Kenney is a past-president of the Pennsylvania Counselor Educators and Supervisors Association and a past-chair of the North Atlantic Region of the American Counseling Association. She is cochair of the Multiracial/Multiethnic Counseling Concerns Interest Network of the American Counseling Association and is serving a second term on the Governing Council of the American Counseling Association.

Mark E. Kenney, MEd, received his master's in counseling in higher education from Kutztown University and is a licensed professional counselor. He is an adjunct professor at Chestnut Hill College/DeSales campus in the Department of Counseling Psychology and Human Services in Center Valley, Pennsylvania, and at Albright College Department of Interdisciplinary Studies in Reading, Pennsylvania. He is founder/director of Rainbow Support Network Diversity Training and Consulting of Reading, Pennsylvania. He is a coauthor of the book *Counseling Multiracial Families* and the counseling training videotape *Counseling the Multiracial Population: Couples, Individuals, and Families.* He is also coauthor of several book chapters and other publications on counseling the multiracial population. Mr. Kenney is a past-president of the Pennsylvania Counseling Association and has also served as the North Atlantic Region representative for the Association for Multicultural Counseling and Development. He is currently cochair of the Multiracial/Multiethnic Counseling Concerns Interest Network of the American Counseling Association.

David Kuhl, MD, MHSC, PhD, is associate professor in the Department of Family Practice, Faculty of Medicine, University of British Columbia, and the director of the Centre for Practitioner Renewal, a joint venture between Providence Health Care and the University of British Columbia. For the past several years, Dr. Kuhl has also been involved in developing the Veterans Transition Program, a group-based program designed to assist former members of the Canadian Military in their transition to life as civilians. Dr. Kuhl graduated with a master's in health sciences (community health and epidemiology) from the University of Toronto in 1981 and received his medical degree from McMaster University in 1985. In 1996 he became a Soros Faculty Scholar, Project on Death in America. This award allowed him to conduct a qualitative study, Exploring Spiritual and Psychological Issues at the End of Life. The study served as the basis for his doctoral dissertation as well as for two books, titled *What Dying People Want: Practical Wisdom for the End-of-Life* and *Facing Death, Embracing Life: Understanding What Dying People Want.* Through his work at the Centre for Practitioner Renewal, Dr. Kuhl is working to combine his interests in medicine and psychology to develop a program of service, education, and research that sustains health care providers in the workplace.

Song E. Lee, PhD, is an assistant professor in counselor education at California State University, Fresno. She received her MS in counseling with a concentration in marriage and family therapy and the Pupil Personnel Services Credential in School Counseling from California State University, Fresno. Dr. Lee earned her PhD in counselor education from North Carolina State University. Dr. Lee's clinical experiences include providing counseling services to diverse groups of children, families, and couples. She has presented at international, national, state, and regional conferences on topics relating to identity development, the Hmong population, multicultural counseling issues, and culturally and linguistically appropriate interventions. Dr. Lee has been involved with the community by advising several student organizations, providing pro bono counseling services to non-English-speaking Hmong clients, cohosting a radio show for the elderly Hmong population, and conducting research on the needs and issues of Hmong elders. Her publications include a cowritten book chapter on counseling diverse clients and an article on Hmong women. She is a recipient of the Courtland C. Lee Multicultural Excellence Scholarship Award.

William Ming Liu, PhD, is a professor and program coordinator of counseling psychology at the University of Iowa. He received his doctorate in counseling psychology from the University of Maryland in 2000. His research interests are in social class and classism, men and masculinity, and multicultural competencies. He has published in journals such as the *Journal of Counseling Psychology, Cultural Diversity and Ethnic Minority Psychology,* and *Psychology of Men and Masculinity.* In recent reviews, he was identified as one of the most frequent producers of research on the psychology of men and masculinity and multicultural competency. He received the Emerging Leader award from the Committee on Socioeconomic Status of the American Psychological Association (APA), the Emerging Young Professional Award (Division 45, APA), and the Researcher of the Year Award (Division 51, APA). He is the associate editor of *Psychology of Men and Masculinity* and has served on the editorial boards of *The Counseling Psychologist, Cultural Diversity and Ethnic Minority Psychology,* the *Journal of Multicultural Counseling and Development,* the *Journal of Counseling Psychology,* and the *Clinician's Research Digest.* He is an editor of the *Handbook of Multicultural Competencies in Counseling and Psychology* (2003, Sage); an editor of *Culturally Responsive Counseling With Asian American Men* (2010, Routledge); author of *Social Class and Classism in the Helping Professions: Research, Theory, and Practice* (2011, Sage); and editor of the forthcoming *Handbook of Social Class in Counseling* (Oxford University Press). He is the past–program chair for the National Multicultural Summit and Conference (2007). He is a licensed psychologist in Iowa, and his present clinical work is with clients at a transitional shelter, where he coordinates a counseling practicum and life skills and self-development curriculum for shelter residents and clients.

Mary M. Misenhimer is currently working on her PhD at North Carolina State University. She has a wide range of clinical experience, including counseling children and adolescents, eating disorders, substance abuse, and family therapy. She currently works at a treatment facility in Durham, North Carolina. Mary is a very active member of Chi Sigma Iota and has served as treasurer, president, and past-president of the Nu Sigma Chi chapter. She is a member of the American Counseling Association and a board member of the Chi Sigma Iota–Task Force Committee and the Association for Creativity in Counseling. Mary's research interests include religious, gender, and ethnic identity development; eating disorders; substance abuse; and career selection and life satisfaction.

Jane E. Myers, PhD, LPC, NCC, is a professor of counselor education at the University of North Carolina at Greensboro, a National Certified Counselor, a National Certified Gerontological Counselor, and a Licensed Professional Counselor. She is a Fellow of the American Counseling Association and a Charter Fellow of the Chi Sigma Iota Academy of Leaders for Excellence. She is also a past-president of the American Counseling Association and two of its divisions, the Association for Assessment in Counseling and the Association for Adult Development and Aging, of which she was founding president. Dr. Myers also served as chair of the Council for Accreditation of Counseling and Related Educational Programs and was the second president of Chi Sigma Iota. In 2003 she was selected for inclusion in *Leaders and Legacies in Counseling,* a book that chronicles the contributions of 25 individuals selected as among the most significant leaders in the counseling profession over the past century. Dr. Myers developed a model and curriculum resources for the infusion of gerontological counseling into counselor education, coauthored the national competencies for training gerontological counselors, and coproduced eight training videotapes in gerontological counseling. She has written and edited numerous publications, including 16 books and monographs and more than 125 refereed journal articles, and was noted twice (most recently in 2010) as being in the top 1% of contributors to the *Journal of Counseling & Development,* the flagship journal of the American Counseling Association. Her books include *Adult Children and Aging Parents; Empowerment for Later Life;* the coauthored *Handbook of Counseling;* and *Developmental Counseling and Therapy: Promoting Wellness Over the Lifespan,* coauthored with Allen and Mary Ivey and Tom Sweeney. She is coauthor with Dr. Sweeney of one theoretical and two evidence-based models of wellness and assessment instruments based on these models.

Sylvia Nassar-McMillan, PhD, is a professor and program coordinator of counselor education at North Carolina State University. She earned her PhD in counseling and counselor education from the University of North Carolina at Greensboro in 1994. She has served in a variety of clinical mental health, school, and college settings over the past 25 years. Her scholarship spans multicultural, gender, and career development issues, with a special focus on Arab American acculturation and ethnic identity development, and she has published more than 50 books, refereed articles, and other instructional materials. She currently serves as a member of the Census Information Center advisory board to the Arab American Institute and as senior associate editor for the *Journal of Counseling & Development.* She has served as a board member for the National Board for Certified Counselors and the North Carolina Board of Licensed Professional Counselors. Her current projects include a National Science Foundation project examining stereotypes in science and engineering career fields, a National Aeronautics and Space Administration/National Institute on Aging project evaluating educational science and engineering curriculum tools, and a clinical text on the biopsychosocial health care of Arab Americans.

Denise Park is a doctoral student in the Counselor Education Program at the University of Maryland, College Park. She received her MS in counseling from Johns Hopkins University. Ms. Park is a professional school counselor with an interest in multicultural issues and diversity and the empowerment of youth. She has conducted a number of professional presentations on topics such as data-driven counseling, the American School Counselor Association National Model, and multicultural counseling competency.

Tarrell Awe Agahe Portman, PhD, is of White River Cherokee descent and received her doctorate from the University of Arkansas, Fayetteville. She is an associate professor in counselor education and supervision at the University of Iowa. Her dissertation, *Differences Between Sex Role Attributes, Worldview and Locus of Control Among American Indian Women of Oklahoma,* is housed in the Smithsonian Institution's National Museum of the American Indian. She is the author of seven articles on Native American counseling issues. She has published 3 books and 61 articles and book chapters and has conducted more than 130 national and international presentations. Dr. Portman is the vice-president for Native American concerns of the Association for Multicultural Counseling and Development. She has served as the chair of the University of Iowa Native American Faculty and Staff council. She is currently the director of the Office of Graduate Ethnic Inclusion in the Graduate College at the University of Iowa.

Laura R. Shannonhouse is a doctoral student at the University of North Carolina at Greensboro and a National Certified Counselor specializing in crisis intervention and disaster response. She has participated in culture-centered clinical outreach efforts within the United States (post–Hurricane Katrina New Orleans and post-earthquake with Haitian communities in Florida), Southern Africa and Botswana (illness-related trauma), and Mexico (prolonged grief work). She completed a 2-year Gestalt Training program and volunteered at the Alachua County Crisis Center in Gainesville, Florida, both training and supervising other volunteers. Her experiences with disaster response naturally lend themselves to social justice concerns. Her interest and passion for advocacy and aging developed through her work with marginalized peoples and her desire to make a difference.

Duncan Shields, MA, is a counselor in private practice in British Columbia (BC), Canada, who specializes in the treatment of men with mood and anxiety disorders. He is a co-facilitator of the University of British Columbia/Legion Veterans Transition Program, which assists soldiers dealing with traumatic experiences. He serves as president of the BC Association of Clinical Counsellors and as treasurer for the BC Alliance on Mental Health/Illness and Addictions, a coalition of professional, nonprofit, police and criminal justice organizations working to influence public policy and increase system access and accountability. He also sits on the Leadership Council of the Community Action Initiative, which stewards a community development fund, and is a member of the BC Task Group on Counsellor Regulation, which is working to establish a new professional

College of Counselling Therapists in BC. Mr. Shields has received several awards in recognition of his contribution to the profession from his professional association.

Anneliese A. Singh, PhD, LPC, NCC, is an assistant professor in the Department of Counseling and Human Development Services at the University of Georgia. She received her doctorate in counseling psychology from Georgia State University in 2007. Her clinical, research, and advocacy interests include LGBTQ youth, Asian American/Pacific Islander counseling and psychology, multicultural counseling and social justice training, qualitative methodology with historically marginalized groups (e.g., people of color, LGBTQ individuals, immigrants), feminist theory and practice, and empowerment interventions with survivors of trauma. Dr. Singh has been the president of the Association for Lesbian, Gay, Bisexual and Transgender Issues in Counseling. She is the recipient of the 2007 Ramesh and Vijaya Bakshi Community Change Award and the 2008 O'Hana Award from Counselors for Social Justice for her organizing work to end child sexual abuse in South Asian communities and to increase visibility of South Asian LGBTQ people. She is also a recipient of the Courtland C. Lee Multicultural Excellence Scholarship Award.

Julie F. Smart, PhD, CRC, LPC, NCC, CCFC, ABDA, ABDA, LVRC, is professor and director of the Rehabilitation Counseling Program at Utah State University. She was awarded a postdoctoral research fellowship from the National Institute on Disability and Rehabilitation Research. She was cited as the most prolific author on multicultural issues in rehabilitation by the *Journal of Applied Rehabilitation Counseling.* Dr. Smart is the author of a widely used textbook, *Disability, Society, and the Individual* (2nd ed.), and her second book, *Disability Across the Developmental Lifespan,* published by Springer in 2011. She is the author of more than 11 chapters in textbooks and the author or coauthor of more than 40 articles in professional journals of general counseling and rehabilitation counseling. Dr. Smart translated into Spanish and field tested two rehabilitation instruments, the Acceptance of Disability Scale and the Client Satisfaction With Rehabilitation Services Scale. Her research interests include models of disability, Latino Americans with disabilities, and adjustment to disability.

Shawn L. Spurgeon, PhD, received his doctorate from the University of North Carolina at Greensboro. He is an assistant professor of counselor education at the University of Tennessee at Knoxville. He has published articles on counseling African American men and has presented on the subject at several national and regional conferences. Dr. Spurgeon serves on the editorial board of the *Journal of Counseling Research and Practice* and the *Journal of the Professional Counselor.* Dr. Spurgeon is a past-cochair of the American Counseling Association Ethics Committee and currently serves as treasurer of Chi Sigma Iota International. He is the first recipient of the Courtland C. Lee Multicultural Excellence Scholarship Award.

Albert Valencia, PhD, was born in South Central Los Angeles, California; received his doctorate in counseling psychology from the University of the Pacific; and is professor and chair of the Department of Counseling, Special Education, and Rehabilitation at California State University, Fresno. He received a master's degree in counselor education from San Jose State University. His clinical experience includes 18 years of private and public practice providing counseling services to diverse groups of children, families, and couples. He served on the editorial board of the *Journal of the Association of Mexican American Educators* and completed a term of service as division representative to the American Psychological Association (APA) Council of Representatives. He is nominated as a Fellow of The Society for the Study of Peace, Conflict, and Violence: Peace

Psychology Division 48 of APA, and served as board president of the K–12 Gilroy Unified School District. He is a published author with 30 years of teaching experience. He consults in mediation, mentoring, domestic violence, immigration, multicultural issues in student success development, and multicultural issues in counseling.

Sherry K. Watt, PhD, is an associate professor in the Higher Education and Student Affairs program at the University of Iowa. She earned a bachelor's degree in communication studies from the University of North Carolina at Greensboro and master's and doctoral degrees in counselor education with an emphasis in student affairs from North Carolina State University. In addition to her academic degrees she holds a counseling license in the state of North Carolina. Prior to becoming a faculty member, she worked as a residence life director and a career counselor at the University of North Carolina at Greensboro, North Carolina State University, and Shaw University. Her research examines participant reactions to difficult dialogues on race, sexual orientation, and disability. Dr. Watt applies her expertise as a researcher and a facilitator in the area of designing and leading educational experiences for educators who facilitate difficult dialogues intended to eradicate social oppression.

Marvin Westwood, PhD, is a professor in the Counselling Psychology Program at the University of British Columbia (UBC) and an associate member of UBC Faculty of Medicine. Prior to coming to UBC, he held a faculty position in counseling psychology at McGill University. His teaching and research areas currently focus on counseling men, group counseling, trauma repair, and therapeutic applications of the guided autobiographical life review method to the counseling process. His most recent work includes the development and evaluation of a group-based approach to trauma repair, which is UBC's Veterans Transition Program. In addition, he has developed several professional development programs for a wide range of groups (counselors/psychologists, nurses, human resources personnel, physicians, military, corrections workers, clergy, etc.) using guided autobiography and group-based therapeutic enactment methods. His research and teaching has been included in many invited presentations at numerous national and international conferences (U.K. Malta, Argentina, Chile, Israel, the United States, Australia, and Indonesia). His research has been supported by grants from a number of different sources, including Humanities and Social Sciences and the Social Sciences and Humanities Research Council of Canada.

Cheryl L. Wu, PhD, is a first-generation American-born Chinese woman with an MA in mental health counseling from Gallaudet University and a doctorate in clinical psychology with a multicultural emphasis from the California School for Professional Psychology. She cochaired the first national Asian Deaf Conference (1994) and taught at the Taiwan School for the Deaf for several years. She cofounded Cultural Intersections in Oakland, California. She serves as an associate professor in the Department of Counseling at Gallaudet University. A licensed clinical psychologist, she has provided mental health, education, and community-based services to multicultural deaf and hard of hearing children, youth, and their families for more than 26 years. Dr. Wu is hard of hearing and is fluent in Mandarin, Taiwan Sign Language, as well as English and American Sign Language.

Part
1

Introduction

A Conceptual Framework for Counseling Across Cultures

Courtland C. Lee and Denise Park

"What is multicultural counseling?"
"How is it different from any other form of counseling?"

• • •

"Do I really need to view clients of color as being different from White clients?"
"Shouldn't race or ethnic background be unimportant in working with people?"

• • •

"Can a counselor from one culture really counsel a person who is from another cultural background?"

• • •

"Why all the fuss about culture? Isn't counseling the same for everybody?"

• • •

Questions such as these are often asked by graduate students as they enter their first class session in a multicultural counseling course. They illustrate the confusion and skepticism students often experience as they are confronted with having to complete this program requirement. Such confusion and skepticism often stem from students' naiveté concerning the importance of issues of cultural diversity or their resistance to having to deal with issues of human difference that are often uncomfortable to confront either individually or in group interactions.

Of all the issues facing contemporary professional counselors, addressing the mental health and educational needs of the growing number of clients from culturally diverse backgrounds is perhaps the most challenging. Counseling theory and practice has been greatly impacted by changing demographics and social dynamics that characterize the 21st century. For example, data from the 2010 Census underscore the nation's changing racial and ethnic diversity. A review of racial and ethnic group distributions nationally shows that although the non-Hispanic White population is still numerically and proportionally the largest major racial and ethnic group in the United States, it is also growing at the slowest rate. In contrast, the Hispanic and Asian populations continue to grow, in part because of relatively higher levels of immigration (Humes, Jones, & Ramirez, 2011).

The 2000 Census marked the first time people could describe themselves by selecting more than one racial category (Root & Kelley, 2003). According to 2010 census data, 9 million people—or 2.9% of the population—chose more than one race on the census form, a change of about 32% since 2000 (Humes et al., 2011).

Although changes are occurring in the racial/ethnic makeup of the country, it is important to note that other changes are contributing to a new awareness of cultural diversity. Data indicate that groups of people long marginalized or disenfranchised along dimensions other than race or ethnicity are now being recognized. For example, an estimated 3.5% of adults in the United States identify as lesbian, gay, or bisexual, and an estimated 0.3% of adults are transgender. This implies that there are approximately 9 million lesbian, gay, bisexual, or transgender Americans, a figure roughly equivalent to the population of New Jersey (Gates, 2011).

In addition, individuals with disabilities make up a notable portion of the U.S. population. According to the 2010 Census, 36 million people have a disability (U.S. Census Bureau, 2010). It is important to note that large numbers of individuals experience deafness. Although this condition is often looked at as a disability, advocates strongly assert that deafness comprises a distinct cultural reality (Christensen, 2000; Ladd, 2003).

Although the United States continues to be the most affluent country in human history, large numbers of individuals still experience socioeconomic disadvantage, and a culture of poverty has long been recognized (Lewis, 1971; Valentine, 1968). Underscoring this notion of poverty as culture are census data that indicate that the official poverty rate in 2010 was 15.1%—up from 14.3% in 2009. This was the third consecutive annual increase in the poverty rate. Since 2007, the poverty rate has increased by 2.6 percentage points, from 12.5% to 15.1%. In 2010, 46.2 million people lived in poverty, up from 43.6 million in 2009—the fourth consecutive annual increase in the number of people living in poverty (DeNavas-Walt, Proctor, & Smith, 2011).

As greater awareness has grown of marginalized or oppressed groups and these groups have made significant strides toward social inclusion, other social movements have changed the fabric of American life. For instance, in the past several decades there have been significant changes in the roles of men and women (Collins, 2009; Freedman, 2003; Pease & Pringle, 2001; Rabinowitz & Cochran, 1994). In addition, as large segments of the population age, the needs and challenges of older Americans are becoming more apparent (Rowe & Kahn, 1997; Schulz & Heckhausen, 1996).

Finally, it has been reported that as of March 2011 there were 1,130,135 men and women serving in the U.S. armed forces (U.S. Department of Defense, 2011). Major geopolitical events of the first decade of the 21st century (e.g., 9/11, the wars in Iraq and Afghanistan) have brought about a new awareness of military life. It has been graphically demonstrated that the realities of men and women in military service are vastly different from those of individuals in civilian life. These realities constitute a distinct culture, and men and women in the service of their country face issues and challenges that are unique to this culture.

In concrete terms, data and issues such as these mean that, perhaps as never before, the United States has become a social arena in which individuals who represent truly diverse behavioral styles, attitudinal orientations, and value systems interact on a daily basis. Cultural pluralism, therefore, has become widely recognized as a major factor deserving of increased understanding on the part of individuals in all professions. Within this context, professional counselors must provide services that help people to solve problems or make decisions in the midst of such sweeping demographic and sociological change.

The past several decades have seen a growing realization that counseling services often do not have broad applicability across the range of cultural backgrounds represented by clients (Katz, 1985; Pedersen, Lonner, & Draguns, 1976; Sue, 1977, 1992; Vontress, 1969, 1976). With this awareness has come frustration that when counselors attempt to promote human development, the values inherent in counseling and those of culturally diverse clients often come into conflict in the helping process. In order to resolve this conflict and the frustration that often accompanies it, counselors must effectively address cultural differences in the provision of counseling services. It is evident that professional counselors need a conceptual framework from which to operate to ensure that clients from culturally diverse backgrounds have access to competent services.

This chapter provides such a conceptual framework. It explores the acquisition of multicultural counseling competence from a developmental perspective. First the nature of multicultural counseling is examined. Next a conceptual framework is presented that examines the foundational aspects as well as the cultural aspects that must form the basis of multicultural counseling competency.

The Nature of Multicultural Counseling

Multicultural counseling can be operationally defined as the working alliance between counselor and client that takes the personal dynamics of the counselor and client into consideration alongside the dynamics of the cultures of both of these individuals. Multicultural counseling, therefore, takes into consideration the cultural backgrounds and individual experiences of diverse clients and how their psychosocial needs might be identified and met through counseling (Lee, 2006; Sue & Sue, 2012).

The concept of multicultural counseling has become the impetus for the development of a generic theory of multiculturalism that has become recognized as the fourth theoretical force in the profession (Pedersen, 1991a). As such, multicultural theory joins the other three major traditions—psychodynamic theory, cognitive behavior theory, and existential–humanistic theory—as a primary explanation of human development. Basic to the theory of multiculturalism is the notion that both client and counselor bring to the therapeutic dyad a variety of cultural variables related to things such as age, gender, sexual orientation, education, disability, religion, ethnic background, and socioeconomic status. In essence, cultural diversity is a characteristic of all counseling relationships; therefore, all counseling is multicultural in nature (Pedersen, 1991b).

This evolution of multicultural counseling into a theoretical force implies some important principles for theory and practice. According to the definition discussed previously, there are six basic principles of multicultural counseling:

1. *Culture* refers to any group of people who identify or associate with one another on the basis of some common purpose, need, or similarity of background.
2. Cultural differences are real, and they influence all human interactions.
3. All counseling is cross-cultural in nature.
4. Multicultural counseling places an emphasis on human diversity in all its many forms.

5. Culturally competent counselors develop the awareness, knowledge, and skills to intervene effectively in the lives of people from culturally diverse backgrounds.
6. Culturally competent counselors are globally literate human beings.

Reflecting on the definition and principles of multicultural counseling, it is important to note that the American Counseling Association (ACA) has adopted the following definition of counseling: "Counseling is a professional relationship that empowers diverse individuals, families, and groups to accomplish mental health, wellness, education, and career goals" (ACA, 2010). This definition makes explicit the idea that counselors will encounter individuals from diverse cultural backgrounds in helping relationships. Implicit in this idea is the importance of counselors having the awareness, knowledge, and skill to help empower individuals, families, and groups in ways that are sensitive to and inclusive of cultural realities.

Within this context, ACA has adopted a set of competencies that forms the context for best practice when counseling across cultures (Arredondo et al., 1996; Sue, Arredondo, & McDavis, 1992). These competencies describe the awareness level, knowledge base, and skill set that enable a counselor to provide culturally responsive service to clients. The following section describes a conceptual framework for the development of the competencies deemed necessary for counseling across cultures.

The Conceptual Framework

The conceptual framework described here focuses on the development of culturally competent counselors who practice in a diverse society. The framework is composed of eight themes organized into three areas: the foundational dimension, the multicultural dimension, and multicultural counseling competency. The conceptual framework appears in Figure 1.1.

Foundational Dimension

The foundational dimension consists of four themes. Although these themes are the foundation of multicultural counseling competency, they can also be considered the essence of competent counseling in general.

Self-Awareness

The basis for culturally competent counseling practice is counselor self-awareness. It is important that counselors fully experience themselves as cultural beings. An individual who expects to work cross-culturally must first be anchored in his or her own cultural realities. This process should start with explorations of how one's own cultural background has influenced one's psychosocial development. It is critical that a person consider the role that cultural heritage and customs play in shaping his or her personality characteristics. It is also crucial that a person assess his or her own process of cultural identity development (Lee & Na, 2011). The significant questions that one must ask in this regard are "How do I experience myself as a member of Cultural Group X?" "How do I experience other members of Cultural Group X?" and "How do I experience people of other cultural backgrounds?"

As part of this self-exploration process, it is also important that a counselor evaluate the influences that have shaped the development of his or her attitudes and beliefs about people from different cultural backgrounds. It is important to evaluate the explicit, as well as the often subtle, messages one has received throughout one's life about people who are culturally different. A counselor must evaluate how his or her personal attitudes and beliefs about people from different cultural groups may facilitate or hamper effective counseling.

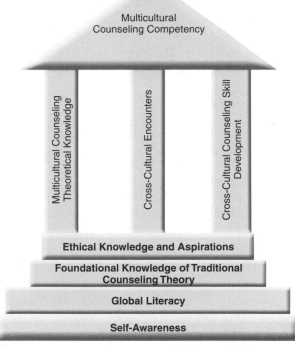

Figure 1.1 • A Conceptual Framework for Counseling Across Cultures

Attaining multicultural competency begins with an exploration of personal issues and questions, no matter how uncomfortable, in an attempt to discern how one's own cultural heritage, values, and biases might impact on the counseling process. Self-exploration leads to self-awareness, which is crucial in developing a set of personal attitudes and beliefs to guide culturally competent counseling practice. Culturally competent counselors are sensitive to cultural group differences because they are aware of their own identities as cultural beings.

Global Literacy
Global literacy refers to the knowledge base that every culturally competent individual should possess in today's interconnected world. It is a reflection of one's exposure to and knowledge of the contemporary world. Global literacy is the breadth of information that extends over the major domains of human diversity. In modern society, a globally literate person has a knowledge of ethnic variations in history, has travel experience, and is knowledgeable about current world events. The concept of global literacy, which is a key foundational aspect of multicultural competency, is explored in further detail in Chapter 19.

Foundational Knowledge of Traditional Counseling Theory
Multicultural counseling competency must also rest on an understanding of traditional counseling theory. Although the Eurocentric nature of traditional counseling theories has been criticized (Sue, Ivey, & Pedersen, 1996), each theory has important aspects that contribute to best practice in counseling. Therefore, it is important that the foundation of counseling practice laid down by pioneering thinkers and practitioners such as Freud, Adler, Rogers, Perls, and the behaviorists is incorporated into culturally diverse ways of thinking and approaches to helping.

Ethical Knowledge and Aspirations
Another crucial foundational aspect of multicultural counseling competency is knowledge of ethical standards. Indeed, the integrity of the counseling profession rests on ethical prac-

tice. It is important to note that the ethical standards of the ACA call on counselors to actively attempt to understand the diverse cultural backgrounds of the clients they serve (ACA, 2005). Best practice in counseling, therefore, involves putting ethics at the forefront of all professional activity. It is safe to assume then that counselors who are culturally competent aspire to high ethical standards. The importance of ethical knowledge and aspirations is underscored throughout this book, and Chapter 18 deals specifically with this issue.

Multicultural Dimension

The multicultural dimension consists of three themes. These themes reflect the theory and practice of multicultural counseling.

Multicultural Counseling Theoretical Knowledge

In addition to knowledge of traditional counseling theory, it is imperative that counselors have a knowledge base that includes culturally diverse ideas on the nature of helping and its impact on human development from which to plan, implement, and evaluate services in a cross-cultural context. Sue et al. (1996) proposed a theory of multicultural counseling. This metatheory of counseling recognizes that both counselor and client identities are embedded in multiple levels of experience and context. It posits that cultural identity development is a major determinant of both counselor and client attitudes, which are also influenced by the dominant and subordinate relationships among groups. *Cultural identity* refers to an individual's sense of belonging to a cultural group and the part of one's personality that is attributable to cultural group membership. Cultural identity may be considered the inner vision a person possesses of himself or herself as a member of a cultural group and as a unique human being. It forms the core of the beliefs, social forms, and personality dimensions that characterize distinct cultural realities and worldviews for an individual. Cultural identity development is a major determinant of a person's attitudes toward himself or herself, others of his or her cultural group, and those of different cultural groups (Sue et al., 1996).

The development of a cultural identity has been theorized within the context of several dimensions of culture. Thus, there are developmental models that explain various aspects of cultural identity, including racial/ethnic identity (Atkinson, Morten, & Sue, 1993; Cross, 1995; Helms, 1995), homosexual/gay/lesbian/bisexual identity (Cass, 1979; Coleman, 1982; Marszalek & Cashwell, 1999; McCarn & Fassinger, 1996; Troiden, 1988), feminist and womanist identity (Downing & Roush, 1985; Ossana, Helms, & Leonard, 1992), biracial identity (Kerwin & Ponterotto, 1995; Poston, 1990), and disability identity (Gill, 1997; Vash, 1981).

Multicultural theoretical knowledge must also include an understanding that counseling is most likely enhanced when modalities and goals are consistent with the life experiences and cultural values of the client. Multicultural theoretical knowledge must therefore also include an awareness of the importance of the multiple helping roles of culturally diverse groups of people.

Another crucial aspect of multicultural knowledge is an understanding of how social systems operate with respect to their treatment of culturally diverse groups of people (Lee, 2007; Ratts, Toporek, & Lewis, 2010). Culturally competent counselors must have an understanding of the impact that systemic forces such as racism, sexism, heterosexism, classism, and ableism can have on psychosocial development and wellness.

Cross-Cultural Encounters

Multicultural competency must be predicated on one's ability to acquire working knowledge and information about specific groups of people. This should include information about the histories, experiences, customs, and values of culturally diverse groups. However, the acquisition of such knowledge must not be limited to books, classes, and workshops. A crucial way to acquire such knowledge is through ongoing professional and, perhaps more important, personal encounters with people from diverse cultural backgrounds. Having such encounters may entail getting outside of the familiarity of one's own cultural realities and experiencing diversity first hand. An important component of any cross-cultural encounter is the ability to get beyond stereotypes and ensure that one sees people as individuals within a cultural context.

Cross-Cultural Counseling Skill Development

It is imperative that counselors enter into a cross-cultural helping relationship with a repertoire of skills. They should develop counseling strategies and techniques that are consistent with the life experiences and cultural values of their clients. Such skill development should be based on the following premises. First, cultural diversity is real and should not be ignored in counseling interactions. Second, cultural differences are just that—differences. They are not necessarily deficiencies or pathological deviations. This suggests having the ability to meet clients where they are, despite obvious cultural gaps between helper and helpee. Third, when working with clients from culturally diverse groups, it is important to avoid stereotypes and a monolithic perspective. It is crucial that counselors consider clients as individuals within a cultural context.

A number of theoretical approaches should be included in the helping repertoire of a culturally competent counselor. It is important that one's counseling approach be eclectic enough that one can use a variety of helping interventions. Any counseling approach should incorporate diverse worldviews and practices.

On actually encountering a client from a different cultural context, a counselor's skill set must proceed from important answers to the following questions: What buttons, if any, does this client push in me as a result of the obvious cultural difference between us? What are some cultural blind spots I may have with respect to this client? As a result of my cultural realities, what strengths do I bring to this counseling relationship? As a result of my cultural realities, what limitations do I bring to this counseling relationship?

The remainder of this book provides direction for enhancing the development of skills in culturally competent counseling. It must be pointed out, however, that the following chapters are not intended to be a cookbook or a how-to manual for working with culturally diverse clients. Rather, they are intended to offer insights into how to translate personal awareness and cultural knowledge into culturally competent practice.

Multicultural Counseling Competency

The apex of the conceptual framework proposed here is multicultural counseling competency. This construct has received significant attention in the cross-cultural literature (Arredondo et al., 1996; Roysircar, Arredondo, Fuertes, Ponterotto, & Toporek, 2003; Sue et al., 1992). Multicultural counseling competency defines a set of attitudes and behaviors indicative of the ability to establish, maintain, and successfully conclude a counseling relationship with clients from diverse cultural backgrounds. Therefore, counselors who are culturally competent have heightened awareness, have an expanded knowledge base, and use helping skills in a culturally responsive manner. In the developmental process described by this conceptual framework, three important questions summarize the essence of the evolution of multicultural competency. First, those counselors who demonstrate multicultural competency possess self-awareness that is grounded in an exploration of the question, Who am I as a cultural being? Second, in addition to knowledge of counseling theory and ethical principles, multiculturally competent counselors consider the question, What do I know about cultural dynamics? Third, the counseling practice of counselors who exhibit multicultural competency is predicated on the question, How do I promote academic, career, and personal–social development in a culturally competent manner?

Conclusion

American society in the 21st century is characterized by ever-increasing diversity and cultural pluralism. These phenomena have had a profound effect on the counseling profession. No longer can counseling theory or practice be considered exclusively within the confines of one cultural perspective. Instead, important aspects of diversity, such as race/ethnicity, sexual orientation, disability, and socioeconomic disadvantage, to name a few, must be factored into effective counseling practice. If counselors are to have an impact on the development of increasingly diverse client groups, then counseling practice must be grounded in multicultural competency. The development of such competency must be an integral part of the personal and professional growth process of all counselors. This process involves acquiring not only the awareness and knowledge but also the skills for effective multicultural intervention.

References

American Counseling Association. (2005). *ACA code of ethics.* Alexandria, VA: Author.

American Counseling Association. (2010). *20/20: A vision for the future of counseling.* Retrieved from http://www.counseling.org/20-20/definition.aspx

Arredondo, P., Toporek, M. S., Brown, S., Jones, J., Locke, D. C., Sanchez, J., & Stadler, H. (1996). Operationalization of the Multicultural Counseling Competencies. *Journal of Multicultural Counseling and Development, 24,* 42–78.

Atkinson, D. R., Morten, G., & Sue, D. W. (1993). *Counseling American minorities: A cross-cultural perspective* (4th ed.). Madison, WI: Brown and Benchmark.

Cass, V. (1979). Homosexual identity formation: A theoretical model. *Journal of Homosexuality, 4,* 219–235.

Christensen, K. (Ed.). (2000). *Deaf plus: A multicultural perspective.* San Diego, CA: Dawn Sign Press.

Coleman, E. (1982). Developmental stages of the coming out process. *Journal of Homosexuality, 7,* 31–43.

Collins, G. (2009). *When everything changed: The amazing journey of American women from 1960 to the present.* New York, NY: Little, Brown.

Cross, W. E. (1995). The psychology of Nigrescence: Revising the Cross model. In J. G. Ponterotto, J. M. Casas, L. A. Suzuki, & C. M. Alexander (Eds.), *Handbook of multicultural counseling* (pp. 93–122). Thousand Oaks, CA: Sage.

DeNavas-Walt, C., Proctor, B. D., & Smith, J. C. (2011). *Income, poverty, and health insurance coverage in the United States: 2010.* Washington, DC: U.S. Census Bureau.

Downing, N., & Roush, K. (1985). From passive acceptance to active commitment: A model of feminist identity development for women. *The Counseling Psychologist, 13,* 695–709.

Freedman, E. (2003). *No turning back: The history of feminism and the future of women.* New York, NY: Ballantine Books.

Gates, G. J. (2011). *How many people are lesbian, gay, bisexual, and transgender?* Los Angeles, CA: The Williams Institute.

Gill, C. J. (1997). Four types of integration in disability identity development. *Journal of Vocational Rehabilitation, 9,* 39–46.

Helms, J. E. (1995). An update of Helms's White and People of Color racial identity models. In J. G. Ponterotto, J. M. Casas, L. A. Suzuki, & C. M. Alexander (Eds.), *Handbook of multicultural counseling* (pp. 181–198). Thousand Oaks, CA: Sage.

Humes, K. R., Jones, N. A., & Ramirez, R. R. (2011). *Overview of race and Hispanic origin: 2010.* Washington, DC: U.S. Census Bureau.

Katz, J. H. (1985). The sociopolitical nature of counseling. *The Counseling Psychologist, 13,* 615–624.

Kerwin, C., & Ponterotto, J. (1995). Biracial identity development. In J. G. Ponterotto, J. M. Casas, L. A. Suzuki, & C. M. Alexander (Eds.), *Handbook of multicultural counseling* (pp. 199–217). Thousand Oaks, CA: Sage.

Ladd, P. (2003). *Understanding deaf culture: In search of deafhood.* Tonawanda, NY: Multilingual Matters.

Lee, C. C. (Ed.). (2006). *Multicultural issues in counseling: New approaches to diversity* (3rd ed.). Alexandria, VA: American Counseling Association.

Lee, C. C. (Ed.). (2007). *Counseling for social justice* (2nd ed.). Alexandria, VA: American Counseling Association.

Lee, C. C., & Na, G. (2011). Identity development and its impact on the therapy relationship. In C. Lago (Ed.), *The handbook of transcultural counseling and psychotherapy* (pp. 54–64). Berkshire, England: McGraw-Hill.

Lewis, O. (1971). The culture of poverty. In M. Pilisuk & P. Pilisuk (Eds.), *Poor Americans: How the White poor live* (pp. 20–26). New York, NY: Transaction.

Marszalek, J. F., & Cashwell, C. S. (1999). The gay and lesbian affirmative development (GLAD) model: Facilitating positive gay identity development. *ADULTSPAN Journal, 1,* 13–31.

McCarn, S. R., & Fassinger, R. E. (1996). Revisiting sexual minority identity formation: A new model of lesbian identity and its implications for counseling and research. *The Counseling Psychologist, 24,* 508–534.

Ossana, S. M., Helms, J. E., & Leonard, M. M. (1992). Do "womanist" identity attitudes influence college women's self-esteem and perceptions of environmental bias? *Journal of Counseling & Development, 70,* 402–408.

Pease, B., & Pringle, K. (Eds.). (2001). *A man's world? Changing men's practices in a globalized world.* New York, NY: St. Martin's Press.

Pedersen, P. B. (1991a). Multiculturalism as a fourth force in counseling. *Journal of Counseling & Development, 70,* 4–5.

Pedersen, P. B. (1991b). Multiculturalism as a generic approach to counseling. *Journal of Counseling & Development, 70,* 6–12.

Pedersen, P., Lonner, W. J., & Draguns, J. G. (Eds.). (1976). *Counseling across cultures.* Honolulu: University of Hawaii Press.

Poston, W. S. C. (1990). The biracial identity development model: A needed addition. *Journal of Counseling & Development, 69,* 152–155.

Rabinowitz, F. E., & Cochran, S. V. (1994). *Man alive: A primer of men's issues.* Belmont, CA: Thomson Brooks/Cole.

Ratts, M. J., Toporek, R. L., & Lewis, J. A. (2010). Advocacy and social justice: A helping paradigm for the 21st century. In M. Ratts, R. L. Toporek, & J. A. Lewis (Eds.), *ACA advocacy competencies: A social justice framework for counselors* (pp. 3–10). Alexandria, VA: American Counseling Association.

Root, M. P. P., & Kelley, M. (2003). *Multiracial child resource book: Living complex identities.* Seattle, WA: MAVIN Foundation.

Rowe, J. W., & Kahn, R. L. (1997). Successful aging. *The Gerontologist, 37,* 433–440.

Roysircar, G., Arredondo, P., Fuertes, J. N., Ponterotto, J. G., & Toporek, R. L. (2003). *Multicultural counseling competencies 2003: Association for Multicultural Counseling and Development.* Alexandria, VA: Association for Multicultural Counseling and Development.

Schulz, R., & Heckhausen, J. (1996). A life span model of successful aging. *American Psychologist, 51,* 702–714.

Sue, D. W. (1977). Barriers to effective cross-cultural counseling. *Journal of Counseling Psychology, 24,* 420–429.

Sue, D. W. (1992). The challenge of multiculturalism: The road less traveled. *American Counselor, 1,* 7–14.

Sue, D. W., Arredondo, P., & McDavis, R. J. (1992). Multicultural counseling competencies and standards: A call to the profession. *Journal of Counseling & Development, 70,* 477–486.

Sue, D. W., Ivey, A. E., & Pedersen, P. B. (Eds.). (1996). *A theory of multicultural counseling and therapy.* Pacific Grove, CA: Brooks/Cole.

Sue, D. W., & Sue, D. (2012). *Counseling the culturally diverse: Theory and practice* (6th ed.). New York, NY: Wiley.

Troiden, R. (1988). Homosexual identity development. *Journal of Adolescent Health Care, 9,* 105–113.

U.S. Census Bureau. (2010). *2010 American community survey.* Washington, DC: Author.

U.S. Department of Defense. (2011). *Active duty military personnel strengths by regional area and by country.* Retrieved from http://siadapp.dmdc.osd.mil/personnel/MILITARY/history/hst1103.pdf

Valentine, C. A. (1968). *Culture and poverty: Critique and counter-proposals.* Chicago, IL: University of Chicago Press.

Vash, C. L. (1981). *The psychology of disability* (Springer Series on Rehabilitation Vol. 1). New York, NY: Springer.

Vontress, C. E. (1969). Cultural differences: Implications for counseling. *Journal of Negro Education, 37,* 266–275.

Vontress, C. E. (1976). Racial and ethnic barriers in counseling. In P. Pedersen, J. G. Draguns, W. J. Lonner, & J. E. Trimble (Eds.), *Counseling across cultures* (pp. 42–64). Honolulu: University of Hawaii Press.

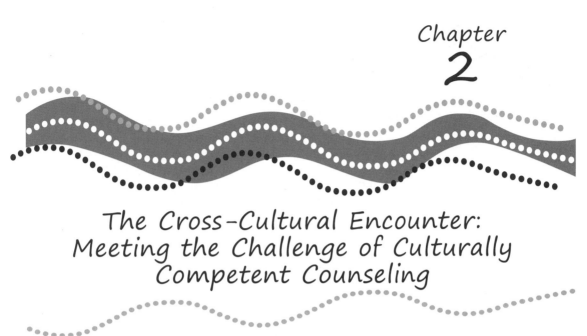

2

The Cross-Cultural Encounter: Meeting the Challenge of Culturally Competent Counseling

Courtland C. Lee

Understanding the complex role of culture in the helping process is a major challenge in counseling practice. Having knowledge of cultural realities has become a professional imperative as counselors encounter increasingly diverse client groups. However, when culture is considered a variable in the counseling process, it has the potential to become a source of conflict and misunderstanding. This may create barriers between helpers and helpees who differ in terms of cultural background. The purpose of this chapter is threefold: first, to present a conceptual analysis of counseling across cultures (The Cross-Cultural Encounter); second, to examine some important issues that should be considered in addressing the challenges of culturally competent counseling in such an encounter; and third, to provide specific guidelines for enhancing the working alliance when one finds oneself engaging in a cross-cultural counseling encounter.

The Cross-Cultural Encounter: Challenges of Culturally Competent Counseling

Entering into a counseling relationship with a person from a different cultural background brings with it certain unique challenges and inherent opportunities. Engaging in such a relationship involves entering into an important and potentially problematic zone of helping (Lee & Chuang, 2005; Lee & Diaz, 2009). This helping space can be conceptualized as the *cross-cultural encounter*. In much of the multicultural counseling literature this helping space has been traditionally conceptualized as involving a White counselor engaging in a helping relationship with a client of color (Atkinson, Morten, & Sue, 1993; Lee, 1997; Locke, 1990; McFadden, 1993; Sue & Sue, 1981). However, the cultural gaps that exist between counselor and client in a cross-cultural encounter may also consist of distinct differences in aspects such as sexual orientation, ability status, socioeconomic status, gender, or age. In addition, it has been argued by Pedersen (1991) that multiculturalism is a basic aspect of all counseling and that every counselor–client relationship is a cross-cultural encounter.

Regardless of how they are perceived, what is clearly evident in cross-cultural encounters is that the cultural differences between counselor and client, when not fully appreciated or understood, can be a significant impediment to the counseling process. Metaphorically speaking, the counselor–client differences in a cross-cultural encounter can be perceived of as a wall that impedes or negates counseling. This wall underscores the cultural distance between the counselor and the client. In many instances, these cultural differences are ignored or misunderstood, thereby widening the distance between the helper and helpee.

Given this metaphorical wall, a cross-cultural counseling encounter can produce one of two possible outcomes. The first of these is underscored by multicultural incompetence on the part of a counselor, which can spawn unintended cultural disregard or, worse, cultural disrespect. Such cultural insensitivity may result in early termination of the relationship on the part of the client. Such an outcome would be considered unethical counseling practice (American Counseling Association, 2005). The second possible outcome, however, reflects multicultural competence on the part of the counselor, which should result in a working alliance between the helper and helpee. Respect and validation of a client's culture through culturally competent counseling practice increases the likelihood of problem resolution or effective decision making. Cultural competence also promotes ethical counseling practice.

The goal when entering into a cross-cultural encounter, therefore, is to acknowledge the wall and decrease the cultural distance between the counselor and client. It is important that cultural differences are acknowledged and factored into the counseling relationship as appropriate. In order to accomplish this and increase the effectiveness of counseling in a cross-cultural encounter, one must consider several important issues (see Figure 2.1). Competent counseling practice in a cross-cultural encounter must be predicated on an understanding of these issues.

Issues to Consider When Entering Into a Cross-Cultural Encounter

Cultural Characteristics of Counseling

It has been long been noted that the theoretical and practical traditions of counseling reflect Euro-American middle-class culture (Atkinson, Morten, & Sue, 1989; Pedersen, 1987; Sue, 1977; Vontress, 1971). In many respects the counseling process is uniquely reflective of major North American cultural, class, and language values (Sue, 1977). Some of these culture-bound characteristics of counseling are the individual-centered nature of the helping process, openness and intimacy between helper and helpee, long-range goal setting, and the use of Standard English and verbal communication in the counselor–client interaction (Sue & Sue, 1981).

For people whose cultural, class, or language values may not be consistent with those found in counseling, an encounter with a counselor can often be an alienating and dissonant experience. Although they have the potential to enhance a working alliance, differences in the values of the counselor and client far too often become an impediment to problem resolution or decision making (Sue, 1977; Vontress, 1976; Whaley, 2001).

Sociopolitical Nature of Counseling

It is important to point out that a cross-cultural encounter in counseling can be a sociopolitical process related to a power differential between the counselor and client (Katz, 1985;

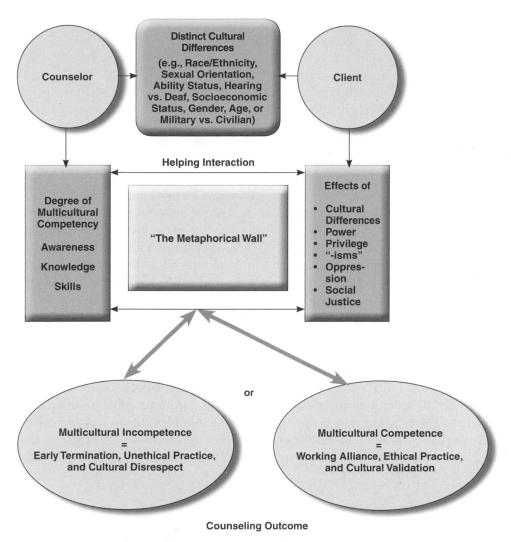

Figure 2.1 • The Cross-Cultural Encounter

Lee, 2006, 2007; Ratts, Lewis, & Toporek, 2010). This is particularly true if, because of race/ethnicity, gender, sexual orientation, age, or disability status, a client occupies a subordinate cultural position in society. Such a position is usually characterized by forces of racism, sexism, ageism, classism, heterosexism, or ableism that impact negatively on academic, career, or personal–social development. In many instances, counseling practice is perceived as a tool of power, oppression, or social control among many groups of people. Often a cross-cultural counseling encounter is a forced—as opposed to a voluntary—experience, with a counselor perceived as a culturally insensitive or unresponsive agent of the broad and repressive social welfare system. Therefore, rather than being an empowering process, counseling can become disenfranchising, contributing to social marginalization for scores of client groups (Lee & Diaz, 2009).

Power and Privilege

Given the often sociopolitical nature of counseling, two pervasive concepts that underlie the helping process in the cross-cultural encounter must be considered: power and privilege. Power is a major theme in any counseling relationship. However, often counselors tend to conceal or deny the fact that there is unequal power in the helping relationship. An individual who needs help with problem resolution or decision making voluntarily comes or is referred (often by a powerful other) to a counselor for that assistance. By default, therefore, that individual places the counselor in a position of power. It is therefore crucial when entering into a cross-cultural encounter that a counselor acknowledge his or her power and ensure that it is competently directed toward helping the client become empowered (Lee & Diaz, 2009). The dynamics of power, therefore, must be acknowledged in a cross-cultural counseling encounter. This is particularly the case for those clients whose counseling issues relate to the stress of prejudice, discrimination, or social injustice (Cartenuto, 1992; Lee, 2006; Lee & Diaz, 2009).

With respect to the concept of privilege, it is important that counselors reflect on the nature of the cultural privilege they may possess because of their race/ethnicity, gender, sexual orientation, age, socioeconomic status, religion, ability status, or other social or cultural characteristics. Privilege can be conceived along several dimensions. First, it is generally unearned. In most cases individuals are born with it, and it tends to be innate. This is certainly the case with skin color or gender, for example. Second, individuals with privilege generally tend to be unaware of the unearned benefits that accrue from their privileged status. Third, privilege gives the individuals who have it distinct cultural, social, and economic advantages. Individuals with privilege are generally seen to be in a position of social dominance compared with those who lack it (McIntosh, 1989). In the United States, privilege generally comes as a result of one's race/ethnicity (White), gender (male), religion (Christian), sexual orientation (heterosexual), ability status (able bodied), and socioeconomic status (affluent).

The prerequisite for entering into a cross-cultural encounter must be that counselors consider the nature of the possible power differential between themselves and their client. Equally important is an understanding of the extent of the cultural privilege distinctions between counselor and client. The dynamics of both power and privilege may significantly impact the counseling process.

Social Justice

Counselors who are aware of the sociopolitical nature of counseling and who acknowledge their potential power and privilege in a cross-cultural encounter must appreciate the importance of social justice to culturally competent counseling. Broadly defined, *social justice* involves promoting access and equity to ensure full participation in the life of a society, particularly for those who have been systematically excluded on the basis of race/ethnicity, gender, age, physical or mental disability, education, sexual orientation, socioeconomic status, or other characteristics of background or group membership. Social justice is based on a belief that all people have a right to equitable treatment, support for their human rights, and a fair allocation of societal resources (Lee & Hipolito-Delgado, 2007; Rawls, 1971).

Social justice places a focus on issues of oppression, privilege, and social inequities. For counselors, social justice implies professional conduct that opposes all forms of discrimination and oppression. Counseling practices that are rooted in social justice seek to challenge inherent inequities in social systems. Such practices are often of great importance in cross-cultural counseling encounters when the etiology of client problems is ultimately linked to oppressive social, economic, or cultural environments that serve to negatively impact academic, career, or personal–social development (Lee, 2007).

A culturally competent counselor must also be an agent of social justice who possesses the awareness, knowledge, and skill to intervene not only at an individual client level but at a systemwide level as well. Whether in partnership with or on behalf of disempowered clients, a culturally competent counselor challenges cultural, social, historical, or economic barriers that stifle optimal human development and wellness (Lee, 2012).

Social justice is a foundational aspect of the cross-cultural counseling encounter. From a theoretical perspective, social justice is now considered the fifth force in the counseling field, following the paradigms of the psychodynamic approach, cognitive behavior theory, humanism, and multiculturalism (Lee, 2012; Ratts, D'Andrea, & Arredondo, 2004; Ratts, Toporek, & Lewis, 2010).

Guidelines for Culturally Competent Counseling in a Cross-Cultural Encounter

If counselors are to be effective in cross-cultural encounters, then they must approach helping from a perspective that simultaneously acknowledges human similarity and celebrates human difference. They must adopt a philosophy that views each client as a unique individual while at the same time taking into consideration the client's common experiences as a human being (i.e., the universal developmental challenges that all people face regardless of cultural background) and the specific experiences that come from his or her cultural background. It is important that counselors consider each client within a cultural group context and a broader global human perspective (Lee, 2006). The following is a set of guidelines for facilitating the working alliance between the counselor and client in a cross-cultural helping encounter. These guidelines represent a foundation for best counseling practice in a cross-cultural counseling encounter.

- *Consider cultural factors in any counseling interaction.* It is important to remember that cultural differences between counselors and clients are just that—differences. These differences are not necessarily deficiencies or pathological deviations.
- *Examine and evaluate one's own cultural "baggage."* All people have preconceived notions and prejudicial assumptions about people who are different. These notions and assumptions can be considered the cultural baggage one unconsciously travels with throughout life. This baggage has the potential to impact the nature of one's social interactions with people from diverse cultural backgrounds. It is imperative, therefore, that one examine the origins of this baggage, acknowledge it, and attempt to move beyond it when working with people who are different.
- *Examine and evaluate cultural privilege.* All people have a degree of privilege in society based on some demographic or cultural characteristic(s). It is important to evaluate what privilege one might enjoy in society and how this might affect one's ability to understand or empathize with the realities of a client whose cultural background is different from one's own.
- *Examine and evaluate the relevance of one's theoretical orientation.* It is important to consider how issues of racism, sexism, classism, ageism, heterosexism, and so on may impact one's theoretical approach to helping. One should consider whether one's theoretical orientation reflects diverse cultural realities in its applicability with a wide range of clients.
- *Avoid stereotypes and adopting a monolithic perspective.* It is important when exploring culture to avoid the pitfall of assuming that all people from a cultural group share the same reality. Such an assumption will lead to approaching culturally diverse clients in a stereotypical as opposed to genuine manner. Although people from a cultural group may share similar characteristics, each person is a unique human being. It is therefore necessary to always consider the individual within a cultural context.

- *Be willing to learn from culturally diverse clients.* In a cross-cultural counseling encounter it is critical to let clients tell their story. This is particularly important when they are discussing cultural issues with which one may not be familiar. Never be afraid to say to a client whose cultural background is different from one's own, "I do not understand."
- *Be an advocate for culturally diverse clients.* For many culturally diverse clients, problematic behavior and challenges can often be traced to negative environmental effects. Clients' issues, therefore, are often merely reactions to or symptoms of deep-seated problems in the social environments in which they must interact. Being culturally competent often entails being able to accurately perceive environmental influences on client development and to intervene at that level to challenge systemic barriers that block development. When necessary, it is important to be an advocate to help culturally diverse clients confront the system.

These guidelines are not merely aspects of best practice in a cross-cultural encounter; they can also be considered the essence of quality counseling in general. As counselors strive to be aware of and responsive to the needs of culturally diverse client groups, they raise the standard of the profession for all.

Conclusion

An important question that must be considered with respect to culturally competent counseling is this: As a counselor, what feelings do you have, have you had, or do you contemplate having when entering into a cross-cultural encounter? In most instances, it is feelings of anxiety and fear. The cross-cultural encounter can be a very challenging one for a counselor. He or she must understand the personal and cultural dynamics of his or her worldview while simultaneously attempting to comprehend those of his or her client. This process can be compounded when the counselor and client differ significantly in terms of their cultural realities.

The next two sections of this book are intended to address the challenges of culturally competent counseling. They expand on the challenges and issues of the cross-cultural counseling encounter presented in this chapter. The remainder of the book explores counseling concepts, issues, and practices needed to effectively meet the challenges—as well as seize the opportunities—of the cross-cultural encounter.

References

American Counseling Association. (2005). *ACA code of ethics.* Alexandria, VA: Author.

Atkinson, D. R., Morten, G., & Sue, D. W. (1989). *Counseling American minorities: A cross-cultural perspective* (3rd ed.). Dubuque, IA: Brown.

Atkinson, D. R., Morten, G., & Sue, D. W. (1993). *Counseling American minorities: A cross-cultural perspective* (4th ed.). Madison, WI: Brown and Benchmark.

Cartenuto, A. (1992). *The difficult art: A critical discourse on psychotherapy.* Wilmette, IL: Chiron.

Katz, J. H. (1985). The sociopolitical nature of counseling. *The Counseling Psychologist, 13,* 615–624.

Lee, C. C. (Ed.). (1997). *Multicultural issues in counseling: New approaches to diversity* (2nd ed.). Alexandria, VA: American Counseling Association.

Lee, C. C. (2006). Entering the cross-cultural zone: Meeting the challenge of culturally responsive counseling. In C. C. Lee (Ed.), *Multicultural issues in counseling: New approaches to diversity* (3rd ed., pp. 13–19). Alexandria, VA: American Counseling Association.

Lee, C. C. (Ed.). (2007). *Counseling for social justice* (2nd ed.). Alexandria, VA: American Counseling Association.

Lee, C. C. (2012). Social justice as the 5th force in counseling. In C. Y. Chang, A. L. Dixon, C. B. Minton, J. E. Myers, & T. J. Sweeney (Eds.), *Professional counseling excellence through leadership and advocacy* (pp. 109–120). New York, NY: Routledge.

Lee, C. C., & Chuang, B. (2005). Counseling people of color. In D. Capuzzi & D. R. Gross (Eds.), *Introduction to the counseling profession* (4th ed., pp. 465–483). New York, NY: Allyn & Bacon.

Lee, C. C., & Diaz, J. M. (2009). The cross-cultural zone in counseling. In C. C. Lee, D. A. Burnhill, A. L. Butler, C. Hipolito-Delgado, M. Humphrey, O. Muñoz, & H. Shin (Eds.), *Elements of culture in counseling* (pp. 95–104). Columbus, OH: Pearson.

Lee, C. C., & Hipolito-Delgado, C. P. (2007). Counselors as agents of social justice. In C. C. Lee (Ed.), *Counseling for social justice* (2nd ed., pp. xiii–xxviii). Alexandria, VA: American Counseling Association.

Locke, D. C. (1990). A not so provincial view of multicultural counseling. *Counselor Education and Supervision, 30,* 18–25.

McFadden, J. (Ed.). (1993). *Transcultural counseling: Bilateral and international perspectives.* Alexandria, VA: American Counseling Association.

McIntosh, P. (1989). White privilege: Unpacking the invisible knapsack. *Peace and Freedom, 2,* 10–12.

Pedersen, P. (1987). Ten frequent assumptions of cultural bias in counseling. *Journal of Multicultural Counseling and Development, 15,* 16–24.

Pedersen, P. (1991). Multiculturalism as generic approach to counseling. *Journal of Counseling & Development, 70,* 6–12.

Ratts, M., D'Andrea, M., & Arredondo, P. (2004, September 13). Social justice counseling: 'fifth force' in the field. *Counseling Today, 47,* 28–30.

Ratts, M. J., Lewis, J. A., & Toporek, R. L. (2010). Advocacy and social justice: A helping paradigm for the 21st century. In M. J. Ratts, R. L. Toporek, & J. A. Lewis (Eds.), *ACA advocacy competencies: A social justice framework for counselors* (pp. 3–10). Alexandria, VA: American Counseling Association.

Ratts, M. J., Toporek, R. L., & Lewis, J. A. (Eds.). (2010). *ACA advocacy competencies: A social justice framework for counselors.* Alexandria, VA: American Counseling Association.

Rawls, J. A. (1971). *A theory of justice.* Cambridge, MA: Harvard University Press.

Sue, D. W. (1977). Barriers to effective cross-cultural counseling. *Journal of Counseling Psychology, 24,* 420–429.

Sue, D. W., & Sue, D. (1981). *Counseling the culturally different: Theory and practice.* New York, NY: Wiley.

Vontress, C. E. (1971). Racial differences: Impediments to rapport. *Journal of Counseling Psychology, 18,* 7–13.

Vontress, C. E. (1976). Racial and ethnic barriers in counseling. In P. Pedersen, J. G. Draguns, W. J. Lonner, & J. E. Trimble (Eds.), *Counseling across cultures* (pp. 42–64). Honolulu: University of Hawaii Press.

Whaley, A. L. (2001). Cultural mistrust and mental health services for African Americans: A review and meta-analysis. *The Counseling Psychologist, 29,* 513–521.

Part
11

Direction for
Culturally Competent
Counseling

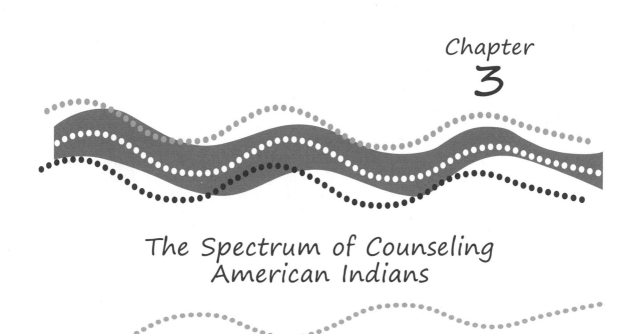

The Spectrum of Counseling American Indians

Tarrell Awe Agahe Portman

Tradition and Change

A *spectrum* is commonly defined as wide range of related values, activities, or ideas. Early usage of the word *spectrum* referred primarily to the array of colors revealed when a prism is exposed to light. Colors, like values, fall on a continuum, such as from dark red to pale pink. *Spectrum* soon entered into everyday language as a descriptive word representing an unlimited variety existing across a continuum. This concept can be applied to American Indian cultures as well as the practice of counseling. Approaches to Native American mental health issues require insight into the variety of beliefs, values, and traditions of Indigenous populations. The literature on counseling is diverse and encompasses many theories, techniques, and interventions, but it is lacking in terms of specific counseling interventions to use with Native American clients. Thus, the spectrum of counseling that shines through the prism of helping others must be applied carefully to Native American people.

Researchers of counseling have long attempted to empirically isolate best practices or validate interventions for use with specific diagnosis or functional wellness concerns. However, the spectrum of counseling approaches has targeted primarily the values, beliefs, and worldviews of the majority cultural group as the impetus to assessing healthy performance. This predominant focus on majority cultural values has been recognized by professionals in the multicultural counseling field (Dixon & Portman, 2010; Lokken & Twohey, 2004; Peregoy, 1993). Cultural populations with opposing value systems have been held at the professional mercy of counselors who in many ways lack training in practical culture-specific approaches to serving people from these populations. Indigenous people's cultural perspectives may appear foreign to many practicing counselors, particularly because of the vast array of differences in culture and values found across tribal affiliations, Nations or geographic locations—the continuum. The purpose of this chapter is to cast light through the spectrum of counseling on the cultural continuum found among American Indian peoples.

Historical Overview of American Indian Populations

According to the 2010 Census, 5.2 million people in the United States identified as American Indian and Alaska Native, either alone (2.9 million people) or in combination with one or more other races (2.3 million people). The latter population has experienced rapid growth, increasing by 39% since 2000 (Norris, Vines, & Hoeffel, 2012). American Indians as a population are validated by various governmental or community acknowledgements. These acknowledgements consist of federal (by the U.S. government), state (by a state government), and community recognition of Native American Indian status (Dixon & Portman, 2010; M. T. Garrett & Portman, 2010). Some tribal groups are not recognized because of the dissolution of their tribal registries or a lack of genealogical connection to federal census rolls taken for American Indians between 1877 and 1910. Recognition historically was determined by each individual group of Native Americans. In the past 100 years, recognition or proof of American Indian identity has been determined by direct linkage to incomplete government documents. Clients seeking help from counselors may or may not fully understand their own American Indian identity based on their family genealogy.

Collecting and analyzing demographic data on American Indian populations has historically been difficult. The colonial fathers of our country determined at the First Continental Congress in 1774 that accurate records should be collected for determining representation for governance (Kromkowski, 2002). These records were used to distribute governmental resources in the form of money, military, and materials until the restructuring of the U.S. Census Bureau under the U.S. Department of Commerce in 1913 (Kromkowski, 2002). The purpose of the U.S. Census Bureau is to "collect, compile and publish demographic, social, and economic data for the U.S. Government" (Kromkowski, 2002, p. 1). Collection of demographic data from American Indians was problematic.

The quantification of American Indian peoples has been a problem for many years. Confusion in defining American Indians continues to be perpetuated by the U.S. Office of Management and Budget, the U.S. Bureau of Indian Affairs, and the U.S. Census Bureau, with each governmental group having different definitions (Dixon & Portman, 2010). Relying on individual self-proclamation, better known as *self-definition,* appears to have brought some uniformity to numerical counts. However, some consider the increase in the number of American Indians to be directly related to the issue of *self-identification,* which is the process of allowing individuals not acknowledged by governmental or community groups to proclaim American Indian status. Self-identification has played an important role in the census numeration regarding American Indian populations (Sandefur, Rindfuss, & Cohen, 1996).

American Indian identity issues are found not just in the majority U.S. population but more often within the Indigenous populations. These internal struggles with identifying who is and is not American Indian cause divisiveness and cultural acrimony within and between Native individuals. Internalized identity dynamics among American Indian communities can be the presenting issue in counseling sessions with individuals from any tribal group.

American Indian peoples have a rich and tumultuous history, a barely recognized present, and a continuous struggle for the future. There is truth in the idiom that history is written by the conqueror—particularly for many Indigenous peoples. Thus, many counselors may not be aware of historical events from an American Indian perspective. Genocide, conquest, oppression, and discrimination all represent the history of Native American peoples.

Five historical stages have been documented in the literature on American Indians' interactions with the U.S. government (M. T. Garrett & Portman, 2010). Prior to the 1840s, genocide occurred predominantly across the coastal states during the Removal Period. The general philosophy of the dominant culture was "the only good Indian is a dead Indian." This period is often romanticized in children's literature with cowboys, cavalry, and *savage* Indians, which continue to be a part of American media to this day. Between the 1860s and the 1920s, U.S. governmental policy moved toward a cultural deficit model in the Reservation Period. Eliminating or destroying the cultural identity of the Indian by reconstructing him into a man (meaning *White* man) characterized the Reservation Period. During this period American Indians became designated as a protected class of citizens—meaning they required *taking care of* or *oversight* for their own good. Other protected classes include prisoners, children, and mentally incompetent individuals. It was during this period when Native American children were physically taken from their families and placed in boarding schools. The education of these children and their reintegration back into their home communities brought about the Reorganization Period from the 1930s to 1950s. Schools were allowed on reservations, and the U.S. government offered assistance in reorganizing tribal governments into mirror governments of the United States in an attempt to expedite acculturation. This was a policy era characterized by killing the community. In the postwar 1950s and 1960s, Native Americans were offered the opportunity to leave poverty and third-world living conditions on the reservations for more populated city areas. Temporary work opportunities and financial resources became incentives for American Indians to move to more urban regional centers in an attempt at integration. This was called the Relocation Period, and it led to an increase in tribal dependence on the federal government and the loss of many American Indian Nation resources. The civil rights movement and the American Indian Movement followed, leading to political involvement and media attention in the United States for the siege at Alcatraz and the Wounded Knee occupation. The U.S. government's reaction to these incidents increased the existing distrust due to historical dishonoring of treaties. American Indians gained political support during this time from the majority population, which led to policies for the current period, the Self-Determination Period (1973 to the present), and the upholding of tribal sovereignty. Sovereignty among American Indian Nations allows for government-to-government interaction between the U.S., international, and tribal governments. Thus, sovereignty also sets the stage for American Indians to hold dual citizenship (U.S. and tribal Nation citizenship).

Current Trends in the American Indian Population

According to the 2010 Census, 15 states have more than 100,000 American Indian and Alaska Native residents (Norris et al., 2012). These states are California, Oklahoma, Arizona, Texas, New York, New Mexico, Washington, North Carolina, Florida, Michigan, Alaska, Oregon, Colorado, Minnesota, and Illinois. Most tribal Nations have fewer than 10,000 members. The largest tribal Nations, each exceeding 100,000 members, are the Cherokee, Chippewa, Navajo, and Sioux Nations (Baruth & Manning, 2007). Because of historical oppression by the U.S. government, most American Indians reside west of the Mississippi River (Baruth & Manning, 2007).

The male-to-female ratio among Native Americans is 99.4 males to every 100 females. Approximately 40% of the U.S. population who report being of two or more races included American Indian or Alaska Native. Among American Indians aged 5 or older, 23.4% have a disability. Fetal alcohol syndrome is 33 times more likely to occur among American Indians than the general population. Diabetes and tuberculosis are both about 7% more likely to occur among American Indians.

About 26% of American Indians live below the poverty line (the U.S. poverty rate is 12.4%), placing them at the highest poverty level among the races in the United States. More than 60% are unemployed, although some own their own businesses. Native Americans who operate their own businesses are most likely to be in service industries. The rate of grandchildren living with their grandparents is 40% higher among American Indians than the national average.

Approximately 1% of the public K–12 population are American Indian children. However, 5.5% of private school K–12 enrollments are Native American children. Moreover, 70% of American Indians have completed a high school education or more, with 11% having earned a bachelor's degree or higher. Only 3.9% have acquired an advanced degree (M. T. Garrett & Portman, 2010).

Collecting demographic information on American Indian populations is fraught with challenges. Similarly, gathering demographic information on individual American Indian clients may create challenges for helping professionals. Sandefur et al. (1996) identified four challenges of gathering information on American Indian populations: (a) American Indians are not as segregated or as concentrated as some other populations, (b) they are very culturally diverse, (c) the more than 300 tribal groups recognized by the federal government and the approximately 200 other entities that are not federally recognized have very diverse histories, and (d) visual inspection is often not a good way to identify American Indians because of the long history of intermarriage. These challenges may account for the limited emergence of American Indian clients in counseling. Particularly problematic is the tendency of counselors to rely on visual attributions for identification, which may cause American Indian clients to go untreated because of their lack of stereotypic features. Counselors must develop an understanding of working with Native American clients with the knowledge that any client could self-identify in this population.

Similarities and Differences Across American Indian Nations

Native Americans are experienced with tradition and change. Acknowledging tradition and change is an important aspect of counseling American Indians, but the multitude of differences among Indigenous peoples must be considered. These differences fall along a continuum that can be measured on multiple lines of similarities. For example, American Indian tribal groups are recognized at Native American activities by their style or type of dance regalia. There is enough difference for specific tribal identification for those involved in the culture. Another example has to do with adherence to oral traditions or spiritual beliefs surrounding death. Cherokees may embrace the spirits of ancestors and welcome them into their homes, whereas Arapahoe tribal members may avoid interacting with the remains of relatives. The Ottawa Nation is known for digging up the bones of their ancestors during the Removal Period. Similarities are noted in the counseling literature as cultural values and expectations (M. T. Garrett & Pichette, 2000). These are often presented in charts comparing American Indians as a homogenous population with the majority American mainstream population. Counselor awareness of majority and minority group comparisons is necessary. In addition, counselors working in areas with more diverse populations of American Indian tribes need to understand the values and expectations of the tribal groups across each continuum. Some traditional common themes include (a) harmony with nature, (b) cooperation, (c) noninterference/privacy, (d) collectivism, (e) humility, (f) reliance on relationships, and (g) the use of nonverbal or high-context language for communication (M. T. Garrett & Pichette, 2000). Counselors working with American Indian clients are encouraged to gather information from the many authors who have provided more complete listings of American Indian values (DuBray, 1985; M. T. Garrett, 1999; Heinrich, Corbine, & Thomas, 1990; Oswalt, 1988; Peregoy, 1993; Sue & Sue, 2007; Thomason, 1991). American Indian clients may display these values or expectations but to varying degrees based on the differences between tribal Nations or just their individual family beliefs.

Although a diverse population of people, American Indians do share a history of externalized oppression across groups. In particular, American Indians in the United States and possibly Mexico and Canada collectively suffer from postcolonial romanticizing or degradation of their cultures. This is found in modern media or retro media depicting American Indians in historical contexts of wearing feathers, beads, and animal skins and constantly seeking to kill non-Indians. Men are seen as warriors or drunkards, and women are viewed as princesses or prostitutes (Portman & Herring, 2001). In fact, many retro television episodes depicting cowboys or wagon trains present actor credits as "Indian 1" and "Indian 2."

The current media tends to depict American Indians in gangs, involved in the drug culture, or as drunken and helpless. This media representation is exacerbated by the continued use of sports mascots depicting American Indians. The social construction of American Indian identity across the life span is inundated with these negative visual images, which may vary depending on the age of the individual. Native American clients undoubtedly will have been exposed to a barrage of media downplaying their human value. This impacts cultural identity as well as feelings of self-worth for clients.

Counselors must assess the level of acculturation of their Native American clients. Trimble (2010) stated that American Indians fall somewhere on a continuum of acculturation: "In the sense that they reflect an understanding and appreciation of culture-specific folkways yet recognize the need to adopt the values and beliefs of the dominant, mainstream culture" (p. 247). Acculturation can be forced on populations or voluntarily accepted (Garcia & Ahler, 1992; M. T. Garrett & Portman, 2010). Although there are instruments for measuring one's level of acculturation (M. T. Garrett, 1999), one of the best methods of doing this may be asking the client to discuss his or her level of involvement in traditional American Indian life. This may be referred to as the client's level of "Indianness" or his or her propensity to choose active involvement with other Native American peoples (J. T. Garrett & Garrett, 1994). A client's ethnic heritage and life choices can only be examined through a cultural dialogue, which generally occurs during the early rapport- and relationship-building sessions.

Counseling American Indian Peoples

Counseling Native American clients can be an enjoyable experience depending on the cultural competence and awareness of the counselor. Initial assumptions regarding the counselor–client relationship need to be understood through an American Indian cultural lens. "American Indians often judge people by who they are, rather than by what they are" (Baruth & Manning, 2007, p. 19). Native American clients may not automatically accept a counselor's educational degree as an indication of his or her proficiency. Trimble (2010) wrote, "For many Indian and Native clients, interpersonal and interethnic problems can emerge when a counselor's lack of culturally resonant experience and knowledge, deeply held stereotypes, and preconceived notions interfere with the counseling relationship and impede counseling effectiveness" (p. 243). Counselors must face issues of cultural resonance by working with the American Indian client and learning from the client's experiences. Counselors need not fear asking questions of American Indian clients to gain understanding, but they should monitor their own socially constructed beliefs regarding this population. The American Indian client is not fully understood until the counselor gains knowledge of the client's connection to the collective population. This constructed reality of the American Indian in the collective may be overlooked by counselors who have been trained to consider their clients from an individualistic perspective. For this reason, it is necessary for counselors to have knowledge relevant to American Indian peoples, not to form stereotypical clinical impressions but to eliminate inappropriate interventions and to be open to Indigenous healing practices. Many authors have provided information on understanding the American Indian client in a counseling relationship (see Dixon & Portman, 2010; Dixon Rayle, Chee, & Sand, 2006; M. T. Garrett & Herring, 2001; Thomason, 1991).

Counselors need to be open to utilizing American Indian community resources in interventions with their clients. These resources may include family or kinship relationships, tribal leaders, or Indigenous healers (called various names by different tribal Nations). Trimble (2010) stated,

> The collaboration with an indigenous healing system can take several forms: The counselor may (a) support the viability of traditional healing as an effective treatment system, (b) actively refer clients to indigenous healers, or (c) actively work together with indigenous healers. (p. 247)

Counselors need to seek opportunities to gain an understanding of Native American healing practices across Nations and along the continuum (M. T. Garrett, 1999). Native American healing traditions cannot be taken out of the context of their relationship to the four constructs of spirituality (Creator, Mother Earth, Great Father), community (family, tribe), environment (daily life, nature, balance), and self (inner passions, thoughts, and values). In fact, many Native American traditional healing practices performed without these spiritual relationships might prove ineffective for treatment. As the American Cancer Society (2008) acknowledged, Native American healing takes place within the context of the relationship with the healer (Garrett & Portman, 2010).

American Indian clients may discuss counseling interventions in the context of medicine. Good medicine is viewed as helping the individual or group; bad medicine is believed to hurt or hinder the life of the individual or group. Medicine in this context is not a tangible object but holds a spiritual or mystical place on the continuum depending on the client's level of acculturation. J. T. Garrett and Garrett (1994) described medicine as a life force or essence that exists in all natural objects. Harmony and balance embody the relationship of all things—wellness of the mind, body, spirit, and natural environment; when this balance is disturbed, illness may occur (J. T. Garrett & Garrett, 1994; Locust, 1988). Harming someone's spirit may be viewed by American Indian clients as bad medicine (M. T. Garrett, 1999). Therefore, counselors should explore guilt in sessions with Native American clients to determine the potential underlying medicine behind the presenting issues.

Levels of Intervention

Counseling interventions utilized with Native Americans span the counseling strategies available for particular behaviors or diagnosis. Culturally competent practice may require subtle differences in the manner in which strategies are employed and by whom. Counselors need to be open to multiple providers and avoid their own resistance to non-counselor helpers. Counseling interventions with American Indians require multiple levels of involvement from others from within the individual's social network system. To help clients, it may be necessary to include family, friends, extended family, and tribal leaders, including leaders from other Nations. Working with American Indian clients at the individual level requires that a counselor develop rapport and a mutual understanding of how cultural similarities or differences will enter into the counseling process.

Working with American Indian families, siblings, parents, and grandparents can be very risky. A counselor will need to explore openly their client's perspectives with regard to including family members in treatment or interventions. In some cases, the American Indian client may be best served by including respected tribal members or leaders. The counselor needs to consult with tribal counselors prior to choosing this option depending on the client's issue. For example, tribal leaders might become involved in a counselor intervention if a client needs to be forgiven for embarrassing the tribal Nation at a local benefit dance. The inclusion of a respected tribal leader in the intervention may allow for collective forgiveness for the client.

The next section of this chapter presents several case examples of counseling Native American clients. It is always difficult to include cases in educational materials out of fear of perpetuating stereotypes. Yet the benefit remains in that the reader may be able to transfer a skill or concept from a case to help him or her in counseling American Indians.

Invitation to My World: Inside Views of American Indians

Practical clinical experience with American Indian clients is not readily available to most counselors. Many cultural systemic issues, such as an individual's racial identity development, level of tribal affiliation and involvement, geographic proximity to other American Indians, and family-of-origin cultural identity, need to be considered to understand each client and to avoid cultural stereotyping. The following case examples provide insight into the world of American Indian peoples. The cases were created from a combination of cases to help counselors process counseling with American Indian clients. Each case study incorporates cultural traditions and counseling techniques across the life span.

The Case of Melissa: Disconnection—Adoption—"Lost Identity"

Melissa is 20 years old. She was adopted at 18 months of age through the U.S. Department of Human Services by a German family. Melissa is not her birth name. She has been told her mother was Anishinabe, but she only knows her birth mother's last name. Because her birth mother lived in Detroit and felt ashamed of being disconnected from the tribe, the Indian Child Welfare Act of 1978 was not enacted with the case. The Anishinabe Tribal council was never contacted.

Melissa has physical features and coloration that others immediately perceive as American Indian. This has created a constant identity crisis for her because of her German upbringing. Her adoptive family valued Melissa's heritage but did not have a connection to her birth family or the Anishinabe Nation primarily because of geographic distance. Melissa describes feeling lost and disconnected while growing up.

As a young adult in college, Melissa is trying to reclaim her American Indian heritage by learning traditions without help and without understanding intertribal differences. She has sought help from a college counselor for her identity issues. The counselor, Dr. Shin, has never counseled an American Indian student.

Case Intervention and Outcome

Without breaking confidentiality, Dr. Shin immediately contacted an American Indian faculty member from the Lakota Nation to consult about the case. The faculty member offered to meet with Melissa to help her learn more about American Indian traditions and to connect her with Anishinabe leaders.

Dr. Shin began working with Melissa on self-awareness concerning identity issues surrounding adoption. She also asked Melissa whether she would like to meet with the American Indian faculty member from the Lakota Nation. Melissa took the man's contact information and scheduled an appointment with him.

Over a period of 6 months, Melissa learned more about Anishinabe history and traditions. She began to understand the American Indian population as a compilation of many individual Nations. Melissa developed a plan to reconnect with and visit the Anishinabe. She began to show more pride in her appearance, and her attitude toward academic work improved. Melissa continued to meet with Dr. Shin and was able to build her academic self-esteem. When Melissa visited the Anishinabe Nation near Lake Superior, she was introduced to tribal members with her birth name. Even more surprising is that Melissa's grandparents were able to identify her and share the family history. Melissa described the experience as a "rebirth."

Case Reflections

How would you have reacted to Melissa's initial session? What other options could have been considered by Dr. Shin for approaching Melissa? What do you think about contacting an outsider to help in cultural interventions? What are the ethical considerations for the counselor working with Melissa?

The Case of Margie: Self-Worth—"Not Enough"

Margie, age 95, self-identifies as Choctaw. Margie loves to attend American Indian intertribal events at the local intertribal community center. She has developed several friendships with members of other American Indian groups. Margie has recently been diagnosed with kidney failure. She has been visited by the Area Aging Program in-home counselor to help her adjust to the news. Margie has expressed that she only wants to do one thing before she dies: dance in the American Indian social dances at the community center. The in-home counselor is an enrolled member of the Ponca Nation. She encourages Margie to dance. Margie eventually lets the counselor know her deepest fears: The lack of a tribal-issued certificate degree of Indian blood card has weighed heavily on Margie. She feels embarrassed and less than a "real" American Indian around others. This feeling is reinforced when Margie overhears American Indians at the center making jokes about non-Indians who want to be Indians. Margie's low cultural self-esteem has created negative self-talk for her. She feels convinced that she is not good enough to be involved in American Indian activities. She says, "I don't want to be known as a wannabe Indian."

Case Intervention and Outcome

The in-home counselor agreed to attend the next intertribal benefit dance with Margie. While there Margie was encouraged to dance in the intertribal dances beside the counselor. Margie expressed a feeling of joy and accomplishment, which increased her cultural self-esteem.

Case Reflections
What life-span development issues does Margie's case present? How would you have approached Margie based on your training as a counselor? How would you handle the cultural issues presented in this case if you are not American Indian? What is the role of community in this case? How does your counseling orientation incorporate community issues for individuals?

The Case of Larry: Learned Helplessness—"Lay Low"

Larry, age 45, has been nicknamed "Lay Low"" by his Kiowa familial group. Whenever work is to be done or decisions are to be made, Larry disappears. He self-describes as being a laid-back free floater who in general is not worried about life. Larry has been able to find work as a laborer on construction jobs but does not stay with any one job very long. He dropped out of high school after getting heavily involved in drinking with friends. Today Larry says that schoolwork was just hard for him. Larry was encouraged by an Indian Health Services counselor to attend adult education classes to get his high school equivalency degree. Larry showed up for class the first night but quickly became frustrated with the work. The Indian Health Services counselor was present and recognized Larry's frustration. She began working with Larry before class to understand his frustration. Larry shared with the counselor that he felt the words and the numbers just jumbled together. He said his brain was not able to keep up and he just could not do it. Larry expressed being comfortable with accepting his inability to move forward. He placed the blame on his previous teen drinking. He said, "I just killed too many brain cells. It is too late now."

Case Intervention and Outcome
Larry agreed to take some assessments, and a visual learning disability was identified. This information allowed Larry to reassess his learning patterns and over time develop more self-confidence to pursue the completion of his general equivalency diploma.

Case Reflections
What is the presenting issue for Larry? How would you develop an intervention for Larry? As a counselor, what would you focus on as a priority for Larry? What are the cultural implications for this case?

The Case of Rose: Grandiosity—"Unique Rose"

Rose, age 35, is Cheyenne/Arapaho. Rose has always been perceived as a beautiful young woman. She began winning American Indian shawl dance contests at age 6. Rose was named the junior Cheyenne/Arapaho Annual Pow Wow princess when she was 8 years old and the young adult princess when she was 14 years old. Rose had multiple successes with American Indian princess competitions as well as many school beauty competitions. Her celebrity status had an impact on Rose's personality that was not perceived as culturally appropriate by her tribal community. Rose was often disrespectful to elders, was rude to peers, and held herself up as better than others. These personality issues began to catch up with Rose after high school when she often found herself shunned or left out of groups. Rose began to get bitter and demanded to be included in activities. She volunteered for committees and then maneuvered herself into self-selected leadership positions within the intertribal groups. Finally, Rose was so rude to members of an intertribal benefit dance committee that the entire group quit. Rose was told by the committee members that she was "no longer the beauty queen and should grow up." This comment had an impact on Rose, and she sought the help of a local counselor. The counselor listened to Rose, who painted a grandiose picture of her life accomplishments. Eventually Rose self-disclosed to the counselor that her life has always been filled with people telling her how beautiful she is. Rose felt that others did not see that she was specially gifted with beauty and should be held up by her people.

Case Intervention and Outcome

Rose's counselor was at a loss for treatment options but decided to ask Rose if she would meet with a group of other American Indian women who had similar histories. A small intertribal group of American Indian women was formed. This group was intergenerational, with ages spanning from 25 to 55. Rose was able to discuss her frustration with others and gain insight into her behaviors from a cultural perspective. One point presented by the group prompted Rose to reflect that she "embraced the majority view of beauty more than the Native view of beauty." Rose began to evaluate her life choices through a new lens and determined that she had never learned to walk in both worlds.

Case Reflections

If Rose were not an American Indian, how would you approach this case? What would you report as the primary issue in counseling sessions with Rose? How do you view group work with culturally diverse clients? What pulls you toward Rose or pushes you away from her as a counselor? How does grief and loss fit into this case?

The Case of Sharon: Addiction—"Because I Can"

Sharon, age 56, is an alcoholic and often engages in recreational substance use. He explains his addiction to others by saying, "It is my choice. I just like to drink and party." Sharon receives a monthly stipend from the Osage Nation, which provides him moderate income without the necessity of being employed. He says, "I have the money and I am free to do as I please regardless of what the government says." Family interventions have continually failed with Sharon. His peers accept the fact that he has chosen to live the way he wants to live. Sharon does not leave his home and expects others to visit him. Often his visitors are peers from his high school days who just want to party with him. Recently, a friend brought over an all-terrain vehicle. Sharon decided to drive the vehicle after drinking and was stopped by the local sheriff. Sharon was charged with driving without a license and being under the influence. As restitution, Sharon had to pay a fine and agree to see a substance abuse counselor.

Case Intervention and Outcome

The substance abuse counselor met with Sharon for an initial meeting. Sharon reported that he did not view himself as having a problem with misusing alcohol or other drugs. The counselor suggested that Sharon join a substance abuse support group. Sharon did agree to meet with other American Indians in a small group. Sharon participated in the meetings but was more interested in completing the required number of sessions for the legal system. One of the group members announced that a sweat lodge was going to be held. Sharon attended the sweat lodge with a group of recovering alcoholics. His experience with the sweat lodge was life changing. Sharon began to acknowledge his substance use as bad medicine in his life and sought out Indigenous healers to help him in his recovery. Sharon continued with the small group and was able to maintain sobriety.

Case Reflections

What are your views of substance abuse counseling? How does culture interplay with the use or misuse of substances? How would you begin building rapport with Sharon? What would you consider possible treatment interventions for Sharon?

The Case of Winona: Abuse—"Expectations"

Winona, age 48, is Cherokee. Her life history is composed of serial relationships with abusive men. She has six children, each with different fathers. They are all living on their own or with relatives. After a recent intertribal celebration, Winona was beaten and left on the side of a parking lot. She was found by the local police and taken to the hospital. The police report indicated that Winona was ranting about "all men being teepee creepers and woman beaters." She told the police that she did not know her assailant's name but that he was not Indian. Winona has come to expect that her relationships will be abusive from the beginning. She reports seeking out partners who are less than desirable. Winona expresses that she loves to flirt and to go "snagging at powwows." Winona was referred to a counselor at the hospital. Winona discloses that the abuse she has received has always been her fault. She has very low self-worth and feels that women should be stronger than she has been.

Case Intervention and Outcome

Winona was placed in a domestic violence shelter with other women. She entered group counseling and was able to identify her faulty thoughts regarding her self-worth. This happened as a result of talking with another Cherokee woman who taught Winona about the strength of Cherokee women.

Case Reflections

What are some of the cultural issues of this case? How would you begin to help Winona? What is the relationship between a collectivist worldview and individualism in this case? How would you determine an intervention plan for Winona?

The Case of Charlie: Depression—Withdrawal—"Untouchable"

Charlie, age 17, is a Seneca Cayuga young man. He has an active family life and is often involved in Seneca Cayuga social gatherings. Charlie suffers from depression and feels unclean. When Charlie becomes depressed he feels cursed with bad medicine and has suicidal thoughts. Charlie's family is at a loss as to how to help him overcome the bad medicine. When asked what is wrong, Charlie frequently tells his family, "I am an untouchable and filled with bad medicine." The family is concerned about Charlie's lack of school attendance and is fearful that the Department of Human Services will get involved. His parents approach the school counselor for help.

Case Intervention and Outcome

The school counselor met with Charlie for a couple of sessions. He then referred Charlie to a psychiatrist at the local hospital who prescribed medication for the depression. The psychiatrist also worked with an Indigenous healer from the Seneca Cayuga Nation. Charlie agreed to begin meeting with the Seneca Cayuga Indigenous healer. He had difficulty complying with the medicine regime until the Indigenous healer became involved. The Seneca Cayuga people gathered around Charlie to help him feel connected to the group and to encourage his success. The tribal council requested a private meeting with Charlie to help him understand his special gifts. Charlie began to acknowledge his gifts and looked forward to his daily purpose in helping others.

Case Reflections

How would you approach this issue from a counseling perspective? What do you know about the concept of bad medicine among American Indian peoples? How can you as the counselor work with the family to help Charlie?

Conclusion

The spectrum of counseling American Indian peoples is very broad. As American Indian persons face a variety of issues and concerns in the 21st century, it is likely that they may experience higher risks for mental health problems and substance abuse than other ethnic groups. For many American Indians, the goals of counseling may center on achieving greater harmony and balance among their minds, bodies, spirits, and relationships and environments.

References

American Cancer Society. (2008). *Native American healing.* Retrieved from http://www.cancer.org/Treatment/TreatmentsandSideEffects/ComplementaryandAlternativeMedicine/MindBodyandSpirit/native-american-healing

Baruth, L. G., & Manning, M. L. (2007). The culturally effective counselor. In L. G. Baruth & M. L. Manning (Eds.), *Multicultural counseling psychotherapy* (4th ed., pp. 3–32). Upper Saddle River, NJ: Pearson.

Dixon, A. L., & Portman, T. A. A. (2010). The beauty of being native: Native American and Alaska Native identity development. In J. G. Ponterotto, J. M. Casas, L. A. Suzuki, & C. M. Alexander (Eds.), *Handbook of multicultural counseling* (3rd ed., pp. 215–226). San Francisco, CA: Sage.

Dixon Rayle, A. L., Chee, C., & Sand, J. K. (2006). Honoring their way: Counseling American Indian women. *Journal of Multicultural Counseling and Development, 34,* 66–79.

DuBray, W. H. (1985). American Indian values: Critical factor in casework. *Social Casework, 66,* 30–37.

Garcia, R. L., & Ahler, J. G. (1992). Indian education: Assumptions, ideologies, strategies. In J. Reyhner (Ed.), *Teaching American Indian students* (pp. 13–32). Norman: University of Oklahoma Press.

Garrett, J. T., & Garrett, M. (1994). The path of good medicine: Understanding and counseling Native American Indians. *Journal of Multicultural Counseling and Development, 22,* 134–144.

Garrett, M. T. (1999). Understanding the "medicine" of Native American traditional values: An integrative review. *Counseling and Values, 43,* 84–98.

Garrett, M. T., & Herring, R. D. (2001). Honoring the power of relation: Counseling native adults. *Journal of Humanistic Counseling, Education and Development, 40,* 139–151.

Garrett, M. T., & Pichette, E. F. (2000). Red as an apple: Native American acculturation and counseling with or without reservation. *Journal of Multicultural Counseling and Development, 78,* 3–13.

Garrett, M. T., & Portman, T. (2010). *Counseling and diversity: Native American.* Wadsworth, CA: Cengage Learning.

Heinrich, R. K., Corbine, J. L., & Thomas, K. R. (1990). Counseling American Indians. *Journal of Counseling & Development, 69,* 128–133.

Kromkowski, J. (Ed.). (2002). *Annual editions: Race and ethnic relations* (12th ed.). New York, NY: Guilford Press.

Locust, C. (1988). Wounding the spirit: Discrimination and traditional American Indian belief systems. *Harvard Educational Review, 58,* 315–330.

Lokken, J. M., & Twohey, D. (2004). American Indian perspective of Euro-American counseling behavior. *Journal of Multicultural Counseling and Development, 32,* 320–331.

Norris, T., Vines, P. L., & Hoeffel, E. M. (2012). *The American Indian and Alaska Native population: 2010.* Washington, DC: U.S. Census Bureau.

Oswalt, W. H. (1988). *This land was theirs: A study of North American Indians* (4th ed.). Mountain View, CA: Mayfield.

Peregoy, J. J. (1993). Transcultural counseling with American Indians and Alaska Natives: Contemporary issues for consideration. In J. McFadden (Ed.), *Transcultural counseling: Bilateral and international perspectives* (2nd ed., pp. 163–191). Alexandria, VA: American Counseling Association.

Portman, T. A. A., & Herring, R. D. (2001). Debunking the Pocahontas Paradox: The need for a humanistic perspective. *Journal of Humanistic Counseling, Education and Development, 40,* 185–199.

Sandefur, G. D., Rindfuss, R. R., & Cohen, B. (1996). *Changing numbers, changing needs: American Indian demography and public health.* Washington, DC: National Academies Press.

Sue, D. W., & Sue, D. (2007). *Counseling the culturally diverse: Theory and practice* (5th ed.). New York, NY: Wiley.

Thomason, T. C. (1991). Counseling American Indians: An introduction for non-American Indian counselors. *Journal of Counseling & Development, 69,* 321–327.

Trimble, J. E. (2010). Bear spends time in our dreams now: Magical thinking and cultural empathy in multicultural counselling theory and practice. *Counselling Psychology Quarterly, 23*(3), 241–253.

Additional Resources

The following websites provide additional information related to counseling American Indian peoples.

American Indian Movement
    www.aimovement.org
Indians.org
    www.indians.org
National Congress of American Indians
    www.ncai.org

Counseling People of the African Diaspora in the United States

Courtland C. Lee and Kimberly N. Frazier

This chapter provides direction for counseling people in the contemporary United States who trace their cultural roots to Africa. These are people whose individual or collective realities are linked to the African diaspora. The *African diaspora* refers to the movement of sub-Saharan Africans to places throughout the world—predominantly to the Americas, as well as other places around the world. The term is applied in particular to the descendants of those Africans who were enslaved and shipped to the Americas by way of the Atlantic slave trade (Manning, 2010). However, this movement is still seen today in the number of individuals from sub-Saharan Africa who immigrate to the United States.

Demographic Profile of the African Diaspora in the United States

In 2010 there were approximately 39 million Black Americans, who made up 12.6% of the U.S. population. Of this number, roughly 33 million were identified as *African American* (Humes, Jones, & Ramirez, 2011). In addition, according to Dodson and Diouf (2005b), 1.7 million people nationwide claim sub-Saharan ancestry. People of sub-Saharan African ancestry, therefore, now represent almost 5% of the African American community. Of these Americans of African descent, 1.5 million were identified as *African Caribbean* and a little more than 600,000 were identified as *African*.

The largest of the Black groups in the United States is identified as *African American*. These people are citizens or residents of the United States who have origins in any of the Black populations of Africa. In the United States, the term *African American* is generally used to describe Americans with at least partial sub-Saharan African ancestry. Most African Americans are the direct descendants of captive Africans who survived the slavery era, which began in the early 17th century and ended in the mid-19th century (Rastogi, Johnson, Hoeffel, & Drewery, 2011). Contemporary African Americans have made considerable social and economic advances in U.S. society, culminating in the election of Barack Obama as the first African American president in 2008. Despite these advances, however, the traditions of oppression and racism that have characterized much of the African experience in America still exert profound negative pressure on the lives of many African Americans (National Urban League, 2010; Robinson, 2010). Recent data on crime, education, and labor suggest an ongoing stifling of human potential in many African American communities and underscore the fact that there continue to be serious challenges to academic, career, and personal–social development among this population (National Center for Education Statistics, 2010; National Urban League, 2010; U.S. Department of Justice, 2011; U.S. Department of Labor, 2011).

The challenges that confront African Americans are inextricably linked. There is no doubt that continued economic disadvantage and social discrimination are the ultimate source of the psychosocial challenges facing many African Americans. Despite an African American in the White House and scores of solidly middle-class families, many Black people still find themselves abandoned in the backwaters of career, educational, and social progress (Robinson, 2010).

Black people identified as *African Caribbean* or *West Indian American* are those with origins in the Dutch-, English-, and French-speaking lands of the Caribbean. They include individuals with cultural roots in the Bahamas, Barbados, the Dutch West Indies, Haiti, Jamaica, Trinidad and Tobago, and the Virgin Islands. African-Caribbean Americans face many issues associated with both their immigrant and minority group status. These include economic challenges, family problems, and educational difficulties (Holger, 2001; Mitchell, 2005; Waters, 1999).

Those Black people identified as *African* are generally recent immigrants to the United States from Africa. This group is to be distinguished from African Americans and African Caribbeans, who are descended from Black Africans who survived the Atlantic slave trade within the United States and the Caribbean. Countries with the most immigrants to the United States are Nigeria, Ghana, Ethiopia, Eritrea, Egypt, Somalia, and South Africa (U.S. Census Bureau, 2011). The influx of African immigrants to the United States began in the latter part of the 20th century. About 57% immigrated between 1990 and 2000 (Dodson & Diouf, 2005b). Africa-to-U.S. migration patterns are influenced by five major factors: (a) economic globalization and integration, (b) the failure of African nations to develop economically and politically, (c) U.S. immigration and refugee policies, (d) linguistic ties, and (e) historic connections between sending nations and the United States (Gordon, 1998). African immigrants tend to be the most educated population group in the United States—50% have bachelor's or advanced degrees compared to 23% of native-born Americans (Dodson & Diouf, 2005a). Although significant numbers of African immigrants have high levels of education and are employed in higher level occupations, they face many of the same challenges associated with immigrant and minority group status in the United States (Robinson, 2010; Takyi, 2002; Uwah, 2002). Recent African immigrants are confronted with challenges in terms of employment (Andemariam, 2007; Kent, 2007; Takougang, 2002), family (Kamya, 2005; Nwadiora, 1996), and education (Njue & Retish, 2010; Traoré, 2006; Traoré & Lukens, 2006).

Counseling people of the African diaspora who reside in the United States presents counselors with an opportunity to become more aware of the cultural issues that form a basic worldview for this client group. Although these issues impact each individual differently, they underlie the psychosocial development of people of African origin and are important in establishing a cultural context for counseling interactions. This chapter provides a cultural framework for counseling people of the African diaspora in the United States. It first presents an overview of the concept of Afrocentricity and its relationship to mental health for people of African descent. This is followed by a discussion of several important issues that must be considered in culturally competent counseling with people of the African diaspora in the United States. The next part of the chapter focuses on counseling practices with clients of African descent. Case studies and specific guidelines for culturally competent counseling highlight this part of the chapter.

Afrocentricity: A Theoretical Overview

Afrocentricity Defined

There is an old saying: "You can take the Black man out of Africa, but you cannot take Africa out of the Black man." To varying degrees, people of the African diaspora in the United States possess attitudes, values, and behaviors that are characteristic of their African heritage. Any discussion of culturally competent counseling with individuals of the African diaspora, therefore, must begin with an examination of Afrocentricity. Afrocentricity is an existential point of view that puts Africa at the center of one's cosmology (Asante, 1992). The central theme of Afrocentrism is the idea that people of African descent must acknowledge, understand, and love their "Africanness" in order to understand and effectively deal with the past, present, and future. Afrocentricity reframes many psychoeducational concepts often considered deviant or pathological in a Eurocentric context into positive developmental notions for people of African descent.

Scholars of Afrocentricity are in general agreement that there exists a composite of African-oriented existential tendencies, philosophies, behaviors, ideas, and artifacts among people worldwide who trace their roots to Black Africa (Asante, 1991, 1992; Asante & Asante, 1993). The fact that these African universal concepts are theorized to exist suggests that mental health and psychosocial development among people of African descent is related to the degree and nature of these people's awareness of and responsiveness to Afrocentricity (Akbar, 1979; Baldwin, 1981; Belgrave et al., 1994; Brookins, 1994; Nobles, 1986, 2004).

As a psychological resource, Afrocentricity represents what Jung (1958) would have referred to as the "collective unconscious" among African peoples. This collective unconscious is composed of African folklore and mythology as well as historical, social, and political events.

Afrocentricity is evident in a number African-oriented traditions and customs. These include such concepts as perception of reality, concept of time, spirituality, human relations, family membership, and holism. In traditional African societies, these concepts are significant representations of a collective African cultural ethos. The work of Mbiti (1970) on African religion and philosophical traditions offers perhaps the best explanation of these concepts.

Perception of Reality

The traditional African-oriented perception of reality can be described as field dependent or field sensitive. This pattern of conceptualizing and processing reality tends to take into consideration the interactions between and among objective and subjective realities as well as the consequences or implications of such interactions. Among the Ibo of eastern Nigeria, for example, a common way to test the manner in which a child perceives reality is with the "birds on a tree" quiz. The child is told that 100 birds are on a tree when a hunter shoots one of them. The child is then asked, "How many birds are left on the tree?" In Western thinking, the obvious answer would be 99. However, for an Ibo child the correct answer is always zero, because the child is expected to factor in all other realities, not just the numerical. In this case, it would be the birds' natural behavior to fly away if one of them is shot.

Concept of Time

The African concept of time embodies a people-oriented or event-oriented utility. Time is fluid and gets its meaning and importance from the essence of people and events. Social events, as opposed to fixed calendars or mechanical devices, control responses to time.

Most traditional African cultures are concerned with two dimensions of time: the past and the present. The concept of the future is considered "no time." Individuals can only reflect on what has been and what is. What will be, however, is generally out of the realm of consideration.

Spirituality

In traditional African societies, religion or spirituality permeates human existence. An individual's entire life is a spiritual phenomenon. Spirituality is an integral part of a unity principle in which humans, animals, plants, and natural phenomena are interrelated in a natural order with God as the driving force.

A strong belief in a spirit world pervades traditional African worldviews. Spirits belong to the ontological realm of existence between human beings and God. Africans generally recognize two categories of spiritual beings: those who were created as spirits and those who were once human beings. Human fate is controlled by the spirit world.

Human Relations

The African-oriented view of human nature is characterized by cooperative interdependence and group-centeredness in human relationships. Every human life is deemed to be existentially relevant to the functioning, well-being, and dynamics of a community.

Achieving adult status has considerable social implications because African societies are adult oriented as opposed to youth oriented. Age and maturity affect leadership selection, social interaction, respect, responsibility, and cultural education. A younger person is expected to respect older persons unconditionally. Advanced age in and of itself is deemed respectable and honorable. Young people who show disrespect for their elders encounter different forms and degrees of social sanctions and isolation.

Family Membership

The traditional African family is extended in nature. For example, individuals with a strong African identity tend to take financial responsibility for even distant relatives as obligatory. Most African languages do not have words for *cousin, nephew, second cousin, niece, uncle, aunt,* and so on. In many cases, these family relations are described simply as *brother* or *sister.* This not only is done for simplicity but reflects the true African-oriented family structure and close sense of family belongingness.

Holism

Generally speaking, traditional Africans make little distinction between body, mind, and spirit. Africans perceive a strong interconnectedness between the cognitive, affective, and behavioral realms of personality. The traditional African personality responds to external stimuli in a holistic fashion. In social gatherings, for example, Africans are more likely to participate rather than merely observe. A traditional African is more likely than not to become cognitively, affectively, and behaviorally expressive to music or other affective stimuli.

It is important to note that given the vast cultural and ethnic group differences among African people, these concepts may be manifested in a variety of ways. There are significant geographic, linguistic, religious, ethnic, and historical variations in the manifestation of these concepts throughout sub-Saharan Africa. The concepts Afrocentricity are also reflected differently in the attitudes, behaviors, and lifestyles of people of the African diaspora in the United States.

Over the years scholars have suggested that the counseling profession seek new directions in its efforts to help Black clients empower themselves (Barnes, 1972; Harley & Dillard, 2005; Lee, 2004; Pasteur & Toldson, 1982; White & Parham, 1990). These scholars have called for counseling interventions that incorporate Afrocentric elements as a way to promote psychosocial development (Belgrave et al., 1994; Lee, 2003; Pasteur & Toldson, 1982).

Prelude to Counseling Practice

In addition to the importance of Afrocentricity, two other issues must be understood if effective counseling with Americans of African descent is to take place. These issues provide an important prelude to counseling practice.

Pitfalls of a Monolithic Perspective

In discussing counseling people of the African diaspora, there is a danger of assuming that all Black people are the same and that one methodological approach is universally applicable in any counseling intervention. Indeed, if one reviews much of the psychological or counseling literature related to Black issues, one might be left with the impression that there is an all-encompassing Black reality and that all Americans of African descent act, feel, and think in a homogenous fashion. Such an impression invariably leads to a monolithic perspective on the Black experience in America as well as to stereotypic thinking in which Black people are considered indistinguishable from one another in terms of attitudes, behaviors, and values. Professional counselors who possess such a perspective run the risk of approaching Black clients not as distinct human beings with individual experiences but rather merely as stereotypes.

Like all people, people of the African diaspora in the United States differ from one another in terms of experiences. Each American of African descent is a unique individual who is the sum total of his or her common human experiences, specific cultural experiences, and personal life experiences. Attempting to identify common experiences among Americans of African descent is a precarious enterprise, because people of the African diaspora in the contemporary United States are not a homogeneous group (Robinson, 2010). The counseling process with Americans of African descent, therefore, must be predicated on the notion that there is a high degree of intragroup variability and that interventions must be client and situation specific. The body of knowledge on the African diaspora in the United States suggests that although African American, African-Caribbean American, and African immigrant worldviews are minimally connected through the concepts of Afrocentricity, significant variability is reflected in the lifestyles and values of these cultural groups (Robinson, 2010; Shaw-Taylor & Tuch, 2007; Waters, 1999). This body of knowledge underscores the importance of approaching counseling with African American clients in an individualistic as opposed to a monolithic manner.

Racism as a Precipitating Factor of Psychoeducational Challenges for Americans of African Descent

When discussing important issues in counseling with people of the African diaspora, it is important to stress again that, as a client group, these individuals differ significantly in terms of their culture, socioeconomic status, educational attainment, lifestyles, and value orientations. However, all Americans of African descent, regardless of their cultural origins, share the common reality of racism (Bobb, 2001; Crocker & Quinn, 1998; Feagin & Sikes, 1994; Harrell, Merritt, & Kalu, 1998; Lewis-Trotter & Jones, 2004; Obiakor & Grant, 2005; Waters, 1999).

Despite claims of a postracial society in the wake of the election of Barack Obama as president, African Americans, African-Caribbean Americans, and African immigrants continue to face race-based economic and social discrimination in the United States (National Urban League, 2010). Although reactions to this oppressive dynamic may differ, its persistence significantly impacts the quality of life of Americans of African descent and should be considered a significant factor in both problem etiology and counseling intervention. The stresses of daily life are compounded for Black people by both overt and covert racism. Racism may operate to limit people of African descent from experiencing a full measure of employment, educational, and social opportunity. The historical persistence of racism has profoundly impacted the mental health of Black Americans. It is important to note that Americans of African descent have developed a number of ways of coping with and adapting to the dynamics of racism and its inherent challenges. These coping and adaptation mechanisms could manifest during counseling.

A Framework for Counseling With Americans of African Descent

Although the issues discussed previously may present challenges to culturally competent counseling with clients from the African diaspora in the United States, they also provide the basis of a framework for effective intervention with this client group. A number of key factors make up this framework (Lee, 2004):

1. *Development of rapport.* Given the possible degree of racism-based alienation or distrust of the counseling process among Black clients, it is important to find ways to make an initial personal connection. Counselors may need to adopt an interpersonal orientation when counseling with Black individuals. Such an orientation places the primary focus on verbal and nonverbal interpersonal interactions between the counselor and client as opposed to counseling goals or tasks (Gibbs, 1980).
2. *Pacing of the counseling process.* It is important to pace the counseling relationship and be mindful of engaging too rapidly in therapeutic work with many Black clients. The counseling process is often more effective if it evolves naturally from an interpersonal relationship based on openness and trust that emerges between the counselor and the client.
3. *Counselor self-disclosure.* It is often important that a counselor be prepared to self-disclose, often on a deep and personal level, to a Black client. A counselor's willingness to forthrightly answer direct and often intimate questions about his or her life increases his or her credibility and promotes rapport with many Black people in counseling. However, a counselor should only self-disclose to the extent he or she is comfortable and should maintain a sense of appropriate boundaries when revealing personal information to a client.
4. *Spirituality.* Counseling with Black individuals can often be enhanced if a counselor can engage in an exploration of how clients approach living and dying (i.e., spirituality). Helping clients to explore their sense of spirituality or personal meaning in life can provide a focus for processing issues of alienation, anger, or frustration. Such an existential or philosophical exploration can only be facilitated if rapport and trust have been established.

5. *Racism-sensitive counseling.* Counseling with Black clients must be predicated on sensitivity to the dynamic of racism. Although there is a great deal of variation in the effects of racism on the psychosocial development of people of the African diaspora, the influence of racism on the quality of these individuals' lives cannot not be overstated. A culturally competent counselor, therefore, should factor this variable into problem etiology and resolution as appropriate. It is important to avoid discounting clients' perceptions of how this dynamic impacts their lives.

6. *Psychoeducational counseling.* Counseling with many Americans of African descent should be viewed as an educative process. The primary focus of the process may need to be on developing new skills or behaviors to deal more effectively with social and economic challenges.

Directions for Professional Counseling Practice

The following case studies present contemporary issues confronting people of the African diaspora in the United States. Each case is followed by an analysis of the dynamics presented and guidelines for counselor intervention.

African American Case Study: Wanda

Wanda is 40 years old, divorced, and raising a teenage son by herself. She lives in a middle-class neighborhood in a large city. She has recently been laid off from her job as a middle school language arts teacher because of budget cuts in the city's public school system.

Wanda is interested in obtaining a master's degree and ultimately teaching English at a community college. However, health problems (diabetes and high blood pressure) and challenges related to raising her son alone have kept her from pursuing her goal.

When she presents for counseling her primary complaints are feelings of depression and low self-esteem. She is experiencing a great deal of anxiety with regard to her job loss and health. She is also feeling overwhelmed with the responsibilities associated with being a single mother.

Case Analysis

Wanda's background and experience appear to refute, to a large extent, negative stereotypes about urban African American women who are single parents. There seem to be several important sources of motivation and strength for her. She has an employment record, the result of a solid educational background. She appears to be motivated to advance both educationally and professionally. It appears, however, that a number of situational forces have converged to present major emotional challenges for Wanda. The budget cuts on the part of the school system, her health problems, and the challenges of single parenthood have contributed to her precarious life position. There is no doubt that Wanda feels disempowered given the roadblocks she perceives to furthering her education in light of her health problems and job loss. Because these issues are closely tied to her financial status, it is little wonder that she is feeling depressed and anxious about the well-being of her family. This, coupled with the demands of raising an adolescent son alone, has left her feeling overwhelmed. The disempowering nature of these challenges has seriously affected her sense of self-efficacy (i.e., "I am what I can do").

Directions for Counseling Practice With Wanda

Counseling with Wanda should be framed within the context of psychoeducational intervention. The major goal is to help Wanda become empowered. Empowerment is a developmental process by which people who are powerless or marginalized become aware of the power dynamics at work in their lives. They then develop the skills and capacity to gain a degree of control over their lives (McWhirter, 1994). The ultimate goal of counseling with Wanda, therefore, involves helping her to become empowered for personal mastery and competence.

Initial Contact. At the outset it is important to gain Wanda's trust and allay her fears about talking about "her business." The counselor should attempt to get Wanda to see him or her as a person first and a mental health professional second. The counselor should adopt an interpersonal approach, focusing more on the relationship between the two of them rather than any specific counseling goals. The counselor may want to engage Wanda in conversations about a variety of nonthreatening issues (e.g., her son, events in her community, things she likes to do in her free time).

Appraisal. As Wanda and the counselor continue to talk and develop rapport over the first few sessions, the counselor may need to be forthcoming with information about his or her own family origin, educational background, and work experience. If Wanda were to ask direct questions about the counselor's home and family life, the counselor needs to consider being open and honest with her, although he or she is perhaps not altogether comfortable revealing such information. It is important for the counselor to be open with Wanda in a personal way. Finding ways to equalize the status between Wanda (an African American woman) and the counselor (who may or may not be an African American or a woman) should be an important aspect of establishing a working alliance.

Involvement. As Wanda begins to reveal her feelings about the loss of her teaching position, her health issues, and her son, her anger, frustration, and anxiety become increasingly evident. It would be important at this point for the counselor to allow Wanda to tell her story.

Commitment. After the counselor spends several sessions listening to Wanda's story, it should become obvious to Wanda that the counselor is someone who is open and who she can definitely talk to and possibly work with. It is at this point that the counselor should elicit a commitment to counseling from Wanda.

Engagement. This is where the empowerment work begins. The counselor should begin by encouraging Wanda to explore meaning in her life. Wanda might be asked to consider how she sees herself as a human being, as a woman, and as an African American. She may then be asked what meaning being an African American woman has for her. The counselor should encourage Wanda to consider what gives her life meaning as an African American woman.

As the meaning and purpose of her life become more focused, the counselor can help Wanda to see the interrelatedness of her challenges. Wanda bears the sole financial responsibility for herself and her son. Career advancement would no doubt make this responsibility easier to bear. However, the loss of her teaching position, complicated by her physical challenges, appears to be preventing her from achieving greater economic reward. In addition, having to be both mother and father to a teenage son has placed additional stressors on her, as she feels she must devote significant time and energy to ensure her son's well-being and positive development. All of this contributes to her depression and also has her questioning her worth as a person.

At this point, it is time to engage Wanda in a plan of action. The counselor should engage her in a concrete problem-solving process designed to help her deal with her immediate challenges on the way to achieving her long-term goals. Her first step is to deal with her health issues. Diabetes and high blood pressure are major health challenges for African Americans (Cain & Kingston, 2003; Rajaram & Vinson, 1998). Because so much of her family situation depends on her being healthy, it is important to help Wanda establish a wellness regime that will control her diabetes and blood pressure. The counselor can help Wanda make a commitment to herself that she will work as hard as she can to take control of her health issues and not let them define or disempower her. In order to make this a viable strategy, however, Wanda and the counselor may need to explore health insurance options given her employment situation.

Her second step is to explore ways to more effectively manage the stress of single motherhood, in particular being the single parent of a young African American male. It is estimated that 67% of African American children live in a single-parent family (Annie E. Casey Foundation, 2011). In addition, it has been well documented that young African American males face formidable challenges to their psychosocial development (Lee, 2003; Schott Foundation for Public Education, 2010). It is important to help Wanda process her feelings related to the pressure she feels about raising a son alone and any fears she may have about her son becoming another negative Black male statistic. The goal is to help Wanda gain a sense of self-efficacy with respect to raising a healthy and productive son alone.

It would be important, therefore, to assure Wanda that she is not alone in dealing with the challenges of single motherhood. Finding a supportive group of mothers who, like her, are raising sons alone would be an important way for Wanda to learn from the experiences of other individuals of dealing with single parenting issues and challenges. Such communal support groups for African American women have been identified as important psychotherapeutic and educational interventions (Bradley & Lipford-Sanders, 2006; Jordan, 1997).

It might also be beneficial to help Wanda find a mentoring program for her son that would put him in contact with positive adult African American male role models. In recent years the number of such programs has increased throughout the country (Lee, 2003). Such a program would be a critical complement to Wanda's parenting because it would provide her son with important male guidance that could enhance his academic and personal–social development.

With respect to Wanda's employment situation, the third step in the plan of action should focus on helping Wanda explore her interests, abilities, and options with respect to a job search. While Wanda engages in a search for employment, it is important that the counselor help her secure unemployment benefits and other resources, such as child support, that will help her maintain the integrity of family life for her and her son. The counselor should help Wanda develop a sense of empowerment as she seeks to gain control over her employment possibilities given the challenging economic times.

As Wanda begins to develop the skills and capacity for gaining a degree of control over her life with these three interrelated action steps, the counselor should help her begin to focus on her long-range plan of furthering her education and obtaining a teaching position at a community college. Although at present these goals may not be obtainable, it is important that Wanda feel that the foundation is in place to seize opportunities at the appropriate time. If she develops self-efficacy with respect to her health, the positive development of her son, and employment, then she can look to the future with a sense of hope.

West Indian American Case Study: Colin

Colin is a 26-year-old immigrant to the United States from Jamaica who is attending a local college part time. He is the first person in his family to attend college. Colin has been referred to the college counseling center by an academic advisor after several professors have reported that he has been turning in assignments late, has been missing classes, and appears distracted when he is in class.

Colin possesses a student visa that allows him to work in the college student union. When he is not attending class or working in the union, he washes dishes at a restaurant near the campus in order to make extra money. The owner of the restaurant pays Colin off the books because this job violates his visa status. Making money is very important to Colin because in addition to paying his college and living expenses, he sends money home each month to his mother, who has a disability and who is attempting to provide for herself and Colin's younger brother and sister.

Recently Colin was laid off at the restaurant. Several men he met while working there have been offering him the opportunity to make extra money by selling drugs. As Colin has limited job prospects given his student visa status, this drug-selling option is becoming more appealing. Colin states that he is "feeling a great deal of pressure."

Case Analysis

Although Colin is a unique individual, his challenge reflects the reality of many West Indian immigrants. It is evident that Colin has come to the United States in search of educational opportunity, as is the case with many immigrants from the Caribbean (Mitchell, 2005). Likewise, like many Caribbean immigrants Colin holds multiple jobs in order to maintain a degree of economic security (Mitchell, 2005). Economic security is a major theme for Colin, as he is helping to support his family back in Jamaica. Sending money to family back home is another common theme of the West Indian immigrant experience (McKenzie, 1986; McLaughlin, 1981). It is not surprising, therefore, that Colin presents for counseling experiencing a great deal of stress that is obviously affecting his academic performance.

Directions for Counseling Practice With Colin

In order to engage Colin in the counseling process, the counselor should follow the same steps for contact, appraisal, involvement, and commitment outlined in the previous case. It would be important to engage him on an interpersonal level, find ways to equalize the counselor–client status to establish a working alliance, and allow Colin to tell his story in his own time and his own way. The goal of counseling should be to help Colin relieve the pressure he is feeling.

A plan of action for Colin should entail sorting out the issues that are exerting pressure on him and impeding his performance in the classroom. To begin the counselor should explore with him the nature and meaning of his education both to him and to his family. As a first-generation college student Colin should ask himself, "What does it mean to me and to my family to be the first person to attend college?" His answer to this question should help him gain important perspective on the significance of his education and his sense of responsibility to his family.

Next Colin should be assisted in examining the nature of his financial commitment to his family back in Jamaica. It is important for the counselor to understand that such a commitment reflects the collectivist nature of the culture in which Colin was raised. Although Colin's obligation to his family must be honored, he needs to consider how it is impacting his efforts to obtain a college degree. He needs to critically assess the jeopardy in which he is placing himself and his family by considering becoming involved in selling drugs. It is vital for him to consider the negative educational and economic consequences for himself and his family of such illegal activity.

In order to ease the stress of his financial obligations the counselor might explore with Colin some alternative ways that his family might be assisted. Such alternatives might be a way to possibly take some of the financial burden off of his shoulders. The counselor might help Colin in contacting the Jamaican embassy or consulate to consult with officials about possible social service resources back home that could provide assistance for his family. Similarly, he could be encouraged to contact Caribbean nongovernmental organizations about possible resources that might help his family. In addition to nongovernmental organizations, the counselor might direct Colin to religious or social and cultural organizations in the local community that could be of assistance. It would be important to help Colin find assistance that might help him see that he may not have to bear this financial responsibility by himself.

In addition, the counselor might consider advocating for Colin with U.S. immigration officials about greater job opportunities. It is important to explore whether it would be possible for Colin to make more money without jeopardizing his visa status or his ability to progress academically. Moreover, the counselor may need to consult with the financial aid office on campus to determine whether other employment options are available to Colin.

Helping Colin find a balance between his educational goals and his family obligations should relieve some of the pressure he is feeling. It should also help to prevent him from putting himself, his family, and his educational plans in serious jeopardy to meet his financial obligations. Through a counseling intervention that focuses on helping him to find this balance, it is crucial that a counselor understand Colin's cultural worldview as well as the realities that confront many immigrants in contemporary U.S. society.

African Immigrant Case Study: Jhodi

Jhodi is a 17-year-old female immigrant from South Africa who has been living with relatives in the United States since age 12. She came to the country for the opportunity to obtain a U.S. education, and she is now applying for admission to local colleges. She is sent to counseling because her grades have slipped and her grade point average is now impacting her ability to successfully gain acceptance into a local college.

Jhodi is feeling homesick for her mother, father, and brother since she has only been able to visit them in South Africa twice since coming to the United States. She is feeling stressed at the thought of disappointing her parents and her extended U.S. family because her college admission is in jeopardy because of her falling grades. She states that she is uncomfortable talking to her U.S. relatives because they have done so much by allowing her to live with them and being supportive of her studies. She does not want to burden them or appear ungrateful.

Case Analysis

Jhodi has been sent to live in the United States by her family in South Africa to take advantage of educational opportunities. It is common for many African immigrants who do this to live with their extended families in the United States. Because her family has given up a great deal to send her to the United States, Jhodi has felt the pressure to make sure her family's sacrifice pays off by earning good grades and getting into a college so she can get a job and start helping to support her family in South Africa. This constant pressure to not disappoint her family and to get into college has resulted in falling grades and anxiety about applying to college.

Directions for Counseling Practice With Jhodi

In order to engage Jhodi in counseling it is important to follow the same steps outlined in the previous two case studies for contact, appraisal, involvement, and commitment. Jhodi needs to be engaged on a personal level so that a working alliance can be naturally established between her and her counselor at a pace with which Jhodi feels comfortable.

A plan of action for Jhodi must include an exploration of her feelings of pressure to not disappoint her family both in South Africa and the United States and how that pressure has led to anxiety about falling grades and applying to college. The counseling intervention should also explore her feelings of homesickness and how these feelings might impact the pressure and anxiety she feels regarding her grades and applying to college. It is clear that education is important to her family, because Jhodi was sent to the United States specifically to be educated. Jhodi needs to be encouraged to express her feelings about being sent to the United States and being away from her family. She also needs to reflect on the responsibility being placed on her to perform well knowing the sacrifices that were made by her family to give her this educational opportunity.

Looking specifically at how pressure and stress manifest themselves in relation to her grades will allow the counselor and Jhodi to develop coping skills to mediate the stress she feels in school. Also, suggesting that Jhodi seek help in applying to college from her high school counselor will be helpful in increasing her chances of being admitted to college. It is also important to help identify resources and programming that will allow Jhodi to explore interests outside of school and help her find activities that will allow her to relieve the stress associated with school and education. It is important for the counselor to understand Jhodi's worldview as it relates to her culture, family, and education while aiding her in finding a balance between the expectations of her family and the realities of being an immigrant in the United States.

Conclusion

Counseling with African Americans must be conducted with the knowledge that the African American culture fosters attitudes, behaviors, and values that are psychologically healthy and that within this culture are the resources for addressing mental health challenges and problems. Counseling interventions, therefore, should be undertaken from an Afrocentric perspective that focuses on promoting optimal mental health and well-being. Counselors should strive to promote African American development within an Afrocentric context of kinship, behavioral and emotional expressiveness, and holistic development.

References

Akbar, N. (1979). African roots of Black personality. In W. D. Smith, K. Burlew, M. Mosley, & W. Whitney (Eds.), *Reflections on Black psychology* (pp. 79–98). Washington, DC: University of America Press.

Andemariam, E. M. (2007). The challenges and opportunities faced by skilled African immigrants in the U.S. job market: A personal perspective. *Journal of Immigrant & Refugee Studies, 5,* 111–116.

Annie E. Casey Foundation. (2011). *Children in single-parent families by race (percent)—2009.* Retrieved from http://datacenter.kidscount.org/data/acrossstates/Rankings.aspx?ind=107

Asante, M. K. (1991). Multiculturalism: An exchange. *The American Scholar, 60,* 267–272.

Asante, M. K. (1992). *Afrocentricity.* Trenton, NJ: African World Press.

Asante, M. K., & Asante, K. W. (1993). *African culture: The rhythms of unity.* Trenton, NJ: African World Press.

Baldwin, J. A. (1981). Notes on an Africentric theory of Black personality testing. *Western Journal of Black Studies, 5,* 172–179.

Barnes, E. J. (1972). The Black community as the source of positive self-concept for Black children. In R. L. Jones (Ed.), *Black psychology* (pp. 106–138). New York, NY: Harper & Row.

Belgrave, F. Z., Cherry, V. R., Cunningham, D., Walwyn, S., Letlaka-Rennert, K., & Philips, F. (1994). The influence of Africentric values, self-esteem, and Black identity on drug attitude among African American 5th graders. *Journal of Black Psychology, 20,* 143–156.

Bobb, V. B. (2001). Neither ignorance or bliss: Race, racism, and the West Indian immigrant experience. In H. R. Cordero-Guzman, R. C. Smith, & R. Grosfoguel (Eds.), *Migration, transnationalization and race in a changing New York* (pp. 212–238). Philadelphia, PA: Temple University Press.

Bradley, C., & Lipford-Sanders, J. (2006). Counseling African American women and girls. In C. C. Lee (Ed.), *Multicultural issues in counseling: New approaches to diversity* (3rd ed., pp. 79–91). Alexandria, VA: American Counseling Association.

Brookins, C. C. (1994). The relationship between Afrocentric values and racial identity attitudes: Validation of the Belief Systems Analysis Scale on African American college students. *Journal of Black Psychology, 2,* 128–142.

Cain, V. S., & Kingston, R. S. (2003). Investigating the role of racial/ethnic bias in health outcomes. *American Journal of Public Health, 93,* 191–192.

Crocker, J., & Quinn, T. (1998). Racism and self-esteem. In J. E. Eberhardt & S. Fiske (Eds.), *Confronting racism: The problem and the response* (pp. 169–187). Thousand Oaks, CA: Sage.

Dodson, H., & Diouf, S. A. (Eds.). (2005a). *The brain drain.* Retrieved from http://www.inmotionaame.org/migrations/topic.cfm;jsessionid=f83016492311959145180041?migration=13&topic=4&tab=image&bhfv=7&bhfx=&bhpc=0&bhqs=1

Dodson, H., & Diouf, S. A. (Eds.). (2005b). *The waves of migration.* Retrieved from http://www.inmotionaame.org/migrations/topic.cfm?migration=13&topic=3&tab=image&bhfv=7&bhfx=&bhpc=0&bhqs=1

Feagin, J., & Sikes, M. (1994). *Living with racism: The Black middle-class experience.* Boston, MA: Beacon Press.

Gibbs, J. T. (1980). The interpersonal orientation in mental health consultation: Toward a model of ethnic variations in consultation. *Journal of Community Psychology, 8,* 195–207.

Gordon, A. (1998). The new diaspora: African immigration to the United States. *Journal of Third World Studies, 15,* 79–103.

Harley, D., & Dillard, J. (2005). *Contemporary mental health issues among African Americans.* Alexandria, VA: American Counseling Association.

Harrell, J., Merritt, M., & Kalu, J. (1998). Racism, stress, and disease. In R. Jones (Ed.), *African American mental health: Theory, research, and intervention* (pp. 247–280). Hampton, VA: Cobb & Henry.

Holger, H. (2001). *The West Indian Americans.* Westport, CT: Greenwood Press.

Humes, K. R., Jones, N. A., & Ramirez, R. R. (2011). *Overview of race and Hispanic origin: 2010.* Washington, DC: U.S. Census Bureau.

Jordan, J. M. (1997). Counseling African American women from a cultural sensitivity perspective. In C. C. Lee (Ed.), *Multicultural issues in counseling: New approaches to diversity* (2nd ed., pp. 109–121). Alexandria, VA: American Counseling Association.

Jung, C. (1958). The archetypes and the collective unconscious. In G. Adler, M. Fordham, & H. Reed (Eds.), *Collective works* (Vol. 9, Pt. 1, Bollingen Series XX). New York, NY: Pantheon Books.

Kamya, H. (2005). African immigrant families. In M. McGoldrick, J. Giordano, & N. Garcia-Preto (Eds.), *Ethnicity and family therapy* (3rd ed., pp. 101–116). New York, NY: Guilford Press.

Kent, M. M. (2007). Immigration and America's Black population. *Population Bulletin, 62,* 3–16.

Lee, C. C. (2003). *Empowering young Black males III: A systematic modular training program for Black male children and adolescents.* Alexandria, VA: American Counseling Association Foundation, Education Resources Information Center/Counseling and Student Services.

Lee, C. C. (2004). Counseling African Americans. In R. L. Jones (Ed.), *Black psychology* (4th ed., pp. 631–650). Hampton, VA: Cobb & Henry.

Lewis-Trotter, P. B., & Jones, J. M. (2004). Racism: Psychological perspectives. In R. L. Jones (Ed.), *Black psychology* (4th ed., pp. 559–588). Hampton, VA: Cobb & Henry.

Manning, P. (2010). *The African diaspora: A history through culture.* New York, NY: Columbia University Press.

Mbiti, J. S. (1970). *African religions and philosophy.* Garden City, NY: Doubleday.

McKenzie, V. M. (1986). Ethnographic findings on West Indian-American clients. *Journal of Counseling & Development, 65,* 40–44.

McLaughlin, M. E. (1981). *West Indian immigrants: Their social networks and ethnic identification.* New York, NY: Columbia University Press.

McWhirter, E. (1994). *Empowerment in counseling.* Alexandria, VA: American Counseling Association.

Mitchell, N. (2005). Academic achievement among Caribbean immigrant adolescents: The impact of generational status on academic self-concept. *Professional School Counseling, 8,* 209–219.

National Center for Education Statistics. (2010). *NAEP summary data tables.* Retrieved from http://nces.ed.gov/nationsreportcard

National Urban League. (2010). *The state of Black America report 2010: Jobs.* New York, NY: Author.

Njue, J., & Retish, P. (2010). Transitioning: Academic and social performance of African immigrant students in an American high school. *Urban Education, 45,* 347–370.

Nobles, W. W. (1986). *African psychology: Toward its reclamation, reascension, and revitalization.* Oakland, CA: Black Family Institute.

Nobles, W. W. (2004). African philosophy: Foundation for Black psychology. In R. L. Jones (Ed.), *Black psychology* (4th ed., pp. 57–72). Hampton, VA: Cobb & Henry.

Nwadiora, E. (1996). Therapy with African families. *Western Journal of Black Studies, 20,* 117–124.

Obiakor, F. E., & Grant, P. A. (Eds.). (2005). *Foreign-born African Americans: Silenced voices in the discourse on race.* Hauppauge, NY: Nova Science.

Pasteur, A. B., & Toldson, I. L. (1982). *Roots of soul: The psychology of Black expressiveness.* Garden City, NY: Anchor Press/Doubleday.

Rajaram, S. S., & Vinson, V. (1998). African American women and diabetes: A sociocultural context. *Journal of Health Care for the Poor and Underserved, 9,* 236–247.

Rastogi, S., Johnson, T. D., Hoeffel, E. M., & Drewery, M. P. (2011). *The Black population: 2010.* Washington, DC: U.S. Census Bureau.

Robinson, E. (2010). *Disintegration: The splintering of Black America.* New York, NY: Doubleday.

Schott Foundation for Public Education. (2010). *Yes we can: The Schott 50 state report on Black males and education.* Retrieved from http://blackboysreport.org/

Shaw-Taylor, Y., & Tuch, S. A. (Eds.). (2007). *The other African Americans: Contemporary African and Caribbean immigrants in the United States.* Lanham, MD: Rowman & Littlefield.

Takougang, J. (2002). *Contemporary African immigrants to the United States.* Retrieved from http://www.africamigration.com/archive_02/j_takougang.htm

Takyi, B. K. (2002). The making of the second diaspora: On the recent African immigrant community in the United States of America. *Western Journal of Black Studies, 26,* 32–43.

Traoré, R. (2006). Voices of African students in America: "We're not from the jungle." *Multicultural Perspectives, 8,* 29–34.

Traoré, R., & Lukens, R. J. (2006). *This isn't the America I thought I'd find: African students in the urban U.S. high school.* Lanham, MD: University Press of America.

U.S. Census Bureau. (2011). *2009 American Community Survey, B04006, People Reporting Ancestry.* Washington, DC: Author.

U.S. Department of Justice. (2011). *Preliminary semiannual uniform crime report, January-June 2011.* Retrieved from http://www.fbi.gov/about-us/cjis/ucr/crime-in-the-u.s/2011/preliminary-annual-ucr-jan-jun-2011

U.S. Department of Labor. (2011). *Civilian labor force level—Black or African American.* Retrieved from http://research.stlouisfed.org/fred2/series/LNU01000006

Uwah, G. O. (2002). Reflections of an African-born immigrant: Story of alienation. In O. E. Festus & G. A. Patrick (Eds.), *Foreign-born African Americans: Silenced voices in the discourse on race* (pp. 15–27). New York, NY: Nova Science.

Waters, M. C. (1999). *Black identities: West Indian immigrant dreams and American realities.* New York, NY: Russell Sage Foundation.

White, J. L., & Parham, T. A. (1990). *The psychology of Blacks: An African American perspective* (2nd ed.). Englewood Cliffs, NJ: Prentice Hall.

Chapter 5

Counseling Asian and Pacific Islander Americans

Song E. Lee and Albert Valencia

Asian and Pacific Islander (API) Americans are those people whose origins are the Asian continent and islands in the Pacific Ocean. API Americans include, but are not limited to, people who represent Chinese, Japanese, Korean, East Indian, Filipino, Vietnamese, Cambodian, Hmong, Laotian, Thai, Samoan, and Malaysian cultural backgrounds. There are more than 17.3 million API Americans in the United States (Humes, Jones, & Ramirez, 2011).

According to Reeves and Bennett (2003), it is impossible to characterize the API population in the United States as a homogeneous group. This growing population includes groups of people who differ with respect to culture, language, values, level of acculturation, socioeconomic status, and length of residency in the United States. A few Asian groups, such as the Chinese and Japanese, have resided in the United States for several generations. Other Asian groups, such as Cambodians, Laotians, Vietnamese, and Hmong, are comparatively recent immigrants. Of the Pacific Islander groups, only a few are foreign born. Within the API population, there are more than 14 subpopulations, each made unique by different cultural, linguistic, and sociodemographic backgrounds and different histories of immigration to the United States. Zhou, Siu, and Xin (2009) cautioned researchers and mental health providers that they run the risk of arriving at erroneous conclusions if they attempt to aggregate Asian Americans into a single monolithic category.

Providing counseling to API Americans requires that counselors identify cultural variables, themes, values, and standards. This chapter introduces API American groups and provides some practical counseling considerations. The goal of the chapter is to ensure that counselors understand the diversity between and within these groups in order to provide culturally competent services.

Chinese Americans

Chinese Americans were one of the first Asian groups to immigrate to the United States. During the 1800s, Chinese came to the United States to work on sugar plantations in Hawaii and as laborers during the California Gold Rush (Chan, 1992). Although the Chinese were the first to arrive in the United States, only 29.1% of the Chinese American population was born in the United States (Reeves & Bennett, 2004). About 70.8% of Chinese Americans are foreign born. Furthermore, 75.6% of foreign-born Chinese entered the United States as recently as the 1980s. Therefore, a large percentage of Chinese Americans are first-generation Americans.

Currently there are 2,422,970 Chinese Americans in the United States, making them the largest Asian American cultural group (Reeves & Bennett, 2004). Because a large number of Chinese were born abroad and speak languages other than English at home, many Chinese families may still value Chinese cultural and religious traditions (Reeves & Bennett, 2004). In addition, although Chinese Americans are more educated and earn more than many other Asian groups, their poverty rate is 13.5%. It is also important to note that the Chinese immigrants who came to the United States during the 1990s were educated and had transferable job skills, which often sets them apart from other recent immigrants or refugees (Zhou et al., 2009).

Chinese culture is influenced by Confucianism, and its moral and social concepts influence Chinese behavior and the Chinese worldview (Huang & Charter, 1996). In contrast to Western cultural notions of autonomy and independence, Chinese culture expects individuals to "focus on ancestral veneration, respect for authority, and duty to the group" (Huang & Charter, 1996, p. 36). Chinese American parents often expect their children to embrace filial piety (the duty and honor owed to elders), education, hard work, and discipline in order to help the family increase its status (Zhou et al., 2009).

Chinese culture is also influenced by Buddhism, Taoism, and ancestral worship. The Chinese religious belief system is a combination of Chinese folk religion, Buddhism, Taoism, and Confucianism (Hsu, O'Conner, & Lee, 2009). Christianity has also played a role in the religious belief system of many Chinese families. Religious beliefs shape the views and values of Chinese and also may contribute to the development of appropriate coping skills (Lee & Chan, 2009).

Japanese Americans

In 1990, there were 847,562 Japanese Americans in the United States. Ten years later, in 2000, the population had decreased by 6% to 796,700. Japanese Americans were the only Asian American group to show a decrease in their numbers over this period (Reeves & Bennett, 2003).

The Japanese began arriving in the United States in the late 1800s. Many Japanese refer to themselves by the number of generations they have resided in the United States. The first generation, or *Issei*, arrived in the United States about 100 years ago. The second generation, *Nisei*, represents the U.S.-born children of the Issei. Educated in U.S. schools and speaking English, the Nisei tend to see themselves as bicultural individuals. The third generation, *Sansei*, and the fourth generation, *Yonsei*, are children of parents who either were direct victims of the unconstitutional practice of U.S. government internment during World War II or knew relatives, friends, or neighbors who were rounded up by the military in a mass evacuation and placed in internment camps (Ina, 1997).

This mass evacuation, largely from the U.S. West Coast, was a reaction to Japan's attack on Pearl Harbor on December 7, 1941. The evacuation was enacted by Executive Order 9066 signed by President Franklin D. Roosevelt on February 19, 1942. This order enabled the military to circumvent the U.S. Constitution and military law to move 110,000 Japanese Americans from their homes, businesses, and property into internment camps. In the years following World War II, the internment of Japanese Americans was characterized as a profoundly hysterical, racist, and economically exploitative measure. Later, it became known that the U.S. government had proof that not one Japanese American was ever found to have engaged in espionage or sabotage (Ina, 1997).

Vital to the worldview of many Japanese Americans is the influence of the philosophical concepts of Confucianism and Buddhism. In Confucian and Buddhist philosophy, which arrived in Japan in the 6th century, the individual is superseded by the family, hierarchal roles are specifically established for individual family members, and rules for behavior and conduct are formalized. In the hierarchy of the family, the father is the prescribed leader and decision maker. His authority to enforce family rules and discipline is not questioned, nor is his responsibility for the welfare of the family. Successes or failures of the family and of its individual members are seen as the father's responsibility. The mother in a traditional Japanese American family is viewed as an emotionally devoted, nurturing parental figure and caregiver. Strong emotional attachments that are developed within the family tend to be developed with the mother (Ina, 1997).

Highly developed feelings of obligation serve to govern many aspects of Japanese Americans' interpersonal relationships. The concepts of loss of face and shame are frequently used to gain acceptance of or adherence to prescribed sets of obligations. Quality and harmony within these relationships are thought to be best achieved through conduct and attitudes that are viewed and recognized as proper. Important and often unspoken in the lives and relationships of many Japanese Americans is the concept of reciprocity of obligation. This reciprocity is a serious relational quality for Japanese Americans, as is the showing of respect and obedience to parents and other authority figures. Demonstrations of respect and obedience go beyond the reflection of indebtedness, as they also express gratitude and affection. Japanese Americans tend to avoid direct confrontation and talk around a point; their communication styles are often indirect, and problem solving occurs within the prescribed family structure. The resolution of a problem is often viewed as a sacrifice for the good of the whole and rests on unwavering loyalty and the ability to stoically endure hardship (Ina, 1997).

Korean Americans

In 1990, there were 798,849 Korean Americans in the United States, and this number increased to 1,076,872 in 2000. Accordingly, Korean Americans rank as the fifth largest Asian American subgroup after Chinese, Asian Indians, Filipinos, and, Vietnamese. Korean Americans have higher scores than other racial/ethnic groups on inventories of depressive symptoms and may be at particular risk for mental distress (Jang, Chiriboga, & Okazaki, 2009). Complicating this scenario are three additional findings. First, Korean Americans tend to underutilize mental health services. Second, Korean Americans have negative perceptions of the use of mental health services. Third, there is a lack of theoretical models appropriate to the psychological experiences of Korean Americans (Jang et al., 2009). These findings are in line with a 2001 report of the U.S. Surgeon General (Office of the Surgeon General, 2001) and a report by Thomas (2009) regarding the disparities and marginalization experienced by Asian Americans in the delivery of mental health services.

In 1997, Toarmino and Chun presented a concise and well-considered overview of the history, cultural values, and mental health status of Korean Americans. The authors cited Confucianism, Buddhism, and Shamanism as being basic to the foundation of traditional Korean culture as demonstrated in hierarchal relationships and gender roles. Based on the cultural practice of collectivism and on hierarchy-defining relations, human relationships place the interests of the group above the interests of the individual, and, taken as a whole, hierarchal relationships create an interdependent network among family members and others in Korean society.

South Asian Americans

South Asian Americans are individuals whose origins are India, Pakistan, and Bangladesh (Singh, 2003). Individuals with origins in India are called *Asian Indians* or *East Indians*. Those from Pakistan are called *Pakistani,* and those from Bangladesh are called *Bangladeshi*. Like other API Americans, South Asians have different languages and cultures. There have also been different waves of South Asian immigrants to the United States. Currently there are 1,645,510 Asian Indians, 155,909 Pakistani, and 57,412 Bangladeshi residing in the United States (Singh, 2003).

After a change in immigration laws in 1965, the first large wave of South Asians immigrated to the United States. South Asian immigrants are mostly well-educated and professional individuals (Reeves & Bennett, 2004; Saran, 1985). They are among the most educated and economically successful Asian Americans. The percentage of people with a college degree is 63.9% among Asian Indians ages 25 and older and 54.3% among Pakistani, putting them ahead of all other Asian groups. In addition, more than 50% of Bangladeshi older than 25 have a bachelor's degree (Reeves & Bennett, 2004). In terms of family income, Asian Indians surpass Pakistani and Bangladeshi (Reeves & Bennett, 2004).

South Asians are diverse in terms of their language and culture. For example, some of the languages that Pakistani Americans speak are Urdu, Punjabi, Sindhi, Pashto, Hindko, Balochi, Kashmiri, and Seraiki. Asian Indians are also linguistically diverse. Although Hindi is the official language of India, Asian Indians may speak any of the other hundreds of dialects in India. Other languages of Asian Indians are Gujarati, Punjabi, Bengali, Urdu, Marathi, Oriya, Kannada, Tamil, and Malayalam (Alagiakrishnan & Copra, n.d.). Most Bangladeshi speak Bangali, or Bangla (Bangladesh-America, 2007).

The religious beliefs of South Asians are influenced mostly by Hinduism, Buddhism, and Islam. Most Asian Indians practice Hinduism, and most Pakistani and Bangladeshi practice Islam. Other religious beliefs of Asian Indians are Sikhism, Buddhism, Jainism, or Christianity (Alagiakrishnan & Copra, n.d.). Other religions of Pakistani are Hinduism, Christianity, and Zoroastrianism.

Like other Asian groups, South Asians also face acculturation issues and culture clash with their children (Das & Kemp, 1997; Saran, 1985). As a result of the September 11, 2001 attack in New York, emergent issues that face South Asians are hate crimes and discrimination (Singh, 2003). Research findings focusing on South Asians also include the following results: Common issues among Asian Indian college students were dating, arranged marriage issues, acculturation concerns, and school related concerns (Tewari, 2002); Stressors in the lives of South Asian second-generation college students were related to concerns with identity, autonomy, academic performance, study skills based on perfectionism, procrastination, and physical health problems (Meunier, 1998). Attitudes toward counseling seem to be more positive with Asian Indians who had come to the United States before age 10 (Panganamala & Plummer, 1998).

Southeast Asian Americans

Southeast Asian Americans consist of ethnic groups from countries such as Laos, Thailand, Vietnam, Cambodian, and Myanmar (Burma). Like many Asian countries, each Southeast Asia country includes several ethnic groups with different cultures and languages. For example, 100 different ethnic groups reside in Laos (Central Intelligence Agency, n.d.). As a result of war in Laos, Vietnam, and Cambodia as well as civil war in Myanmar, many Southeast Asian ethnic groups have sought refuge in the United States.

Southeast Asian Americans are the most recent Asians to enter the United States, beginning in the mid to late 1970s. They include the Vietnamese, Cambodians, Laotians, Hmong, Miens, Lahus, and Khmus, among others. Recently, more Hmong and Myanmar refugees have been admitted into the United States. In 2005, 15,000 Hmong refugees were admitted into the United States (Martin, 2005), and in 2007, 13,896 Myanmar refugees were admitted (Associated Press, 2007). Southeast Asian Americans make up about 17% of the Asian American population (Reeves & Bennett, 2004). The Vietnamese are the largest group of Southeast Asian Americans, making up 10.9% of the Asian American population. Southeast Asian Americans such as the Mien, Lahu, and Khmu were not included in the census. They may represent less than 1% of the Asian population.

Many Southeast Asian Americans struggle financially and have difficulties adjusting to life in the United States. Among Southeast Asian Americans, the Vietnamese and Thai are the most educated and financially stable, whereas the Hmong and other Southeast Asians who resided in mountainous areas in their former countries are the least educated and financially stable. Many of these refugees came from an agricultural lifestyle and may have difficulty adjusting to life in the United States. Furthermore, most Southeast Asian Americans were born outside of the United States, which may make it difficult for them to adjust to the Western culture. In addition, some Southeast Asians, such as the Hmong, lived in remote areas before immigrating to the United States. Therefore, adjusting to life in the United States is difficult because they are often illiterate and lack appropriate job skills (Mouanoutoua & Brown, 1995).

Southeast Asian Americans include diverse ethnic groups that share many similarities as well as differences in terms of culture, language, traditions, and religious beliefs. Their ways of life are mostly influenced by Confucian and Buddhism philosophies. Most Southeast Asian Americans have a patriarchal family system, but because of shifts in roles in the United States, Southeast Asian American women are starting to take part in making family decisions. Despite these shifts in roles, however, men still hold official positions in the clan and familial structure in many Southeast Asian American communities. Yet, traditionally, despite the power differential between Southeast Asian men and women, both genders are often respected and esteemed for their life experiences in their older years.

Some issues Southeast Asian American families face before and after migrating include trauma, grief and loss, adjustment difficulties, generation gaps, and financial difficulties (Reeves & Bennett, 2004). Another important emergent issue among Southeast Asian Americans is the needs of elders. Most Southeast Asian American elders are illiterate and endured major trauma and adjustment as they escaped atrocity in their country of origin.

Pacific Islanders

In the 2000 U.S. Census, 874,000 people, or 0.3% of the population, reported being Native Hawaiian and Other Pacific Islander. This number included 399,000 people, or 0.1%, who reported being only Pacific Islander and 476,000 people, or 0.2%, who reported being Native Hawaiian and Other Pacific Islander as well as one or more other race. According to Grieco (2001), the term *Native Hawaiian and Other Pacific Islander* refers to people with origins among any of the original peoples of Hawaii, Guam, Samoa, or other Pacific Islands. Pacific Islanders differ in terms of culture and language. Their different populations are of Polynesian, Micronesian, and Melanesian cultural backgrounds (Grieco, 2001).

A total of 401,000 respondents to the 2000 U.S. Census reported being Native Hawaiian alone or in combination with one or more other races or Pacific Islander groups (Grieco, 2001). Samoan and Guamanian or Chamorro were the next two largest groups: 91,000 people reported being Samoan alone and an additional 42,000 reported being Samoan in combination with one or more other races or Pacific Islander groups. Moreover, 58,000 people reported being Guamanian or Chamorro, and an additional 34,000 reported being Guamanian or Chamorro in combination with one or more other races or Pacific Islander groups. Combined, Native Hawaiians, Samoans, and Guamanians or Chamorro accounted for 74% of all respondents who reported being of a single Pacific Islander group (Grieco, 2001).

Although there is limited research on Native Hawaiians and Pacific Islanders, it is evident that health education and health care are needed among this population. Moy, Sallis, and David (2010) found a higher prevalence of obesity and chronic conditions such as hypertension in Native Hawaiians and Pacific Islanders than in the general population. Other challenges that face this ethnic group are "parental language barriers, cultural expectations, community demands, and the often economically deprived family circumstances" (Vakalahi, 2009, p. 1259). Acculturation issues and the need to navigate two cultures are also issues for many Native Hawaiians and Pacific Islanders. In addition, Native Hawaiian and Pacific Islanders youth are at risk for being high school dropouts and show high rates of delinquent behaviors (Vakalahi, 2009).

Commonalities Found Among API American Groups

Although API groups are linguistically and culturally diverse, they share many similarities. The following are selected commonalities among API Americans that may impact the counseling process.

Family and Religion

Family and religious beliefs are strong among many API Americans because they serve as a bridge connecting younger generations to their ethnicity and culture (Saran, 1985). Although some API Americans may not be religious, they may engage in religious activities to maintain the culture. Likewise, strong ties to families often help people deal with the strains of life (Saran, 1985). Therefore, many API Americans do not believe in seeking outside professional help because they have support at home.

Viewing the Self in Relation to Others

API Americans view the self in relation to others, which is qualitatively different from the Western worldview in which the self is independent of others (Markus & Kitayama, 1991). The API view of the self is associated with the goal of Buddhism "to forget the self" (Lillard, 1998, p. 11). Therefore, many API Americans identify themselves in relation to their clan or family, and many strive to succeed for the family rather than for themselves. Because of the influence of this philosophy, younger generations may experience pressure to choose a profession, choose a location of residence, or make other decisions based on their families' needs rather than their own.

Although many API Americans may have an interdependent view of the self, this does not mean that they are not efficient as individuals or have a low self-concept (Markus & Kitayama, 1991). Therefore, it is imperative that counselors understand how individuals shape themselves rather than trying to shape them into being healthy within a Western context.

Gaps Between Children and Parents

An issue that is characteristic of traditional Asian American families and recent refugees or immigrants is the cultural gap that often exists between parents and children. As discussed previously, some characteristics of API Americans, such as being interdependent, stand in stark contrast to Western views. Therefore, parents may expect their children to be cooperative and give in to others, whereas children may see this as a sign of weakness because self-assertion is a positive attribute in the Western worldview (Markus & Kitayama, 1991). The generational difference in views between traditional API American parents and their children who have been influenced by Western worldviews may negatively impact family relationships and communication, often resulting in stress, misunderstandings, and conflicts.

Differences Found Among API American Groups

There are noteworthy differences among API American groups. Issues that distinguish these groups stem from their pre- and postmigration experiences. For instance, many Southeast Asians came to the United States as refugees as a result of the Vietnam War. These API Americans experienced trauma and hardship before entering the United States. Furthermore, most Southeast Asians who arrived in the United States after the end of the Vietnam War did not have formal education or transferable job skills. Therefore, as a result of a lack of exposure to Western philosophies, limited education, and being illiterate in English they are believed to have suffered greatly in their postmigration experiences.

Other API Americans, such as the Chinese and Asian Indians, came to the United States as immigrants seeking greater opportunities and economic mobility. Therefore, many Chinese and Asian Indians came to the United States equipped with professional job skills, formal education, and knowledge of the English language. Their postmigration experiences were different from and in some cases not as difficult as those of Southeast Asians.

Another major difference in the experience of API American cultural groups pertains to economic and educational attainment. The term *model minority* is a common stereotype that asserts that Asian Americans, as an aggregated group, are able to gain educational attainment without special assistance and are thereby positioned as a model for other minority groups to emulate. According to Ngo and Lee (2007), this stereotype "is used to silence and contain Asian Americans even as it silences other racial groups" (p. 416) and minimizes "the fact that America is a fundamentally racist society" (p. 416).

Yet the term *model minority* does not apply to every API American group. This is particularly true when the data for Asian Americans are disaggregated. For example, although some Chinese, Japanese, and Asian Indians may have higher educational and economic attainment than the general population, other API American groups, such as the more recently arrived Southeast Asians, have the lowest educational and economic attainment (Reeves & Bennett, 2004).

In addition, there are diverse languages and dialects among API American cultural groups. Likewise, there are major differences among API American cultural groups with respect to religious practices. Although some API Americans may share similar religious beliefs, religious practices vary across cultural groups and across generations in the United States.

Counseling Considerations

Counseling API Americans presents important challenges. These include the underutilization of counseling services among this population, the retention of API American clients in counseling, the inconvenient location of counseling services, language issues, the need to respect individual and group differences among API Americans, and the need to modify Western interventions to fit the worldviews and needs of API Americans. Counseling services are often not understood by many API American groups, and mental health illness often has a negative connotation that prevents individuals from seeking needed services. Furthermore, illness and well-being are viewed differently in each API American culture (Spector, 2000).

Limitations of Western Interventions

Whereas counseling methods taken from Euro-American culture are based on "lateral human relationships, individuation, independence, and self-disclosure," API American culture is based on "hierarchal relationships, interdependence, self-control, and acceptance" (Toarmino & Chun, 1997, p. 249), and this is further complicated by the dynamic of immigration. Therefore, a culturally competent counseling methodology for use with API Americans might need to be directive, structured, and more clearly defined as opposed to client centered, nondirective, neutral, and explorative.

Counseling methods that are more consistent with API American cultural expectations include cognitive therapy and cognitive behavior therapy. In addition, because individual issues are often embedded in family dynamics, family therapy may be more culturally consistent with the hierarchal structure and traditional values and beliefs of many API Americans. According to Toarmino and Chun (1997), this model of family therapy could avoid internal conflicts and focus on external stressors, teaching "problem solving techniques and active problem management" (p. 250) and assisting family members to achieve solutions that are external and concrete.

The idea of American individualism is contrary to the API Americans values of individual sacrifice and collective and cooperative hierarchal family structures. Trying to balance two very different cultures can be overwhelming, as API Americans can be ignored or redirected for exhibiting behaviors that historically have received appreciation and value in their ethnic communities. Because American counseling systems and modalities cater largely to individual and inner-directed decision-making processes, methods of counseling API Americans need to be different by being culturally sensitive, responsive, and consistent. Neutral and ambiguous explorations into feelings may need to be replaced with culturally sensitive assessments and followed with direct, structured, and defined approaches.

Even though a typical Eurocentric counseling process of weekly visits may be helpful to some, counseling consultation visits may be perceived as more useful to API American clients. Counseling consultation in our practice deals less with processing and focuses on educating the clients to better understand their issues, providing ideas on how to strengthen their relational skills, and providing suggestions on how to more effectively cope with their situation. Often, the suggestions include encouraging clients and linking them to weekly counseling services. In agreement with this, Lin (1998) found that some API Americans tend to seek consultation regarding their own and their family's mental health needs rather than seeking counseling services. Many API Americans set appointments to seek advice on how to deal with the issues but do not want to attend continuous sessions. For example, a Hmong client once asked one of us (Song E. Lee) whether counseling would be beneficial for him and his wife. He also asked about issues that may have contributed to his failing marriage and possible strategies to improve his relationship. He wanted to be educated on his issues before making a decision on how to deal with them. After being helped to conceptualize his issues with his wife, receiving tips on how to improve his communication by using "I statements" and focusing conversations on the needs of the couple instead of blaming, the client thanked me for the consultation. Although he was advised to seek counseling with his wife, he never did. Before ending his first session he said, "I'll come again if I have any other questions." Therefore, typical counseling sessions or appointments may not be relevant to the needs of many API Americans. Using a consultation model in counseling may fit some of the needs of API Americans and may be a bridge between the API community and counseling services (Lin, 1998).

Modifying Western Interventions

Incorporating traditional healing practices and religious beliefs in counseling helps to motivate and fulfill the needs of many API American clients. Preisser (1999) also supported the use of Eastern interventions with Western methods. The counseling goal is to help clients understand and deal with their issues by using concrete and direct methods. It is important for the counselor to try to understand a client's traditional views, using culturally consistent and linguistically appropriate inquiry. The following integrative approach is recommended for ongoing counseling sessions with API American clients.

Assessment Sessions
When working with API American clients it is important to explore their level of acculturation, their degree of acculturation stress, their religious beliefs, their belief in traditional healing practices, their cultural values, their views about their presenting issues, the transgenerational impact of immigration in their lives, and their views of counseling.

Conceptualization
After obtaining a clear view of who clients are, what their issues are, and how they view their issues, it is important to help them gain a better understanding of their issues. A counselor should strive to demystify his or her role by providing education to clients regarding the process of counseling and helping them to understand their issues in terms of their traditional beliefs.

Intervention
Once the presenting issue is conceptualized in relation to clients' family and environment, a cognitive behavior therapy approach is recommended as a way to work on some of their thoughts and behaviors. Cognitive behavior therapy is more directive and has strategies that are tangible and relatively easy for clients and their families to use.

Integration
In addition to Western counseling interventions, if needed and/or expected by clients, the counselor might suggest seeking the assistance of a traditional healer or religious guide. For example, while working with Hmong clients using Cognitive Behavioral Therapy, if clients believe that soul loss is a reason for their diminished mental health status, the

counselor could suggest that they consider the help of a shaman. For clients who have other religious beliefs, their own spiritual practices should also be considered while they attend counseling sessions.

Another way to incorporate an integrative counseling approach is to help clients resolve their issues to benefit themselves and their family. When any of the parties are not benefiting from a behavioral or cognitive change through counseling, it might be useful for the counselor to explore the range of consequences by examining individualist and collectivist needs. By exploring these consequences, clients can better understand the effects of their decisions. As a result, they are generally able to make better choices and to set counseling goals that are more culturally appropriate for their needs.

Consultation

When API American clients are only seeking a few counseling sessions, a consultative approach might be useful. When consulting it is important to conduct a brief assessment of a client's issues, views, and needs. The counselor may then make recommendations, provide education, and/or provide the client with coping skills. If warranted, it might also be suggested that the client look at his or her own resources, such as families or traditional approaches, to deal with the presenting issues. It is important to advise the client to seek further counseling to ensure that he or she has support for his or her issues, understands his or her coping mechanisms, and receives some education on the process and content of counseling.

Psychoeducation

Psychoeducation is another direct approach that may appear more acceptable to API American clients. The following experience illustrates a psychoeducational technique for working with API American clients.

In 2008, I (Song E. Lee) collaborated with a local nonprofit organization to provide psychoeducation in Hmong via a Hmong AM radio station. The target audience was Hmong elders because they lack transportation to see a counselor in the community and often listen to the radio. Therefore, I went on air once a week at the radio station to educate the elders on mental health issues, symptoms, and coping mechanisms. The program included additional elements to make the show livelier and included guest speakers on numerous topics. The listeners were encouraged to call in to share knowledge and insights they had gained and to provide feedback to improve the show. In a 1-year review, the comments from listeners were positive and supportive. In addition, the callers found the information to be relevant and some of the coping techniques to be novel and useful.

The radio show proved to be a good idea because I knew this population was unaware of counseling services and did not have the means to seek counseling. Therefore, the radio program provided mental health education to the listeners as well as bridged the gap between them and available counseling services.

Conclusion

As you think about this chapter, reflect on your experiences of being misunderstood and stereotyped. Were there times during these experiences when you became angry, felt like you needed to correct others, or felt like you just needed to walk away? If so, you may understand how many API Americans feel when others do not understand them. API American clients may not return to counseling if they feel misunderstood or perceive that counseling is of no value to them.

As counselors, it is important to understand certain aspects of the clients with whom we work. Counseling services need to be culturally sensitive and relevant to the situations of clients, such as in terms of filial duty, lack of transportation, limited English proficiency, and lack of trust in or knowledge of counseling. In order to understand any cultural group, it is also imperative that counselors continue to be self-aware and educated on the ethnic groups with whom they work. Self-awareness and education need to go beyond your reading of this book. In addition, remember that not all API Americans or their issues were discussed in this chapter. For more detailed information regarding the different API groups, please refer to the additional Web resources at the end of this chapter.

References

Alagiakrishnan, K., & Copra, A. (n.d.). *Health and health care of Asian Indian American elders.* Retrieved from http://www.stanford.edu/group/ethnoger/asianindian.html

Associated Press. (2007). *Myanmar refugees strain U.S. aid groups: Communities fear backlash as asylum-seekers flood Ind., Minn., N.Y.* Retrieved from http://www.msnbc.msn.com/id/21281062/

Bangladesh-America. (2007). *Bangladesh country profile.* Retrieved from http://www.bangladesh-america.com/content.php?pagename=bangladesh

Central Intelligence Agency. (n.d.). *The world factbook: Ethnic groups.* Retrieved from https://www.cia.gov/library/publications/the-world-factbook/fields/2075.html

Chan, S. (1992). Families with Asian roots. In E. W. Lynch & M. J. Hanson (Eds.), *Developing cross-cultural competence* (pp. 181–257). Baltimore, MD: Brookes.

Das, A., & Kemp, S. (1997). Between two worlds: Counseling South Asian Americans. *Journal of Multicultural Counseling and Development, 25,* 23–33.

Grieco, E. M. (2001). *The Native Hawaiian and other Pacific Islander population: Census 2000 brief.* Retrieved from http://www.census.gov/prod/2001pubs/c2kbr01-14.pdf

Hsu, C. Y., O'Conner, M., & Lee, S. (2009). Understanding of death and dying for people of Chinese origin. *Death Studies, 33,* 153–174.

Huang, D., & Charter, R. (1996). The origin and formulation of Chinese character: An introduction to Confucianism and its influence on Chinese behavior patterns. *Cultural Diversity and Mental Health, 2*(1), 35–42. doi:10.1037/1099-9809.2.1.35

Humes, K. R., Jones, N. A., & Ramirez, R. R. (2011). *Overview of race and Hispanic origin: 2010 Census Briefs.* Retrieved from http://www.census.gov/prod/cen2010/briefs/c2010br-02.pdf

Ina, S. (1997). Counseling Japanese Americans: From internment to reparation. In C. C. Lee (Ed.), *Multicultural issues in counseling: New approaches to diversity* (2nd ed., pp. 189–206). Alexandria, VA: American Counseling Association.

Jang, Y., Chiriboga, D. A., & Okazaki, S. (2009). Attitudes toward mental health services: Age-group differences in Korean American adults. *Aging & Mental Health, 13*(1), 127–134.

Lee, E. K., & Chan, K. (2009). Religious/spiritual and other adaptive coping strategies among Chinese American older immigrants. *Journal of Gerontological Social Work, 52,* 517–533.

Lillard, A. (1998). Ethnopsychologies: Cultural variations in theories of mind. *Psychological Bulletin, 123,* 3–32.

Lin, J. (1998). Descriptive characteristics and length of psychotherapy of Chinese American clients seen in private practice. *Professional Psychology: Research and Practice, 29,* 571–573. doi:10.1037/0735-7028.29.6.571

Markus, H., & Kitayama, S. (1991). Culture and the self: Implications for cognition, emotion, and motivation. *Psychological Review, 98,* 224–253.

Martin, D. (2005). *The US refugee program in transition.* Retrieved from http://www.migrationinformation.org/feature/display.cfm?ID=305

Meunier, V. (1998). South Asian and other Asian students' use of university counseling services. *Dissertation Abstracts International, 58* (9), 5131B.

Mouanoutoua, V. L., & Brown, L. (1995). Hopkins Symptom Checklist 25, Hmong Version: A screening instrument for psychological distress. *Journal of Personality Assessment, 64,* 376–383.

Moy, K. L., Sallis, J. F., & David, K. J. (2010). Health indicators of Native Hawaiian and Pacific Islanders in the United States. *Journal of Community Health, 35*(1), 81–92.

Ngo, B., & Lee, S. (2007). Complicating the image of model minority success: A review of Southeast Asian American education. *Review of Educational Research, 77,* 415–453.

Office of the Surgeon General. (2001). *Mental health: Culture, race, and ethnicity: A supplement to Mental health, a report of the surgeon general.* Rockville, MD: U.S. Public Health Service.

Panganamala, D., & Plummer, D. (1998). Attitudes toward counseling among Asian Indians in the United States. *Cultural Diversity and Mental Health, 4,* 55–63.

Preisser, A. (1999). Domestic violence in south Asian communities in America: Advocacy and intervention. *Violence Against Women, 5,* 684–699. doi:10.1177/10778019922181437

Reeves, T., & Bennett, C. (2003). *The Asian and Pacific Islander population in the United States: March 2002.* Retrieved from http://www.census.gov/prod/2003pubs/p20-540.pdf

Reeves, T., & Bennett, C. (2004). *We the people: Asians in the United States.* Retrieved from http://www.census.gov/prod/2004pubs/censr-17.pdf

Saran, P. (1985). *The Asian Indian experience in the United States.* Cambridge, MA: Schenkman.

Singh, J. (2003). Bangladeshi & Pakistani Americans. *Asian-Nation: The Landscape of Asian America.* Retrieved from http://www.asian-nation.org/bangladeshi-pakistani.shtml

Spector, R. E. (2000). *Cultural diversity in health and Illness.* Upper Saddle River, NJ: Prentice Hall Health.

Tewari, N. (2002). Asian Indian American clients presenting at a university counseling center: An exploration of their concerns and a comparison to other groups. *Dissertation Abstracts International. Section B: The Sciences and Engineering, 62*(7-B), 3391.

Thomas, S. (2009). From the editor: Introduction of special issue on minority mental health. *Issues in Mental Health Nursing, 30,* 69. doi:10.1080/01612840802595055

Toarmino, D., & Chun, C. (1997). Issues and strategies in counseling Korean Americans. In C. C. Lee (Ed.), *Multicultural issues in counseling: New approaches to diversity* (2nd ed., pp. 233–254). Alexandria, VA: American Counseling Association.

Vakalahi, H. F. O. (2009). Pacific Islander American students: Caught between a rock and a hard place? *Children and Youth Services Review, 31,* 1258–1263.

Zhou, Z., Siu, C., & Xin, T. (2009). Promoting cultural competence in counseling Asian American children and adolescents. *Psychology in the Schools, 46*(3), 290–298. doi:10.1002/pits.20375

Additional Resources

The following websites provide additional information related to Asian Pacific Islander Americans.

Asian Nation: Indian Americans
http://www.asian-nation.org/indian.shtml

Asian Pacific American Heritage Teaching Resources
    http://www.smithsonianeducation.org/educators/resource_library/asian_american_
    resources.html
The Chinese Experience
    http://www.pbs.org/becomingamerican/chineseexperience.html
Countries and Their Cultures: Asian Indian Americans
    http://www.everyculture.com/multi/A-Br/Asian-Indian-Americans.html
Exploring the Japanese American Internment Through Film and the Internet
    http://www.asianamericanmedia.org/jainternment/
Japanese American National Museum
    www.janm.org
National Association of Korean Americans
    www.naka.org
Southeast Asia Resource Action Center
    www.searac.org
Virtual Hilltribe Museum
    http://www.hilltribe.org/index.shtml

A Conceptual Approach to Counseling With Latina/o Culture in Mind

Carlos P. Hipolito-Delgado and Jessica M. Diaz

What does it mean to be Latina/o? What is the Latina/o experience? These are questions with which many clients and counselors struggle. We ourselves have also struggled with these questions at various points in our lives. In fact, we have come to understand our ethnic identity and what it means to be Latina/o in different ways.

As we examined our unique experiences as Latinas/os, it became clear that a general discussion of Latinas/os would not be appropriate for this chapter. Thus, a conceptual approach to counseling is presented. This is done to teach practitioners and counselors-in-training how to honor the individual client while keeping Latina/o culture in mind. This chapter highlights the heterogeneity of Latinas/os. It also provides a basic understanding of this ethnic community by discussing ethnic labels, presenting the demographic profile of Latinas/os, presenting the U.S. experience, discussing traditional cultural considerations, and presenting some counseling considerations and interventions. We anticipate that this chapter is not the endpoint of your study of Latinas/os and their culture; rather, we hope that it inspires a continued interest in and investigation of this ethnic community.

Ethnic Labels

Various terms are used to describe people living in the United States who can trace their ancestry to Latin America; the most common are *Latina/o, Chicana/o,* and *Hispanic.* Although a full exploration of the history and meaning of these terms is beyond the scope of this chapter, given the confusion about these terms and the debate as to which is politically correct, we briefly consider the origins and usage of each term. Ultimately it is recommended that you use the term with which your client identifies.

The term *Latina/o* originally referred to the Latins, a small cultural community from the land of Latium that existed in ancient Rome (Gracia, 2000). *Latino* was also used in 19th-century Europe to describe persons from countries whose official language derived from Latin (Gonzales & Gandara, 2005; Gracia, 2000). During the 1970s, *Latina/o* became an umbrella term used to express solidarity of interest across national lines for people who trace their ancestry to Latin America (Alaniz & Cornish, 2008). Although *Latina/o* is historically most popular in Chicago and New York and with the politically left and center (Shorris, 1992), the term seems to have gained acceptance throughout the United States.

The term *Chicana/o* is most often used to refer to people of Mexican American heritage. However, such a narrow definition neglects the vital role that political consciousness and social activism play in Chicana/o identity (Huerta, 2002). In fact, Acuña (2003) and Duncan-Andrade (2005) described *Chicana/o* as a sociopolitical identity, one that is more concerned with political action than with ethnic heritage. *Chicana/o* was embraced as an ethnic identifier during the 1960s (Acuña, 2003; Duncan-Andrade, 2005; Huerta, 2002)—it represented empowerment, a rejection of Eurocentrism, a connection to indigenous ancestry, and a commitment to the struggle for civil rights (Alaniz & Cornish, 2008; Garcia, 1997). Furthermore, Chicanas/os are often characterized as militants and political radicals representing the left and the far left (Garcia, 1997). *Chicana/o* seems to be most popular in California (Shorris, 1992).

Hispanic was introduced as an ethnic identifier in the United States in the 1970 census to classify people of Mexican, Cuban, Puerto Rican, or Central or South American ancestry (Shorris, 1992). Many reject the label *Hispanic* because they believe it refers to Spanish ancestry (Gracia, 2000) or because the label was imposed by the government (Santiago-Rivera, Arredondo, & Gallardo-Cooper, 2002). The term *Hispanic* is historically most popular in Texas, New Mexico, and the U.S. southeast; with political conservatives; and with those of higher socioeconomic backgrounds (Shorris, 1992).

In this chapter we use the term *Latina/o*. The decision to use this term is based on convenience and the popularity of the term nationally and should not be viewed as an endorsement of *Latina/o* or as an argument for this term being politically correct. You are encouraged in your counseling work to use the term(s) with which your clients identify. Malott (2009) noted that it is disrespectful for counselors to apply an ethnic label to a client with which the client does not identify. Furthermore, Ortiz and Santos (2009) described how Latina/o students found it offensive to be called by an ethnic identifier that they did not endorse.

Demographic Profile

According to the 2010 Census, 50.5 million people (or 16% of the U.S. population) are of Hispanic or Latino origin. The Latino population has increased from 35.3 million in 2000, when this group made up 13% of the total population (Ennis, Ríos-Vargas, & Albert, 2011). Note that this estimate does not include the 3.7 million residents of the Commonwealth of Puerto Rico or any of the estimated 10–15 million undocumented Latinas/os in the United States. Latinas/os tend to be younger than the general U.S. population, with a median age of 27.2 years compared with 36.2 for the United States as a whole. Unfortunately, with regard to socioeconomic level, the Latina/o population falls behind the general population. Latinas/os' median income is less than $36,000 per year compared with the U.S. average of $46,326. Also, 22% of Latinas/os live below the poverty line (DeNavas-Walt, Proctor, & Lee, 2006).

Although Latinas/os share similar aspects of their cultural heritage, the Latina/o population in the United States "can often be characterized better by their diversity than by their similarity" (Marcoux, 2006, p. 482). To further stress these distinctions, we briefly outline the circumstances that have contributed to the immigration of the largest Latina/o ethnic groups in the United States. These next sections examine the migration patterns of Mexicans, Puerto Ricans, Cubans, Salvadorians, and Dominicans. The following information is intended to aid you in gaining a general overview of the Latina/o experience; however, remember that individual differences most certainly exist.

Mexicans

As of 2007, Mexicans were the largest population of Latina/o origin living in the United States, accounting for nearly two thirds (64.3%) of the U.S. Latina/o population (U.S. Census Bureau, 2006). The majority of Mexicans (62.6%) arrived in the United States in 1990 or later (Pew Hispanic Center, 2007). The population of Mexico continues to grow (approaching 100 million residents); however, the number of living-wage jobs has not kept pace with this growth. The availability of unskilled or entry-level jobs in the United States and a shared border accounts for the high rate of immigration from Mexico (Marcoux, 2006). Nearly 4 in 10 Mexicans (37.6%) live in California, and 1 in 4 (25.0%) live in Texas (Pew Hispanic Center, 2007).

Puerto Ricans

Puerto Ricans are the second largest population of Latina/o origin living in the United States, accounting for 9.1% (4.1 million) of the U.S. Latina/o population in 2007 (Pew Hispanic Center, 2007). The Puerto Rican immigration story is unique from that of other Latinos in that Puerto Rico is a commonwealth, a self-governing territory of the United States. Following World War II, thousands of Puerto Ricans moved to the continental United States when airfares sold for as little as $75. Because of their commonwealth status, immigrants from the island needed only documentation that they had been born in Puerto Rico to enter the United States. Puerto Ricans are concentrated in the northeast (primarily in New York) and in the south (primarily in Florida).

Cubans

Cubans are the third largest Latina/o population living in the United States, accounting for 3.5% (1.6 million) of the U.S. Latina/o population in 2007. According to the Pew Hispanic Center (2007), Cubans are the most geographically concentrated Latina/o group, with 68.7% living in Florida. This is largely the result of the close proximity of Florida to Cuba. The first wave of Cuban immigrants arrived in the United States after Fidel Castro assumed power in 1959. This first wave of immigration included a mass exodus of much of the country's upper-class, middle-class, and professional and business people. A second wave of immigration began in 1980 with the permission of Castro and President Jimmy Carter. In Florida the Cuban community developed into a powerful economic and political force (Marcoux, 2006).

Salvadorians

Salvadorians are the fourth largest population of Latina/o origin living in the United States, accounting for 3.2% (1.5 million) of the U.S. Latina/o population in 2007. According to the Pew Hispanic Center (2007), 38.5% of Salvadorians live in California, and

13.9% live in Texas. El Salvador was plagued by civil wars and political unrest throughout the 1970s and 1980s. Consequently, Salvadorian citizens and U.S. supporters fought for Salvadorians to be granted the same political asylum rights that the United States offered to Cubans (Wiltberger, 2009).

Dominicans

Dominicans are the fifth largest population of Latina/o origin living in the United States, accounting for 2.6% (1.2 million) of the U.S. Latina/o population in 2007. According to the Pew Hispanic Center (2007), 80.3% of Dominicans live in the northeast, and more than half (52.4%) live in New York. The Dominican Republic is a small Caribbean island nation that relies heavily on the export of goods such as sugar and the tourism industry. However, as the population grows and these industries fail to provide sufficient job opportunities, migration to surrounding countries continues to increase (Itzigsohn, 2005).

Unity and Diversity

The diversity of Latinas/os makes the cultural traditions of this community nuanced and rich. However, this diversity may also prevent Latinas/os from reaching their potential as a political force (Marcoux, 2006; Rodriguez, 2009). Statistics and history have shown that newly immigrated groups prefer to initially remain in homogeneous communities (Lay, 2005); the benefits of becoming a member of these ethnically homogeneous communities include stability, support, familiar language, and identity. However, when Latinas/os remain in ethnic enclaves defined by nationality they are less likely to develop a pan-ethnic Latina/o identity. The Latina/o population is often referred to as the "Sleeping Giant" of the political world; that is, they have the potential to influence legislation, but only if smaller national communities come to adopt a larger Latina/o identity (Rodriguez, 2009).

The U.S. Experience

Vontress (1997) stated that a conceptual approach to multicultural counseling considers the sociopolitical circumstances of clients. In this section some of the sociopolitical issues related to the experience of Latinas/os in the United States are discussed. This section considers the role of language, education, employment, and civil rights, as these issues are likely to influence the worldviews and presenting concerns of Latina/o clients.

Language

Although Latinas/os come from countries with distinct national histories, many share a common linguistic heritage. Note that not all Latin American countries speak Spanish: Some speak Portuguese, French, English, and/or a native language (such as Nahuatl, Mayan, or Quechua). That said, understanding the role language plays in the life of a Latina/o in the United States is a complex issue that involves generational traditions, family compromise, and the need to survive in a country that, for the most part, speaks English only.

Though most second- and third-generation U.S.-born Latinas/os have a good grasp of the English language, Latina/o immigrants often arrive in the United States with limited English language skills. The inability to speak English can hinder a Latina/o's ability to attain education (Bhatia, 2006; Marcoux, 2006; Smith-Adcock, Daniels, Lee, Villalba, & Indelicato, 2006), gain employment (Bardallo-Vivero, 2006), or in general engage in mainstream U.S. culture.

What is interesting is that some Latina/o neighborhoods are large and insular enough in their organization that traditional Latina/o cultural values are more prevalent than dominant U.S. values. Furthermore, Spanish is so widely spoken in these areas that residents do not need to speak English to conduct business, receive medical care, access social services, or travel within the boundaries of these neighborhoods. In general it is believed that increased economic and educational opportunities exist for those Latinas/os who acquire strong English language skills while retaining their fluency in Spanish.

However, the decision to acculturate or assimilate to the mainstream language may be a difficult one for families. For some learning English or losing the native language represents a betrayal of their cultural heritage, whereas for others fully assimilating to the English language represents limitless opportunities in the United States. With passing generations born in the United States, Latina/o families must decide whether the Spanish language will be preserved or forgotten. This decision may be made as a family or by an individual member and may be a source of tension. Although it is not directly tied to ethnic identity, the ability to speak the native language does facilitate access to and retention of cultural values and ethnic identity.

Education

Among Latina/o eighth graders originally surveyed in 1988, 80% had completed high school by the year 2000, 5% had earned a general equivalency diploma, 15% had done neither, and 65% had attended a postsecondary institution (Erisman & Looney, 2007). Although these numbers represent a dramatic improvement over previous generations, dropout continues to be an issue in the Latina/o community, particularly for recent immigrants. In 2006, 36% of foreign-born Latinas/os between the ages of 16 and 24 were classified as dropouts compared with 12% for both first-generation and second-generation or higher Latinos born in the United States (National Center for Education Statistics, 2008).

As of 2006, Latinas/os represented 19.1% of the kindergarten through Grade 12 educational population (Kewal Ramani, Gilbertson, Fox, & Provasnik, 2007). That same year, Latinas/os represented only 11% of students taking the SAT and scored on average 70 points below their White counterparts in mathematics and critical reading and 60 points below White students in writing (College Board, 2007). Given that the SAT is an entrance requirement for many colleges, it is not surprising that Latina/o students are not pursuing college at the same rate as other students. Limited access to financial resources, the need to obtain employment after graduating from high school to contribute to the family income, or decreased access to rigorous courses that prepare Latinas/os academically for college could deter Latinas/os from attaining higher education (O'Connor, Hammack, & Scott, 2010; Marsico & Getch, 2009). Also, Latina/o students are less likely to apply for college even when they have met the academic qualification for admission (National Center for Higher Education Management Systems, 2006).

Latino students represent 30% of undergraduate students in postsecondary education (Santiago, 2008). However, compared to their White counterparts, Latinas/os are more likely to enroll in community colleges and less likely to transfer to 4-year institutions (Kewal Ramani et al., 2007). Latinas/os enrolled in college are less likely than other minority groups to earn a degree (Santiago, 2008)—only 11% of Latinos and 13% of Latinas possess a bachelor's degree (Kewal Ramani et al., 2007).

The educational attainment of Latina/o parents plays a pivotal role in the educational attainment of their children. According to longitudinal studies conducted with Latina/o children, parents' educational level is significantly related to their subsequent educational attainment (Lopez, Gallimore, & Garnier, 2007).

Employment

Unemployment and underemployment continue to be serious issues for the Latina/o community. According to the April 2010 *Employment Situation Summary* from the Bureau of Labor Statistics, Latina/o unemployment is at 12.6%, almost 3 percentage points higher than in the general U.S. population (9.7%). Unemployment is especially high among Latina/o teens, with almost 1 in 3 Latina/o teens unemployed (compared with less than 1 in 4 White teens). Underemployment occurs when a worker is only able to secure part-time employment or is unable to secure sufficient income to sustain his or her family. The prevalence of underemployment is more difficult to capture statistically, but it is estimated that 18%–28% of Latinas/os are underemployed.

Although hope for better employment prospects has brought many immigrants to the United States, recent immigrants often discover barriers and challenges to employment once they arrive in the United States. Some Latina/o immigrants who were professionals in their native countries find that their educational qualifications are not honored by professional industries in the United States. Thus, they find themselves seeking lower level or unskilled jobs. For others, barriers such as an inability to speak English, lack of transportation, inadequate training, and lack of education prove to be difficult to overcome.

Civil Rights

Information in the areas of education, language, and employment begins to provide an understanding of the sociopolitical reality of Latinas/os in the United States. But a more comprehensive understanding of sociopolitical reality of Latinas/os requires attention to the issue of civil rights. Although racism and discrimination are still part of the lived reality of many Latinas/os in the United States, progress toward equality and social justice has been made.

A key moment in Latinas/os' struggle for civil rights was the case of *Méndez et al. v. Westminster School District et al.* (1947). This court decision ended the segregation of White and Mexican students in Orange County, California, schools and set a legal precedent for *Brown v. Board of Education* (Valencia, 2005). However, the greatest gains in the struggle for civil rights occurred during the 1960s and 1970s. In the 1960s a labor organizer named Cesar Chavez began to organize migrant farm workers, bringing national attention to the poor working conditions and substandard living conditions of these largely Mexican and Filipino workers. Since then, Chavez has become a symbol of the Latina/o civil rights movement. Also in the 1960s the Young Lords battled gentrification and the evictions of Puerto Rican residents in the Lincoln Park neighborhood of Chicago. In 1968 Mexican American students in Los Angeles, frustrated with inferior public schools, a lack of representation in the school curriculum, and limited access to college, walked out of schools and took their message to the streets—an event now known as the Chicana/o Blowouts. These events served to mobilize the Latina/o community and led to increased civic participation, political representation, and participation in higher education.

Although progress toward equality has been made on a number of civil rights issues, other issues continue to be sources of struggle for Latinas/os. The issues of immigration, bilingual education, unemployment, voting rights, antidiscrimination and profiling practices, equal access to employment and training programs, lack of political representation, access to postsecondary education, and access to health care and social welfare still need to be addressed.

Cultural Considerations

In earlier editions of this text Lee (2006a) discussed the potential pitfalls of multicultural counseling scholarship, including how the literature often presents ethnic communities as homogenous and monolithic. Thus, it is with reservations that we discuss some of the traditional cultural values of Latinas/os. Here we present the following information on the role of family, shared cultural values, spirituality, and gender roles to aid those with limited exposure to Latinas/os in understanding the cultural values traditionally held by this community. A brief discussion of *familismo, respeto, simpatia, colectivismo, personalismo, vergüenza, machismo,* and *marianismo* is presented. Later we present a more client specific method of working with Latina/o clients. This methodology will aid counselors in being culturally responsive and avoiding stereotypes.

Family Dynamics

Latinas/os traditionally come from a collectivist, family-oriented culture. Furthermore, it has been argued that the family is the basis of Latina/o culture (Gloria & Peregoy, 1996). The importance of family in Latina/o culture is best conveyed in the notion of *familismo.* This concept refers to significance of, attachment to, and identification with family, whether it be nuclear family, extended family, and/or fictive kin (Gloria & Rodriguez, 2000; Lopez-Baez, 2006; Santiago-Rivera et al., 2002). Latinas/os have traditionally felt a sense of obligation to provide material and emotional support to their family (de las Fuentes, Barón, & Vásquez, 2003; Lopez-Baez, 2006), and in turn the family is seen as the primary source of social support (Gloria & Rodriguez, 2000). The notion of family extends to fictive kin. A particularly important familial relationship is that with *compadres* (godparents). *Compadres* often play a significant role in the life of a child (Santiago-Rivera et al., 2002). The *comadre* (godmother) and *compadre* (godfather) are often charged with the spiritual guidance of a child and traditionally care for the child in the event that something happens to his or her parents. Thus, to be offered and to accept the charge of *comadre* or *compadre* is a great honor and responsibility.

Two concepts related to *familismo* are *colectivismo* and *personalismo. Colectivismo* describes the tendency to put the interests and well-being of the group ahead of those of the individual (Lopez-Baez, 2006). It is likely that this value stems back to the indigenous societies of the Americas. In Mayan culture, a system of tribute and redistribution existed: Individuals contributed a portion of their work (whether that be corn or textile) and in turn received an allotment of the remaining resources they would need. *Personalismo* describes a preference for personal relationships and contacts, particularly warm, friendly, and personal relationships (Santiago-Rivera et al., 2002). Interpersonal and social skills are valued (Bean, Perry, & Bedell, 2001; Lopez-Baez, 2006; Santiago-Rivera et al., 2002). Given the values of *colectivismo* and *personalismo* in Latina/o culture, individuals who support and protect their family are valued over those with high social standing and material wealth (Gloria & Peregoy, 1996).

Cultural Values

The cultural values of *respeto, simpatia,* and *vergüenza* have been used to describe the worldview and personal disposition of Latinas/os. *Respeto* refers to a respectful and deferential attitude toward others, particularly elders and respected community figures, such as teachers, political leaders, religious leaders, and business people (de las Fuentes et al., 2003). Children in particular are expected to address all adults formally (de las Fuentes et al., 2003). The notion of *simpatia* describes both the tendency to avoid interpersonal conflict (Lopez-Baez, 2006) and the behaviors that promote smooth and pleasant social relationships (Gloria & Peregoy, 1996). *Vergüenza* can be understood as not bringing shame to the family (Gloria & Peregoy, 1996) or behaving in a humble manner. A person is expected to keep family matters private and to have *respeto* and *simpatia* in interactions with others. Furthermore, a person should have *vergüenza* and not make a spectacle or draw too much attention to himself or herself. When considering these values, one must refrain from taking a Western perspective and assuming that a Latina/o client is passive, unassertive, avoiding, or depressed.

Spirituality

Latinas/os have historically been religious and spiritual people (Arredondo et al., 2003). Although Catholicism is the most widely practiced faith throughout Latin America, other religious orientations exist and are gaining prominence (Arredondo et al., 2003; Santiago-Rivera et al., 2002). Latinas/os often invoke a higher power to understand events in life (Santiago-Rivera et al., 2002). The *dichos* (sayings) *si dios quiere* and *ojalá* (God willing) point to the belief that life events are a product of God's will. Some religious traditions, such as *Día de los Muertos* (Day of the Dead), not eating meat on the Fridays of Lent, and the practice of taking *compadres,* have become embedded in Latina/o culture. For some clients their spiritual or religious identity is of greater importance than their ethnic identity.

Gender Roles

It is said that Latinas/os are the product of and ascribe to strict gender roles and norms (Arredondo et al., 2003; de las Fuentes et al., 2003). In Latina/o households males are typically allowed more social and familial freedoms than females (de las Fuentes et al., 2003). Males are typically encouraged to be independent, self-determined, and emotionally self-restrained (Arredondo et al., 2003). For males the notion of *machismo* is valued. *Machismo* is described as hypersexuality, chauvinism, and sexism (Constantine, Gloria, & Barón, 2006). Unfortunately, U.S. society and the counseling literature have misinterpreted the notion of *machismo.* Although sexism is a problem in Latin America and some men use *machismo* to rationalize sexism, the notion of *machismo* better describes the behavior of a man who is proud, is respectful, and cares and provides for his family.

Marianismo describes ideals to which Latinas are thought to aspire. *Marianismo* is associated with being yielding, deferent, dependent, sentimental, and sexually pure (Lopez-Baez, 2006; Santiago-Rivera et al., 2002). To enact *marianismo* is to seek to be like the Virgin Mary (Arredondo et al., 2003; de las Fuentes et al., 2003; Lopez-Baez, 2006). The paradox is that women are expected to be spiritually superior and simultaneously subservient to men (Constantine et al., 2006; Santiago-Rivera et al., 2002). It is typically expected that women will put the needs of the family before their own (Arredondo et al., 2003; Santiago-Rivera et al., 2002).

Once again, we urge caution in generalizing these values to all Latinas/os. The values described here are those traditionally associated with many Latinas/os. However, a Latina/o client's degree of ethnic identification and level of acculturation are likely to influence the extent to which he or she identifies with these cultural values.

Counseling Considerations

As we stated previously, the Latina/o community is incredibly heterogeneous. This diversity and the individual uniqueness of clients make it unwise for us to describe a particular counseling theory or intervention. Vontress (2009) called for counselors to recognize the influence of culture on the client and to recognize the unique needs of each client. Thus, Vontress called for a conceptual approach to multicultural counseling. The counselor using a conceptual approach is called to understand his or her client's ethnic identity, level of acculturation, and presenting problem. This information is then used to develop a culturally appropriate counseling intervention. In this section we describe the components of the conceptual approach to counseling and how to apply these concepts with Latina/o clients.

Ethnic Identity

Ethnic identity describes how a person understands and interprets his or her ethnic heritage and the extent to which the person identifies with his or her ethnic group (Phinney, 1996). For Latina/o clients, *ethnic identity* describes the degree to which they identify, see themselves as, and/or feel Latina/o. It also describes the extent to which they endorse the values, beliefs, and customs traditionally held by Latinos. Thus, the higher a client's level of ethnic identification, the more likely he or she is to identify and feel Latina/o and to endorse some or all of the traditional beliefs described earlier in this chapter. Ethnic identity development models have traditionally described a process in which an individual goes from a position of low salience of his or her ethnic identity to a position of high salience and commitment to that identity (Lee, 2006b). Although models exist to describe the ethnic identity of Latinas/os, this chapter is concerned with the degree to which a client identifies ethnically.

Counselors are encouraged to understand a client's ethnic identity in order to build rapport and develop effective counseling interventions (Lee, 2006b). The greater the ethnic identity of a Latina/o client, the more necessary it is to understand Latina/o culture, for there is a greater likelihood that the Latina/o culture influences the client's worldview and presenting problem. In addition, clients with high levels of ethnic identity are likely to require culturally specific counseling intervention; often there will be a need to incorporate traditional healers or indigenous support systems. Furthermore, the less culturally identified a Latina/o client is, the more likely he or she is to have values and beliefs that are aligned with the dominant U.S. culture, and the more likely it is that Western approaches to counseling will be efficacious. Also, higher levels of ethnic identity in Latinas/os are related to higher self-esteem (Umaña-Taylor, 2004), increased coping and optimism (Roberts et al., 1999), and increased academic achievement (Zarate, Bhimji, & Reese, 2005). Although it is the belief of one of us (Carlos P. Hipolito-Delgado) that ethnic identification should be promoted by counselors, we recognize that in certain instances a lower level of ethnic identification may be in the best interest of a client—particularly when the client lacks cultural validation or is faced with discrimination in his or her environment.

Acculturation

Acculturation has traditionally described the process of cultural diffusion, borrowing, and conflict that typically occurs when two cultural groups come into continuous first-hand contact (Tremble, 2003). However, in the context of U.S. psychology and counseling, it describes the acceptance of dominant cultural values by ethnic minority communities or, simply, the process of Americanization.

For the purposes of this chapter, *acculturation* describes the adaptation of Latinas/os to Euro-American, middle-class values, practices, and beliefs. It is important to assess a client's level of acculturation (Bean et al., 2001). Such an assessment will allow a counselor to develop a better understanding of a client's worldview and to develop culturally specific counseling interventions. The more acculturated a client is, the more likely he or she is to identify with dominant U.S. culture and values; consequently, the more likely he or she will respond to Western psychological interventions. It is important to take a culturally specific perspective in understanding the worldview of less acculturated clients. Furthermore, less acculturated clients will likely need an introduction to counseling in which the counselor describes what the counseling process entails, what the client can expect, what the boundaries are, and which techniques will be used.

Acculturation may also influence the presenting problem of a client. Because of the significant changes associated with migrating to a new country, some recent immigrants struggle to adapt to the dominant U.S. society (Shin & Muñoz, 2009). This can lead to acculturative stress that manifests as a mild stressor or as posttraumatic stress disorder (Santiago-Rivera et al., 2002). Thus, when working with an immigrant Latina/o client, it is wise for the counselor to frequently assess how the client is adapting to his or her new surroundings.

Another issue for counselors to be aware of when working with Latina/o families is the potential for an acculturation gap and the subsequent conflict that may ensue. The *acculturation gap* is the phenomenon whereby children of immigrants acculturate much quicker than their parents. This tends to lead to parent–child conflict (Shin & Muñoz, 2009) as parents try to promote the ethnic culture and the children attempt to Americanize. Children's better English skills can lead to them becoming interpreters for their parents in various social arenas, with the consequences of the children becoming active in the parent sphere, the children becoming resistant to traditional roles, and the children and parents experiencing increased conflict. When working with Latina/o families dealing with an acculturation gap, it is wise that the counselor broker communication between family members and use a strengths-based perspective to help parents and children see the utility of both the dominant U.S. culture and the Latina/o culture.

It is important to note that language fluency does not determine one's level of acculturation. A Latina/o client may be fluent in English but not identify with U.S. culture and values. In addition, acculturation is often context specific: A client may align with dominant U.S. cultural values in public spheres and may identify more as Latina/o in private spheres. Thus, to gain a comprehensive perspective of a Latina/o client's worldview, a counselor is encouraged to consider the intersection of the client's ethnic identity and level of acculturation.

Ethnic Identity, Acculturation, and Counseling

As Lee (2006a) and Vontress (2009) have addressed, there is no one-size-fits-all method to working with culturally diverse communities. Given varying levels of ethnic identity and acculturation as well as individual differences, the counselor has to balance traditional counseling theory and techniques with culturally centered practice. To aid counselors in striking this balance, Vontress (2009) discussed the importance of viewing a client's problem and its intervention from an emic (racio-ethnic-centered) or etic (dominant U.S.) perspective or approach. The decision to take an emic or etic counseling approach with a Latina/o client should be based on the intersection of the client's ethnic identity and acculturation.

Figure 6.1 is an adaptation of Lee's (2006a) model describing the intersection of ethnic identity and acculturation. Clients in Quadrant III (assimilation) are most likely to respond

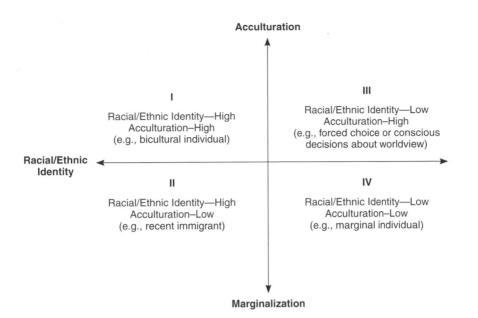

Figure 6.1 • Acculturation Matrix

to an etic approach and Western interventions. Note that although these clients are more connected to the dominant U.S. culture and will likely respond to Western psychological interventions, the counselor cannot rule out the likelihood of their having presenting problems with an emic etiology.

Client in Quadrant II (separation) will most likely require an emic approach. Although these clients may have problems with an etic etiology, they will still need interventions that respect their cultural heritage. A counselor would do well to consider the values outlined earlier in the chapter in working with a client representative of this quadrant. Take extended time to develop rapport, and remember the importance of *personalismo* and *respeto*. Introduce the client to the counseling process, and attempt to normalize counseling so as to minimize the *vergüenza* associated with seeking help outside of the family. Authors have encouraged the practice of family therapy with Latina/o clients (Arredondo et al., 2003; Bean et al., 2001; Santiago-Rivera et al., 2002) using the values of *colectivismo* and *familismo*. In other cases it will be necessary to employ the aid of spiritual healers and religious leaders in counseling interventions.

A client in Quadrant I (bicultural) is likely to respond to some combination of emic and etic approaches. In this case, use the etiology of the problem to decide which perspective or approach is more appropriate. For example if the client feels *vergüenza* for achieving academic success and leaving his or her family behind, an emic approach can be used to help him or her understand the importance of academic achievement in Latina/o culture and the sense of pride the family likely feels in his or her achievements.

Additional Considerations

Because Latinas/os are less likely than people of Euro-American descent to be familiar with counseling, it is suggested that counselors working in Latina/o neighborhoods conduct community outreach. Workshops can provide an opportunity for counselors to introduce themselves to the community and discuss the various services they provide. Such workshops can also foster *personalismo*. Counselors might consider providing informational workshops on topics such as fostering dialogue between parents and children, the role of parents in education, and financing college. These workshops can be offered through social service agencies, schools, and religious institutions. Counselors are also encouraged to seek the assistance of community gatekeepers, prominent figures who can provide entree into the community. Forming a relationship with a trusted community member may make it more likely that others in the community will trust a counselor and seek out his or her services.

In counseling with Latina/o clients, you can use several means to help level the power differential between yourself and the client. First, attempt to make your office feel comfortable. In many Latina/o households important decisions are made in the dining and living rooms, places that are warm and inviting. Second, because important decisions and sensitive topics are often discussed over a meal or *una taza de café* (a cup of coffee), consider offering coffee and bread (maybe even *pan dulce* [sweet bread]) to your clients. These simple actions will do much to increase rapport and ease clients' tensions.

Counseling Interventions

To aid practitioners and counselors-in-training in their work with Latina/o clients, this section goes inside our work with Latina/o students. Here we present strategies and interventions that we have found successful in working with Latina/o clients.

Inside Urban High School

My (Jessica M. Diaz's) doctoral internship experience was in an urban high school. The student population at Urban High School (a pseudonym) was approximately 30% Latino, 65% African American, and 5% White and other. At Urban High School the influx of Spanish-speaking students was a relatively recent development. The school was located at the crossroads of two clearly divided areas: a predominantly African American neighborhood and a predominantly Latina/o neighborhood. Although the school had an English Speakers of Other Languages (ESOL) program, it had few bilingual teachers, and most classes were conducted completely in English. No school counselors spoke Spanish, and although the school district had a Spanish-speaking translator, she was rarely available at the school.

Needs of the Population
In partnership with a local university, Urban High School received a variety of mental health services. A university psychologist and counselors- and psychologists-in-training staffed the school-based mental health program. The program was designed to reduce barriers to learning by preventing and treating mental health and adjustment concerns. Free services were available to any student or family who was referred or sought services. These services, which included initial assessments and individual, group, and parent counseling, were offered on site during the school day.

I was an intern for the school-based mental health program. Within a few weeks I began to notice that, despite the large representation of Latina/o students at the school and their high suspension and absentee rates, we had no referrals for Latina/o students. It seemed as though Latina/o students were invisible in the school. They were rarely seen in the school counseling offices, and Spanish-speaking parents were rarely called in to discuss issues with students. If they were called in, they sometimes waited all day for the interpreter.

One day after walking the halls between counseling sessions I caught the eye of a parent who looked upset. She saw me and in a desperate voice asked, "*¿Habla español?*" (Do you speak Spanish?) When I responded, "Yes," she teared up and told me her story; this was her third visit to the school, and no one was able to understand her. She was trying to enroll her son before his 18th birthday, and she was going to lose her job if she did not return to work soon. This incident prompted an examination of the needs of Latina/o students at the school.

Las Unikas

Soon after this incident I spoke with two of the school counselors and the therapist supervising the internship program, and we agreed to create a psychoeducational group for students in the school. Based on school data on suspensions, dropouts, gang affiliations, and pregnancy rates, we identified Latina students as being most in need. Fifteen girls were identified as potential group candidates. Seven students returned parental consent forms, and six eventually participated in regular biweekly individual and group sessions. The group members, who were in Grades 9 and 10, ranged in age from 14 to 18. Five were in the ESOL program and one was taking mainstream classes. Four of the girls had been in the United States for less than 9 months, one for more than 2 years, and one for more than 5 years.

In the first session we defined group objectives and began to develop group cohesion. During the first session, the girls decided that the group would be used to meet the following objectives: (a) to provide a forum to discuss problems, issues, and concerns they were experiencing at school and at home; and (b) to help each girl explore where she fit in and who she was as an individual. These goals would be met through group discussion, exploration, homework, and activities. The girls also came up with the name, *Las Unikas,* which was a variation on the Spanish phrase *los únicos,* meaning "the only ones." This was significant to the girls for a few reasons: because they were the only ones who were chosen and who followed through with becoming members of the group, and because they shared the feeling of being alone or being outsiders. The girls decided that either Spanish or English could be spoken at any time and that no student would be forced to translate for another group member. However, a student could always request that someone volunteer to translate.

The following conditions helped make *Las Unikas* a success: spending extended group time establishing a safe space to talk about the ladies' life experiences in the United States and providing ample opportunity for discussion of the experience of being a Latina high school student. This also aided the ladies in relating to one another. Developing a personal relationship (*personalismo*) was key in earning the students' trust and respect. This trust later allowed me to challenge the girls to dig deeper into their feelings. Also important was allowing the girls to decide on their goals and objectives and even what language would be used in the group. This permitted them to own the group process, which was especially important given that they felt marginalized in school. The combination of group sessions and individual sessions gave a space to address particular concerns they could not address in the group setting. Two of the students' cases are described in further detail to give deeper insight into what developed throughout the group and individual counseling experience.

Case Study 1: Angela. Angela was a sophomore at Urban High School who was born in Uruguay. Her family immigrated to the United States when she was 11, and she had been in the country for 5 years. Angela spoke English well and was therefore placed in mainstream classes. She was referred to the group because her teachers felt she was not "integrating well" into the school, and they felt she might need help making friends. She received above-average grades and was overall a good student. A teacher reported that Angela was having some behavior issues after an incident in which she had refused to act as the teacher's translator.

During the third group session the topic of identity was discussed. During this discussion Angela stated, "Every moment I am in this place I struggle with who I am and where I fit in. Just when I start to understand myself the world around me changes and I am back at the beginning again." During our individual session Angela and I spent some time exploring this comment. Angela felt that she was seen as "just another Latino student" by most of the students in the school, and she felt rejected by the Latino students for being more American than Latina. In addition, Angela had been put in an awkward place by the teachers, who often called on her to play the role of translator with newly arrived Spanish-speaking students. This forced service caused her to stand out when all she wanted to do was blend in.

Angela discussed labels in our first one-on-one counseling session. Angela questioned why everyone in school felt the need to label her. Couldn't she just be a student? Angela's objective in counseling was to accept herself despite how others might label her. Her homework consisted of tasks that would help her explore what it meant to be Latina. For example, Angela would sit with the girls from the group during lunch. We later discussed the significance of this activity and whether sitting with Latinas changed who she was. Over time Angela began to recognize that she could be Latina, speak Spanish or English in the halls, be a good student, sit with whomever she wanted at lunch, and still be Angela. Although she continued to struggle with feeling intimidated by students who teased her about being too White, she made big gains in feeling comfortable with her identity. She planned on continuing to work on not being so defensive when teachers and students labeled her because she understood better that sometimes individuals label others in an attempt to understand them better.

Case Study 2: Christina. Christina was a student from El Salvador and the most recent immigrant of *Las Unikas.* Her schedule consisted of mostly ESOL classes. According to her Spanish teacher, she never spoke in class and was seldom observed talking with friends. Despite the Spanish teacher's report, Christina was active and engaged in group and individual sessions. She often laughed and made jokes. However, outside of the group she appeared quiet and sullen. In discussing identity Christina stated, "I have three choices: to be invisible, to get in trouble, or to sell out. There is nothing in between. Right now I choose to be invisible. It is the way I get through the day."

For Christina, the topic of identity was closely related to survival in school. Urban High School had issues with gang violence, particularly within the Latina/o student population. When Christina referred to the choice of "getting in trouble," she meant drawing attention from and being forced into a gang. The "selling out" option referred to trying to be someone she wasn't. Christina mentioned that many Latino students tried to fit in with the African American or White students. To Christina this amounted to denying who she was. Thus, her only option was to "be invisible." This entailed doing only enough in school to get by and not enough to draw attention to herself. Thus, she talked to no one and seemed to disappear into the crowded hallways.

Developing rapport with Christina was key to helping her open up about her life outside of school. Christina had spent so much of her time in group discussing her feelings of being lost and invisible in school, it was important to explore whether these feelings existed primarily at school or continued in her daily life. It was not surprising to find out that Christina was feeling invisible outside of school. Her family had left behind a large support system of extended family, and now she had only her mother and her two oldest brothers. She was not adjusting well to the loss of her family and her old routine, which seemed to be a symptom of acculturative stress. We spent much of our individual counseling time discussing her adjustment to the United States and normalizing her yearnings for her family and her mourning of her old lifestyle. Although she did not feel that it was an option to discuss these feelings with her mother, she worked on opening up to the other group members. By the end of our time in group and individual counseling, Christina's goals were to feel less isolated and marginalized and to understand that this was a process that others had experienced as well.

Inside MEChA *Calmecac*

In this section I (Carlos P. Hipolito-Delgado) discuss my experience as a counselor working for the Chicana/o and Latina/o student group MEChA *Calmecac*. I provide background on MEChA *Calmecac*, information on *Calmecac*'s counseling philosophy, information on what about this program worked, and direction for working with Latina/o students.

Background

El Movimiento Estudiantil Chicana/Chicano de Aztlán (MEChA) is a Chicana/o and Latina/o student retention program that, among other things, is committed to the promotion of higher education in the Chicana/o community. MEChA at the University of California, Los Angeles, created *Calmecac* to address the low graduation and retention rates for Chicana/o and Latina/o undergraduates at the university. The name *Calmecac* was chosen for its reference to the Mexica (more commonly but erroneously known as *Aztec*) institution of learning. MEChA *Calmecac* is the first student-run and student-initiated undergraduate retention program in the United States. Furthermore, the program is funded entirely with student fees.

I was first hired as a peer counselor during my sophomore year of undergraduate study. Over the next 2 years I was promoted to counseling coordinator and assistant director.

Counseling Philosophy

During my tenure with *Calmecac*, we worked from a model called *holistic student empowerment*. The idea was to personalize the counseling experience and to move beyond a focus on academic issues. Although academic success was a primary goal, counselors sought to aid students in their personal and social adjustment to higher education. We discussed issues related to family, spirituality, culture, politics, social and professional networking, adjustment to college, and strategies for academic success. We also conducted academic planning.

Cultural validation was a large portion of our work. The *Calmecac* office (a small cubicle) was decorated with icons of Chicana/o and Latina/o history. I frequently shared information with counselees about cultural happenings in the area and engaged in dialogue on how to balance cultural values with the Western values of the institution. Given that *Calmecac*'s programs had Nahuatl (the language of the Mexica) names, I would often discuss precolonial Latin American history.

With the exception of the director, all service providers were undergraduates. The peer counseling model had both symbolic and practical power. At a symbolic level, the peer counselor represented someone who was successfully navigating the university. We sought to hire peer counselors who had struggled academically and/or socially and who, through support, were able to become successful students. This type of peer counselor understood the value of support and of helping their fellow student. On a more practical level, peer counselors were able to more readily establish rapport; we were not seen as agents of the university.

What Worked

It is challenging to dissect the parts of *Calmecac* that most contributed to our success in serving Chicana/o and Latina/o students. However, factors that I felt were significant and could be replicated by other practitioners are taking a holistic approach, using peer helpers, taking a personal approach, and conducting outreach. This section explores how these strategies were used at *Calmecac* and why they are considered to be successful with Latina/o students.

Holistic Approach. Although the theoretical foundation of holistic student empowerment may have been a lofty ideal, the holistic approach was very effective in working with

Chicana/o and Latina/o students. By being willing to discuss all aspects of the self, the student was able to see how these dimensions are interrelated and how difficulty in one area can influence all other areas. Realizing that disconnect and isolation played a role in their academic struggles was powerful for students, as it alleviated concerns of inadequacy, inferiority, and inability.

Furthermore, clients were encouraged to attend to their various needs, not to neglect spirituality and focus solely on academics. This was also useful in helping students balance their various familial, personal, and academic obligations. I was told by numerous students that despite their initial hesitance to discuss personal issues, they later realized how important it was to acknowledge and work on the self as a whole. In addition, students told me how comforting it was to know they had someone to talk with about anything.

Peer Helping. As stated previously, peer counseling facilitated the development of rapport and empathy with Chicana/o and Latina/o undergraduates. Peer counselors are less likely to be viewed as agents of foreign agencies and institutions and more likely to be seen as representatives of the community. When armed with basic counseling skills, peer counselors can provide services to students who would not otherwise seek help. Furthermore, they provide an entry point to counseling services, demystifying the process of counseling and providing referrals to professional counselors when needed.

A Personal Approach. Because of our use of the holistic model and the lack of resources available for *Calmecac,* counseling took a less formal approach. The holistic model facilitated a personal approach by opening up areas of dialogue that a student might not typically share with an academic counselor. Furthermore, encouraging the exploration of spiritual and cultural issues served to increase the personal nature of the counseling services.

As employees of *Calmecac* we took our roles as peer helpers seriously and believed in the mission of increasing graduation rates among Chicanas/os and Latinas/os. Thus, we went the extra mile for our students. Students who entered our offices were greeted warmly and provided with a tour of our modest facilities. I would typically meet with students every 3 to 4 weeks and would briefly call to check in with my students on the weeks we were not meeting. Furthermore, I made it a point to remember key facts, such as names of significant others, important dates, or favorite activities, so that I could ask my clients about these things when they came in. I always took the first few minutes of our sessions to get reacquainted and discuss what was going on in my client's life, avoiding the less personal customer service approach of "What brings you in today?"

Lack of resources also contributed to a less formal approach to counseling. Because of its limited budget, *Calmecac* had little office space and few counseling rooms. If more than three counseling sessions were ever taking place simultaneously, any additional counseling sessions took place outside. This led to many a counseling session sitting on the grassy hill outside of the *Calmecac* office. As paraprofessionals we were well versed in confidentiality and how this could not be guaranteed outside, but some of my best sessions were held on that hill. Sitting on the grass, the student and I were more like friends sharing a conversation in the sun than a counselor and his client. Many of my clients preferred to meet outside; it was an escape from the formality of the institution. Although I am not advocating conducting all counseling with Latinas/os outdoors, I am strongly endorsing making your office space more inviting. Consider how you position chairs and desks, how you place the art that adorns your office, and how you use lighting. All of these contribute to making your office feel more or less formal.

Outreach. One of the challenges we faced at *Calmecac* was reaching out to undergraduate students. Students utilized our services on a voluntary basis; they were not assigned to us, and they had other services to choose from. This required us to constantly reach out to the undergraduate population. Each year *Calmecac* would mail a letter to all incoming students and those experiencing academic difficulty, introducing them to our services and inviting them to come and visit us. Furthermore, peer counselors would call all incoming students, attend student association meetings and campus orientation events, and provide workshops to introduce our services. A primary goal of these activities was to help students make a personal connection with a counselor. There was a much higher likelihood that a student would come in to see me when I had been able to talk to him or her either by phone or at an event than if he or she simply responded to a mailing or discovered our services online. Conducting outreach also helped to demystify the counseling process. During outreach activities potential clients were introduced to the helping relationship, presented with our theories of counseling, informed about confidentiality, and told what they could expect. Thus, when working with Latinas/os you are strongly encouraged to take a proactive approach and actively reach out to the community.

Conclusion

Practitioners and students are often frustrated to learn that there is no road map for counseling Latina/o students or clients. However, given the unique histories, diverse cultural values, and differing rates of acculturation and ethnic identity among this population, it is obvious that a single intervention—no matter how appealing it may seem initially —is unattainable and impractical. Vontress (1997) stressed that culturally sensitive counseling services that follow a conceptual approach must take into consideration the counselor's level of cultural awareness, the client's cultural background, and the societal context in which the client and counselor exist. Within this context, this chapter has attempted to provide an understanding of the U.S. experience and traditional cultural values of the Latina/o community, important counseling considerations for working with this community, and personal insight and suggestions from our own experiences working with Latina/o clients.

References

Acuña, R. F. (2003). *U.S. Latino issues.* Westport, CT: Greenwood Press.

Alaniz, Y., & Cornish, M. (2008). *Viva la raza: A history of Chicano identity and resistance.* Seattle, WA: Red Letter Press.

Arredondo, P., Davison Aviles, R. M., Zalaquett, C. P., Grazioso, M. D. P., Bordes, V., Hita, L., & Lopez, B. J. (2003). The psychohistorical approach in family counseling with Mestizo/Latino immigrants: A continuum and synergy of worldviews. *Family Journal: Counseling and Therapy for Couples and Families, 14,* 13–27.

Bardallo-Vivero, G. (2006). Latinos and employment. In C. L. Bankston, III, D. A. Hidalgo, & R. K. Rasmussen (Eds.), *Immigration in U.S. history* (Vol. 2, pp. 488–493). Pasadena, CA: Salem Press.

Bean, R. A., Perry, B. J., & Bedell, T. M. (2001). Developing culturally competent marriage and family therapists: Guidelines for working with Hispanic families. *Journal of Marriage and Family Therapy, 27,* 43–54.

Bhatia, T. K. (2006). Bilingual education. In C. L. Bankston, III, D. A. Hidalgo, & R. K. Rasmussen (Eds.), *Immigration in U.S. history* (Vol. 1, pp. 85–90). Pasadena, CA: Salem Press.

Bureau of Labor Statistics. (2010, April). *Employment situation summary.* Retrieved from http://www.bls.gov/news.release/empsit.nr0.htm

College Board. (2007). *2007 college-bound seniors: Total group profile report.* Retrieved from http://www.collegeboard.com/prod_downloads/about/news_info/cbsenior/yr2007/national-report.pdf

Constantine, M. G., Gloria, A. M., & Barón, A. (2006). Counseling Mexican American college students. In C. C. Lee (Ed.), *Multicultural issues in counseling: New approaches to diversity* (3rd ed., pp. 207–222). Alexandria, VA: American Counseling Association.

de las Fuentes, C., Barón, A., & Vásquez, M. J. T. (2003). Teaching Latino psychology. In P. Bronstein & K. Quina (Eds.), *Teaching gender and multicultural awareness: Resources for the psychology classroom* (pp. 207–220). Washington, DC: American Psychological Association.

DeNavas-Walt, C., Proctor, B. D., & Lee, C. H. (2006). *Income, poverty, and health insurance coverage in the United States: 2005* (Current Population Reports No. P60-231). Washington, DC: U.S. Government Printing Office.

Duncan-Andrade, J. M. R. (2005). An examination of the sociopolitical history of Chicanos and its relationship to school performance. *Urban Education, 40,* 576–605.

Ennis, S. R., Ríos-Vargas, M., & Albert, N. G. (2011). *The Hispanic population: 2010.* Washington, DC: U.S. Census Bureau.

Erisman, W., & Looney, S. (2007). *Opening the door to the American dream: Increasing higher education access and success for immigrants.* Washington, DC: Institute for Higher Education Policy.

Garcia, I. M. (1997). *Chicanismo: The forging of a militant ethos among Mexican Americans.* Tucson: University of Arizona Press.

Gloria, A. M., & Peregoy, J. J. (1996). Counseling Latino alcohol and other substance users/abusers: Cultural considerations for counselors. *Journal of Substance Abuse Treatment, 13,* 119–126.

Gloria, A. M., & Rodriguez, E. R. (2000). Counseling Latino university students: Psychosociocultural issues for consideration. *Journal of Counseling & Development, 78,* 145–154.

Gonzalez, C., & Gandara, P. (2005). Why we like to call ourselves Latinas. *Journal of Hispanic Higher Education, 4,* 392–398.

Gracia, J. J. E. (2000). *Hispanic/Latino identity: A philosophical perspective.* Malden, MA: Blackwell.

Huerta, J. (2002). When sleeping giants awaken: Chicano theatre in the 1960s. *Theatre Survey, 43*(1), 23–35.

Itzigsohn, J. (2005). The Dominican immigration experience. *Centro Journal, 17*(1), 270–281.

Kewal Ramani, A., Gilbertson, L., Fox, M., & Provasnik, S. (2007). *Status and trends in the education of racial and ethnic minorities* (National Center for Education Statistics Publication No. 2007-039). Washington, DC: National Center for Education Statistics.

Lay, J. (2005, July). *Growing up in racially diverse versus homogeneous communities: Which is better?* Paper presented at the meeting of Southern Political Science Association, New Orleans, LA.

Lee, C. C. (2006a). *Multicultural issues in counseling: New approaches to diversity* (3rd ed.). Alexandria, VA: American Counseling Association.

Lee, C. C. (2006b). Updating the models of identity development. In C. Lago (Ed.), *Race, culture and counselling: The ongoing challenge* (pp. 179–186). Berkshire, England: Open University Press.

Lopez, E., Gallimore, R., & Garnier, H. (2007). Preschool antecedents of mathematics achievement of Latinos: The influence of family resources, early literacy experiences, and preschool attendance. *Hispanic Journal of Behavioral Sciences, 29,* 456–471.

Lopez-Baez, S. I. (2006). Counseling Latinas: Culturally responsive interventions. In C. C. Lee (Ed.), *Multicultural issues in counseling: New approaches to diversity* (3rd ed., pp. 187–194). Alexandria, VA: American Counseling Association.

Malott, K. M. (2009). Investigation of ethnic self-labeling in the Latina population: Implications for counselors and counselor educators. *Journal of Counseling & Development, 87,* 179–185.

Marcoux, C. H. (2006). Latinos. In C. L. Bankston, III, D. A. Hidalgo, & R. K. Rasmussen (Eds.), *Immigration in U.S. history* (pp. 481–488). Pasadena, CA: Salem Press.

Marsico, M., & Getch, Y. (2009). Transitioning Hispanic seniors from high school to college. *Professional School Counseling, 12,* 458–462.

Méndez et al. v. Westminster School District et al. 161 F. 2d 774 (9th Cir.). (1947).

National Center for Education Statistics. (2008). *Dropout and completion rates in the United States: 2006* (National Center for Education Statistics Publication No. 2008-053). Washington, DC: Author.

National Center for Higher Education Management Systems. (2006). *Public high school graduation rates.* Retrieved from http://www.higheredinfo.org/dbrowser/index.php?submeasure=36&year=2006&level= nation&mode=data&state=0

O'Connor, N., Hammack, F., & Scott, M. (2010). Social capital, financial knowledge, and Hispanic student college choices. *Research in Higher Education, 51*(3), 195–219.

Ortiz, A. M., & Santos, S. J. (2009). *Ethnicity in college: Advancing theory and improving diversity practices on campus.* Sterling, VA: Stylus.

Pew Hispanic Center. (2007, May 30). *Indicators of recent migration flows from Mexico.* Retrieved from http://pewhispanic.org/files/factsheets/33.pdf

Phinney, J. (1996). Understanding ethnic diversity: The role of ethnic identity. *American Behavioral Scientist, 40,* 143–152.

Roberts, R. E., Phinney, J. S., Masses, L. C., Chen, Y. R., Roberts, C. R., & Romero, A. (1999). The structure of ethnic identity of young adolescents from diverse ethnocultural groups. *Journal of Early Adolescence, 19,* 301–322.

Rodriguez, A. (2009). Exploring the effects of Latino subgroup diversity on Latino identity and preferences for a co-ethnic candidate. Paper presented at the Southern Political Science Association, New Orleans, LA.

Santiago, D. (2008). *The condition of Latinos in education: 2008 factbook.* Washington, DC: Excelencia in Education.

Santiago-Rivera, A. L., Arredondo, P., & Gallardo-Cooper, M. (2002). *Counseling Latinos and la familia: A practical guide.* Thousand Oaks, CA: Sage.

Shin, H. J., & Muñoz, O. (2009). Acculturation: Context, dynamics, and conceptualization. In C. C. Lee, D. A. Burnhill, A. L. Butler, C. P. Hipolito-Delgado, M. Humphrey, O. Muñoz, & H. J. Shin (Eds.), *Elements of culture in counseling* (pp. 57–76). Columbus, OH: Pearson.

Shorris, E. (1992). *Latinos: A biography of the people.* New York, NY: Norton.

Smith-Adcock, S., Daniels, M. H., Lee, S. M., Villalba, J. A., & Indelicato, N. A. (2006). Culturally responsive school counseling for Hispanic/Latino students and families: The need for bilingual school counselors. *Professional School Counseling, 10,* 92–101.

Tremble, J. E. (2003). Introduction: Social change and acculturation. In K. M. Chun, P. B. Organista, & G. Marín (Eds.), *Acculturation: Advances in theory, measurement, and applied research* (pp. 3–13). Washington, DC: American Psychological Association.

Umaña-Taylor, A. J. (2004). Ethnic identity and self-esteem: Examining the role of social context. *Journal of Adolescence, 27,* 139–146.

U.S. Census Bureau. (2006). *U.S. census of the population.* Washington, DC: U.S. Government Printing Office.

Valencia, R. (2005). The Mexican American struggle for equal educational opportunity in *Mendez v. Westminster:* Helping to pave the way for *Brown v. Board of Education. Teachers College Record, 107,* 389–423.

Vontress, C. (1997). *A conceptual approach to teaching cross-cultural counseling.* Unpublished manuscript.

Vontress, C. E. (2009). A conceptual approach to counseling across cultures. In C. C. Lee, D. A. Burnhill, A. L. Butler, C. P. Hipolito-Delgado, M. Humphrey, O. Muñoz, & H. J. Shin (Eds.), *Elements of culture in counseling* (pp. 19–30). Columbus, OH: Pearson.

Wiltberger, J. (2009). Bringing Latin America into US debates on Latino immigration: Views from El Salvador. *Development, 52,* 519–524.

Zarate, M. E., Bhimji, F., & Reese, L. (2005). Ethnic identity and academic achievement among Latina/o adolescents. *Journal of Latinos & Education, 4,* 95–114.

Additional Resources

A single chapter is insufficient in aiding in the development of competence for working with Latina/o clients. We hope that in addition to using this chapter as a resource, you seek to further develop your Latina/o cultural literacy. Thus, the following websites provide additional information related to the Latina/o culture, Latinas/os' U.S. experience, and counseling Latinas/os.

El Movimiento Estudiantil Chicana/Chicano de Aztlán: The largest Chicana/o student organization in the United States
http://www.nationalmecha.org/about.html

Excelencia in Education: Applying Knowledge to Public Policy and Institutional Insight
www.edexcelencia.org

Hispanic Scholarship Fund
www.hsf.net

iHispano.com: The Professional Latino Network
www.ihispano.com

League of United Latin American Citizens: A Latina/o civil rights and advocacy group
www.lulac.org

Mexican American Legal Defense and Educational Fund: A Latina/o civil rights organization
www.maldef.org

National Association of Latino Arts and Culture: A nonprofit dedicated to promoting and advancing the Latino art field
www.nalac.org

National Council of La Raza: The largest national Latino civil rights and advocacy organization in the United States
www.nclr.org

Pew Hispanic Center: Chronicling Latinos diverse experience in a changing America
http://pewhispanic.org/

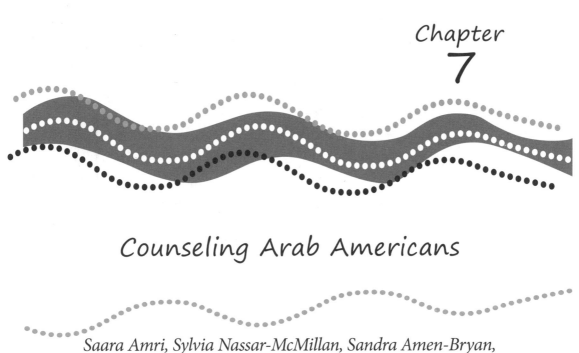

Chapter

7

Counseling Arab Americans

*Saara Amri, Sylvia Nassar-McMillan, Sandra Amen-Bryan,
and Mary M. Misenhimer*

Who Are Arab Americans?

Arab Americans, like many of their ethnic counterparts, are often defined by external entities. Some mistakenly consider individuals of Arab ancestry to have roots in any country within the geographic Middle East. Others define them as those who speak the Arabic language. This chapter defines *Arab Americans* as the 3–4 million Americans who claim ancestry within the League of Arab States. The League of Arab States is composed of 22 countries spanning Asia and northern Africa. This chapter refers to those countries as the *Arab Middle East*. In this chapter, the rich diversity within this culture in terms of religion, family, gender, and sociopolitical history is examined. Next, some of the ways in which these background issues impact individuals' identity development and their mental health are discussed. Finally, several case studies that illustrate some of the information provided are presented.

Religion

The geographic Middle East is the birthplace of several religious traditions, including Islam, Christianity, and Judaism. Thus, it is understandable that there is a range of religious practices among descendants of the Arab Middle East that may or may not overlap those of countries in this region that are not part of the Arab Middle East, such as Pakistan, Afghanistan, Iran, and Turkey. Arab Americans encompass a variety of religious denominations despite the perception some have that *Arab* and *Muslim* are synonymous. The heightened attention to Muslim Americans since the tragic events of September 11, 2001, has brought Arab Americans into the media and other spotlights, and the portrayals of this rich culture

• 87 •

have not always been accurate. Thus, despite misconceptions of Arab Americans as being by default Muslim, many contemporary Arab American communities have roots in the Catholic tradition that lead back to the Crusades of the 12th century. In fact, Catholicism (35%) is the number one religious affiliation among Arab Americans, followed by Islam (20%) and Eastern Orthodox (20%; Arab American Institute, 2002). Some religious scholars have attributed the differences among Arabs to religious distinctions between Christianity and Islam. Here we address some of these differences while also highlighting similarities among Arab Americans that span religious affiliation.

Like members of other U.S. religious groups, some Arab Americans adhere to strong faith practices and traditions, whereas others spend less time attending religious services. The degree of religiosity in the client is an important aspect in the counseling relationship. Unfortunately, stereotypes about extremist Muslims are often amplified by the media, resulting in distorted opinions and perceptions in the United States of all Muslims as being radical extremists (Nassar-McMillan, 2003). However, many see religion as a source of strength and comfort, providing connection to cultural roots and resources for Arab Americans of any faith tradition (Faragallah, Walter, & Farrell, 1997).

Family

Conflict often arises when Arab Americans try to negotiate between old world collectivist values and the individualist attitudes of American culture (Hakim-Larson, Kamoo, Nassar-McMillan, & Porcerelli, 2007). Arab culture typically adheres to a patriarchal family structure. Along with this structure come cultural norms and traditions that may appear different from those traditionally upheld in the mainstream United States. Some of these include different concepts of time and dialects that abound with metaphors and indirect meanings, many of which are expressed through gestures and euphemisms (Nydell, 2006).

The extended family enforces cultural traditions and heritage. Family unit, cohesion, and proximity are valued over and above work and even friendships. In return, emotional support and financial security are afforded by the extended family (Nydell, 2006). Unlike in contemporary U.S. culture, individuals may have limited freedom within extended families (Hakim-Larson et al., 2007). Thus, counselors need to realize that Arab American families may be closer and operate more interdependently in ways that might mistakenly be described as "enmeshed" compared with individualist U.S. families (Nassar-McMillan, Gonzalez, & Mohamed, 2010).

Gender

Arab Americans have encountered negative stereotyping resulting from portrayals of Arab men as heartless oil barons, desert drifters, religious fanatics, and repressive dictators and women as oppressed and abused, wearing dark cloaks, and unable to leave the house (Shakir, 1997). These depictions lack intercultural understanding (Shaheen, 1997). The negative stereotyping and misunderstanding of this population have led many Arab Americans to deny their heritage (Nassar-McMillan & Hakim-Larson, 2003). Some Arab Americans have not only experienced discrimination but also become the byproduct of indirect discrimination (Sarroub, 2002). The fact is that research on Arab and American women has yielded images of modernism, with Arab American women dressing like most other Americans and balancing their time between work, school, community, and family (Read, 2003).

Fathers, elder brothers, and extended male family members, as heads of nuclear or extended families and households, are charged with providing for the family. These financial and family responsibilities and decision-making authority reflect a patriarchal power structure (Hakim-Larson et al., 2007), and individuals in this role are often regarded with great respect.

Psychosocial Development in a Contemporary Context

Many factors influence acculturation and ethnic identity development for Arab Americans. Such factors include country of origin; sociopolitical history; reason for immigration; length of time in the United States; socioeconomic status in the United States; level of education and English language proficiency; level of social support; and premigration experiences, such as trauma (Erickson & Al-Tamimi, 2001; Jamil, Nassar-McMillan, & Lambert, 2007; Nassar-McMillan & Hakim-Larson, 2003). In this section, we explore some of these influences on acculturation and ethnic identity development for Arab Americans, including refugee issues and other current mental health risks and resiliencies among this population.

Acculturation and Ethnic Identity Development

The process of acculturation can take two forms: immersion in or adoption of the dominant society, or immersion in and retention of the ethnic society (Awad, 2010; Berry, 2003). Which process an individual takes depends on the factors mentioned in preceding paragraph. When individuals adopt the dominant society's culture, they are able to successfully integrate into society and find a balance between their culture of origin and the new dominant culture. In contrast, when individuals remain completely attached to their ethnic culture, they may struggle to bridge the gap between their culture of origin and the dominant culture. This rejection of the dominant culture most often leads to marginalization in society (Awad, 2010; Berry, 1984).

Britto and Amer (2007) discussed three levels of acculturation and cultural identity development among Arab Americans as they relate to family functioning: high bicultural, moderate bicultural, and high Arab cultural. Those who identify as high bicultural value both cultures—their culture of origin and the dominant culture—equally. Those who identify as moderate bicultural have the most family acculturative stressors and the least amount of social support, yet the highest level of academic achievement. Those who identify as high Arab cultural value their culture of origin over the dominant culture. This study is important because it highlights the complexity of Arab American identity development and acculturation.

Arab American identity development is influenced by various factors, the most prominent being religion and family (Habboush, 2007). Christianity and Islam are the two major religions among Arab Americans, and the majority of Arab Americans are Christian (Nassar-McMillan & Hakim-Larson, 2003). An Arab American's level of religiosity and family cohesiveness has a significant impact on how he or she identifies with the U.S. culture and how well he or she acculturates. Christian Arabs, for example, are more likely to adapt to the Western culture rather than the Arab culture because the Arab culture identifies more closely with Islam (Habboush, 2007). Furthermore, depending on how recently they immigrated to the United States and their level of acculturation, individuals may be more inclined to identify with their country of origin rather than the larger racial group, or vice versa (e.g., Iraqi or Saudi vs. Arab or Arab American; Witteborn, 2007). However, Arab American identity is also greatly influenced by the international and national political climate (Witteborn, 2007). Since the terrorist attacks of 9/11, many Arabs are reluctant to identify themselves as Arab or Muslim for fear of discrimination and marginalization. Instead, many Arabs prefer to be identified as Arab Americans because this demonstrates an alliance with America and the American culture, thus protecting them from any retaliation as a result of negative sentiments toward Arabs (Witteborn, 2007).

Another dimension of Arab American identity development is the lack of recognition of Arabs as a racial minority group. Unlike other racial minorities in the United States, Arabs are not officially classified as a racial minority; consequently, they are left with no choice but to identify as White or Caucasian on forms or in interviews requesting demographic information (Awad, 2010; Samhan, 1997). Although Arab Americans represent various racial backgrounds (Nassar-McMillan, 2010), it is not hard to imagine the level of confusion they may experience when trying to identify themselves, particularly given that their census classification has changed several times during U.S. history (at one time their classification was "colored"). Among the rationale for the U.S. census and government agencies not identifying this group as an ethnic minority population is its seeming lack of risk (e.g., Arab Americans fare well in educational and economic pursuits compared with mainstream Americans). However, as a result Arab Americans are not considered a protected group. In fact, they often deal with challenges associated with profiling and prejudice in the current U.S. sociopolitical climate, which depicts Arabs and Muslims as the perpetrators of the War on Terror and a group to fear and retaliate against.

Refugee Issues

According to a 2008 United Nations High Commissioner for Refugees report, less than 1% of the world's refugee population (approximately 14 million) are projected to be resettled to a host country each year (Kumin & Hemingway, 2008). Refugee demographics made an abrupt shift, however, after the terrorist attacks of September 11, 2001. Refugees from Iraq and Afghanistan now make up half of the worldwide refugee population; Iraqi refugees currently number at around 1.9 million and primarily seek refuge in neighboring countries in the Middle East (United Nations High Commissioner for Refugees, 2009). The United States only resettled 18,000 Iraqi refugees between 2007 and 2009 (U.S. Citizenship and Immigration Services, 2009). Refugees from the Arab Middle East have been immigrating to the United States since the early 1900s. The earliest groups of immigrants typically came for economic reasons, whereas later groups, such as displaced Palestinians in the 1940s through 1960s and, decades later, Iraqi refugees from the first Persian Gulf War, immigrated to the United States in hopes of beginning a new, safer life.

Given the circumstances under which refugees flee their countries, they are often faced with significant challenges once they resettle in a country such as the United States. Enduring community violence; political torture; and the loss of their homes, livelihood, family, and loved ones, refugees often suffer from depression, anxiety, and posttraumatic stress disorder (PTSD; Daud, Klinteberg, & Rydelius, 2008; Jamil et al., 2002). These mental health issues are often compounded by challenges associated with acculturation and adjustment to their new life, which, in and of themselves, can be quite daunting to overcome (Jamil et al., 2007).

Refugees from the Middle East may resettle to the United States with little notice or time to prepare. Most refugees have no known family or friends in the United States with whom they can live and from whom they can receive support. For those with little to no financial means, resettling in the United States may be more of a challenge than a blessing. Relying on the limited public assistance entitled to refugees from the U.S. Department of State, those without financial resources may struggle to make ends meet. And with the added stressors of limited English language proficiency, limited or nontransferable job skills, social marginalization and discrimination, and isolation, along with, perhaps most important, profiling and prejudice, refugees from the Arab Middle East may face significant mental health challenges that impede their ability to successfully thrive in the United States (Jamil et al., 2002, 2007; Lindencrona, Ekblad, & Hauff, 2008).

Current Mental Health Issues and Status

Trauma

The prevalence of PTSD among Arab American communities is on the rise as the number of individuals and families fleeing war and civil conflict in the Middle East increases each year (Habboush, 2007; Jamil et al., 2002; Norris & Aroian, 2008). Many Iraqi refugees have witnessed the deaths of loved ones, been subjected to torture, and/or witnessed community violence. Some Iraqis have experienced three waves of wars and civil conflicts: the Iraq/Iran war in the 1980s, the first Persian Gulf War in the 1990s, and Operation Iraqi Freedom. These chronic and compounded traumas leave many Arab American immigrants debilitated and struggling to function normally (Daud et al., 2008; Jamil et al., 2002). It should not be surprising that research on various Arab immigrant populations has linked PTSD with depression and anxiety (Jamil, Nassar-McMillan, Lambert, & Hammad, 2006).

Although premigration trauma is a critical factor impacting the mental health of Arab Americans, it is also important to consider postmigration trauma (Nassar-McMillan, 2010). Many Arab Americans experience the trauma of immigration and acculturation. The process of acculturating to a new society can be terrifying, and if one is not prepared or is struggling with previous traumas or mental health issues, the process of acculturation can become overwhelming. Searching for employment and navigating social services and educational systems all can be quite traumatizing for someone who is new to the United States.

Discrimination

Arab Americans have become increasingly traumatized by incidents of discrimination and racism directed toward Arabs (Nassar-McMillan, 2010). Such discrimination takes place on various levels, involving government and national security policies, travel restrictions, and the negative portrayal of Arab Americans in the media (Padela & Heisler, 2010). Struggling with pre- and postmigration traumas can exacerbate other mental health issues such as depression, anxiety, and substance abuse, further alienating individuals from society and putting strain on the individual, family, and community (Daud et al., 2008; Jamil et al., 2002; Nassar-McMillan, 2010).

Substance Abuse

Arab culture may be more permissive than Western societies of cigarette smoking in general, perhaps because of the long-term ritual of engaging in *narguileh* (pronounced *argilah* or *nargeelee*) or smoking a water pipe (also referred to as a hookah or *shisha*). This practice historically occurred in cafes among men, who would discuss politics and play cards or the ancient board game now known as backgammon. According to the American Cancer Society (2011), *argilah* smoking involves more nicotine consumption than cigarette smoking, despite the common misconception that it is less dangerous.

Nicotine has long been considered a gateway drug to other forms of substance abuse. Considering that *argilah* has historically been associated with the Arab culture and has now become more a part of mainstream American social customs, its use among Arab American youth may lead to additional experimentation and use of other substances. The biggest predictor of adolescent use of *argilah* is whether family members smoke one (Rice et al., 2006).

One area that has received little research attention is the subject of drug use among Arab American women. Although alcohol is available for consumption in most Arab countries, there still exists a cultural stigma against its use in public, particularly among women. The expectation is that prohibition would be greatest among Muslim Arab women given the clear Islamic directives to avoid alcohol use. It would be reasonable to assume, then, that Arab Muslim women who exhibit patterns of alcohol abuse or addiction may experience more stigma from their families or communities.

A qualitative study of substance abuse within an Arab American community suggested that, despite the diversity of clients presenting for drug treatment, the major pathways to treatment were criminal justice involvement and health referrals. The clients reported intense stigmatization against alcohol and marijuana use in the Arabic-speaking Muslim community, which may discourage self-referral. The clients also reported language and cultural barriers to accessing and staying in treatment. Thus, underrepresentation within treatment programs is not necessarily due to underidentification (Arfken, Berry, & Owens, 2009). Another study that examined 156 Arab American male clients in treatment for drug-related problems found that higher levels of U.S. acculturation were positively correlated with the incidence of polysubstance abuse (Arfken, Kubiak, & Farrag, 2009).

Domestic Violence

The topic of domestic violence is a complex one from an Arab cultural perspective. It is unlikely that the violence will be the presenting problem or the reason for consultation, unless the referral is from the judicial system. In this case, the perpetrator will probably minimize his role in the violence and explain the circumstances as a misunderstanding.

Perpetrators are as overwhelmingly male, consistent with the prevalence of perpetrators in the general U.S. population (U.S. Department of Justice, n.d.). The question that most frequently arises when one is analyzing the problem of violence within the family or between intimate partners is this: Why does she stay? The answer to this question is not a simple one. Anecdotal stories and research studies have compiled a variety of reasons why women stay, ranging from financial concerns, shame due to self-blame for the abuse, fear of losing custody of children, and an inability to escape because of the barriers the perpetrator constructs.

Arab women report similar rationale in trying to preserve their marriages as well as a number of additional concerns that include fear of losing their legal status, lack of trust in the legal system, possible language barriers, and family pressure to maintain the integrity of the marital union. Moreover, the patrilineal organization of Arab culture gives males ultimate authority in public life and defines women's roles as those connected with child rearing and domestic duties. This dynamic may become internalized to a high degree and create in the woman a mindset that she must tolerate a certain amount of discomfort in life for the sake of her children and future generations. Moreover, a traditionally oriented husband may feel responsible for keeping his wife in line or teaching her a lesson. This attitude encompasses the ideas that a female partner must be patient to solve the problems in her life and that she is responsible for any violence on the part of her spouse. Mistakenly ascribing ownership of the perpetrator's acts to the partner is an error in judgment that is shared by many family members and society in general. This inaccuracy is evident when domestic violence is portrayed as a woman's problem instead of a crime perpetrated mostly against women. Moreover, although this dynamic is somewhat supported by the Arab cultural framework, it is not unlike that of the mainstream United States.

Legal interventions have significantly higher implications as a consequence of the tactics that have been used to fight the War on Terror. Many men have been unfairly profiled, have been questioned by government agencies, have been deported for visa violations, or have lost jobs because they have been interviewed by the government at their place of employment. Suspicion of the true motives of government or police officials has been prevalent within Arab American communities since September 2001. This mistrust has resulted in added harm to those experiencing physical and sexual assault in domestic situations.

Proactive Intervention Strategies

Key counseling strategies need to be taken into consideration when working with Arab American clients. These strategies come from a multicultural competency framework in which culturally responsive and appropriate interventions are used to assist individuals of diverse backgrounds through the counseling process. Like other minorities, Arab Americans may not fit traditional Western client models and may not benefit from traditional Western approaches to counseling (Erickson & Al-Tamimi, 2001; Nassar-McMillan, 2003; Nobles & Sciarra, 2000). This section provides an overview of the critical considerations that one must take in working with Arab Americans.

Initial Rapport

The counselor should strive to ensure that the counseling relationship starts off on a positive note from the very first encounter. If the counselor is female and she is meeting another woman, it is appropriate to shake hands. If there are children present, it is also considered respectful to acknowledge them, greet them, and establish communication with them with some basic questions, such as their name or grade in school. If the female client has an infant or toddler with her, the counselor should also pay attention to the baby but not make too many overt actions. Arab culture tends to be superstitious, and these beliefs intersect for both Christian and Muslim groups with regard to the protection of their very young children. However, if the counselor continues to have contact with the young child over subsequent visits, more affection can be shown.

If the counselor is male or female and is meeting a woman dressed in traditional Islamic attire, it is preferable to initiate with the greeting of *"Asalam Aliekum."* It would also be wise to use this greeting with a man of the Islamic faith. If the counselor is male and greeting a woman dressed in traditional Islamic attire, he should refrain from attempting to shake hands, unless she makes the first move and extends her hand. We make this suggestion because Muslim women vary a great deal in their level of comfort with and acceptance of physical contact with men to whom they are not related. The counselor should give her some initial latitude and allow her to set the parameters. This same advice is extended to female counselors when first meeting Muslim men. If the client's religious orientation is clear, then the counselor might extend the Islamic greeting of *"Asalam Aliekum."* If the client does not respond in kind (with *"Aliekum Salam"*), then the counselor should not continue to extend this greeting.

The very first greetings are likely to take place before the client is escorted to see the therapist. The next phase of rapport building should take place in the counselor's office. If the counselor is drinking or eating something, then the client should be offered the same refreshment. Arab culture is known for its hospitality, particularly within a home environment. A counselor will appear rude if he or she is drinking coffee or soda and does not offer this same level of comfort to a client. Offering a small dish of wrapped candy is an easy ice breaker to use with individuals of any background.

At this point the counselor might engage the new client in small talk. Neutral questions, such as whether the client was able to find the location or the particular floor or office, are useful. Comments or stories about the weather are topics everyone can relate to. This is the point when an Arab American client is most likely to ask personal questions of the counselor. If both the client and counselor are women, the client may inquire about the counselor's marital status, children and their ages, or possibly age if it is obvious there may be a generation gap. The client may be concerned about whether the counselor can relate to the presenting problems. Or, if the counselor is very young, there may be a concern about the counselor's qualifications, namely regarding expertise and experience, to deal with the specific issues.

Counselors should answer questions politely and without too much detail. If confronted with intrusive questions such as why they are not married or why they do not have children, they can respond with very neutral replies such as "This is life" or "This is God's will." Detailed explanations are not obligatory or recommended. This need to tactfully sidestep personal inquiries is a tactic that may need to be utilized frequently during the counseling sessions.

At the same time, if the counselor is of the same ethnic or religious background as the client, making this known can help to build some common ground. In this case, effective self-disclosure can enhance the rapport-building process. For example, if a counselor knows that a new client will be presenting with family or parenting issues, it may be useful to self-disclose some information about his or her own children. On this issue, however, it is important not to proceed too quickly in trying to identify common markers. Personal identity has become more fluid as individuals move to different locales, blend their families, transform their religious ideas and practices, and cultivate ever-changing political ideologies. It is critical to be open to individual differences with each client one encounters. For example, making assumptions about recent immigrant women "under the *chador*" (meaning that they practice veiling, an Islamic tradition practiced by some, but not all, Muslim women) who may, at a glance, appear to be subservient to their spouse or within society may lead to surprise when one finds out that they may have years of education and professional training.

At this point in the initial rapport building, it is appropriate to inquire as to why the individual is seeking services. Although the counselor may possess a basic referral, it is up to the client to elaborate as to why he or she decided to seek counseling services at this time. If there are other family members present, the initial information gathering may be lengthened, as the client might not reveal too much confidential information in front of others. If a woman is the primary client and has been accompanied by her husband, it is better to build some rapport and alliance with him before trying to exclude him for the sake of confidentiality. This can be accomplished by acknowledging his concern and validating his decision to seek counseling. This advice also holds true for parental involvement with an adolescent. Respect the heads of households by listening to their input. Then ask permission to speak to the client alone. This guideline may sound too subservient for some counselors to follow. However, if a counselor is dealing with a dominant or controlling spouse, and that spouse's behavior is fueling current conflicts, by building effective rapport the counselor may diffuse any conflicts that may erupt over a perceived power struggle.

Nonverbal Communication

It is important to consider nonverbal behaviors and communication patterns in the counseling process with Arab Americans. In Arab culture, being direct or confrontational can be perceived as disrespectful or threatening. Therefore, it is important for counselors to be aware of both how they are communicating with the client and how the client is communicating with them. In other words, a client may not express anger overtly but may display his or her feelings nonverbally through facial expressions or body language. Furthermore, it is important that the counselor avoid using clinical jargon or words with negative connotations, such as *depression* or *mental illness,* as they can have very different meanings for each client and may be misinterpreted by or perceived as threatening to the client (Erickson & Al-Tamimi, 2001; Nobles & Sciarra, 2000).

Integrating Family Into the Counseling Process

Considering that Arab Americans are a collectivist people, individual counseling needs to focus not only on the individual and the family unit but also on individuals within the unit. Whenever possible, it may be beneficial to engage the support of community or religious leaders, such as a priest or imam, or other trusted individuals (Nassar-McMillan et al., 2010). In some instances counselors may need to step outside of the tenets of traditional Western counseling by attending a local community event. Such activities may even be incorporated into the treatment plan, if appropriate, and perhaps involve family members. It is important to continually assess the client's perception of the counselor within the community setting and to maintain a balance between using this community role and stature as an advantage and overstepping the bounds of confidentiality (Nassar-McMillan et al., 2010).

Because Arab Americans come from collectivist societies, it is important to consider that they may see their issue as impacting not only themselves but also the larger family system. Also, mental health issues may be stemming from a larger family issue, thus making it that much more important to consider the larger family system in treatment interventions. This may include engaging in family counseling or involving individual family members in the one-on-one counseling process (Erickson & Al-Tamimi, 2001; Nassar-McMillan, 2003, 2008; Nobles & Sciarra, 2000).

Understanding Sociopolitical History

Other important considerations in working with Arab Americans are their sociopolitical history and the current sociopolitical climate. As mentioned earlier, many Arab Americans come from war-torn countries or countries in which there has been constant political and civil strife. Many have fled their homeland in search of safety and a new life. In addition, given the current anti-Arab climate in the United States, many Arab Americans not already traumatized by events in their homeland are becoming traumatized by discrimination and social marginalization. Having a thorough knowledge of the client's social, political, and economic context is critical in effectively counseling Arab Americans (Erickson & Al-Tamimi, 2001; Nassar-McMillan, 2008; Nobles & Sciarra, 2000).

Gender Roles in Counseling Settings

As mentioned earlier, gender considerations are key in developing rapport with Arab American clients. In addition, counselors need to consider the gender identity of their Arab

American clients. Gender is likely to intersect religion, shared values, and the acculturation status of Arab Americans. Individuals striving to negotiate between family heritage and individual expectations may struggle with a clear sense of identity. Mixed messages about gender development may cause additional confusion. These messages may emerge from families, communities, and media. Counselors can encourage clients to have strong role models and mentors (Nassar-McMillan et al., 2010).

Understanding Mental Health Treatment and the Therapeutic Process

For many Arab Americans, counseling may be seen as a last resort (Erickson & Al-Tamimi, 2001). These individuals may seek assistance from religious healers or community leaders, physicians, or family members prior to considering counseling. For many, acknowledging a mental health issue can mean that they are "crazy" or have been hit by "the evil eye," and these beliefs contribute to the avoidance of mental health treatment. Therefore, it is important to provide thorough psychoeducation on the myths of mental health treatment and to validate any fears or concerns (e.g., by explaining confidentiality).

Furthermore, individuals may not have a clear understanding of the role of the counselor or the process of counseling. They may call the counselor "doctor" or "teacher" as a way to justify that the counselor is in fact providing something to them that is tangible or safe. It is important for the counselor to explain his or her role to clients but also to allow clients to find their own way to accept the counselor and the counseling process. Again, psychoeducation is vital to helping clients normalize their feelings about counseling and gain new understandings of the process as one that is collaborative and two way (Erickson & Al-Tamimi, 2001; Nassar-McMillan, 2010; Nobles & Sciarra, 2000).

As mentioned earlier, it is not abnormal for Arab American clients to first seek assistance from religious healers or community leaders prior to seeking out counseling. Clients may also wish to seek assistance from nontraditional healers in conjunction with entering traditional counseling. Thus, it is important for the counselor to be flexible and accepting of nontraditional healing methods and, when possible, align himself or herself with community leaders and religious healers to provide a higher, more culturally responsive quality of intervention for the client (Erickson & Al-Tamimi, 2001; Nobles & Sciarra, 2000).

Boundaries

Traditional Western approaches to counseling require that counselors have stringent boundaries with their clients. These boundaries extend to refusing gifts, not making physical contact, and depending on Western concepts of timeliness relative to appointments and the like. These Western approaches do not, however, mesh well with non-Western cultures such as the Arab or Arab American cultures. It is crucial that counselors working with Arab American clients develop culturally responsive approaches for negotiating such boundaries.

It is customary for an Arab American client to give a gift of appreciation to his or her counselor, especially at termination. Also, it is not abnormal for an Arab American woman to want to hug or give a kiss on the cheek to her female counselor. Termination in and of itself may be challenging for many Arab Americans because it may seem finite and they may not want the relationship to end. In this case, it is appropriate to explain termination as temporary and to state that the client may always contact the counselor in the future, even just to say hello or to check in (Erickson & Al-Tamimi, 2001; Nassar-McMillan, 2008; Nassar-McMillan & Hakim-Larson, 2003; Nobles & Sciarra, 2000).

Social Justice and Advocacy

It is impossible to work with Arab Americans without considering social justice and advocacy issues. Arab Americans are increasingly becoming marginalized in U.S. society, and this is especially true for those who have recently immigrated to the United States and are struggling economically. As social justice agents, it is crucial for counselors to recognize how social injustices negatively impact their clients. In addition, clients can be empowered to recognize the injustices they have experienced and to more fully understand their lives in this context. Moreover, counselors can teach their clients how to stand up against racial and social injustices, advocate for clients who may not be able to advocate for themselves, confront barriers their clients may face to accessing resources and services in the community, connect clients to resources and services they otherwise may not have access to, and join and encourage clients to join community groups that are acting on a community level to advocate for social justice issues in the Arab American community (Ratts & Hutchins, 2009; Toporek, Lewis, & Crethar, 2009).

Case Studies

Case 1: Ahmed

Ahmed is a 47-year-old Iraqi refugee who was resettled to the United States along with his family in the spring of 2009. Ahmed's family includes his wife, his 20-year-old daughter, and his 16- and 8-year-old sons. Ahmed has an older daughter, 24, who resides in Iraq. The rest of his immediate family (his mother and a brother) reside in Egypt. Ahmed and his family fled Iraq in 2007 after receiving death threats from unknown individuals as a result of his work with U.S. coalition security forces in Iraq. The brutal torture and death of one of Ahmed's subordinate officers was the main motivator for Ahmed to flee the country. Ahmed and his family fled with only the clothes on their backs—they left behind all their belongings.

Ahmed was referred for individual counseling by his resettlement agency case worker to address symptoms of posttraumatic stress. At intake, Ahmed reported that since hearing news of his officer's death, he had not been able to sleep more than a couple of hours each night. He reported having nightmares, flashbacks, and uncontrollable crying. In addition, Ahmed reported having severe migraines and intolerable anxiety. He also reported feeling increasingly angry and short tempered. Ahmed has had negative experiences in the past with psychotropic medications and is unwilling to see a psychiatrist for a new evaluation. His main fear is becoming chemically dependent on medications for sleep and anxiety.

Ahmed and his family are also struggling financially, as their expectations of resettlement and life in the United States have not been met. Because of past back injuries, Ahmed is unable to work. In addition, Ahmed's older son and 20-year-old daughter are visually impaired, which impedes their ability to work, and his wife did not complete high school, has limited transferable job skills, and is unwilling to look for employment. No one in the family speaks English. The family does receive public assistance from the county and through local nonprofits, but the resources are coming to an end now that the family is reaching its 1-year anniversary in the United States. Ahmed reported feeling that he is carrying the entire family's burden; he does not feel he can ask for help for fear of appearing incapable or weak. Ahmed reported that he has lost all hope and wishes he could return to Iraq and back to his old life. He reports that he would never commit suicide because he is a Muslim but that he wishes he could die to alleviate his pain.

Counseling Considerations

Ahmed's case is not unlike that of other Iraqis who are resettled to the United States. For this reason, it is extremely important to have a thorough understanding of the sociopolitical environment that Ahmed and his family fled in Iraq. It is likely that Ahmed may have suffered PTSD prior to receiving death threats given his exposure to community violence as a police commander and the fact that he was living in Iraq during the Iran/Iraq war and the first Persian Gulf War. This suggests that Ahmed may be struggling with compounded traumas.

Another important factor in treating Ahmed is addressing his understanding and perceptions of mental health and well-being. Ahmed struggles, as many Arabs do, with the idea that he is unable to function normally or as expected for an Arab man as a result of psychological impairments. This concept of shame and appearance of weakness is a huge barrier to successful treatment and recovery. In addition, his past negative experiences with side effects of psychotropic medications further increase his resistance to undergoing a psychiatric evaluation. In this case, psychoeducation is an absolute necessity. It is important to explain to Ahmed the debilitating effects of PTSD and depression on his ability to function normally and the potential for marked improvement in how he feels should these symptoms be successfully treated through counseling and the use of psychotropic medication. It is also important to validate his concerns and fears of medication, to stress that an evaluation is his chance to assert himself and express his concerns and skepticism toward medication, and to stress that ultimately it is his choice whether he wants to take any medication.

Ahmed is also experiencing a loss of control over his life and hopelessness about his future. It is important to help Ahmed restore his sense of self-efficacy and control. This can be done by taking a social justice and advocacy approach. It is important (a) to help Ahmed learn to advocate for himself and assert his needs with his family and in the community, (b) to assist him in learning how to access community resources, and (c) to assist him in gaining access to these resources. These may include rental assistance, English as a second language classes, or job training programs. Decreasing his feelings of helplessness and hopelessness is integral to Ahmed being able to recover and begin to live his life in the United States.

Case 2: Siham

Siham is a 16-year-old Kurdish-Iraqi girl who immigrated to the United States from Iran with her family when she was 10 years old. Siham's family includes her father and mother (both in their 40s), her 19-year-old sister, her 18- and 17-year-old brothers, and her 14-year-old sister. Siham's father is an Arab Iraqi and her mother is half Kurdish Iraqi and half Arab Iraqi. Siham's older sister is a product of her mother's first marriage to an Iranian man. During Saddam Hussein's regime, Siham and her family had to flee Iraq because of their Kurdish background. In fact, both of Siham's maternal uncles were tortured and assassinated by Saddam's regime for being openly against the Iraqi government's treatment of Kurds in Iraq.

Siham's father was physically, verbally, and sexually abusive to her mother and older siblings while they were in Iran. This behavior continued when they immigrated to the United States; however, 1 year after arriving in the United States, Siham's mother was able to escape her husband with their children and file for divorce. Siham's father was charged with domestic violence and child abuse and was officially diagnosed as paranoid schizophrenic. He is currently homeless and has not had contact with Siham or her siblings.

Since arriving in the United States, Siham and her siblings have struggled academically and socially. Both brothers were incarcerated several times for misdemeanors and minor offenses such as theft, assault, and possession of illegal substances. None of her older siblings completed high school. As Siham reached her teen years, her older brother became increasingly physically and verbally abusive toward her and her mother and sister. The physical abuse turned sexual, and both Siham and her younger sister were sexually molested by their oldest brother. This prompted Child Protective Services to intervene and remove the brothers from the home. After this, Siham ran away from home twice, during which time she was raped by an unknown acquaintance. Siham was subsequently removed from the home and placed in foster care, where she thrived emotionally, socially, and academically. She was also placed in an alternative school for students with emotional and behavioral challenges.

Siham was referred for individual counseling following her transition from foster care back home. Siham reported having anxiety and fears of going back home. She reported feeling that she did not belong in her home any longer (she had been in foster care for a year). Siham also reported that she does not identify with her culture of origin and does not like to be identified as Arab or Iraqi. She reported that the majority of her friends are African American and Latino and that she identifies more with their cultures. Furthermore, Siham reported that she does not identify with the Islamic religion and fears she will be pressured by her mother to practice both her cultural and religious traditions.

Counseling Considerations

It is important to approach Siham's case from two directions, exploring (a) cultural identity development and (b) chronic intergenerational trauma. As with the case of Ahmed, understanding the sociopolitical environment that Siham and her family lived in prior to immigrating to the United States is key. Iraqi Kurds suffered greatly under Saddam Hussein's regime and are marginalized and discriminated against in the region to this day. Having a history of political and ethnic persecution has a significant impact on Siham's identity and has an impact on how her family copes with other life stressors. It is also important to consider any experiences of discrimination Siham or her family members have had in the United States, as these too have an impact on how Siham identifies herself. Working with Siham on developing and understanding her culture and how it is impacted by her environment and past experiences will greatly improve her self-image and self-confidence, which in turn will improve her ability to function more normally and successfully.

It is also important to address the complex and chronic traumas Siham has experienced throughout her life. Her traumatic experiences are ones that were passed down from her parents. Thus, addressing intergenerational traumas from a family perspective is crucial. In this situation, counseling cannot be limited to Siham and must include extended family members who have shared Siham's experiences. This includes her mother and siblings (her father is not available). The family should be assisted in understanding its larger identity and how its past experiences have influenced how members interact with and treat each other. Psychoeducation is key in helping the family move forward.

Case 3: Jamilla

Jamilla is a 35-year-old Egyptian woman of Nubian descent. She immigrated to the United States with her husband and her son and daughter, ages 18 and 16, respectively. Jamilla's family immigrated to the United States by way of the Diversity Visa (or the "lottery," as many call it). Jamilla has a sixth-grade education and does not speak any English. Her son has graduated from high school and is attending community college, and her daughter is a junior in high school. Her husband, who no longer resides with the family, is unemployed.

Jamilla was referred for individual counseling by her case manager, who reported that Jamilla was struggling to cope with her marriage. At intake, Jamilla reported that several months ago her daughter had discovered that her father had been sending romantic e-mails to another Arab woman overseas. After Jamilla confronted her husband, he informed her that he is actually married to the woman and they are expecting twins. He further informed Jamilla that he would like her and the children to leave the home and return to Egypt so his second wife could join him in the United States. Jamilla reported that when she refused to return to Egypt, her husband became verbally and physically abusive toward her. He locked her in their home; removed most of the furniture, except items he used; removed all of the kitchenware to prevent her from cooking; and refused to provide her with any money to purchase food or necessities. However, he did ensure that the children had food to eat.

With the assistance of her case manager, Jamilla was able to go to a hospital for a physical exam to document the abuses. With documentation, she was able to have her husband arrested and removed from the home. She was also able to get a restraining order to prevent her husband from returning to the home.

Jamilla now struggles with being the sole wage earner in the home, as her husband is unable to pay child support because of being unemployed. He has also fled the country and cannot be held accountable unless he returns to the United States. Jamilla believes she will be able to find employment immediately even though she has no language skills or transferable job skills. Jamilla would like to start her own day care center and wants assistance with becoming certified. Yet, without any English language skills, she is unable to participate in the training courses. Jamilla does not believe she needs to take English language classes and intends on relying on her children to interpret when needed.

Jamilla views counseling as additional case management and expects the counselor to assist her in meeting her basic needs despite already having a case manager. She shows up unannounced to see the counselor and calls several times a week asking the counselor to interpret for her or to advocate for her needs. Jamilla also struggles with regulating her emotions and has limited coping skills, which causes her to have meltdowns and temper tantrums in counseling any time she is confronted or something does not go as she expects (e.g., when she learned she was unable to attend child care certification courses because of her limited language skills). She has also become verbally abusive toward her children, especially her son, whom she suspects is in contact with his father and "spying" on her. Jamilla is unable to acknowledge the breakdown in her communication skills and coping behaviors and has a skewed sense of reality and what she can accomplish. Her children are becoming increasingly impatient with her and are beginning to isolate themselves from her.

Counseling Considerations

In the case of Jamilla, it is important to begin by addressing the role of the counselor and the purpose of individual counseling. Jamilla's main focus is having her basic needs met, and she views the counselor as yet another person who will assist in that process. Although this is true to some extent, it is important to provide Jamilla with psychoeducation on how the counselor can assist her in accessing basic needs through developing self-advocacy skills and becoming more self-reliant. In addition, it is essential to explain appropriate boundaries between client and counselor. This needs to be done in a culturally responsive manner, respecting Jamilla's cultural norms for interactions with others, especially those in the helping professions. Jamilla's negative communication skills are affecting her relationship with her children, causing them to distance themselves from her and be reluctant to come to her aid. She needs her children and needs to establish a partnership with them given that they speak English fluently and can assist her with certain tasks and responsibilities.

Furthermore, Jamilla needs to understand the impact that domestic violence has on self-esteem and feelings of helplessness and hopelessness. Jamilla feels as though she will not be able to accomplish anything and that she is not being helped by anyone. It is important to assist Jamilla in developing stronger coping skills and increasing her resilience and hope. This can be achieved through giving Jamilla specific and achievable tasks that she can accomplish on her own (e.g., having her drop off her application for food stamps and Temporary Assistance for Needy Families on her own without a case manager; or, after teaching her how to use the bus, having her take the bus on her own for the first time). Again, this boils down to basic social justice and advocacy skills, empowering the client to take ownership of her life and her circumstances.

Conclusion

Arab Americans are descended from the specific area of the geographic Middle East called the Arab Middle East, which comprises the League of Arab States. Because of their historic immigration patterns, Arab Americans and Muslims share some common cultural traditions, but these two groups are not identical, and the majority of Arab Americans are in fact non-Muslim. This chapter has provided information about the sociopolitical history and climate of Arab Americans and some of the intricate influences these can have on the identity development and mental health of this population. It has also explored some specific cultural and mental health issues and how these translate into considerations for counseling. The case examples illustrate how these considerations are effectively applied. Although these cases might be considered illustrative of newer, less acculturated immigrants, many Arab Americans, regardless of acculturation, face these issues in navigating their identity development. We anticipate that professional counselors will come away from this chapter with a renewed and, most important, accurate perspective on Arab Americans and their cultural realities.

References

American Cancer Society. (2011). *What about more exotic forms of smoking tobacco, such as clove cigarettes, bidis, and hookahs?* Retrieved from http://www.cancer.org/Cancer/ CancerCauses/TobaccoCancer/QuestionsaboutSmokingTobaccoandHealth/questions-about-smoking-tobacco-and-health-other-forms-of-smoking

Arab American Institute. (2002). *Religious affiliation of Arab Americans.* Retrieved from http://www.aaiusa.org/page/file/b8bad613905570ea97_mghwmvb2d.pdf/ancestry.pdf

Arfken, C. L., Berry, A., & Owens, D. (2009). Pathways to substance abuse treatment: Arab-American clients. *Journal of Muslim Mental Health, 4,* 31–36.

Arfken, C. L., Kubiak, S. P., & Farrag, M. (2009). Acculturation and polysubstance abuse in Arab-American treatment clients. *Transcultural Psychiatry, 4,* 608–622.

Awad, G. H. (2010). The impact of acculturation and religious identification on perceived discrimination for Arab/Middle Eastern Americans. *Cultural Diversity and Ethnic Minority Psychology, 16,* 59–67.

Berry, J. W. (1984). Cultural relations in plural societies: Alternatives to segregation and their sociopsychological implications. In N. Miller & M. Brewer (Eds.), *Groups in contact: The psychology of desegregation* (pp. 11–27). Orlando, FL: Academic Press.

Berry, J. W. (2003). Conceptual approaches to acculturation. In K. M. Chun, P. Balls Organista, & G. Martin (Eds.), *Acculturation: Advances in theory, measurement and applied research* (pp. 17–37). Washington, DC: American Psychological Association.

Britto, P. R., & Amer, M. M. (2007). An exploration of cultural identity patterns and the family context among Arab Muslim young adults in America. *Applied Development Science, 11,* 137–150.

Daud, A., Klinteberg, B. A., & Rydelius, P.-A. (2008). Trauma, PTSD and personality: The relationship between prolonged traumatization and personality impairments. *Scandinavian Journal of Caring Sciences, 22,* 331–340.

Erickson, C. D., & Al-Tamimi, N. R. (2001). Providing mental health services to Arab Americans: Recommendations and considerations. *Cultural Diversity and Ethnic Minority Psychology, 7,* 308–327.

Faragallah, M. H., Walter, R. S., & Farrell, J. W. (1997). Acculturation of Arab-American immigrants: An exploratory study. *Journal of Comparative Family Studies, 28,* 182–203.

Habboush, K. L. (2007). Working with Arab American families: Culturally competent practice for school psychologists. *Psychology in the Schools, 44,* 183–198.

Hakim-Larson, J., Kamoo, R., Nassar-McMillan, S. C., & Porcerelli, J. H. (2007). Counseling Arab and Chaldean American families. *Journal of Mental Health Counseling, 29,* 301–321.

Jamil, H., Hakim-Larson, J., Farrag, M., Khafaji, T., Duqum, I., & Jamil, L. H. (2002). A retrospective study of Arab American mental health clients: Trauma and the Iraqi refugees. *American Journal of Orthopsychiatry, 72,* 355–361.

Jamil, H., Nassar-McMillan, S. C., & Lambert, R. G. (2007). Immigration and attendant psychological sequelae: A comparison of three waves of Iraqi immigrants. *American Journal of Orthopsychiatry, 77,* 199–205.

Jamil, H., Nassar-McMillan, S. C., Lambert, R. G., & Hammad, A. (2006). An epidemiological study: Health assessment of three waves of Iraqi immigrants. *Journal of Immigrant and Refugee Studies, 4,* 69–74.

Kumin, J., & Hemingway, B. (2008). EU must do more to help refugees. *Refugees Daily.* Retrieved from http://www.unhcr.org/cgi-bin/texis/vtx/refdaily?pass=463ef21123&id=48896b0a10

Lindencrona, F., Ekblad, S., & Hauff, E. (2008). Mental health of recently resettled refugees from the Middle East in Sweden: The impact of pre-resettlement trauma, resettlement stress, and capacity to handle stress. *Social Psychiatry and Psychiatric Epidemiology, 43,* 121–131.

Nassar-McMillan, S. C. (2003). Counseling Arab Americans. In N. A. Vacc, S. B. DeVaney, & J. M. Brendel (Eds.), *Counseling multicultural and diverse populations* (4th ed., pp. 117–139). New York, NY: Brunner-Routledge.

Nassar-McMillan, S. C. (2008). Arab Americans. In F. T. L. Leong (Ed.), *Encyclopedia of counseling,* Vol. 3 (pp. 985–991). Thousand Oaks, CA: Sage.

Nassar-McMillan, S. C. (2010). *Counseling Arab Americans.* New York, NY: Brooks-Cole/Cengage.

Nassar-McMillan, S. C., Gonzalez, L. M., & Mohamed, R. H. (2010). Individuals and families of Arab descent. In D. Hays & B. Erford (Eds.), *Developing multicultural competency: A systems approach* (pp. 216–245). Upper Saddle River, NJ: Prentice Hall.

Nassar-McMillan, S., & Hakim-Larson, J. (2003). Counseling considerations among Arab Americans. *Journal of Counseling & Development, 81,* 150–159.

Nobles, A. Y., & Sciarra, D. T. (2000). Cultural determinants in treatment of Arab Americans: A primer for mainstream therapists. *American Journal of Orthopsychiatry, 70,* 182–191.

Norris, A. E., & Aroian, K. J. (2008). Avoidance symptoms and assessment of post-traumatic stress disorder in Arab immigrant women. *Journal of Traumatic Stress, 21,* 471–478.

Nydell, M. (2006). *Understanding Arabs.* Boston, MA: Instructional Press.

Padela, A. I., & Heisler, M. (2010). The association of perceived abuse and discrimination after September 11, 2001 with psychological distress, level of happiness, and health status among Arab Americans. *American Journal of Public Health, 100,* 284–291.

Ratts, M. J., & Hutchins, A. M. (2009). ACA advocacy competencies: Social justice advocacy at the client/student level. *Journal of Counseling & Development, 87,* 269–275.

Read, J. (2003). The sources of gender role attitudes among Christian and Muslim Arab-American women. *Sociology of Religion, 64,* 207–222.

Rice, V. H., Weglicki, L. S., Templin, T., Hammad, A., Jamil, H., & Kulwicki, A. (2006). Predictors of Arab American adolescent tobacco use. *Merrill-Palmer Quarterly, 52,* 327–342.

Samhan, H. H. (1997, April 4). *Not quite White: Race classification and the Arab American experience.* Retrieved from http://www.aaiusa.org/foundation/355/not-quite-white

Sarroub, L. K. (2002, Spring). Arab American youth in perspective. *Newsletter of the Society for Research on Adolescence,* pp. 3–6.

Shaheen, J. G. (1997). *Arab and Muslim stereotyping in American popular culture.* Washington, DC: Georgetown University Center for Muslim–Christian Understanding.

Shakir, E. (1997). *Bint Arab: Arab and Arab American women in the United States.* Westport, CT: Praeger.

Toporek, R., Lewis, J., & Crethar, H. (2009). Promoting systemic change through the ACA advocacy competencies. *Journal of Counseling & Development, 87,* 260–268.

United Nations High Commissioner for Refugees. (2009, June 16). *2008 global trends: Refugees, asylum-seekers, returnees, internally displaced, and stateless persons.* Retrieved from http://www.unhcr.org/4a375c426.html

U.S. Citizenship and Immigration Services. (2009, February 11). *Fact sheet: Iraqi refugee processing.* Retrieved from http://www.uscis.gov/portal/site/uscis/menuitem.5af9bb95919f35e66f614176543f6d1a/?vgnextchannel=68439c7755cb9010VgnVCM10000045f3d6a1RCRD&vgnextoid=df4c47c9de5ba110VgnVCM1000004718190aRCRD

U.S. Department of Justice. (n.d.). *Intimate partner violence in the United States.* Retrieved from http://bjs.ojp.usdoj.gov/content/pub/pdf/ipvus.pdf

Witteborn, S. (2007). The situated expression of Arab collective identities in the United States. *Journal of Communication, 57,* 556–575.

Additional Resources

American-Arab Anti-Discrimination Committee
www.adc.org
Civil rights organization committed to defending the rights of people of Arab descent and promoting their rich cultural heritage.

Arab American Institute
www.aaiusa.org
Represents the policy and community interests of Arab Americans throughout the United States and strives to promote Arab American participation in the U.S. electoral system.

Arab American National Museum
www.arabamericanmuseum.org
The first museum in the world devoted to Arab American history and culture, and an affiliate of the Smithsonian Institution.

Arab Community Center for Economic and Social Services
   http://www.accesscommunity.org/site/PageServer)
   Includes resources on cultural arts, employment and training, public health, and
   education.
Institute on Religion and Civic Values (formerly the Council on Islamic Education)
   www.cie.org
   A group of scholars that provide academic information about Islam.
Middle East and Middle Eastern American Center
   http://memeac.gc.cuny.edu/
   Based at the City University of New York, the Middle East and Middle Eastern
   American Center has as its mission to promote the study of the Middle East and
   Middle Eastern Americans.
National Network for Arab American Communities
   www.nnaac.org
   Committed to the development of Arab American community-based nonprofit
   organizations at the local and national levels.
Network of Arab-American Professionals
   www.naaponline.org
   A nonpartisan, volunteer-based organization dedicated to strengthening the Arab
   American community.

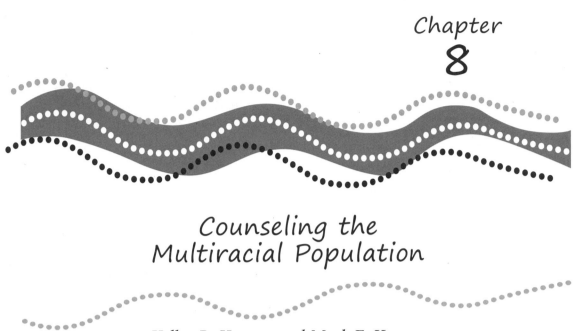

Counseling the Multiracial Population

Kelley R. Kenney and Mark E. Kenney

This chapter examines the counseling issues and concerns of multiracial individuals and families. In exploring this population, it is important to first identify and define who is included.

Definitions

Multiracial individuals are persons whose biological parents are of two or more different racial backgrounds and whose linage encompasses two or more distinctly difference racial backgrounds (Funderburg, 1994; Gibbs, 1989; Root, 1992).

Interracial couples are couples, married or not, in which each partner is of a different racial background (Root, 1992; Spickard, 1989).

Multiracial families are composed of interracial couples and their multiracial offspring; single parents with biological offspring who are multiracial; single parents who have gone through a surrogate pregnancy process or artificial insemination process that results in the birth of a multiracial child; and families in which a cross-racial or transracial adoption has occurred, including gay and lesbian couples or single individuals who have adopted transracially or have gone through a surrogate pregnancy process or artificial insemination process that results in the birth of a multiracial child (Kenney, 2000).

Transracial adoptions are adoptions in which children are placed with families of another race (Stolley, 1993).

As a segment of the U.S. population, multiracial individuals and families, including those that have become multiracial as a result of transracial adoption, are increasing dramatically. According to a 2008 demographic analysis done by the Pew Research Center, approximately 1 in 7 marriages was interracial. This figure is 6 times the intermarriage rate of 1960. Of particular note is the increase in out-marriage rates among Asians and Hispanics as well as the increase in out-marriage rates among African American men (Passel, Wang, & Taylor, 2010). The 2000 Census marked the first time that people in the United States could describe themselves by selecting more than one racial category (Root & Kelley, 2003). Census 2000 data revealed that 2.4% of the country's 281.4 million individuals described themselves as multiracial. Of these, 93% reported being of two racial backgrounds, whereas 7% reported being of three or more racial backgrounds. Census surveys suggest that although these numbers have remained fairly constant since 2000, the number of multiple-heritage marriages has increased 20% since 2000 to 4.5 million, or 8% of total marriages. Census 2010 Data revealed that nine million individuals, or 2.9% of the total population, were identified as being of two or more races. This represents a 32% increase from the 2000 Census.

Transracial adoptions in the United States include adoptions of children born in other countries. Estimates of the numbers of transracial adoptions range from 8% of all adoptions (Evan B. Donaldson Adoption Institute, 2002) to 14% of both domestic and international transracial adoptions (National Adoption Information Clearinghouse, 1994). International adoption figures for 2002 totaled 20,009. This number is more than triple the 1992 figure, with the vast number of these being transracial international adoptions (U.S. Department of State, 2006).

Roughly a third of children adopted through the foster care system are adopted by parents or families of different racial backgrounds (Steinberg & Hall, 2000). Despite ongoing criticism and challenges, both domestic and international transracial adoptions continue to be viable options for individuals, couples, and families interested in raising children (Baden, Thomas, & Smith, 2009).

Issues and Concerns of Interracial Couples

Research conducted by the Pew Research Center and the Gallop Organization has revealed dramatic shifts in societal attitudes and reactions to both interracial dating and marriage and has indicated that rates of acceptance and approval of interracial relationships are increasing (Gallup Organization, 2004; Passel et al., 2010; Taylor, Funk, & Craighill, 2006). Despite this and the growing numbers of multiple-heritage couples, the topic of interracial marriage continues to evoke controversy and meet with opposition, specifically based on a couple's education level, socioeconomic status, and geographical location (Passel et al., 2010; Root, 2001; Zebroski, 1999).

Multiracial individuals and interracial couples have historically evoked controversy and scrutiny, and although interracial unions between Blacks and Whites have been far outnumbered by other interracial partnerships, particularly those between Asians and Whites, Black–White relationships have borne the brunt of much of the controversy and ridicule (Okun, 1996). The historical context of this ridicule in the United States is based on a set of assumptions and societal myths regarding the superiority of Whites (DaCosta, 2007; Davis, 1991; Yancey, 2002). The myths further suggested that individuals who engaged in interracial relationships had ulterior motives for doing so (Wardle, 1992, 1999). These motives included quests for the exotic, sexual curiosity and promiscuity, economic and social status or achievement, domination, potential citizenship, rebellion against society or family, or racial self-hatred (DaCosta, 2007; Root, 1992; Spickard, 1989; Yancey, 2002). Other myths have implied that persons of color are more willing than Whites to accept children of interracial unions (Wardle, 1992, 1999) and that the difficulties faced by interracial individuals and families are based on race (Root, 2001; Wehrly, 1996).

The racial stratification of U.S. society, whereby races are viewed as inherently separate, has always made interactions among and between races a challenge. Societal concerns regarding interracial unions have been representative of many unresolved issues about race (Root, 2001; Spickard, 1992; Yancey, 2002). Interracial couples of all racial compositions have faced overt and covert challenges that seem to be directly related to the maintenance of racial and ethnic categorizations and identifications, sociopolitical hierarchies, and cultural values and mores (Azoulay, 1997; DaCosta, 2007). These concerns, although prevalent in relationships between Whites and Blacks, may be even more prevalent in intermarriages involving Arabs, Asians, Latinos, and Native Americans.

Intermarriage has often been viewed as an indicator of the assimilation process. The degree to which individuals of a particular group are likely to intermarry may be based on issues concerning level of assimilation and acculturation (Bacigalupe, 2003; Kitano, Fujino, & Sato, 1998; Negy & Snyder, 2000; Taylor et al., 2006). Lee (1996) indicated that although some interracial families that include Asians seem to be able to integrate multiple cultures with a high level of success, others experience conflicts related to differences in values, religious beliefs, communication styles, child-rearing practices, and influences of in-laws. This often seems to be related to issues of acculturation and assimilation. For immigrant and first-generation Asians, Latinos, and Arabs married to Euro-Americans, concerns regarding communication styles, language, gender roles, parenting styles, customs, and food may be indicative of profound differences in cultural values and worldviews (Negy & Snyder, 2000; Wehrly, Kenney, & Kenney, 1999). These cultural issues may become more cumbersome when both intermarried partners are persons of color (Blau, 1998).

Issues and Concerns of Multiracial Individuals

U.S. society operates out of a monoracial model of race relations and racial identity development that does not allow for variations in physical appearance (Root, 1997a, 1997b). Multiracial individuals, particularly those whose appearance makes it difficult for mainstream society to project onto them an identity from one of the sociopolitically defined single-race groups, challenge conventional racial ideology. An additional burden for multiracial individuals involves curtailing the ongoing challenges of responding to questions regarding who or what they are (Houston, 1997; Ramirez, 1996; Wijeyesinghe, 2001; Williams, 1996). Many multiracial individuals have reported that questions and concerns about their physical appearance and racial identity have been issues that they as well as their parents have needed to address even before birth (Wehrly et al., 1999). Hence, for many multiracial individuals, concerns and questions regarding identity are lifelong issues (Bradshaw, 1992; Dalmage, 2000; Williams, 1996).

Navigating and integrating multiple heritages in a monoracial society is often a challenge that multiracial individuals face well into adulthood (Henriksen & Paladino, 2009; Nishimura, 1998; Root, 1998). The issues and challenges faced by multiracial individuals as well as how they negotiate and deal with these concerns vary depending on their age and developmental stage in life. Thus, it is important to examine and discuss persons of multiple heritages from a developmental perspective.

Multiracial Children

Multiracial children experience a variety of stressors that are different from those of their parents. Many of these stressors are related to issues of racial identity and to the establishment of a sense of belonging among their peers and the greater society (Funderburg, 1994; Gardner, 2000; Root, 1996; Rosenblatt, Karis, & Powell, 1995). According to McFadden (2001), it is important for interracial partners to recognize in the early stages of their relationship that children from their marriage not only will be racially mixed but also will have to adjust to being identified as "others." A family environment that fosters communication and provides love and security is key to wholesome development and to the emergence of ego strength and resilience in multiracial individuals (Nash, 1997; Rockquemore & Laszloffy, 2003; Root, 1996; Rosenblatt et al., 1995; Wardle & Cruz-Janzen, 2004).

The issues and concerns of multiracial children may vary based on the children's age and developmental stage. Children begin to explore who they are during early childhood. In an attempt to understand their identity and how they fit into the family and other social environments, young children spend a lot of time and energy comparing themselves with others. They may even ask questions about their looks and those of others, specifically their parents, as a way of exploring their identity (Sheets, 2003; Wardle, 1999). Confronted with frequent questions such as "What are you?" or "Are you Black or are you White?" and quizzical and scrutinizing stares, multiracial children experience their uniqueness and discover at a young age that they do not fit traditional patterns of racial identification (Root, 1990; Sheets, 2003; Wehrly, 1996; Wijeyesinghe, 2001). The development of a positive racial identity and ethnic identity is the most salient issue faced by multiracial children. Hence, according to Wardle (1999) and Wardle and Cruz-Janzen (2004), an open, honest, and supportive environment is essential for helping multiracial children to explore their identity.

The complexities of navigating between their multiple heritages and those of their family and social environment can be confusing for young children. Those who are challenged to identify more with one aspect of their racial heritage than another experience an even greater level of confusion and dissonance. To endure these challenges and develop a healthy and positive self-concept, multiracial children must have the benefits of a secure and predictable family environment (Okun, 1996; Sheets, 2003). In addition, Wardle (1999) and Wardle and Cruz-Janzen (2004) pointed out the necessity of giving multiracial children exposure to supportive and positive influences in all aspects of their environments. This includes professionals who are involved in the child's care even before birth. Professionals do not function in a vacuum and may make race-based assumptions, treating the child and his or her family as a stereotype. Beginning at birth, it is important to expose the multiracial child to persons, books, dolls, pictures, and so forth that are reflective of all races and cultures. During childhood, it is important to establish a solid foundation on which to build a strong self-concept in preparation for the more difficult challenges faced in adolescence.

Multiracial Adolescents

Establishing and maintaining social acceptance is one of the major tasks of adolescence. This normal aspect of the development process may be complicated by issues of racial identity (Bracey, Bamaca, & Umana-Taylor, 2004; Okun, 1996; Tefera, 2005). Multiracial adolescents experience this period of their development with varying degrees of anxiety and vulnerability; this is particularly true as involvement with their peer group, dating, and other social interactions become important (Okun, 1996; Root, 1994; Sheets, 2003; Wardle, 1999; Wardle & Cruz-Janzen, 2004). Multiracial adolescents often find themselves redefining and renegotiating their once stable relationships as a result of experiencing societal racism through stereotypical and prejudicial comments and actions directed toward their mixed ancestry (Cheng & Lee, 2009; Wehrly, 1996; Wright, 2000). This is often the first time that multiracial individuals experience the barriers associated with being people of color (Bracey et al., 2004; Root, 1990).

Another major challenge that may be experienced by multiracial adolescents is pressure to choose a racial identity or racial reference group (Gibbs & Hines, 1992; Pinderhughes, 1995). Desires to be accepted by peers, desires to conform to social expectations, or loyalties felt toward one parent over the other are often at the root of this pressure (Steel, 1995; Wehrly, 1996; Wright, 2000). The decision to choose or identify with one aspect of one's heritage over others can result in feelings of disloyalty and guilt. The racial dissonance often experienced by multiracial adolescents who are challenged in this way can be quite painful (Cheng & Lee, 2009; Okun, 1996; Wright, 2000).

Many of the developmental issues and concerns that affect multiracial adolescents are similar to those experienced by all adolescents. Multiracial children who enter adolescence with a strong sense of themselves and their multiracial heritage as well as an ability to respond firmly and assertively to questions, remarks, and pressures have a greater chance of successfully meeting the challenges of adolescence (Bracey et al., 2004; Wardle, 1999). Here again, the support provided within the individual's environment is critical.

Multiracial Adults

The issues that may be faced by multiracial adults are most often related to a lack of resolution of concerns and questions regarding their mixed racial identity and heritage (Wehrly, 1996). Difficulties surviving earlier experiences of rejection or isolation and feelings of inferiority, as well as guilt related to embarrassments about parts (or all) of one's racial heritage, may be manifested in feelings of confusion or insecurity that may be experienced throughout the multiracial individual's lifetime (Okun, 1996; Wehrly, 1996; Wehrly et al., 1999).

The challenge of integrating dual or multiple heritages with other areas of their lives is ongoing for multiracial individuals (McClain, 2004; Paladino & Henriksen, 2009; Root, 1998, 2002). The problem of institutionalized racism continues to permeate societal forces; hence, some multiracial adults continue to have their racial identities assigned for them or experience pressure to self-identify in a particular way. This is often based on their physical appearance (Root, 1997b). According to Root (1990), multiracial men in particular often have a difficult time overcoming social obstacles and constraints. Multiracial women, in contrast, are seen as less threatening and may therefore experience less overt obstacles to their success.

Root (1994) discussed six themes around which issues and challenges often arise for multiracial individuals: uniqueness, acceptance and belonging, physical appearance, sexuality, self-esteem, and identity. Although these themes are not mutually exclusive, any one of them may be operating or related to concerns that a multiracial individual may be experiencing at any developmental stage.

1. *Uniqueness.* According to Root (1994), this theme interfaces with all of the other themes. Multiracial individuals often experience themselves as different from others because they are often treated as special or unique simply because of their multiple heritages. This may lead to behaviors or interactions that may be misinterpreted or misunderstood.
2. *Acceptance and belonging.* Multiracial individuals often feel that they must straddle both or all sides of the racial line. As a result, constant efforts are made to find a place where they can feel and experience a sense of connection or fit.

3. *Physical appearance.* According to Hall (1997), persons of mixed-race heritage often have physical features that are distinctly different than those of people of single-race heritage. Because of societal pressures, women tend to define themselves and their value on the basis of physical appearance; hence, for multiracial women, appearance seems to be of particular significance. Questions or judgments made about multiracial individuals' racial identity are typically based on perceptions of their physical appearance (Root, 1994).

4. *Sexuality.* Multiracial women continue to experience difficulties in relationships related to stereotypical myths about the exotic multiracial female.

5. *Self-esteem.* Self-esteem interfaces with and is affected by the experiences of the multiracial individual with regard to the other five themes. Positive environmental support is essential for the development of a positive self-concept.

6. *Identity.* One's sense of identity can be equated with feelings of connectedness and belonging. Multiracial individuals who have had positive exposure to and support for their exploration of their multiple heritages are more fluid in the affirmation and expression of their identity (Okun, 1996; Wehrly et al., 1999)

Counseling Interracial Couples: The Case Study of Carlos and Sheila

This case study of Carlos and Sheila is a depiction of a married interracial couple dealing with acculturation and assimilation issues.

Carlos, a 33-year-old Latino of Mexican background, and Sheila, a 31-year-old of English heritage, have been married for 9 months. The couple has come to counseling to discuss how to deal with conflicts that have recently surfaced in their relationship. The two met at a singles group offered by their church and dated for about 3 years before getting married.

Carlos was born in a small town outside Mexico City. His family came to the United States when he was 4 years old. Carlos recalls that his mother worked outside of the home on a limited basis because she had to care for four children and a household. She worked as a seamstress and could therefore do much of her work at home. Carlos's father believed that the home and children were the woman's responsibility and that the man was the head of the household and the chief breadwinner. He was a skilled and licensed electrician in Mexico and on arriving in the United States found employment with a contracting firm.

Carlos and his brother Antonio were the only children in the family to attend college. His two sisters were only allowed to attend cosmetology school. After completing college, Carlos pursued a career as a teacher and coach and was very successful. Sheila and her two sisters were encouraged by their parents to go to college. Sheila's mother worked as a registered nurse, and her father was a chemical engineer. Sheila studied accounting as an undergraduate and pursued a master's degree in accounting. She entered into a career as an investments accountant for a high-powered accounting firm.

Carlos and Sheila never talked much before they were married about the number of children they wanted to have or about each other's career or family roles. Shortly after the couple was married, Carlos began to talk about starting a family and spoke of dreams of having at least four children, as his parents had. Sheila was very excited and enthusiastic about her work and the social opportunities it provided her. The couple's conflicts and constant arguments began when Sheila shared at dinner one evening that she had accepted an account that in the future would require travel and long hours at the office. Sheila had difficulty understanding why Carlos was not happy about this new opportunity she had been given, particularly because it was possible that he could accompany her on business trips when he was not teaching.

This case example raises issues and questions regarding the backgrounds, cultural identities, and worldviews of both partners and how couples navigate around concerns in these areas. The counselor working with Carlos and Sheila needs to be aware of and sensitive to the cultural backgrounds of both partners as well as have an understanding of how counseling is viewed in a cultural context. Whereas a White spouse may view counseling as a natural solution to working out problems or difficulties, a non-White spouse may not because of cultural beliefs regarding how one deals with personal and family issues (Okun, 1996). Hence, if Carlos and Sheila remain in counseling, this needs to be assessed and discussed up front.

Another variable that needs to be addressed at the outset of counseling with this couple is the racial and cultural background of the counselor as well as his or her gender. Myths and stereotypes continue to cloud societal views of individuals who enter into interracial relationships and marriages. Counselors have an obligation to examine their own views and the manner in which these views affect their perceptions of clients, their clients' concerns, and the work they do with them (Bacigalupe, 2003; Solsberry, 1994; Wehrly et al., 1999). Similarly, it is important to consider the extent to which clients perceive the racial/cultural background of the counselor as a deterrent to the counselor's ability to understand their issues and concerns (Okun, 1996; Tubbs & Rosenblatt, 2003; Wardle & Cruz-Janzen, 2004). Moreover, when counselors are working with partners whose country of origin is not the United States, they must examine their views regarding acculturation and assimilation. Awareness of the potential to impose American values on others through counseling is key. Hence, the counselor must openly dialogue with clients and assist them in developing goals that are conducive to their values and needs (Okun, 1996; Tubbs & Rosenblatt, 2003; Wardle & Cruz-Janzen, 2004).

Partners who are able to comprehend each other's worldview are often able to function more collaboratively and come up with mutually agreed-on solutions and decisions (Okun, 1996). According to Ibrahim and Schroeder (1990), partners benefit from receiving assistance with clarifying and understanding each other's worldview and cultural background. This provides each with useful information for becoming aware of the values that each brings to the relationship and how these values affect views and interactions. Hence, to assist Carlos and Sheila in diffusing the conflict in their relationship, it is important that the counselor help them to examine the cultural context within which each of them was raised and has continued to operate. It is also important to educate each of them about the other's cultural values and mores. In working with Carlos and Sheila, the counselor should pay specific attention to cultural values related to work, family, child rearing, and gender-role expectations and responsibilities. Once their differing values have been delineated and understood, both partners can be assisted in dealing with disappointments they may experience related to unmet expectations.

Ishiyama (2006) presented a self-validation model that emphasizes the significance of each partner experiencing a sense of self-validation as well as validation from his or her spouse. The model's validation-gram is a tool that can be used to examine and assess the extent to which relationships, activities, things or objects, places, and cultural practices are important to each partner. The validation-gram can be used to facilitate discussion that will assist partners in developing empathic understanding as they work toward understanding attitudes, beliefs, behaviors, and expressions that are culturally based. The model offers another process that can help Carlos and Sheila to further understand the basis for conflicts and to clarify and normalize their different cultural worldview experiences. The model helps partners to acknowledge shared values and worldview experiences that can help strengthen and solidify their relationships (Ishiyama, 2006). According to Okun (1996), helping couples to positively reframe their conflicts as being indicative of cultural differences—rather than being indicative of one partner being right and the other wrong—enables couples to see their conflicts as differences with equal value. Thus, they are able to establish a climate in the relationship that is conducive to negotiation. When they have greater awareness of and respect for their differences and similarities, couples are able to move beyond their conflicts and develop the empathy and tolerance necessary for working more collaboratively on lifestyle choices and decisions (Okun, 1996; Waldman & Rubalcava, 2005).

It is important to address the fact that there has been an increase in the number of gay and lesbian interracial couples. According to Wehrly et al. (1999), the complexities of society's stigmatized perceptions of gays, lesbians, and people of color often result in a level of stress in this type of interracial relationship that is greater than the level of stress experienced by heterosexual interracial couples. Therefore, to be effective in helping these couples deal with the complexities of their relationships, counselors must not only assess their attitudes and views about persons who engage in interracial relationships but also assess their attitudes and views about gay and lesbian relationships.

Counseling Multiracial Children

Counselors working with multiracial children must be sensitive to the possibility that the problems children present may be unrelated to their multiracial status (Wardle, 1999; Wardle & Cruz-Janzen, 2004; Wijeyesinghe, 2001). According to Okun (1996), in assessing the problems or concerns of multiracial children, it is important to determine whether they are related to the children's developmental age or stage; child-rearing practices of the parents, the parents' relationship, or other familial issues; or racial/ethnic issues and concerns. Children's age, their level of understanding of identity, and their cognitive abilities are also important to consider because these influence the children's perceptions and experiences of the problem (Okun, 1996; Wehrly, 1996).

Children need to feel heard and validated; hence, the most important skill to utilize in working with multiracial children is that of supportive and culturally sensitive listening (Harris, 2002; Wehrly et al., 1999). This is particularly necessary for the development of trust and a positive relationship with the child, especially if the issues and concerns being presented are racially or ethnically oriented (Wehrly, 1996; Wehrly et al., 1999).

Establishing a foundation for positive self-concept is crucial to multiracial children's development. Counselors must assist children in identifying and acknowledging their strengths and abilities, in developing effective coping skills for dealing with conflict, and in developing and pursuing their own unique interests (Okun, 1996). According to Herring (1992), in helping children develop positive views of their racial and ethnic heritage, it is important to encourage and assist them in learning about all aspects of their heritage. This may be particularly important in cases in which conflict exists between parents, a parent is absent, and/or a parent's extended family is not available or involved. Working with both the child and significant adults in the child's life may also be crucial (Root, 2003a; Wardle, 1999; Wehrly et al., 1999).

Involving siblings and parents or significant adults in the child's life in the counseling process can be useful for understanding the interactions and dynamics of the family. Counselors may also intervene and work with teachers, specifically if there seems to be a lack of understanding or sensitivity to issues related to the child's multiracial status (Wehrly et al., 1999). Other effective treatment strategies include bibliotherapy, role-playing, journaling, creative writing, and the use of various art mediums (Wehrly, 1996; Wehrly et al., 1999).

Counseling Multiracial Adolescents

Adolescents of mixed-race heritage may have the additional dilemma of dealing with stresses related to their multiple heritages; therefore, it is important that the counselor distinguish between typical developmental concerns of adolescence and concerns that may be related to the adolescents' mixed heritage (Gibbs & Moskowitz-Sweet, 1991; Tefera, 2005). Gibbs (1989) suggested that the counselor's work with multiracial adolescents involve an assessment of potential conflicts in five major psychosocial areas: multiracial identity, social marginality, sexuality and choice of partners, separation from parents, and educational and career goals. This assessment should be conducted in the context of the adolescents' views and perceptions of their multiracial heritage. The perceptions and views of family members, including extended family members, toward family members' multiracial status should also be assessed. In addition, the availability of support resources and networks in the school and community should be examined (Gibbs & Moskowitz-Sweet, 1991; Wardle & Cruz-Janzen, 2004). The support of individual, family, and other social support networks should be established from the start of the counseling process (Pinderhughes, 1995; Wehrly et al., 1999).

Like treatment and intervention with multiracial children, treatment and intervention with multiracial adolescents requires a solid working alliance built on trust and cultural sensitivity. According to Gibbs and Moskowitz-Sweet (1991), intervention must also be considerate of the adolescents' ego strength and should focus on the development of skills related to problem solving, clarification of values, decision making, and goal setting. Of importance is the counselor's ability to validate the adolescents' feelings about their mixed-race status, assist them with understanding the relationship between problematic behavior and challenges they may be experiencing regarding their mixed-race heritage, and assist them in exploring all aspects of their heritage in order to develop a positive self-image (Maxwell & Henriksen, 2009; Pinderhughes, 1995).

Intervention strategies that are useful for assisting multiracial adolescents with exploring their racial identity and developing a positive self-concept include focused discussions, bibliotherapy, and homework assignments (Pinderhughes, 1995). Other useful strategies include role-playing, journaling, storytelling, and behavioral goal setting. Counselors working in school settings can also utilize peer counseling and peer support groups (Gibbs & Moskowitz-Sweet, 1991).

Counseling Multiracial Adults: The Case Study of Cindy Malloy

The case study of Cindy Malloy depicts a multiracial young adult attempting to come to terms with and understand her multiracial heritage.

Cindy is a 23-year-old journalist of Japanese and Irish American ancestry. She has recently come in for counseling in hopes of learning how to cope with anxiety, which she has been experiencing since shortly after plans were made for her to go to Japan to work and meet her Japanese family members for the first time.

Cindy's mother was raised in Kyoto, Japan, as one of six children. Cindy's mother was young when her parents died, leaving her and her siblings to be raised by an aunt and an uncle who had no children. Cindy's father is an Irish American who worked as a teacher in an English language school in Kyoto. Cindy's parents met and secretly dated; 6 months later they fled to Tokyo and were married, despite threats from Cindy's mother's family to disown her.

A couple of years after they were married, Cindy's parents moved from Japan to Mr. Malloy's hometown of Wilton, Connecticut. Despite the estranged relationship that Cindy's parents had with other members of her mother's family, Cindy's mother and father managed to maintain ongoing contact with Mrs. Malloy's two older sisters. Mrs. Malloy attempted to give Cindy and her older brother and sister a sense of connection to their Japanese family by sharing pictures that arrived of their aunts and their families. Cindy recalls occasions when packages would arrive for them from their aunts as well. The environment in which the Malloy children grew up was prototypically American. Despite this, Mr. and Mrs. Malloy attempted to give their children a sense of their Japanese culture and roots, including the language. Cindy and her siblings enjoyed eating Mrs. Malloy's Japanese cooking and hearing their parents' stories about Japan; however, Cindy recalled that she and her siblings thwarted their parents' attempts to teach them the Japanese language and customs.

Mrs. Malloy eventually resumed contact with all of her siblings. This was followed by a trip home to Japan, which Mrs. Malloy made with Cindy's older sister shortly after Cindy's sister finished college. This trip served as an opportunity for Cindy's mother to reconcile with her family. On returning home, Mrs. Malloy and Cindy's sister shared stories of their experience. Hearing her sister tell stories about her Japanese aunts, uncles, and cousins as well as stories about the places she had visited made Cindy long for an opportunity to meet and see the people and places she had only heard about.

Cindy majored in journalism during college. A year before graduation, she learned from a Japanese exchange student about opportunities available for English-language journalists in Japan. Excited about the prospects that this would present, Cindy began investigating the idea of going to Japan to work. After graduating from college, she was fortunate to get a position working full time for the newspaper where she had done her internship. This allowed her to gain additional experience and to save money for the trip that she was hoping she could make to Japan. With the help of cousins in Japan and a Japanese placement service referred by the career services officer at her alma mater, Cindy continued to explore possibilities for employment in Japan and eventually landed a position.

As her grew closer, Cindy began to worry about how she would be perceived and accepted by her family in Japan. More so than her siblings, Cindy has spent the majority of her life dodging curious questions about her background. Although she has always had a circle of friends, Cindy has always felt that she has had to make an extra effort in order to be accepted. At times, she has wondered whether she is really accepted anywhere.

Multiracial individuals seldom use counseling to deal with overt issues related to their mixed heritage; however, it is important that counseling professionals be aware of the potential influence that being of mixed-race heritage may have on one's life (Root, 1994). The six themes discussed in "Multiracial Adults" (Root, 1994) provide an essential framework for counselors to use to assess and conceptualize the issues and concerns presented by multiracial individuals. These themes are important to consider in Cindy's case because of their possible relevance to her interpersonal style, her perceptions of her environment, and her symptoms of anxiety. Consideration should also be given to the possible relevance of these themes in Cindy's life on the basis of the geographical area in which she grew up; the level of contact she has had with other multiracial individuals; and the degree to which her family has provided her with support, preparation, and validation for a multiracial existence (Root, 1992). Exploring the underlying issues related to these themes will be helpful in reducing Cindy's anxiety and will be useful for developing problem-solving strategies to help her prepare positively for the journey that she is about to take (Root, 1994).

Root's (1998) ecological framework for understanding multiracial identity development is also useful for exploring the issues and concerns underlying Cindy's anxiety. Although this model may be applicable for use with other multiracial individuals, it was developed specifically from Root's work with multiracial Asian Americans. Root (1998) outlined numerous factors that influence the identity of multiracial Asians, including the historical conditions in the country of origin at the time of the Asian ancestor's immigration to the United States, the historical conditions of the United States at the time of the Asian immigrant's arrival in the United States, and the historical conditions in the United States since the time of the Asian immigrant's arrival. Other factors that can affect a multiracial Asian individual's identity are generation in the United States, age, physical appearance, gender, gender and ethnicity of each of the individual's parents, acceptance or rejection of the individual by paternal and maternal family members, and whether the individual had or has a reclaimed Asian name.

Root's 2002 model is an updated and expanded version of the 1998 model and provides a framework for understanding the complexity of racial identity development for all multiracial individuals. Hence, it can assist in determining both the factors influencing Cindy's identity development and the potential impact that Cindy's identity development has had on her current difficulties. The model comes out of sociological constructs of interaction and looks at invisible factors and other common influences that affect identity. In understanding Root's (2002) model, it is important to look at the influencing variables as lenses through which the experiences of multiracial individuals can be viewed, remembering that no two multiracial individuals—even siblings from the same family—will be the same. The macro lenses of the model are geographical region and generational history of race and ethnic relations, sexual orientation, gender, and class. These variables are fundamental influences of identity development and are central contexts through which multiracial people learn social norms and rules regarding their racial and ethnic identities (Root, 2003a). Both geographical region and generational history provide a context and framework for understanding the sociopolitical issues that have confronted the multiracial population and have impacted their identity options throughout U.S. history. The politics of sexual orientation are further exacerbated by those of race and vice versa. How and where an individual finds the support necessary to navigate issues related to sexual orientation may be strongly influenced by his or her racial and ethnic affiliations and experiences (Root, 2003b). Gender is a dynamic variable from the standpoint of power differentials and race relations. Similarly, class figures prominently in people's understanding of how the social construct of race is experienced in the United States (Root, 2003b).

The middle lenses of the model include family functioning, family socialization, traits and aptitudes, community attitudes and racial socialization, identity, and phenotype (Root, 2003a, 2003b). Family functioning was added to the revised model and includes consistency of parental availability; extended family acceptance; losses and disruptions; sense of belonging and acceptance; and extent of violence, abuse, or neglect (Root, 2002). Inherited influences in the 2002 model consist of family socialization factors such as languages used in the home, parent's identity, parent's nativity, extended family, given names, values/spirituality, family racial socialization, and family racial and ethnic identity. Factors included under traits include temperament, social skills, coping skills, giftedness, health, learning difficulties, and physical attractiveness (Root, 2002). The influence of the factors in these three variables, and their relationship to and interaction with one another, is of crucial significance to the identity development of the multiracial individual over the life span (Root, 2003b).

Although the family has the greatest influence on individual identity, the community within which the individual navigates has significant influence on both the family and the individual (Root, 2003b). The middle lens variable community attitudes and racial social-ization consists of factors such as school/work, community, friends, and new community. According to Root (2003b), five potential identities may result from multiracial individu-als' experiences with all of the variables of the model, including their experiences based on phenotype. In the 2002 version of Root's model, phenotype is both a middle lens variable and a magnifying lens that cuts across all other lenses and variables. It is a major experien-tial component of multiracial identity that, when considered in conjunction with the other variables, significantly influences the five potential identities that may emerge from an indi-vidual's experience. Furthermore, the potential identities are affected by the generation into which the individual is born (Root, 2003a). The potential identities are as follows:

1. *Assignment by hypodescent/one-drop rule.* The multiracial individual who identifies in this manner has accepted the racial identity assigned by society. This identity is typically a monoracial minority identity based on the one-drop rule and hypodescent (Root, 2003a). In this system, multiracial individuals were assigned or forced to iden-tify with the racial group of their heritage perceived as having the least social status (Root, 1996). According to Root (2003b), for older generations of multiracial indi-viduals this identity was the only option.

2. *Monoracial fit self-assignment.* This identity is the self-selected declaration of a monoracial minority identity by the multiracial individual; it is based on fit and is consistent with the experience of the individual over time. This identity option may present challenges if it is different from how others perceive the multiracial indi-vidual based on phenotype (Root, 2003a).

3. *New group/blended.* According to Root (2003a), because of circumstances one aspect of the multiracial individual's identity may be more salient than another; hence, the identity that emerges or is claimed at a particular time varies and is fluid. This identity is a more recent option for multiracial individuals.

4. *Biracial/multiracial.* This identity is part of a more recent and radical phenomenon. For younger generations, the declaration of a bicultural or multiracial identity is both a refusal to break racial and ethnic identity down into categories and a celebration of all of one's racial and ethnic heritages (Root, 2003b).

5. *White with symbolic identity.* According to Root (2003b), this is the newest of the potential identities and may be indicative of identification with a class lifestyle and values or a lack of exposure to and experience with an ethnic background to which one belongs. This identity may be problematic if the individual selecting it does not have another salient identity related to a special talent or aptitude or does not have the temperament to deal with the scrutiny and opposition that may come from others as a result of him or her making such a selection (Root, 2003b).

Logan, Freeman, and McRoy's (1987) ecological approach may also be beneficial in working with multiracial clients like Cindy. This approach has three components—the genogram, ecomap, and cultural continuum—that can be utilized to assist multiracial individuals in exploring what it means to be multiracial (Logan et al., 1987). These com-ponents offer tools that may be used in conjunction with the Root (2002) model. The genogram is a useful tool for helping the client to examine the potential impact of fam-ily relationships and dynamics, roles, and significant life events. The genogram can also be used to examine the racial and ethnic backgrounds of family members, the attitudes of immediate and extended family toward the multiracial individual, and the level of functioning of family relationships. The relationships that the multiracial individual and his or her family have had with social networks, including the community, the neighborhood, schools, and other community institutions, may also be explored. Specifics pertaining to the individual and his or her family's overall development and lifestyle may also be examined (Logan et al., 1987).

The ecomap is a tool that utilizes connecting lines and symbols, similar to those used in the genogram, to illustrate relationships. The multiracial individual's family is shown in a large circle, with smaller circles drawn around it that signify connections with other family and social support networks. Connecting lines are used to show the individual's and family's relationships to other family and sources of social support. The ecomap allows the counselor to explore with the client the client's and family's relationships with external networks. Information that can be gleaned regarding the positive or negative experiences that the client and his or her family have had with these networks can provide useful data about where and to whom the individual can go for empowerment and support. It can also provide information regarding the potential need for reevaluating or reframing relationships (Logan et al., 1987).

The cultural continuum is a tool that consists of four cultural response categories: denial of cultural or racial significance, assimilation with the dominant culture or race, assimilation with the minority culture or race, and multiracial identification. There are advantages and disadvantages associated with each response category. Utilizing these response categories, the counselor can help clients explore how they have responded to circumstances in their lives in which they have felt challenged about their mixed-race heritage while also examining the pitfalls and outcomes of earlier and more recent choices and decisions made related to aspects of their heritage (Logan et al., 1987).

Counseling Multiracial Individuals and Their Families

Counseling intervention with multiracial families varies depending on the issues and concerns of the family members (Wehrly et al., 1999; Wijeyesinghe, 2001). It is important to note that although the issues presented by multiracial families may at times differ from those presented by monoracial families, the fact that a multiracial family is coming for counseling is not indicative of pathology or dysfunction. Rather, multiracial families may often deal with issues concerning their multiple heritages, experience bouts of racism, and be challenged about their racial loyalties (Okun, 1996; Wardle & Cruz-Janzen, 2004; Wehrly et al., 1999).

Counselors must examine their own views of interracial couples and their offspring. If the therapeutic environment is perceived as unaccepting or biased, the family is not likely to continue in counseling (Okun, 1996; Wardle & Cruz-Janzen, 2004; Wehrly et al., 1999). In addition, the strategies utilized by the counselor must take into consideration the multiple racial and cultural backgrounds that may be present in the session and the multiple worldviews and perspectives that may be operating (Wehrly, 1996).

Multiracial families often present with child-related issues and concerns. In these instances, assessments should include an examination of whether the concerns are related to developmental factors, inadequate parenting, marital or relationship conflicts in the environment, academic difficulties, or racial/ethnic-related challenges (Laszloffy, 2005; Okun, 1996; Wardle, 1999; Wardle & Cruz-Janzen, 2004). The therapeutic strategies of structural family therapy, experiential family systems therapy, and extended family systems therapy are useful with multiracial families (Wehrly, 1996). Ibrahim (1998) advocated the use of general systems theory in counseling multiracial families and suggested that the pragmatic and psychoeducational approach of primary intervention may be valuable in that it is proactive and prevention oriented and it focuses on empowerment. Primary intervention should involve the home, the schools, and the community and entails educating parents, teachers, school personnel, community agencies, recreation groups, sports groups officials, and others who may be knowledgeable about the issues and challenges faced by multiracial youngsters and their family members (Henriksen & Rawlins, 2003; Ibrahim, 1998; Wardle, 1999; Wardle & Cruz-Janzen, 2004).

Gibbs and Moskowitz-Sweet (1991) and Wardle and Cruz-Janzen (2004) discussed the benefits of complete family involvement in activities that provide a sense of family pride and enhance children's self-esteem. They made suggestions for family participation in ethnic and cultural activities as well as multiracial and multicultural social activities. They also made recommendations for family involvement in religiously oriented activities that provide a spiritual component to cultural enhancement and politically oriented activities that emphasize the need for improvement of the social climate for multiracial families (DaCosta, 2007; Gibbs & Moskowitz-Sweet, 1991; Yancey & Yancey, 2002).

Kenney (2000) and Kenney and Kenney (2010) suggested that as advocates for multiracial families, counselors need to be familiar with resources available to provide support and affirmation for multiracial individuals and families. These resources include support groups and organizations (more than 30 across the country) and websites. Many of these are organized and facilitated by interracial couples, multiracial individuals, and multiracial families (Root & Kelley, 2003).

Transracial Adoption

For decades, both domestic and out-of-country transracial adoptions have met with extreme controversy. Domestic adoptions have typically involved White parents adopting Black, Latino, or Native American children. Prior to 1994, when the U.S. Congress approved the Multiethnic Placement Act, which prevented child welfare agencies from discriminating against prospective parents on the basis of race, color, or national origin, restrictions existed that curtailed placements of Black and mixed-race Black children with White families (Baden et al., 2009; Okun, 1996).

In the early 1970s, the National Association of Black Social Workers passed a resolution against transracial adoptions involving Black and mixed-race Black children. The opposition of the National Association of Black Social Workers toward these adoptions was largely related to concerns about the racial identity of these children and a fear that these adoptions would lead to cultural genocide (Baden et al., 2009; McRoy & Hall, 1996). Similar concerns regarding the adoption of Native American children resulted in the passage of the 1978 Indian Child Welfare Act, which forbade the transracial adoption of Native American children (Baden et al., 2009; McRoy & Hall, 1996). The 1994 Multiethnic Placement Act was revised in 1996 as the Interethnic Placement Act (Baden et al., 2009). Despite the existence of the Interethnic Placement Act and the continued prevalence of transracial adoptions, there is still opposition to these adoptions, particularly from groups with political agendas and from factions of the Black community (Wardle, 1999).

International or out-of-country adoptions started in the United States as a response to the increased number of orphans in war-torn Europe after World War II. The Korean War gave rise to the phenomena of international and transracial adoptions. Since the Korean War, international and transracial adoptions have taken place from such countries as Vietnam, Guatemala, Colombia, South Korea, Ethiopia, India, Haiti, and Kazakhstan, with the largest number of adoptees coming from China (Baden et al., 2009). The controversy surrounding these adoptions is mainly related to the dramatic cultural differences that often exist between the child's country of origin and the United States. In addition, concerns have been raised about cultural exploitation in the adoptions of children from underdeveloped countries in need of political and economic reforms (Okun, 1996). Moreover, some have suggested that such adoptions are indicative of American imperialism (DellaCava, Phillips, & Engel, 2004).

According to Okun (1996) and Steinberg and Hall (2000), a major issue for domestic transracial adoptees is the development of a positive racial identity and the ability to handle the challenges of racism. For intercountry transracial adoptees, issues are most often related to a loss of cultural heritage and identity. According to Baden et al. (2009), research conducted on racial/ethnic identity development has concluded that transracial adoptees tend to identify with their racial/ethnic group differently than nonadopted individuals of the same racial/ethnic background. Wehrly (1996) indicated that cross-racial and cross-cultural adjustment is the most salient issue confronted by both domestic and out-of-country transracial adoptive children and families. Opponents of transracial adoption have typically negatively linked racial identity development and adjustment. According to Baden et al., research does not suggest that the different racial/ethnic identification of transracial adoptees is associated with psychological maladjustment or self-esteem difficulties.

The age of the child at the time of the adoption may present some concerns, particularly with regard to the changes and adjustments that must be made by both the child and his or her new family. How these changes and adjustments are attended to will determine the success of the placement (Miranda, 2003; Steinberg & Hall, 2000; Wardle, 1999). Silverstein and Kaplan (1988) identified seven core issues around which concerns often arise for adoptees, adoptive families, and birth parents: loss, rejection, guilt and shame, grief, identity, intimacy, and control. Although these issues may be significant for all adoptees and their families, the manner in which they are manifested may be different for transracial adoptees and their adoptive families and birth parents and must therefore be explored and addressed (Baden et al., 2009; Steinberg & Hall, 2000).

According to Crumbley (1999) and Steinberg and Hall (2000), a number of issues should be addressed when the suitability of prospective adoptive parents is being considered. Similar to other multiracial families, transracial adoptive families often encounter challenges associated with the racial and cultural makeup of their families. Hence, transracial adoptive parents must examine their motivation to adopt, the racial diversity of the community in which they live, the level of acceptance of family and friends, their own knowledge of the child's cultural heritage and ancestry, their commitment to exposing the child to his or her racial and cultural roots, and their commitment to helping the child develop a positive sense of racial and cultural identity. The feelings that the biological children in the family have regarding the transracial adoption are also important to consider.

The feelings, comfort level, and welfare of the transracial adoptive child must come first. Therefore, parents must be able to prepare the child to face racism and discrimination and teach the child how to respond. To do this effectively, parents must acknowledge that racism exists and not make excuses for prejudice and discrimination, and they must have a sense of their own values and attitudes (Crumbley, 1999; Miranda, 2003; Steinberg & Hall, 2000; Vonk, 2001). They must also expose their adoptive child to aspects of his or her racial and cultural heritage in a consistent, positive, and meaningful way in order to help the child develop a positive identity and a strong sense of racial and cultural pride (Miranda, 2003; Steinberg & Hall, 2000; Vonk, 2001; Wardle, 1999).

Counseling a Transracial Adoptee and Family: The Case Study of Carl Hagerman

The following case study is an example of the potential issues faced by transracial adoptive families.

Carl, an 8-year-old African American child, was adopted as an infant by an affluent young White couple who are both physicians. Carl and his parents live in a predominantly White suburb of a small city in the midwestern region of the United States. Carl's parents are bringing him for counseling because they have begun to notice that he is becoming isolated and withdrawn and does not want to go to school. Mornings at the Hagerman house have become challenging for all of them.

The school that Carl attends is predominantly White, with the exception of only a few other African American and Asian American students. Carl is in the third grade and is now the only student of color in his class. An Asian American student who had been in his class previously, and with whom Carl got along, is no longer there because his family has moved. All of the teachers, administration, and support personnel at Carl's school are White and have had little preparation for working with diverse students and their families.

Although it has been no secret to Carl that he is adopted, the Hagermans have made an effort not to call attention to Carl's racial background. The Hagermans' extended family have all been very positive and supportive of Carl's adoption. However, Mrs. Hagerman's sister, a social worker who lives in the southwest, expressed concern about the Hagermans adopting an African American child and suggested that they might need additional support, just as the adopting caseworker had recommended. Mrs. Hagerman's retort was that love and a financially secure environment were sufficient. The Hagermans have not sought out support or resources available to cross-racial adoptive families.

During his first session with the counselor Carl discloses that he is unhappy at school and afraid of the children. Further probing reveals that some of the boys in his class and their older siblings have been calling him names and saying that "brown people are disgraceful and disgusting." Carl further reveals that he has become fearful of going to school because a few of the older boys have made threats to hurt him. On one occasion, while in the lavatory, one of Carl's male classmates tripped him. Carl indicates having shared this incident with his teacher, who did nothing to intervene.

Individuals who are adopted transracially may present for counseling to deal with a vast array of issues related to their adoption and/or their racial/ethnic heritage, including concerns related to Silverstein and Kaplan's (1988) seven core issues discussed in the previous section (Baden et al., 2009; Steinberg & Hall, 2000). In working with Carl and his adoptive parents, the counselor must assess the manner in which the issues related to Carl's adoption and his obvious racial difference have been addressed. The counselor must also assess the views that the extended family have about the adoption and determine the relationship that exists with the extended family as well as the level of support provided by the extended family. In addition, the counselor should explore the extent to which Carl's adoptive parents are aware of and have made use of the support resources available to transracial adoptive families (Miranda, 2003; Okun, 1996; Steinberg & Hall, 2000; Vonk, 2001).

In this case example, Carl has informed the counselor that his unhappiness at school is a result of teasing and harassment that he is receiving because of his racial background. In trying not to call attention to Carl's racial background, his adoptive parents have not talked with Carl about prejudice and discrimination and how others may respond to the fact that he is Black. Thus, Carl is not prepared to deal with the onslaught of racial negativity that he experiences at school. Although the Hagermans have a close relationship with and receive support from extended family, the fact that they have not sought out resources available to transracial adoptive families may be problematic.

In continuing to work with Carl and his parents, the counselor must assist the Hagermans in becoming aware of the implications of their lack of attention to addressing Carl's racial background. The counselor must also emphasize the availability of resources to assist transracial adoptive families in providing the level of support necessary not only for the success of the placement but also for the positive growth and development of their adoptive child (Miranda, 2003; Steinberg & Hall, 2000; Vonk, 2001; Wardle, 1999). The counselor can serve as an advocate for the family by identifying and assisting the Hagermans in getting connected to appropriate support resources geared toward helping transracial adoptive families (Kenney & Kenney, 2010).

Deborah Haynor and Lorie Miller provided a four-stage model of cultural socialization useful for working with families of transracially adopted children (as cited in Paolino, 2007). The stages are not meant to be followed in a linear fashion, but are fluid.

> *Stage 1: We Are a Family.* This stage involves helping the parents to get to know their children and encourage the extended family to see the child as a member of the family.
>
> *Stage 2: We Are a Multicultural Family.* This stage involves the parents learning to acknowledge racial and cultural differences and to create opportunities for the entire family to get to know and become involved in the birth culture and heritage of the adopted child. This entails making a concerted effort to participate in culturally based celebrations and festivals, special holiday activities, and camps.
>
> *Stage 3: We Are an Antiracist Family.* This stage requires the family to explore and deal with issues of race, racism, and White privilege and how these may be manifested in the family. It also requires them to speak openly about the differences between them and the transracially adopted child as well as to openly examine and discuss issues of prejudice and racism with the child.
>
> *Stage 4: We Are a Multiracial Family.* This stage requires the adoptive parents and family to spend more time in the birth culture of the transracially adopted child. In this stage adoptive parents become more conscious and appreciative of diversity in their lives. Thus, steps may be taken to change and provide a more diverse and inclusive environment and network for the family.

According to Okun (1996) and Steinberg and Hall (2000), the specific strategies utilized in working with children in transracial adoptive families depend on the ages or development stages of the children. In working with transracial adoptive families with young children like the Hagermans, play therapy, art therapy, and other expressive therapies may be useful. In addition, bibliotherapy is recommended for the entire family and can be particularly helpful as the family works through the Haynor and Miller model. When working with older transracial adoptees, counselors must be sensitive to special concerns that the children may have related to adjusting to the new environment and all that it encompasses. Some transracial adoptees experience conflicted and ambivalent feelings regarding their identities as they get older. They and their families need support, reassurance, and validation as they deal with these complex issues (Okun, 1996; Steinberg & Hall, 2000). The therapeutic environment must be sensitive and conducive to allowing family members to freely express their feelings and concerns (Wehrly et al., 1999). This is further substantiated in Wiley and Baden (2005) and Baden and Wiley (2007), both of which emphasize the importance of counselors and other practitioners working with adoptees and their families in a competent and sensitive manner.

Gay and lesbian individuals and couples have been increasingly involved in transracial adoptions. These transracial adoptive families encounter the same issues faced in other transracial adoptive families; therefore, the same recommendations given for counseling with other transracial adoptive families should be followed. It should be noted, however, that these families may face additional challenges related to societal homophobia. Counselors working with these families may need to assess their own attitudes related to gay and lesbian relationships and transracial adoption by gay and lesbian individuals and couples (Wehrly et al., 1999).

Conclusion

With the continued increase in the numbers of interracial couples, multiracial individuals, multiracial families, and families that have become multiracial through transracial adoption comes an increasing need for counseling professionals to have an awareness of the unique issues, concerns, and strengths of this population. In gaining greater awareness about this group and the history of oppression experienced by its members, counselors are challenged to examine their roles not only as counselors but also as advisers, advocates, consultants, and agents of social change. Kenney and Kenney (2010) emphasized the necessity for counselors to get involved in advocacy work with this population at the micro, meso, and macro levels. Oriti, Bibb, and Mahboubi (1996) suggested that the therapeutic strategy or approach utilized may not be as salient an issue in working with multiracial families as the extent to which the services provided are sensitive to and accepting of the diverse heritages, orientations, and worldviews of this population.

References

Azoulay, K. G. (1997). *Black, Jewish, and interracial: It's not the color of your skin, but the race of your kin and other myths of identity.* Durham, NC: Duke University Press.

Bacigalupe, G. (2003). Intercultural therapy with Latino immigrants and White partners: Crossing borders coupling. In V. Thomas, T. A. Karis, & J. L. Wetchler (Eds.), *Clinical issues with interracial couples: Theories and research* (pp. 131–149). New York, NY: Haworth Press.

Baden, A. L., Thomas, L. A., & Smith, C. (2009). Navigating heritage, culture, identity, and adoption: Counseling trans-racially adopted individuals and their family. In R. C. Henriksen, Jr., & D. A. Paladino (Eds.), *Counseling multiple heritage individuals, couples, and families* (pp. 125–144). Alexandria, VA: American Counseling Association.

Baden, A. L., & Wiley, M. O. (2007). Counseling adopted persons in adulthood: Integrating practice and research. *The Counseling Psychologist, 35,* 868–901.

Blau, M. (1998, December/January). Multiracial families. *Child, 12*(10), pp. 96, 98, 103.

Bracey, J. R., Bamaca, M. Y., & Umana-Taylor, A. J. (2004). Examining ethnic identity and self-esteem among biracial and monoracial adolescents. *Journal of Youth and Adolescence, 33,* 123–132.

Bradshaw, C. K. (1992). Beauty and the beast: On racial ambiguity. In M. P. P. Root (Ed.), *Racially mixed people in America* (pp. 77–99). Newbury Park, CA: Sage.

Cheng, C., & Lee, F. (2009). Multiracial identity integration: Perceptions of conflict and distance among multiracial individuals. *Journal of Social Issues, 65*(1), 51–68.

Crumbley, J. (1999). *Transracial adoption and foster care.* Washington, DC: Child Welfare League of America Press.

DaCosta, K. M. (2007). *Making multiracials: State, family, and market in the redrawing of the color line.* Stanford, CA: Stanford University Press.

Dalmage, H. M. (2000). *Tripping on the color line: Black-White multiracial families in a racially divided world.* Piscataway, NJ: Rutgers University Press.

Davis, P. J. (1991). *Who is Black? One nation's definition.* University Park: Pennsylvania State University Press.

DellaCava, F. A., Phillips, N. K., & Engel, M. H. (2004). Adoption in the U.S.: The emergence of a social movement. *Journal of Sociology & Social Welfare, 31*(4), 141–160.

Evan B. Donaldson Adoption Institute. (2002). *Overview of adoption in the United States.* Retrieved from http://www.adoptioninstitute.org/FactOverview.html

Funderburg, L. (1994). *Black, White, other: Biracial American talk about race and ethnicity.* New York, NY: Morrow.

Gallup Organization. (2004). *Civil rights and race relations.* Washington, DC: Author.

Gardner, L. (2000). *White/Black race mixing.* St. Paul, MN: Paragon House.

Gibbs, J. T. (1989). Biracial adolescents. In J. T. Gibbs, L. N. Huang, & Associates (Eds.), *Children of color: Psychological interventions with minority youth* (pp. 322–350). San Francisco, CA: Jossey-Bass.

Gibbs, J. T., & Hines, A. M. (1992). Negotiating ethnic identity: Issues for Black-White biracial adolescents. In M. P. P. Root (Ed.), *Racially mixed people in America* (pp. 223–238). Newbury Park, CA: Sage.

Gibbs, J. T., & Moskowitz-Sweet, G. (1991). Clinical and cultural issues in the treatment of biracial and bicultural adolescents. *Families in Society, 72,* 579–591.

Hall, C. C. I. (1997). Best of both worlds: Body image and satisfaction of a sample of Black-Japanese biracial individuals. *Amerasia Journal, 23*(1), 87–97.

Harris, H. L. (2002). School counselors' perceptions of biracial children: A pilot study. *Professional School Counseling, 6,* 120–129.

Henriksen, R. C., & Paladino, D. A. (2009). History of racial classification. In R. C. Henriksen, Jr., & D. A. Paladino (Eds.), *Counseling multiple heritage individuals, couples, and families* (pp. 1–16). Alexandria, VA: American Counseling Association.

Henriksen, R. C., & Rawlins, M. (2003, November). *Understanding multicultural issues: Awareness, theory and practical implications.* Paper presented at the annual conference of the Illinois Counseling Association, Springfield, IL.

Herring, R. D. (1992). Biracial children: An increasing concern for elementary and middle school counselors. *Elementary School Guidance and Counseling, 27,* 123–130.

Houston, H. R. (1997). "Between two cultures": A testimony. *Amerasia Journal, 23*(1), 149–154.

Ibrahim, F. A. (1998, March). *Counseling multiracial adolescents.* Paper presented at the annual conference of the American Counseling Association, Indianapolis, IN.

Ibrahim, F. A., & Schroeder, D. G. (1990). Cross-cultural couples counseling: A developmental, psychoeducational intervention. *Journal of Comparative Family Studies, 21,* 193–205.

Ishiyama, F. I. (2006, March). *Cultural diversity, intermarriage, and intercultural complexity in family: Self-validation model and counseling implications.* Paper presented at the Learning Institute of the annual conference of the American Counseling Association and the Canadian Counseling Association, Montreal, Quebec, Canada.

Kenney, K. (2000). Multiracial families. In J. Lewis & L. Bradley (Eds.), *Advocacy in counseling: Counselors, clients, community* (pp. 55–70). Greensboro, NC: Education Resources Information Center/Counseling and Student Services Clearinghouse.

Kenney, K. R., & Kenney, M. E. (2010). Advocacy with the multiracial population. In M. J. Ratts, R. L. Toporek, & J. A. Lewis (Eds.), *ACA advocacy competencies: A social justice framework for counselors* (pp. 65–74). Alexandria, VA: American Counseling Association.

Kitano, H. H. L., Fujino, D. C., & Sato, J. T. (1998). Interracial marriages: Where are the Asian Americans and where are they going? In L. C. Lee & N. W. Zane (Eds.), *Handbook of Asian American psychology* (pp. 233–260). Thousand Oaks, CA: Sage.

Laszloffy, T. A. (2005, March-April). Multiracial families. *Family Therapy Magazine,* pp. 38–43.

Lee, E. (1996). Asian American families: An overview. In M. McGoldrick, J. K. Pearce, & J. Gidordano (Eds.), *Ethnicity and family therapy* (2nd ed., pp. 227–248). New York, NY: Guilford Press.

Logan, S. L., Freeman, E. M., & McRoy, R. G. (1987). Racial identity problems of biracial clients: Implications for social work practice. *Journal of Intergroup Relations, 15,* 11–24.

Maxwell, M., & Henriksen, R. C. (2009). Counseling multiple heritage adolescents. In R. C. Henriksen, Jr., & D. A. Paladino (Eds.), *Counseling multiple heritage individuals, couples, and families* (pp. 65–81). Alexandria, VA: American Counseling Association.

McClain, C. S. (2004). Black by choice: Identity preferences of Americans of Black/White parentage. *Black Scholar, 34*(2), 43–54.

McFadden, J. (2001). Intercultural marriage and family: Beyond the racial divide. *The Family Journal: Counseling and Therapy for Couples and Families, 11*(1), 39–42.

McRoy, R. G., & Hall, C. C. I. (1996). Transracial adoptions—In whose best interest? In M. P. P. Root (Ed.), *The multiracial experience: Racial borders as the new frontier* (pp. 63–78). Newbury Park, CA: Sage.

Miranda, G. E. (2003). Domestic transracial and multiraciality. In M. P. P. Root & M. Kelley (Eds.), *Multiracial child resource book: Living complex identities* (pp. 108–115). Seattle, WA: MAVIN Foundation.

Nash, R. D. (1997). *Coping with interracial dating.* New York, NY: Rosen.

National Adoption Information Clearinghouse. (1994). *Trans-racial and trans-cultural adoption.* Retrieved from http://www.adoption.org/adopt/national-adoption-clearinghouse.php

Negy, C., & Snyder, D. (2000). Relationship satisfaction of Mexican American and non-Hispanic White American interethnic couples: Issues of acculturation and clinical intervention. *Journal of Marital and Family Therapy, 26*(3), 293–304.

Nishimura, N. J. (1998). Assessing the issues of multiracial students on college campuses. *Journal of College Counseling, 1*(1), 45–53.

Okun, B. F. (1996). *Understanding diverse families: What practitioners need to know.* New York, NY: Guilford Press.

Oriti, B., Bibb, A., & Mahboubi, J. (1996). Family-centered practice with racially/ethnically mixed families. *Families in Society, 76,* 573–582.

Paladino, D. A., & Henriksen, R. C. (2009). Counseling multiple heritage adults. In R. C. Henriksen, Jr., & D. A. Paladino (Eds.), *Counseling multiple heritage individuals, couples, and families* (pp. 101–110). Alexandria, VA: American Counseling Association.

Paolino, M. (2007, November). *Parenting across race: The identity development of White parents.* Retrieved from www.baystateparent.com/news/2007-11-01/articles/023.html

Passel, J. S., Wang, W., & Taylor, P. (2010). *Marrying out: One-in-seven new U.S. marriages is interracial or interethnic.* Washington, DC: Pew Research Center.

Pinderhughes, E. (1995). Biracial identity—Asset or handicap? In H. W. Harris, H. C. Blue, & E. E. H. Griffith (Eds.), *Racial and ethnic identity: Psychological development and creative expression* (pp. 73–93). New York, NY: Routledge.

Ramirez, D. A. (1996). Multiracial identity in a color-conscious world. In M. P. P. Root (Ed.), *The multiracial experience: Racial borders as the new frontier* (pp. 49–62). Newbury Park, CA: Sage.

Rockquemore, K. A., & Laszloffy, T. L. (2003). Multiple realities: A relational narrative approach to therapy with Black-White mixed-race clients. *Family Relations, 52*(2), 119–128.

Root, M. P. P. (1990). Resolving "other" status: Identity development of biracial individuals. In L. S. Brown & M. P. P. Root (Eds.), *Diversity and complexity in feminist therapy* (pp. 185–205). New York, NY: Haworth Press.

Root, M. P. P. (Ed.). (1992). *Racially mixed people in America.* Newbury Park, CA: Sage.

Root, M. P. P. (1994). Mixed-race women. In L. Comas-Diaz & B. Greene (Eds.), *Women of color: Integrating ethnic and gender identities in psychotherapy* (pp. 455–478). New York, NY: Guilford Press.

Root, M. P. P. (Ed.). (1996). *The multiracial experience: Racial borders as the new frontier.* Thousand Oaks, CA: Sage.

Root, M. P. P. (1997a). Contemporary mixed-heritage Filipino Americans: Fighting colonized identities. In M. P. P. Root (Ed.), *Filipino Americans: Transformation and identity* (pp. 80–94). Thousand Oaks, CA: Sage.

Root, M. P. P. (1997b). Multiracial Asians: Models of ethnic identity. *Amerasia Journal, 23*(1), 29–41.

Root, M. P. P. (1998). Multiracial Americans: Changing the face of Asian America. In L. C. Lee & N. W. Zane (Eds.), *Handbook of Asian American psychology* (pp. 261–287). Thousand Oaks, CA: Sage.

Root, M. P. P. (2001). *Love's revolution: Interracial marriage.* Philadelphia, PA: Temple University Press.

Root, M. P. P. (2002). Methodological issues in multiracial research. In G. C. Nagayama Hall & S. Okazaki (Eds.), *Asian American psychology: The science of lives in context* (pp. 171–193). Washington, DC: American Psychological Association.

Root, M. P. P. (2003a). Multiracial families and children: Implications for educational research and practice. In J. A. Banks & C. A. McGee Banks (Eds.), *Handbook of research on multicultural education* (2nd ed., pp. 110–124). San Francisco, CA: Jossey-Bass.

Root, M. P. P. (2003b). Racial identity development and persons of mixed race heritage. In M. P. P. Root & M. Kelley (Eds.), *Multiracial child resource book: Living complex identities* (pp. 34–41). Seattle, WA: MAVIN Foundation.

Root, M. P. P., & Kelley, M. (Eds.). (2003). *Multiracial child resource book: Living complex identities.* Seattle, WA: MAVIN Foundation.

Rosenblatt, P. C., Karis, T. A., & Powell, R. D. (1995). *Multiracial couples: Black and White voices.* Newbury Park, CA: Sage.

Sheets, R. H. (2003). Multiracial adolescent perception: The role of friendship in identification and identity formation. In K. Wallace (Ed.), *Working with multiracial students: Critical perspectives on research and practice* (pp. 137–154). Greenwich, CT: Information Age.

Silverstein, D. N., & Kaplan, S. (1988). Lifelong issues in adoption. In L. Coleman, K. Tilbor, H. Hornby, & C. Boggis (Eds.), *Working with older adoptees: A source book of innovative models* (pp. 45–53). Portland: University of Southern Maine.

Solsberry, P. W. (1994). Interracial couples in the United States of America: Implications for mental health counseling. *Journal of Mental Health Counseling, 4,* 304–307.

Spickard, P. R. (1989). *Mixed blood: Intermarriage and ethnic identity in 20th century America.* Madison: University of Wisconsin Press.

Spickard, P. R. (1992). The illogic of American racial categories. In M. P. P. Root (Ed.), *Racially mixed people in America* (pp. 12–23). Newbury Park, CA: Sage.

Steel, M. (1995). New colors: Mixed race families still find a mixed reception. *Teaching Tolerance, 4*(1), pp. 44–46, 48–49.

Steinberg, G., & Hall, B. (2000). *Inside trans-racial adoption.* Indianapolis, IN: Perspectives Press.

Stolley, K. S. (1993). Statistics on adoption in the United States. *The Future of Children: Adoption, 3*(1), 26–42.

Taylor, P., Funk, C., & Craighill, P. (2006). *Guess who's coming to dinner: 22% of Americans have a relative in a mixed-race marriage.* Washington, DC: Pew Research Center.

Tefera, N. A. (2005). A phenomenological study of the life experiences of biracial adolescents. *Dissertation Abstracts International, 66,* 2882B.

Tubbs, C. Y., & Rosenblatt, P. C. (2003). Assessment and intervention with Black-White multiracial couples. In V. Thomas, T. A. Karis, & J. L. Wetchler (Eds.), *Clinical issues with interracial couples: Theories and research* (pp. 115–129). New York, NY: Haworth Press.

U.S. Department of State. (2006). *Immigrant visas issued to orphans coming to the U.S.* Retrieved from http://travel.state.gov/family/adoption/stats/stats_451.html

Vonk, M. E. (2001). Cultural competence for trans-racial adoptive parents. *Social Work, 46,* 246–255.

Waldman, K., & Rubalcava, L. (2005). Psychotherapy with intercultural couples: A contemporary psychodynamic approach. *American Journal of Psychotherapy, 59*(3), 227–245.

Wardle, F. (1992). Supporting biracial children in the school setting. *Education and Treatment of Children, 15,* 163–172.

Wardle, F. (1999). *Tomorrow's children.* Denver, CO: Center for the Study of Biracial Children.

Wardle, F., & Cruz-Janzen, M. I. (2004). *Meeting the needs of multiethnic and multiracial children in schools.* Boston, MA: Pearson Education.

Wehrly, B. (1996). *Counseling interracial individuals and families.* Alexandria, VA: American Counseling Association.

Wehrly, B., Kenney, K. R., & Kenney, M. E. (1999). *Counseling multiracial families.* Thousand Oaks, CA: Sage.

Wijeyesinghe, C. L. (2001). Racial identity in multiracial people: An alternative paradigm. In C. L. Wijeyesinghe & B. W. Jackson, III (Eds.), *New perspectives on racial identity development: A theoretical and practical anthology* (pp. 129–152). New York: New York University Press.

Wiley, M. O., & Baden, A. L. (2005). Birth parents in adoption: Research, practice, and counseling psychology. *The Counseling Psychologist, 33,* 13–50.

Williams, M. G. (1996). Race as process: Reassessing the "What are you?" encounters of biracial individuals. In M. P. P. Root (Ed.), *The multiracial experience: Racial borders as the new frontier* (pp. 191–210). Newbury Park, CA: Sage.

Wright, M. (2000). *I'm chocolate, you're vanilla: Raising healthy Black and biracial children in a race-conscious world.* Hoboken, NJ: Jossey-Bass.

Yancey, G. A. (2002). Debunking the top stereotypes about interracial couples. In G. A. Yancey & S. W. Yancey (Eds.), *Just don't marry one: Interracial dating, marriage, and parenting* (pp. 39–53). Valley Forge, PA: Judson Press.

Yancey, G. A., & Yancey, S. W. (Eds.). (2002). *Just don't marry one: Interracial dating, marriage, and parenting.* Valley Forge, PA: Judson Press.

Zebroski, S. A. (1999). Black-White intermarriages: The racial and gender dynamics of support and opposition. *Journal of Black Studies, 30,* 123–132.

Chapter 9

Issues in Counseling Men

Shawn L. Spurgeon

Since the beginning of time, men have played a vital role in the development of society. This chapter is designed to explore the critical, cultural, and clinical issues currently affecting the male population. The chapter explores the use of theoretical approaches with this population and provides case studies to help the reader understand these approaches.

Analysis of the Population

Population Parameters

According to the National Center for Health Statistics (NCHS; 2010), there are 148.7 million men living in the United States. Men currently make up 48.5% of the U.S. population and continue to serve as an important part of societal development. The majority of men (67%) are between 15 and 64 years old.

Vital Statistics

Men's life expectancy at birth (75.65 years) is approximately 5 years less than women's (80.69 years), and this has been consistent since the 1980s (NCHS, 2010). Of the 2,426,264 registered deaths in the United States in 2006, men accounted for 1,201,942. The infant mortality rate is higher among males (6.9 deaths/1,000 live births) than females (5.5 deaths/1,000 live births), and mortality rates are consistently higher for men than for women. The most common causes of death for men are heart disease, cancer, and accidents (NCHS, 2010).

Cultural Issues Within the Population

Within-Group Differences

Given the changes in the economy and the reconceptualization of socially acceptable behaviors, social class has become a significant factor for men in a number of arenas, including access to educational opportunities and economic viability (Blustein et al., 2002). This is one example of the within-group differences that permeate the male population. Other evidence supports the notion that men's within-group differences are more profound than their differences with women. Wester (2008) noted the contextual experiences of African American men and how those experiences are relevant aspects of their development. Erera and Baum (2009) highlighted the powerlessness that divorced fathers feel and how this influences their development and gender-role socialization. Good, Thomson, and Brathwaite (2005) concluded that working with men in a counseling setting requires a thorough understanding of the influence of race, ethnicity, and gender roles on their development. These differences help counselors understand the need for assessment strategies that take into consideration within-group differences.

Socialization

Men receive messages about normal masculine socialization from society, from their family of origin, and from peers (Good et al., 2005). Wester (2008) stated that men have the requisite skills to display emotions but are taught from an early age to avoid disclosing them so that they will not be challenged by others. For example, boys are taught not to cry when they get hurt and understand early in life that they will be teased by their peers if they show too much emotion. These internalized gender roles play an important role in men's development in society; for example, providing for the family and discipline are still considered by many to be men's roles (Burn & Ward, 2005). As a result of this, many men lack the ability to display a full range of emotions, which puts them at a disadvantage in the counseling relationship.

Mejia (2005) reported that the socialization experience can often be traumatic for men in part because of an early adherence to a code of behaviors deemed masculine by their peers. The media play an important role in this socialization process by reinforcing the stereotype that men need to be macho and sometimes violent to prove their toughness. Dutton (2000) reported that boys often experience traumatic situations and do not deal with them in a healthy manner because of the curtailing of trauma in the male socialization process. Counselors need to increase their awareness of the relevance of socialization in the development of their male clients so that they can develop effective interventions to help this population (Good et al., 2005).

Critical Issues Within the Population

Educational Concerns

There were no differences in high school dropout rates between men and women in 2005; however, men currently drop out of high school at a higher frequency than women. Burn and Ward (2005) argued that the need to conform to traditional masculine roles (e.g., provider, father) has a profound influence on men's willingness to pursue their education. Also, teenage males identify high school as the most stressful time in their lives (Peckham, 2008). The increased dropout rate among males has implications for their educational development and pursuits beyond high school.

The graduation rate for all men who entered college in 1998 and expected to complete college by 2004 was 54%, compared with 63% for women. Men consistently lag behind women in terms of graduation from every category of institution except for private schools, from which men graduate at a rate of 36% and women graduate at a rate of 29% (National Center for Education Statistics, 2009). The lack of formal educational pursuits has created situations in which men find themselves struggling to maintain economic viability.

Economic Concerns

The United States has the largest and most powerful economy in the world, with private individuals and business firms providing the most decision-making power (World Factbook, 2010). The recession in 2008 along with the global economic downturn correlates highly with the economic downturn during the Great Depression. The 2008 recession resulted in the loss of a number of industrial and business opportunities for men, thereby increasing their anxiety about the state of the economy (World Factbook, 2010).

Changes in the economic structure have resulted in a change in the workforce for men, who have traditionally held positions of status and importance. Though unmarried women continue to maintain the highest level of economic need, many men feel a sense of despair when thinking about economic stability (Dodson & Borders, 2006). This despair manifests itself in a number of ways for men, including increased medical and health problems.

Medical and Health Concerns

According to a 2008 national health survey, 12% of all men older than 18 are considered to be in either fair or poor health (NCHS, 2010). In 2006, 31% of men older than 20 were diagnosed with hypertension, and 32% of men in the same age category were diagnosed with obesity. In 2008, 23% of men aged 18 and older admitted to smoking on a regular basis.

Though modern technology and science have contributed greatly to marked changes in men's health, major concerns still exist within the population. These concerns highlight the importance of professional counselors increasing their awareness of the medical problems that exist within this population. The methods used to help deal with problems often manifest themselves in pervasive, destructive behaviors.

Clinical Issues Within the Population

Depression

Approximately 3% of all men in the United States can be diagnosed with some form of depression, including major depressive disorder; 9%–12% of men will experience depressive symptomatology at some point during their lives (Good et al., 2005). Depression is diagnosed less frequently in men than in women. The incidence of depression in men is significant, given the fact that men are 4 times more likely than women to die from suicide and often choose more lethal means of attempting suicide than women (Baughman, 2008). Males represent 79% of all suicides in the United States (NCHS, 2010).

Substance Abuse

In 2007, 10.4% of males used illicit drugs compared with 5.8% of females. Males were twice as likely as females to use marijuana and to engage in binge alcohol drinking. Moreover, 35% of males used tobacco and tobacco-related products as opposed to 22% of females.

Only 16.7% of all men qualified as lifetime alcohol abstainers compared with 30.4% of women. Sharpe, Heppner, and Dixon (1995) highlighted the relationship between gender-role identification and substance abuse for the male population.

Gender Role Identity

According to Wester (2008), *gender role identity* is defined as a state in which gendered individuals come to understand socialized gender roles. For many men, conflict occurs when they try to resolve this social phenomenon with the life demands that are placed on them. The difficulty of trying to live up to masculine standards set by society leads to gender role strain (Burn & Ward, 2005).

The internalization of social beliefs about what constitutes masculinity can have a pervasive affect on male development. For example, men are socialized to be competitive, to value winning while avoiding intimacy, and to limit emotional expressiveness (Ludlow & Mahalik, 2001). This can lead men to express lower levels of intimacy with others, which has a direct influence on the emotional expressiveness and self-disclosure necessary for building strong marital relationships (Perrone, Wright, & Jackson, 2009).

One current trend highlights the decreasing role of the traditional breadwinner and the increased need for men to place a higher value on the homemaker role (Lease, 2003). Social norms have changed markedly; as a result, the roles that men and women play in the familial structure are currently in flux (Gordon & Whelan-Berry, 2005). For example, more men are choosing to stay at home to care for their children when they are laid off as a way of supporting the family system rather than pursuing alternative careers that may not provide the necessary monetary compensation. Also, more women are choosing to pursue careers because they have better opportunities than their spouses and can provide better financial support for the family. Related to this flux is the constant notion that men avoid seeking help for mental health services, a trend that has been and continues to be a major concern for this population (McKelley, 2007).

Help-Seeking Behaviors

Generally speaking, men do not seek professional psychological help for issues such as substance abuse and depression (Pederson & Vogel, 2007). McKelley (2007) reported that 1 in 7 men will seek the help of a mental health professional as opposed to 1 in 3 women. There has been much debate about why this disparity exists. Freud (1937) framed men's resistance to seek help as resistance to a potential loss of power for the male ego. Silverberg (1986) argued that characteristics such as lack of motivation or fear of intimacy need to be considered. Whatever the case may be, men continue to struggle with their attitudes toward help-seeking behaviors.

Good et al. (2005) supported the notion that this struggle is due in part to men's socialization toward stoicism, interpersonal dominance, and internal self-reliance. Researchers have agreed that the strength of the therapeutic relationship is the best predictor of therapeutic outcomes (Cochran & Cochran, 2006; Messer & Wampold, 2002; Young, 2009). Therapeutic relationships are strong when there is mutual sharing, an emotional connection between the counselor and client, and empathy (Corey, 2009). These attributes can often be daunting and challenging for male clients.

The current social climate influences the level of empathy men can experience and can make it difficult for them engage in empathic behavior. For example, Walker (2001) highlighted the fact that men are often seen as perpetrators, regardless of whether they are the victims of a crime. Men are socialized not to value feminine characteristics and therefore struggle with making emotional connections with other individuals (Real, 2002). Thus, it is easy to understand why men display fewer skills associated with emotional expression, which is a vital part of the therapeutic relationship (Good, 1998). Men tend to struggle with the basic aspects of emotional connection that serve as key ingredients for strong therapeutic relationships in counseling; therefore, they are often unwilling to enter into these types of relationships.

These clinical issues serve as a snapshot of the challenges men face in an ever-changing society. Men are expected to become involved interpersonally as fathers, friends, and co-workers in ways that require high levels of emotional awareness (Good et al., 2005). The issues men face can serve as both a detriment to their development and an impetus for pursuing social and personal change as they matriculate through society.

Theoretical Perspectives on Counseling Men

Developmental Approaches

Counselors who understand the developmental approach know that psychosocial factors play a role in human growth and awareness and that key needs and developmental tasks need to be addressed (Corey, 2009). Development includes the social and life-span issues individuals face and their ability to effectively navigate through those issues. According to Erikson (1963), the choices people make at key points in their development help determine what happens in their lives. Three key phases of development for men are young adulthood, middle age, and later life. When counselors are aware of the tasks associated with each phase of development, they can use this information to aid both assessment and intervention.

Young Adulthood

The key aspect of this stage of development for men is the formation of intimate relationships, which normally occurs between the ages of 18 and 35. This stage of development is characterized by moving away from dependence on parents and friends to adulthood, which involves the freedom of decision making and work. Individuals who do not accomplish this life task have problems connecting with society and often isolate themselves (Erikson, 1963).

This is a critical area of development for men and one that often does not fully develop, in part because of the social strain felt by men from society (Good, 1998). Men who are successful in this area of development have a strong sense of self, have a high level of emotional intelligence, and are willing to allow themselves to be vulnerable in relationships (Burke, Arkowitz, & Dunn, 2002). The inability to develop intimate relationships with others has been correlated with violence, depression, and deviant behavior (McKelley, 2007).

Middle Age

Normally occurring between the ages of 35 and 60, this stage is characterized by an individual's willingness to engage in activities designed to help the next generation. It is important to achieve some level of productivity to avoid psychological stagnation (Corey, 2009). Examples of such productivity include a job promotion, the birth and academic achievement of one's children, or the achievement of a personal goal. Individuals at this stage of development typically recognize the discrepancy between dreams and accomplishments and are willing to reconcile the difference in order to move forward in life.

This area of development is vital for men because of the psychological distress they face in society. The ability to resolve this phase of development can lead to a healthy life and longevity; the inability to do so can lead to gender role conflict (Heppner & Heppner, 2009). Burn and Ward (2005) conceptualized *gender role conflict* as "a psychological state in which socialized gender roles have negative consequences on the person" (p. 255). Men who struggle with gender role conflict in this stage of development are less emotionally expressive, which reduces the intimacy of relationships with family and friends (Rochen & Mahalik, 2004). This lack of emotional expressiveness can lead to social isolation and stagnation, so it is important that men achieve some level of productivity early in this stage of development.

Later Life

The key aspect of this stage of development is that the individual is able to achieve ego integrity, which is the ability to feel some sense of worth after taking stock of one's life achievements. Individuals in this stage, which usually occurs around age 60, can achieve ego integrity when they can look back on their lives with minimal regrets. Those who cannot do so fail to achieve ego integrity and can spend inordinate amounts of time dealing with hopelessness, guilt, resentment, and self-loathing (Corey, 2009).

A key aspect of this stage is the ability of the individual to engage in a life review designed to evaluate his or her life and to highlight critical aspects of development that influenced life outcomes. Gray (2005) emphasized the importance of using narrative therapy with men in this stage of development and considered it a valuable tool for dealing with the resistance men normally have when working through clinical issues and concerns. Good et al. (2005) concluded that the unique experiences men face in society can best be addressed with an approach that does not challenge their role definition. Men at this stage of development rely heavily on the roles they have developed in their lives and take solace in how these roles have shaped their growth.

It is important for counselors to be aware of the different aspects of development that affect men's lives. Being keenly aware of the developmental issues men face can serve as an impetus for building a stronger therapeutic relationship as well as a tool for intervening in dealing with the resistant behaviors men bring with them to the counseling session. In a similar fashion, Carlson and Englar-Carlson (2008) advocated for the use of an Adlerian approach when working with men because of its emphasis on holism and phenomenology.

Adlerian Approaches

Adler believed that individuals are not held captive by their past; everyone is born with innate qualities and unique abilities that help them move toward a positive future (Sweeney, 1998). According to Adler (1964), humans behave in a way that is goal directed and purposeful toward a subjective finality. This drive results in the development of behaviors that compensate for feelings of inferiority developed during childhood experiences. A major goal of his approach is to help the individual overcome feelings of inferiority and thereby naturally move toward meaningful relationships with others (Sweeney, 1998).

The use of this approach is very effective with men who struggle with building and maintaining intimate relationships in counseling (McKelley, 2007). Adler's focus on building relationships through trust and his emphasis on encouragement and self-interest connect with Brooks's (2001) belief in the importance of these traits in dealing with mental health issues that plague men. Pederson and Vogel (2007) asserted that men often experience gender role conflict because they do not believe anyone is willing to understand, hear, and acknowledge their concerns. The Adlerian approach can serve as the impetus for helping men open up more about the problems they face (McKelley, 2007).

Rogerian Approaches

Rogers believed in *phenomenology*, which is the notion that reality is individually constructed and is a function of an individual's understanding of his or her world (Rogers,

1957). Throughout their lives individuals assess interactions according to whether they are positive or negative and tend to move toward those experiences that are positive (Neukrug, 2011). This assessment leads to self-actualization, though Rogers believed that individuals never become truly self-actualized but tend to develop a need for positive regard as a result of these experiences (Rogers, 1957). The highlight of this approach is the belief that individuals are able to resolve their own issues as a result of their experiences, and therefore trust serves as a cornerstone of this approach (Corey, 2009). The core conditions—unconditional positive regard, congruence, and empathic understanding—serve as a catalyst for growth and actualization by promoting a positive atmosphere and enhancing the potential for positive growth in the client.

Johnson (2006) supported the relevance of this approach for use with African American men because of its nondirective nature and its ability to provide an open forum for them to discuss their concerns. Good et al. (2005) agreed that men need more avenues for expression in the counseling setting because they do not enter into the counseling relationship on equal footing with women. Thus, it is important for the counselor to understand and view men's issues from men's perspective, taking into account the experiences men face that are uniquely different from those women face. For example, Englar-Carlson and Shepard (2005) encouraged counselors to use strategies that focus on respect, understanding, and empathy when working with men in couples counseling. This approach allows men to engage more with the counselor and to increase their emotional expression to their wives or partners.

Cognitive–Behavioral Approaches

Though there are different cognitive–behavioral approaches, they all share the common attributes of a collaborative relationship; an understanding of the nature of psychological distress; a focus on using cognitions to bring about changes in behavior; and the use of a focused, educational, time-limited approach to counseling (Corey, 2009). Cognitive behavior therapy focuses on restructuring one's thoughts in such a way that promotes growth and healing (Neukrug, 2011). It uses a number of techniques, such as behavioral rehearsal, modeling, cognitive mapping, and stress inoculation training.

The cognitive–behavioral approach can be challenging for men who have been socialized to hide their true thoughts and feelings as a way to show mental toughness. Burn and Ward (2005) concluded that men are less likely than women to self-disclose thoughts and feelings in the counseling relationship. They highlighted the importance of establishing a strong therapeutic relationship with men before delving into deeper clinical issues. Dodson and Borders (2006) believe that a cognitive–behavioral approach is useful in helping men explore the gender role conflict they experience in their careers. Beck (1987) demonstrated the effectiveness of cognitive therapy in helping men deal with depression. He advocated an approach that focuses on dealing effectively with cognitions, faulty interpretations, and negative self-views by using a problem-focused, behavior-enhanced approach.

These theoretical approaches can serve as an avenue to help counselors deal more effectively with the clinical issues men face in society. The strength of the relationship serves as the foundation for all of these theoretical approaches, and counselors need to be aware of the importance of the relationship. Good et al. (2005) purported that the most important aspect of counseling with men is developing a therapeutic relationship that is collaborative and that allows men to express their innermost feelings without fear of rejection. Researchers have highlighted the need for counselors to increase their awareness of the clinical issues men face in society if they want to work effectively with them in a counselor–client relationship (Burn & Ward, 2005; Englar-Carlson & Shepard, 2005; Good et al., 2005; Johnson,

2006). Within this context, the following case studies are presented to help the reader better understand these theoretical perspectives on working with men in counseling relationships.

Case Study: Michael

Michael is a 39-year-old African American male who recently lost his job because his company had to downsize in response to changes in the economy. Michael is angry because he believes that he was singled out for termination and that other people in the company who were less qualified did not lose their jobs. Michael has both a bachelor's and master's degree in his chosen field but has decided not to look for work because he does not believe he will find any. He states, "I am so tired of fighting this battle, it seems like every time I take two steps forward someone pulls me back down again." He admits to being depressed and is attending counseling at the recommendation of his wife, who is very frustrated with his recent behavior. He believes that no one will give him an opportunity to display his talents and often laments the future and what it holds for his three children (two boys and a girl). Michael has talked about the importance of his provider role in his family and relates it to that of his father, who "worked two jobs and had a little hustle on the side" to keep them in a middle-class lifestyle. He is concerned that he has let his father down with this recent termination and does not know what his next step will be. He states, "One thing I have learned in all of this: Trust no one."

Counseling Considerations With Michael

Michael is a hard worker who is committed to providing for his family. He is frustrated by what he perceives as a slight by his company because he believes he was singled out for termination. His current behavior is different from his typical behavior, and his spouse has encouraged him to seek professional help. Achieving adequate employment and a middle-class lifestyle for his family seems to be an ongoing struggle for him. He does not believe that he will get the support he needs from others and has learned over time to trust his own instincts. His role as the provider for his family is very important to him and can be tied to his need to find proper employment. Also, he models his work ethic after that of his father, whom he considers a good provider and an example to follow.

When working with Michael, the counselor needs to consider certain aspects of his development. First, Michael is an African American male who has obtained a master's degree; this is significant because only two thirds of all African American males graduate from high school, and only one third of those who enter college graduate with a degree (Johnson, 2006). Second, he does not trust anyone because of his life experiences. Third, he has a supportive spouse who cares about him and wants him to feel better. Fourth, the provider role is definitely important to him. And finally, his experiences with his father have a profound effect on the way he views his current situation.

When considering a theoretical approach for working with Michael, the counselor needs to select one that fits his current dilemma. For example, a Rogerian approach would allow Michael the freedom to talk about his experiences and problems from his perspective and not to feel judged or challenged by the counselor. This approach would help to provide a strong therapeutic connection for Michael and his counselor because the counselor would work to understand Michael's worldviews, thereby reducing the resistance men typically feel when engaging in the counseling process. The open forum provided by the counselor would help Michael move toward self-actualization and toward the development of effective strategies for dealing with his concerns.

However, a cognitive–behavioral approach would allow Michael to organize his thoughts and feelings in a way that promotes growth and healing. This approach advocates a strong therapeutic bond between the client and the counselor. This is the support Michael would need to engage in the counseling process and to consider exploring his thoughts and feelings. Because Michael has been socialized to hide his true feelings, a collaborative relationship is essential in helping him focus on positive changes. Given his depression and his discontent with external forces, the cognitive–behavioral approach can provide a problem-focused, behavior-specific system for exploring the conflicts that exist in his life.

It is also important for the counselor to consider aspects of his or her own personal values that will affect the relationship with Michael. The values counselors hold can serve as a support or detriment to effective work with their clients. Michael grew up in a system in which the father's role as provider was very important to the outcome of the family. Also, the most important things in his life are rooted in his current family system and in his family of origin. Michael's perceptions of oppression, prejudice, and racial microaggressions as an African American male serve as an important part of his development. In working with Michael, a counselor needs to be aware of these issues and aware of how his or her own values around these issues will influence the counseling intervention.

Case Study: Philip

Philip is a 57-year-old White male who has decided to come to counseling because of increased anxiety and outbursts of anger over the past 6 months. He has a PhD in history and admits to living an upper-class lifestyle. Approximately 6 months ago, Philip lost his position as a faculty member at a large southeastern university because of budget cuts and departmental changes. He had taught in the history department for 5 years. Moreover, this was the third university he has had to leave. His first position as a tenure-track assistant professor did not go well because he did not get along with his colleagues. His second position as tenure-track assistant professor did not go well because he believed the research requirements were too difficult for him to meet. His wife is angry with him because he chose to take a nontenured faculty position and now is being asked to leave 5 years later. Philip laments, "I can't do anything right. My kids probably think I am a loser. I am tired of running around the country looking for work. This economy sucks." Philip considers himself a hard worker and devoted father and husband; he is the first one in his family to graduate from college and admits that his siblings have always looked up to him. Also, he states that he is a little embarrassed by his parents' lack of education, even though he loves them dearly for all the sacrifices they made to help him achieve his dream of becoming a professor.

Counseling Considerations With Philip

Philip is an accomplished professor who is concerned about his current state of affairs. He is frustrated by a repeated pattern of teaching positions at universities that do not seem to work out for one reason or another. He is also embarrassed by his outbursts of anger. He has worked hard to maintain his upper-class lifestyle, something that was not afforded to him as a child. The way his wife and children see him is very important to him, and he takes pride in his achievements. He values the relationship he has with his parents and is very comfortable in his role as the educational leader for his family of origin.

When working with Philip, the counselor needs to consider certain aspects of his development. First, Philip is the first individual in his family of origin to graduate from college and to attain a PhD. Second, his relationship with his current family is tied to his status. Third, his current behaviors are alarming to him and he wants to change them. Fourth, the lifestyle he has worked to provide for his family is a source of pride and is viewed by him as an indication of his success as a Caucasian male. And finally, he has been unable to pursue his dreams of becoming a professor because of different challenges he has faced.

When considering a theoretical approach for working with Philip, the counselor needs to select one that fits his current dilemma. For example, an Adlerian approach would allow Philip the freedom to experience the encouragement and support he needs to talk about the current challenges he faces. The counselor could explore any feelings of inferiority with Philip by exploring his family of origin and his beliefs about those relationships. An Adlerian perspective would help Philip tap into the innate qualities that helped him move toward a positive future (e.g., being the first one in his family to achieve a PhD).

However, a developmental approach would allow Philip to organize his thoughts and feelings in a way that promotes growth and healing. It is clear that Philip is currently experiencing stagnation because of his inability to achieve productivity in his career. This is a critical time for him because intimate relationships and family bonds can become disrupted and stagnant. The counselor needs to process with Philip his current achievements and how those achievements have helped to structure his life up to this point. This would allow him to further address his outbursts of anger and anxiety and to understand the source of those behavioral problems. Also, the counselor can use Philip's strong sense of self as a point of emphasis in helping him work through this stage of development.

It is important for the counselor to consider aspects of his or her own personal values that will affect the relationship with Philip. Philip grew up with supportive parents who worked hard to help him achieve his dreams. The upper-class lifestyle he has worked hard to achieve is very important to him and is a vital part of his identity. His views as a White male of the nuclear family and roles within the family unit are important for his survival. In working with Philip, a counselor needs to be aware of these issues and aware of how his or her own values around these issues will influence the counseling intervention.

Conclusion

Men have been and will continue to be a very important part of U.S. society. Being aware of the issues that affect their development is crucial to gaining a better understanding of their needs in therapeutic interactions with counselors. Counselors need to be aware that economic concerns can hinder men's development because of men's need to serve as providers and caretakers. This need can lead to medical and emotional problems that have a detriment on their development. Substance abuse and depression are major clinical issues within this population that merit understanding and increased awareness on the part of counselors. A number of theoretical approaches are effective for working with men in the counseling relationship. These approaches highlight the importance of the counseling relationship and how that relationship can serve as either an impetus for growth and change or an impetus for further resentment, frustration, and anger.

References

Adler, A. (1964). Advantages and disadvantages of the inferiority feeling. In H. L. Ansbacher & R. R. Ansbacher (Eds.), *Superiority and social interest: A collection of later writings* (pp. 50–58). Evanston, IL: Northwestern University Press.

Baughman, S. (2008). *Essential topics for the helping professionals.* Boston, MA: Pearson Education.

Beck, A. T. (1987). Cognitive models of depression. *Journal of Cognitive Psychotherapy, 1,* 5–37.

Blustein, D. L., Chaves, A. P., Diemer, M. A., Gallaher, L. A., Marshall, K. G., Sirin, S., & Bhati, K. S. (2002). Voices of the forgotten half: The role of social class in the school-to-work transition. *Journal of Counseling Psychology, 49,* 311–323.

Brooks, G. R. (2001). Masculinity and men's mental health. *Journal of American College Health, 49*(6), 285–297.

Burke, B. L., Arkowitz, H., & Dunn, C. (2002). The efficacy of motivational interviewing and its adaptations: What we know so far. In W. Miller & S. Rollnick (Eds.), *Motivational interviewing* (2nd ed., pp. 217–250). New York, NY: Guilford Press.

Burn, S. M., & Ward, A. Z. (2005). Men's conformity to traditional masculinity and relationship satisfaction. *Psychology of Men and Masculinity, 4,* 254–263.

Carlson, J. D., & Englar-Carlson, M. (2008). Adlerian therapy. In J. Frew & M. D. Spiegler (Eds.), *Contemporary psychotherapies for a diverse world* (pp. 93–140). Boston, MA: Lahaska Press.

Cochran, J. L., & Cochran, N. H. (2006). *The heart of counseling: A guide to developing therapeutic relationships.* Belmont, CA: Thomson Wadsworth.

Corey, G. (2009). *Theory and practice of counseling and psychotherapy* (8th ed.). Belmont, CA: Thomson Brooks/Cole.

Dodson, T. A., & Borders, L. D. (2006). Men in traditional and nontraditional careers: Gender role attitudes, gender role conflict, and job satisfaction. *The Career Development Quarterly, 54*(4), 283–296.

Dutton, D. G. (2000). Witnessing parental violence as traumatic experience in shaping the abusive personality. *Journal of Aggression, Maltreatment and Trauma, 3,* 59–67.

Englar-Carlson, M., & Shepard, D. S. (2005). Engaging men in couples counseling: Strategies for overcoming ambivalence and inexpressiveness. *The Family Journal, 13*(4), 383–391. doi:10.1177/1066480705278467

Erera, P. I., & Baum, N. (2009). Chat-room voices of divorced non-residential fathers. *Journal of Sociology and Social Welfare, 36*(2), 63–83.

Erikson, E. H. (1963). *Childhood and society* (2nd ed.). New York, NY: Norton.

Freud, S. (1937). Analysis terminable and interminable. In P. Rieff (Ed.), *Freud: Therapy and technique* (pp. 233–272). New York, NY: Collier.

Good, G. E. (1998). Missing and underrepresented aspects of men's lives. *SPSMM Bulletin, 3*(2), 1–2.

Good, G. E., Thomson, D. A., & Brathwaite, A. D. (2005). Men and therapy: Critical concepts, theoretical frameworks, and research recommendations. *Journal of Clinical Psychology, 61,* 699–711.

Gordon, J. R., & Whelan-Berry, K. S. (2005). Contributions to family and household activities by the husbands of midlife professional women. *Journal of Family Issues, 26,* 899–923.

Gray, M. C. (2005). Narrative couple's therapy with feeling resistant men. *McGill Journal of Education, 40*(1), 120–130.

Heppner, M. J., & Heppner, P. P. (2009). Taking the road less traveled. *Journal of Career Development, 36*(1), 49–67.

Johnson, P. D. (2006). Counseling African American men: A contextualized humanistic perspective. *Counseling and Values, 50,* 187–196.

Lease, S. H. (2003). Testing a model of men's nontraditional occupational choices. *The Career Development Quarterly, 51,* 244–258.

Ludlow, L. H., & Mahalik, J. R. (2001). Congruence between a theoretical continuum of masculinity and the Rasch model: Examining the Conformity to Masculine Norms Inventory. *Journal of Applied Measurement, 2,* 205–226.

McKelley, R. A. (2007). Men's resistance to seeking help: Using individual psychology to understand counseling-reluctant men. *Journal of Individual Psychology, 63*(1), 48–58.

Mejia, X. E. (2005). Gender matters: Working with adult male survivors of trauma. *Journal of Counseling & Development, 83,* 29–40.

Messer, S. B., & Wampold, B. E. (2002). Let's face the facts: Common factors are more potent than specific therapy ingredients. *Counseling Psychology: Science and Practice, 9,* 21–25.

National Center for Education Statistics. (2009). *The condition of education.* Retrieved from http://nces.ed.gov/fastfacts/display.asp?id=40

National Center for Health Statistics. (2010). *Men's health.* Retrieved from http://www.cdc.gov/nchs/fastats/mens_health.htm

Neukrug, E. S. (2011). *Counseling theory and practice.* Belmont, CA: Brooks/Cole.

Peckham, S. (2008). Teenagers cite school as greatest source of stress. *The Education Digest, 73*(6), 76.

Pederson, E. L., & Vogel, D. L. (2007). Male gender role conflict and willingness to see counseling: Testing a mediation model on college-aged men. *Journal of Counseling Psychology, 54,* 373–384.

Perrone, K. M., Wright, S. L., & Jackson, Z. V. (2009). Traditional and nontraditional gender roles and work family interface for men and women. *Journal of Career Development, 36,* 8–24.

Real, T. (2002). *How can I get through? Reconnecting men and women.* New York, NY: Scribner.

Rochen, A. B., & Mahalik, J. R. (2004). Women's perceptions of male partners' gender role conflict as predictors of psychological well-being and relationship satisfaction. *Psychology of Men & Masculinity, 5,* 147–157.

Rogers, C. R. (1957). The necessary and sufficient conditions of therapeutic personality change. *Journal of Consulting Psychology, 21,* 95–103.

Sharpe, M. J., Heppner, P. P., & Dixon, W. A. (1995). Gender role conflict, instrumentality, expressiveness, and well-being in adult men. *Sex Roles, 33,* 1–8.

Silverberg, R. A. (1986). *Psychotherapy for men: Transcending the masculine mystique.* Springfield, IL: Charles C Thomas.

Sweeney, T. (1998). *Adlerian counseling: A practitioner's approach* (4th ed.). Philadelphia, PA: Accelerated Development.

Walker, L. E. A. (2001). A feminist perspective on men in emotional pain. In G. Brooks & G. Good (Eds.), *The handbook of counseling and psychotherapy approaches for men* (pp. 683–695). San Francisco, CA: Jossey-Bass.

Wester, S. R. (2008). Male gender role conflict and multiculturalism: Implications for counseling psychology. *The Counseling Psychologist, 36*(2), 294–324.

World Factbook. (2010). *Economy—United States.* Retrieved from https://www.cia.gov/library/publications/the-world-factbook/geos/us.html

Young, M. E. (2009). *Learning the art of helping: Building blocks and techniques* (4th ed.). Upper Saddle River, NJ: Pearson.

Issues in Counseling Women

Kathy M. Evans

Who Are U.S. Women?

In 2007, women in the United States numbered 153.6 million, or 50.7% of the total population. Of that number, 65% were reported as White, 14.2% as Latina, 12.9% as African American, and 4% as Asian. Older women outnumbered older men; of women older than 65, White women made up a little more than 58%, African American women 8.9%, and Latinas 6.5%. At 55%, White women younger than 15 outnumbered other age groups but not as significantly as their older-than-65 counterparts. Latinas accounted for 21.5% of women younger than 15, followed by African Americans at 14.6% (Health Resources and Services Administration, 2009). More than half of U.S. women were married and living with a spouse. However, 12% of Whites, 36% of African Americans, 8% of Asians, and 19% of women of other racial groups were single heads of household.

In terms of health, most White women (62.1%) said they were in good or excellent health, whereas only 53.1% of Latinas and 51% of African American women reported that status. White women were more likely than minority women to have arthritis and heart disease, whereas African American women were more likely to have hypertension and Latinas and African American women were more likely to have diabetes. Low-income women of all racial groups reported conditions such as poorly managed asthma (Health Resources and Services Administration, 2009).

With regard to mental health, women are more likely than men to be diagnosed with depression, anxiety, phobias, eating disorders, borderline personality disorders, dissociative disorders, somatization disorders, agoraphobia, and posttraumatic stress disorder (PTSD). In 2007, poor women were even more often diagnosed with depression and anxiety than those who had higher incomes (Health Resources and Services Administration, 2009).

Often women are diagnosed with mental disorders based on "exaggerations or stereotyping of female gender roles and behavior" (American Psychological Association [APA], 2007, p. 8). African American women are more likely than other women to be diagnosed with schizophrenia, and minority women in general typically receive more pharmacological treatment than they do psychotherapy (Homma-True, Greene, Lopez, & Trimble, 1993).

Domestic Violence and Sexual Abuse

As previously mentioned, PTSD is a psychological diagnosis found more often in women than men. The fact is, there were 18 million reports by women of domestic violence by an intimate partner in 2006 (Tjaden & Thoennes, 2006). In addition, girls are 2.5 times as likely as boys to experience childhood sexual abuse (Boney-McCoy & Finkelhor, 1995). It seems reasonable that women who have suffered from traumas such as domestic violence or sexual abuse are twice as likely as those who have not to develop PTSD (Kimerling, Ouimette, & Wolfe, 2002). Brown and May (2009) found that women whose income was at or below the poverty line were more likely to experience intimate partner violence than women whose income was higher.

Gender Bias

Unfortunately, gender bias in counseling and psychotherapy is still apparent in research. Danzinger and Welfel (2000) found that mental health professionals believe that their female clients are less competent than male clients. Seem and Clark (2006) found that counselors-in-training tended to have different definitions of what constitutes a healthy woman and a healthy man based on gender stereotypes. Yet another study has shown that men and women are diagnosed differently even when they present the same symptoms: Women received a diagnosis of histrionic or borderline more often than men (Becker & Lamb, 1994). Moreover, for years counselors have complained about gender stereotypes in the *Diagnostic and Statistical Manual of Mental Disorders* (Ancis, Szymanski, & Ladany, 2008) that could lead to gender bias in diagnosis. Ancis et al. (2008) noted that gender bias typically is not overt but that when it occurs it is more likely the result of omissions to gender fair counseling, for example "fostering traditional roles, not accepting women's anger, and lack of consideration of the sociocultural context of problems" (p. 721).

In 2007, a joint task force of APA Divisions 17 and 35 published *Guidelines for Psychological Practice With Girls and Women* (APA, 2007). These guidelines were intended to not only reduce potential harm but result in "improved treatment [that] will also likely benefit women and girls, particularly through greater awareness, education and prevention" (p. 4) given the changing demographics of women in the United States and changes in sexism, racism, and other "-isms."

Cultural Issues for Women

Minority Status

The women of the United States epitomize multiculturalism. They represent every race, culture, ethnicity, religion, level of ability or disability, sexual orientation, social class, political party, and occupation. What they have in common is that they are women, and in U.S. society, though they outnumber men, they are considered an oppressed minority group. The oppression of women is a fact that some choose to deny and others cannot believe, especially in a day and age when oppression is subtle and justified in socially acceptable terms. However, women's oppression is clear when one considers the gap in earnings between men and women; the fact that women are more likely than men to experience sexual harassment, rape, and domestic violence; and the fact that women are more likely than men to be challenged by role conflicts (Herlihy & Watson, 2006; Tjaden & Thoennes, 2006; U.S. Department of Commerce, Economics and Statistics Administration, 2011). Moreover, women heads of household are overrepresented among poor and homeless families (Health Resources and Services Administration, 2009). In addition, many women belong to more than one oppressed group. Not only are they oppressed because of their gender, but they may be oppressed because of their race, ethnicity, culture, ability status, sexual orientation, religious beliefs, and/or socioeconomic status as well. Women who identify with multiple oppressed groups face challenges that can be truly overwhelming.

Gender Socialization

Many believe that the cause of the oppression of women is due in part to the socialization of men and women in the United States. In U.S. society, males are taught behaviors and attitudes that are more highly valued than those that are taught to females. Women, however, are criticized and devalued when they exhibit the same behaviors and attitudes that are valued in men (Evans, Kincade, & Seem, 2011).

More likely than not, individuals are unable to pinpoint how they learned gender-appropriate behavior, but it most likely began in infancy, with a pink or blue blanket. Gender socialization typically begins at home and is carried out by both the same-sex and opposite-sex parent. Parents of infants think of their baby girls differently than they do their baby boys (Wester & Trepal, 2008). As they grow, girls and boys are rewarded for different behaviors. Whereas boys are harshly criticized for displaying feminine characteristics and behaviors (such as playing with dolls), girls who exhibit tomboy behavior before puberty (such as playing with trucks) are seldom admonished for it (Campenni, 1999; Sandnabba & Ahlberg, 1999). Girls are expected to set aside those tomboy behaviors during puberty once they show signs of becoming women. Even families who attempt an androgynous upbringing for their children at home find it challenging once children start to attend school. Schools tend to reinforce what society has defined as acceptable behavior for boys and girls (Maher & Ward, 2002). It has been found that teachers and counselors alike unconsciously reinforce stereotypical gendered behaviors in their students.

The fact that boys and girls learn different behaviors and attitudes according to their gender is not problematic in itself. The problem is that the behaviors identified as appropriate for males are highly valued but exclusively in males (Robinson-Wood, 2009). In U.S. society, it is good to be strong, independent, assertive, competitive, and ruthless if one is male. Women who display these characteristics to the same extent as men are typically devalued and criticized for it. They are valued more when they are accommodating, caring, and supportive.

Career and Socioeconomic Status

The devaluation of women is also seen in the salaries that are paid for jobs that are considered women's work. The traditionally female fields of nursing, kindergarten–Grade 12 teaching, secretarial work, and social work are historically low paying. The most significant indicator that women are devalued is that no matter their level of education, no matter their occupation, women earn less than men (Institute for Women's Policy Research, 2010). Men earn more than women even in those fields that are traditionally female (e.g., kindergarten–Grade 12 teaching, nursing, secretarial work). Men who engage in occupations that require the same levels of skill and education receive higher pay than women. According to the Institute for Women's Policy Research, in 2009 women earned 80.2% of what men earn. Women of color— African Americans, Latinas, Native Americans—typically earn even less than White women. This 80% figure is an average; the gap is larger between White men and women of color. Although 80.2% is an improvement over previous years, the gap continues to exist.

There have been several suggestions as to why the wage gap exists. One suggestion is that women are their own enemies because they do not negotiate higher salaries. Women who do ask for higher salaries, however, tend to be less successful at it than men. Another suggestion is that women believe they can increase their income once they show their worth, but this rarely happens (Herlihy & Watson, 2006). Another explanation is that they do not ask for more for fear that an offer or promotion will be withdrawn—an indication that they have bought into the idea that they are not worthy of the higher salaries offered to men.

Socioeconomic Status and Careers

When it comes to socioeconomic status, all one needs to know is that no matter what a woman's career might be, she will earn less than a man in that same career (Institute for Women's Policy Research, 2010). The unfortunate reality that accompanies this knowledge is that because of racial discrimination, the wage gap between men of color and women of color is smaller than it is for White men and White women because men of color earn less than White men. Latinas typically earn the least of all groups regardless of occupation. Poverty levels for women are higher than they are for men, and women in poverty are more likely to be hit hard in times of recession. Unmarried women have the highest poverty rate of all women. African American women represent the largest group of women in poverty at 30%; Latinas do not fare much better at 29.5%, and 18.5% of unmarried White women are poor. Unmarried women with children younger than age 6 are 5 times as likely than married women with young children to be poor (Health Resources and Services Administration, 2009).

An April 2010 news release by the U.S. Census Bureau touted the fact that 58% of the advanced degrees awarded in 2009 were awarded to women. Women are thus more likely than men to earn a high school diploma, a bachelor's degree, and an advanced degree. Although this trend may appear to be positive, even a woman with an advanced degree makes 80 cents for every dollar a man makes with that same degree. More women are entering higher paying male-dominated fields, such as law and accounting. More women are bus drivers and letter carriers. However, women are still outnumbered in science, engineering, and construction. In fact, 40% of women still work in traditionally female careers such as teaching, nursing, and social work, which are the lowest paid professions.

Body Image

As a result of gender socialization, girls learn that to be accepted, loved, and admired they need to meet a standard of beauty that is typically based on an exaggerated notion of northern Euro-American woman (Brown & May, 2009). The media is ripe with images of unrealistically thin bodies that girls and women may internalize and set as a goal to achieve. For women of color, this standard of beauty is even more elusive. As a consequence of their inability to achieve the ideal, many girls and women develop body dissatisfaction, low self-esteem, and/or eating disorders. It was once believed that women of color, especially African American women, were not prone to developing eating disorders because full-figured women are culturally accepted. Such thinking represents a limited view of eating disorders. For example, obesity is a tremendous problem among African Americans, and overeating needs to be included among the eating disorders. That said, increasing numbers of African American teens are developing bulimia and anorexia (Brown & May, 2009; Perez & Joiner, 2003).

Multiple Oppressions

Many women have multiple identities and can be the target of multiple oppressions. These women include but are not limited to women of color, women with disabilities, lesbians, and women living in poverty. Of course some women may identify with all of these oppressed groups. Because these women may be multiply oppressed, their struggles are multiplied. Women of color tend to experience oppressions to a greater degree than White women. Compared to White women, they are poorer, have more severe mental illness, and are more likely to be abused by an intimate partner (Evans, 2010; Sue & Sue, 2008). The multiple oppressions of women with disabilities include the belief that they are incapable of fulfilling traditional women's gender roles or career duties. Martin (2003) described women with disabilities as "role-less": "They are not merely undervalued but valueless on every level" (p. 75). Lesbians not only experience the same oppressions that all women face but face the possibility of being physically abused by strangers because of their sexual orientation. In addition, lesbians are not protected under the law for being discriminated against because of their sexual orientation. Therefore, they can lose their jobs and their housing simply because they are lesbian (Evans, 2006). Women living in poverty are oppressed in so many ways. Women who lack money or means must live in neighborhoods with the worst living conditions; they are exposed to street violence and have little access to supermarkets and transportation. Women living in poverty have the worst health and mental health care but high levels of physical illness and psychological stressors (Hopps & Liu, 2006; Liu & Estrada-Hernandez, 2010).

However, the greatest danger for women who are multiply oppressed is buying into the negative beliefs, attitudes, and expectations associated with themselves and internalizing those beliefs. According to Vasquez and Magraw (2005), women who internalize these negative beliefs tend to engage in self-destructive behavior, develop eating disorders, engage in substance abuse, associate with gangs, and more.

Strategies for Working With Women

The APA (2007) *Guidelines for Psychological Practice With Girls and Women* are used here as an outline for this discussion of strategies. The headings from these guidelines are outlined here.

1. Psychologists strive to be aware of the effects of socialization, stereotyping, and unique life events on the development of girls and women across diverse cultural groups.
2. Psychologists are encouraged to recognize and utilize information about oppression, privilege, and identity development as they may affect girls and women.
3. Psychologists strive to understand the impact of bias and discrimination on the physical and mental health of those with whom they work.
4. Psychologists strive to use gender and culturally sensitive, affirming practices in providing services to girls and women.
5. Psychologists are encouraged to recognize how their socialization, attitudes, and knowledge about gender may affect their practice with girls and women.

6. Psychologists are encouraged to use interventions and approaches that have been found to be effective in the treatment of issues of concern to girls and women.
7. Psychologists strive to foster therapeutic relationships and practices that promote initiative, empowerment, and expanded alternatives and choices for girls and women.
8. Psychologists strive to provide appropriate, unbiased assessments and diagnoses in their work with women and girls.
9. Psychologists strive to consider the problems of girls and women in their sociopolitical context.
10. Psychologists strive to acquaint themselves with and utilize relevant mental health, education, and community resources for girls and women.
11. Psychologists are encouraged to understand and work to change institutional and systemic bias that may impact girls and women.

Note. Adapted from *Guidelines for Psychological Practice With Girls and Women: A Joint Task Force of APA Divisions 17 and 35,* by the American Psychological Association, 2007. Retrieved from http://www.apa.org/practice/guidelines/girls-and-women.pdf

These guidelines serve as a good foundation for effectively counseling girls and women. Among the theoretical approaches that parallel these guidelines are feminist therapy and womanist therapy.

Feminist Therapy and Womanist Therapy

Feminist therapy developed during the second wave of feminism in the 1970s and has evolved continuously since that time (Evans, Kincade, Marbley, & Seem, 2005). Although feminist therapy has its critics because it ignored the plight of women of color in the first decade of its evolution, it is now seen as an approach that is multicultural and appropriate for use with all women. Evans et al. (2011) suggested that a multicultural feminist approach to therapy can be used to eliminate the internal and external oppression of men and women of all races and cultures. Grounded in feminist philosophy, feminist therapy has four basic tenets. The first is that the personal is political. Feminist therapists believe that personal problems have a social cause and a political solution. Rather than encouraging clients to adjust to the status quo, counselors encourage clients to change the status quo. Rather than focusing on the internal causes of a psychological problem, counselors focus on the context of the client's life that resulted in the problem. The second tenet is the egalitarian relationship. Feminist therapists believe that therapy should be demystified for the client and that the client is an equal partner in his or her treatment. Feminist therapists treat the counseling relationship as one in which the client and counselor work collaboratively on the problem. The third tenet is that of privileging women's experience. Women's issues and oppressed people's issues are not seen by the therapist as an afterthought. Instead, these unique experiences are brought front and center. Feminist therapists actually privilege the client's lived experience (Evans et al., 2011). The final tenet is empowerment. Women in U.S. society lack power, and feminist therapists help clients to understand and use power in ways that strengthen them.

Three strategies make multicultural feminist therapy unique from other therapies. These are gender-role analysis, power analysis, and cultural analysis. In gender-role analysis, counselors help clients understand how their training as females or males of their personal cultural group has influenced their lives for better or worse. Gender-role analysis helps clients discover how to take from their gender socialization those beliefs that enhance their lives and how to resocialize themselves to reject those beliefs that hinder or hurt them

(Evans, 2010). In power analysis clients learn about how they use power and how power is used against them. They learn how to exert their power in ways that increase their self-esteem and self-efficacy but that still fit with their beliefs about themselves (Evans, 2010). In cultural analysis clients' multiple identities are discussed, clients explore the cultural messages they have received, and clients determine which cultural beliefs strengthen them and which negatively affect their well-being.

Support Groups

Support groups have traditionally been effective in counseling women, especially when clients discover more about how they have been oppressed. Clients can normalize their symptoms and face challenges in changing themselves and the contexts in which they live. Support groups contribute significantly to clients' ability to let go of beliefs and behaviors that are harmful to them.

Empowerment Groups

Feminist therapy is often conducted in empowerment groups. Groups are especially effective in helping women explore stereotyped gender roles and the importance of those roles in their lives. Gender roles are deeply embedded for many people because gender socialization begins at infancy and it is difficult to turn away from ideas that have long been held. Through empowerment groups, clients not only address gender-role issues but learn more about what they can do to change society to alleviate their problems.

Case Study: Sara

Sara is a 27-year-old White married woman with two children whose husband Jim is a batterer. Sara and Jim got married right out of college and immediately moved away from family to another state so that Jim could take a position at a prestigious accounting firm. Sara had majored in science education and found it easy to secure a job once they made their move. Jim had always been critical of Sara, but not long after their move he became more verbally abusive. Sara attributed this to the stress of the job and his "having to take it out on someone." Just after the birth of their first child, Jim hit Sara for the first time. Sara forgave him because she took responsibility for provoking him and because they both were exhausted from getting too little sleep. He did not hit her again for more than a year, during which time she conceived their second child. Then the attacks began to come more often. Sara showed up at the women's center after Jim beat her badly enough for her to be hospitalized for 2 days. Sara refused to attend group counseling but came for individual counseling instead.

Sara's counselor Sue practices feminist therapy, and at first Sara was not sure she would continue with Sue. She resented her husband for beating her, but she did not hate all men. She finally decided that she would try counseling with Sue because Sue seemed very honest and open with her and explained everything she would do during counseling. Sue even offered to suggest some good counselors if Sara decided not to continue with her.

During counseling, Sara discovered how angry she was not only with her husband but with the people in her life who had condoned his behavior when it had first started and those who had chosen to look the other way as it had gotten worse. Sara was also full of her own guilt for not telling people what was wrong and seeking help sooner. But after all, she had two little children and she could not raise them without Jim. After a few sessions with Sue, in which they did a gender-role analysis and a power analysis, Sara understood more about why she felt so dependent on Jim and why Jim may have thought that battering was something he could do to her. Sara was always praised for making people happy, for letting others have their way when she disagreed, and for being a good sport. All the women in her family were married, and everyone in the family frowned on divorce. She belonged to a church that also denounced divorce and promoted women being submissive to their husbands. She was proud of her home and the fact that her children were in private school. Everyone praised Jim for being a good man and providing handsomely for his family. All of these beliefs helped keep her with Jim even though he was beating her. Sara had a hard time fighting the draw to go back to Jim, who had not sought counseling but who continuously begged her to come back.

When Sue and Sara began to talk about changes Sara could make to support her changing ideas about her gender roles and her responsibilities to her children, she began to gather strength. The first thing Sara did was change churches—she found one that was supportive of her needs but that also was involved in a battered women's ministry. She started working with the church on that project and with the women who came in for assistance. Sara soon decided to inform Jim that she would not consider reconciliation until he got help. That decision seemed right to her, and although she was not sure she could completely sever her relationship with Jim, she felt better about her ability to support herself and her children.

Case Study:
An African American Women's Support Group

A group of 30-something professional African American women began a leaderless support group when they learned about one another's isolation in their careers. Two women were lawyers, one a college professor, one a social worker, one a second-grade teacher, and one a college student with two children. Three of the women belonged to the same church, two went to the same hairdresser, and the others were friends of one or more of the other members. They had in common the fact that they were all highly educated, single African American women in their 30s. They were the only African American women at their jobs, they all owned their own homes, and they felt discriminated against in many ways in almost every place they went.

At their first meeting they discussed how they wanted the group to run. They would do a thermometer check to see how everyone was doing at the beginning of every session and then they would discuss the special topic. Each person would take turns hosting the group, and the host would be responsible for coming up with the topic. They would meet formally like that once a month and then socially one other time each month.

The group met twice a month for more than a year, not including two weekend retreats to the beach. The women discussed their isolation in being the only African American women at their jobs and the discrimination they experienced on the job from colleagues, bosses, clients, and students. They discussed the isolation they felt being left out of social activities by coworkers because these activities were for couples, and single women—especially Black single women—just would not fit in. They discussed the rejection they felt from African American men because they were highly educated and owned property.

The women gained understanding and camaraderie by attending the support group sessions, and they rarely missed a meeting. Their experiences were normalized and they were able to cope better with the oppressions they felt by sharing and brainstorming ideas and strategies.

Case Study:
A Racially Diverse Adolescent Empowerment Group

This group was formed by a school counselor for girls who had been referred by their teachers as being "un-ladylike." The group included two African Americans adolescents aged 14 and 15, one Puerto Rican aged 15, and two White adolescents aged 14 and 15. Although not a feminist therapist, the school counselor believed that these young women were being admonished for not living up to someone else's idea of what it meant to be female, and she wanted to give them the opportunity to be themselves without judgment and to discover their own meanings of womanhood. She read up on strategies for counseling girls and women and put the group together with those strategies in mind.

The group met for eight sessions. The first session was spent getting to know one another and finding similarities among the members. The second session was devoted to discussing their differences. By the end of the second session the young women were truly forming into a group and were connecting with one another. They respected one another culturally and shared cultural information.

During the third session the counselor brought up gender identity and the group discussed what it meant to be a girl and a woman. It was a lively session: Sometimes there was perfect agreement, and at other times there opinions differed. During the fourth session the counselor introduced the idea of gender socialization and dos and don'ts for girls and women. Most of the group members disagreed with the dos and don'ts but agreed that "some people do think that way."

In the fifth session the counselor discussed sexism and played videotapes that demeaned women. They had a lively discussion about the images of women on MTV and in popular music videos and whether they were endorsing of women or demeaning of women. The sessions continued with discussions of gender, gender roles, and expectations of women and men.

By the last session, the young women in the group were knowledgeable about gender discrimination, domestic abuse, eating disorders and body image, verbal abuse, rape, date rape, and limitations externally imposed on women's careers and income. The counselor was not sure whether there was any change in the girls' un-ladylike behavior, but she felt that the girls were far more equipped to handle threats to their gender identity and gender discrimination than they had been when the group had started.

Conclusion

Counseling women involves having an understanding of the sociopolitical, economic, and historical contexts that women experience in their lives. The focus on multiculturalism in counseling has been extremely beneficial in increasing awareness of contextual issues. As a profession, the field of counseling and psychotherapy has made enormous progress in serving the population of U.S. women. Unfortunately, there is much more to do before it can be said that the profession offers women the best mental health care possible.

References

American Psychological Association. (2007). *Guidelines for psychological practice with girls and women: A joint task force of APA Divisions 17 and 35*. Retrieved from http://www.apa.org/practice/guidelines/girls-and-women.pdf

Ancis, J., Szymanski, D. M., & Ladany, N. (2008). Development and validation of the Counseling Women Competencies Scale. *The Counseling Psychologist, 36*, 719–744.

Becker, D., & Lamb, S. (1994). Sex bias in the diagnosis of borderline personality disorder. *Professional Psychology: Research and Practice, 25*, 55–61.

Boney-McCoy, S., & Finkelhor, D. (1995). Psychosocial sequelae of violent victimization in a national youth sample. *Journal of Consulting and Clinical Psychology, 63*, 726–727.

Brown, S. L., & May, K. M. (2009). Counseling with women. In C. M. Ellis & J. Carlson (Eds.), *Cross cultural awareness and social justice in counseling* (pp. 61–88). New York, NY: Routledge.

Campenni, E. C. (1999). Gender stereotyping of children's toys: A comparison of parents and nonparents. *Sex Roles, 40,* 121–138.

Danzinger, P. R., & Welfel, E. R. (2000). Age, gender and health bias in counselors: An empirical analysis. *Journal of Mental Health Counseling, 22*(2), 135–149.

Evans, K. M. (2006). Career counseling with couples and families. In D. Capuzzi & M. D. Stauffer (Eds.), *Career counseling: Foundations, perspectives and applications* (pp. 336–359). Boston, MA: Pearson Education.

Evans, K. M. (2010). ACA competencies and women. In M. J. Ratts, R. L. Toporek, & J. A. Lewis (Eds.), *ACA advocacy competencies: A social justice framework for counselors* (pp. 85–96). Alexandria, VA: American Counseling Association.

Evans, K. M., Kincade, E. A., Marbley, A. F., & Seem, S. R. (2005). Feminism and feminist therapy: Lessons from the past and hopes for the future. *Journal of Counseling & Development, 83*, 269–277.

Evans, K. M., Kincade, E. A., & Seem, S. (2011). *Introduction to feminist therapy: Strategies for social and individual change.* Thousand Oaks, CA: Sage.

Health Resources and Services Administration. (2009). *Women and poverty—Women's health USA 2009.* Retrieved from http://mchb.hrsa.gov/whusa09/popchar/pages/104wp.html

Herlihy, B. R., & Watson, Z. P. (2006). Gender issues in career counseling. In D. Capuzzi & M. D. Stauffer (Eds.), *Career counseling: Foundations, perspectives and applications* (pp. 363–385). Boston, MA: Pearson Education.

Homma-True, R., Greene, B., Lopez, S. R., & Trimble, J. (1993). Ethnocultural diversity in clinical psychology. *The Clinical Psychologist, 46*, 50–63.

Hopps, J. A., & Liu, W. M. (2006). Working for social justice from within the health care system: The role of social class in psychology. In R. L. Toporek, L. Gerstein, N. Fouad, & G. Roysircar (Eds.) *Handbook for social justice in counseling psychology* (pp. 318–332). Thousand Oaks, CA: Sage.

Institute for Women's Policy Research. (2010). *The gender wage gap by occupation April 2010.* Retrieved from http://www.iwpr.org/publications/pubs/the-gender-wage-gap-by-occupation-updated-april-2011

Kimerling, R., Ouimette, P., & Wolfe, J. (Eds.). (2002). *Gender and PTSD.* New York, NY: Guilford Press.

Liu, W. M., & Estrada-Hernandez, N. (2010). Counseling and advocacy for individuals living in poverty. In M. J. Ratts, R. L. Toporek, & J. A. Lewis (Eds.), *ACA advocacy competencies: A social justice framework for counselors* (pp. 43–53). Alexandria, VA: American Counseling Association.

Maher, F. A., & Ward, J. V. (2002). *Gender and teaching.* Mahwah, NJ: Erlbaum.

Martin, T. P. (2003). Counseling women with disabilities. In M. Kopala & M. A. Keitel (Eds.), *Handbook of counseling women* (pp. 74–86). Thousand Oaks, CA: Sage.

Perez, M., & Joiner, T. (2003). Body image dissatisfaction and disordered eating in Black and White women. *International Journal of Eating Disorders, 33,* 342–350.

Robinson-Wood, T. L. (2009). *The convergence of race, ethnicity, and gender: Multiple identities in counseling* (3rd ed.). Upper Saddle River, NJ: Pearson Education.

Sandnabba, K. N., & Ahlberg, C. (1999). Parents' attitudes and expectations about children's cross-gender behavior. *Sex Roles, 40,* 249–263.

Seem, S. R., & Clark, M. D. (2006). Healthy women, healthy men, and healthy adults: An evaluation of gender role stereotypes in the 21st century. *Sex Roles, 55,* 247–258.

Sue, D. W., & Sue, D. (2008). *Counseling the culturally diverse: Theory and practice* (4th ed.). Hoboken, NJ: Wiley.

Tjaden, P., & Thoennes, N. (2006). *Extent, nature, and consequences of intimate partner violence: Findings from the National Violence Against Women Survey.* Washington, DC: National Institute of Justice.

U.S. Census Bureau. (2010). *Census Bureau reports nearly 6 in 10 advanced degree holders age 25-29 are women.* Retrieved from http://www.census.gov/Press-Release/www/releases/archives/education/014731.html

U.S. Department of Commerce, Economics and Statistics Administration. (2011). *Women in America: Indicators of social and economic well-being.* Retrieved from http://www.whitehouse.gov/sites/default/files/rss_viewer/Women_in_America.pdf

Vasquez, H., & Magraw, S. (2005). Building relationships across privilege: Becoming an ally in the therapeutic relationship. In M. Mirkin, K. L. Suyemoto, & B. Okun (Eds.), *Psychotherapy with women: Exploring diverse contexts and identities* (pp. 64–83). New York, NY: Guilford Press.

Wester, K., & Trepal, H. (2008). Gender. In G. McAulliffe (Ed.), *Culturally alert counseling: A comprehensive introduction* (pp. 429–465). Thousand Oaks, CA: Sage.

Additional Resources

Books

Julia, M. (Ed.). (2000). *Constructing gender: Multicultural perspectives in working with women.* Belmont, CA: Brooks/Cole.

Kopala, M., & Keitel, M. A. (Eds.). (20003). *Handbook of counseling women.* Thousand Oaks, CA: Sage.

Mirkin, M. P., Suyemoto, K. L., & Okun, B. F. (2005). *Psychotherapy with women: Exploring diverse contexts and identities.* New York, NY: Guilford Press.

Robinson-Wood, T. L. (2009). *The convergence of race, ethnicity, and gender* (3rd ed.). Upper Saddle River, NJ: Merrill.

Worrell, J., & Goodheart, C. (2006). *Handbook of girls' and women's psychological health.* Oxford, England: Oxford University Press.

Worrell, J., & Remer, P. (2003). *Feminist perspectives in therapy* (2nd ed.). Hoboken, NJ: Wiley.

Journals

Psychology of Women Quarterly
Sex Roles
Women and Therapy
Women in Higher Education

Websites

American Association of University Women
www.aauw.org
Association for Women in Psychology
www.awpsych.org/
Institute for Women's Policy Research
www.iwpr.org
Ms. Magazine
www.msmagazine.com
National Organization for Women
www.now.org
National Research Center for Women and Families
www.center4research.org/
Southern Poverty Law Center
www.splcenter.org
Wellesley Centers for Women
www.wcwonline.org

Chapter
11

Combating Ageism: Advocacy for Older Persons

Jane E. Myers and Laura R. Shannonhouse

The aging of populations is a worldwide phenomenon that is "unprecedented, a process without parallel in the history of humanity" (United Nations, 2007, p. xxvi). Although aging is a global phenomenon, in this chapter the focus is on aging in only one country: the United States. The *graying of America* is a term often used to describe demographic changes over the past 100 years that have resulted in older persons no longer being a small and relatively insignificant minority but an increasing and significant minority group within the total population. At the same time, popular use of the term *gray out* suggests a fading into the background that occurs as one grays. These statements suggest two important issues for exploration: The U.S. population is growing older, and growing older may not be a fully positive experience. It is important for counselors to understand these changing demographics from a macro or societal perspective as well as from a micro or individual perspective.

In this chapter, demographic changes in the United States are explored with a focus on the aging of the population and within-group factors that predispose some older persons to significant personal and social risk. The traditional professional counseling response to the graying of America is described. Ageism, an unreasonable prejudice against persons based on chronological age, is discussed in relation to its personal impact on older individuals. The chapter concludes with a consideration from both macro and micro perspectives of recommended strategies and actions for counselors and with suggestions for counselor advocacy and empowerment relative to population aging and the needs of older individuals. The chapter concludes with a case study that demonstrates the application of these suggestions with an older client.

Demographic Changes:
Aging as a Normative Life Experience

Although only 4% of the population of the United States was older than 65 at the turn of the 20th century, more than 12% were in this age group in the year 2000. Increases in the numbers of older persons have become increasingly dramatic, with a 13% increase between 1998 and 2008 compared to a 10.2% increase between 1992 and 2002. By 2030, the older population will have nearly doubled in number from its current 38.9 million and will make up nearly 20% of the population (Administration on Aging, 2009a). As the population ages, the age structure of society is changing as well. The number of older persons will exceed the number of younger persons in the world as a whole within the next few decades and, in the United States, within the next 10 years (United Nations, 2007).

Changes in the numbers of older persons are due to a variety of factors, the most obvious one being that people are living longer. Improved medical care, enhancements in the ability to treat chronic disease, the ability of persons with disabilities to live long and productive lives, the eradication of diseases such as polio, and decreased infant mortality are among the factors that have prolonged the life span. In addition, increased affluence and better public health measures—including controlled water supplies, inspection of foods in grocery stores and restaurants, and universal inoculations against diseases such as tuberculosis and many varieties of the flu—have resulted in a better and healthier standard of living for most persons.

Persons born in the United States in 1900 could expect an average life span of only 47 years. Persons born in 2001 can expect to live to be more than 78 years of age—31 years longer. What is interesting is that a survivorship phenomenon exists with regard to aging, such that the longer a person lives, the longer he or she can expect to live. A person who reached age 65 in 2008 can expect to live an additional 18.6 years, for a total of more than 83 years of life. Gender differences in life expectancy change this figure significantly, such that women who reach age 65 may expect to live another 19.8 years, whereas men can expect to live another 17.1 years (Administration on Aging, 2009b). Life expectancy also varies by race, and at birth Whites may expect to live 6 years longer than Blacks. This discrepancy declines with age, perhaps because Blacks who survive to old age may be healthier than their White counterparts (Administration on Aging, 2009b).

Currently only 8.3% of the older population is African American, compared to approximately 13% of persons younger than 65. About 80.4% of older Americans are Caucasian, 6.8% are Hispanic, and 3.4% are Asian (Administration on Aging, 2009b). Although the reasons for these differences are complex, a history of poverty, lower socioeconomic status, a lifetime of low-paying employment, lack of access to health care, and poor nutrition are among the reasons for shorter life spans among minority populations. Though the proportion of minorities among older Americans is expected to increase, the results of institutional racism do not disappear in the later years but rather are compounded by the stigma associated with advancing age. Those older individuals who have historically been marginalized because of race, ethnicity, gender, sexual orientation, or so on are now part of another stigmatized group and thus experience multiple forms of oppression and trauma. Older ethnic women of color are most vulnerable to access barriers and represent an increasing proportion of client caseloads for those working with older populations (Brotman, 2003).

The statistics cited here underscore the fact that aging has become a normative life experience. What is interesting is that the negative attitudes toward older persons that have been prevalent throughout history remain in the present day (Nelson, 2002). We all have only two choices: growing old or dying young. If we grow old, all of us will be subject to ageism. Ageism is similar in nature to racism, sexism, ableism, and other "-isms" and refers to an unreasonable prejudice toward persons based on their advanced age. Similar to all prejudices, ageism functions to limit the daily lives and optimal potential of persons as they grow older.

In the United States today, individuals may expect to live three fourths or more of their lives as adults and one third to one half as older adults. As a consequence, some counseling clients, or the families of these clients, will inevitably be older individuals. In addition, counselors who do not die young may expect to experience aging as a personal process. Given these facts, it is important to examine how counselors have responded to aging and to consider how they may respond in the future as the older population increases in size and the phenomenon of ageism continues its traditional historical path.

Counseling and Older Persons: A Tradition of Professional Neglect

There has historically been a lack of interest in issues of aging within the counseling profession, which has had significant consequences. For counselors to assume that the ageism so pervasive in U.S. society either does not affect them or does not apply to them represents a very serious form of denial and makes them all contributors to the problems faced by older persons. Denial of aging until one actually experiences it in the midlife decades and beyond seems to be the norm.

Two excellent examples of denial are found in the work of the major theorists Donald Super and Erik Erikson. Super's early and widely used career development theory incorporated five stages of career development: fantasy, exploration, establishment, maintenance, and decline. As Super neared the age of 60, his theory underwent significant changes. What emerged was a life-career rainbow in which a variety of life roles (e.g., student, parent, worker, leisurite) were defined and shown to be active throughout the life span. In talking about these changes over dinner one evening, Super indicated to me (Jane E. Myers) the importance of what people learn about life as they grow older.

Erik Erikson described eight psychosocial stages of life-span development ending with the challenge of ego integrity versus despair. He described this last stage as a time when healthy older persons look back and gain a sense of well-being with the life they have lived and a sense of wisdom relative to the life span and its various challenges. In recent years, research with older persons has suggested that the struggle for integrity is largely resolved in the late 60s and early 70s, which was the end of the life span when Erikson first wrote his theory. When he reached his seventh, eighth, and ninth decades, Erikson began to reconceptualize the later stages of life, suggesting that a stage beyond that of integrity in fact existed. Though this stage of very old age was not fully defined before his death, both Erikson's wife and others continue to speculate on the challenges of the ninth stage relative to autonomy, particularly given the many possible physical challenges of the later years.

Every year or so I (Jane E. Myers) receive a call from an experienced professional counselor who has, early into her (occasionally his) retirement years, become greatly concerned about the problems of aging. She is certain that counselors need to respond and that the way to get this response is to provide training in how to work with older persons. She notes that curriculum materials and videotapes are badly needed. When I express my agreement with her, along with the fact that this very rationale was used successfully between 1977 and 1990 to gain grant funding to develop training materials and projects for counselors (Myers, 1995) and that all of the materials were disseminated to counselor education programs, her response is not one of surprise. Two of the things she will predictably say are "I never heard of your work" and "Isn't that wonderful—but you were ahead of your time. I think people are ready to listen now." Sadly, we have to disagree. People, predictably, have a wonderful capacity for denial, and denial of aging is a major issue in U.S. society. Almost 20 years ago, Crose (1991) alerted counselors to an important issue in work with older persons: that we respond from a personal knowledge base. As a consequence, we as counselors may fail to recognize our own stereotypes and misconceptions as they affect our older clients, we may fail to meet effectively the mental health and counseling needs of older persons and their families, and we may—and often will—fail to recognize or actualize opportunities to advocate for the needs of older persons. Can we afford to wait until we ourselves grow older to begin to recognize and deal with these concerns? We cannot. Ageism affects all of us now, if we recognize that aging is *a part of* the life span, not *apart from* the life span.

Ageism: What, Where, When, How, and Why?

Ageism was defined earlier as an unreasonable prejudice against persons simply because of their chronological age or perceived chronological age. It is important for counselors to understand what ageism is, as well as where, when, how, and why it occurs, as a first step in combating this irrational but pervasive phenomenon.

Ageism: What?

Robert Butler first described ageism in his 1975 Pulitzer Prize–winning book *Why Survive? Being Old in America.* Numerous studies since that time have confirmed the pervasiveness of negative attitudes toward older people. These attitudes have been identified in persons of all ages, including children, adolescents, young and midlife adults, and older persons themselves. Ageism has been found among a variety of health care providers, including nurses, psychologists, psychiatrists, and counselors.

Old age is viewed as a time of undesirable physical, emotional, social, and financial losses. Older persons are viewed as a group living with poverty, disability, and depression. In spite of abundant research establishing that 4 out of 5 older persons live above the poverty level, that more than 95% of older persons live in the community and only about 5% live in institutional settings, and that rates of depression peak in middle rather than later life (Administration on Aging, 2009a), these stereotypes persist. Older persons are mistakenly viewed as being emotional and financial drains on their adult children (most support their adult children emotionally as well as financially), as wanting to live with their adult children (what adult wants to give up his or her independence after a lifetime of being in charge?), as being disinterested in sex (there is no age limit on sexuality), and as being chronically ill (86% of older persons experience one or more chronic physical impairments, yet most are able to live actively and independently). These stereotypes persist in spite of recent research suggesting that most older people age well and that healthy aging, particularly among the young-old (aged 60–75), is the norm. In fact, even many old-old persons (aged 85+) continue to function independently and enjoy life. In general, older persons are resilient in responding to stress, transitions, and change and experience a lower incidence of mental illness than younger persons (Whitbourne, 2010).

An interesting and widely held stereotype supported by clichés such as "You can't teach an old dog new tricks" is that older persons are set in their ways. Research reveals that reaction time slows with age but that intelligence does not decline. Older persons can learn equally well as younger persons, although the pace of learning and learning styles may need to be modified. After all, sorting through a lifetime of accumulated knowledge in the process of assimilating new information certainly requires more time than sorting through only a few years of information.

Research is available to support the perspective that change is unlikely to occur in later life. Dr. Paul Costa of the National Institute on Aging, a well-known and certainly reputable researcher, reported that "by the time people reach 30, their basic personality traits—anxiety, assertiveness, or openness are virtually 'set like plaster'" (p. 21). This somewhat pessimistic view of development seems to argue against the prospects of continued development throughout the life span. If people do not change, what role is there for counselors in working with adults older than 30? Certainly change is difficult at any age, so the basic question that must be asked is whether change is more difficult in later life. We think that as people get older, they become more and more like themselves and less and less like anyone else. If they are set in their ways when they are younger, chances are excellent that they will be this way when they are older. The preponderance of research suggests that personality is consistent with aging, not discontinuous.

The developmental perspective suggests that individuals are capable of change and growth across the life span, even if that change means becoming more firmly who they are. In the process of coping with changing life circumstances, personal change and growth can certainly be an asset. Those who fail to cope, or who continue to try to resolve new problems with old, tried-and-true but no longer effective coping resources, are likely to be among the older persons who could benefit most from counseling interventions. From an ageist perspective, believing that older persons cannot change relieves service providers of the challenge of trying to help them change. However, multiple studies of mental health interventions have revealed that older persons have the capacity for change and continued growth regardless of chronological age factors (see Myers & Harper, 2004, for a review of these studies).

Ageism: Where, When, How?

Ageism is both formal and informal, obvious and subtle. Formal aspects of ageism, such as mandatory retirement ages in some professions, are easier to identify. I (Jane E. Myers) am a private pilot who frequently attends aviation training seminars and reads aviation publications. One of the most important characteristics of a safe pilot is the ability to exercise good judgment in dealing with the aviation environment, from weather to mechanical systems to navigation to air traffic control. Judgment, from all accounts, is gained only through experience. Thus, it remains an enigma why until 2007 federal legislation mandated that airline pilots, whose reflexes may have slowed a tiny bit from the aging process but whose competence as defined by judgment is at an all-time career high, retire at the age of 60—with an estimated 20 years of useful life remaining! In 2007, the federal government finally responded to advocacy efforts and raised the retirement age of pilots to 65.

How many counselors are aware of and responsive to legislation concerning child abuse in their state? The answer should be 100%. Among these same counselors, how many are familiar with the mandatory laws regarding elder abuse, which also exist in each state? How about the laws concerning grandparent visitation rights or age discrimination in employment (which extends to persons between the ages of 40 and 70)? The fact that the mental health system gives far greater attention to the needs of younger persons rather than older persons reflects the pervasive lack of public awareness of and support for programs for the older population. This is a form of ageism.

The prejudices held by health care providers likewise limit the choices of older persons. Managed care is a particular case in point because medical treatment and hospital-stay limitations are based on studies with younger persons, who heal more quickly and require larger doses of medication. Many of the medical problems and dementias of older persons are thus iatrogenic, or physician induced, such as when prescriptions calibrated for use with young persons (usually males in their 20s) are prescribed for older persons. Fortunately, these problems can be alleviated or reversed with proper medical care, especially under the treatment of trained geriatric physicians.

Family, friends, and neighbors of older persons—the informal support network—are also a source of ageism that acts to limit the lives of older people. Family members often are among the first to suggest to older people that they "can't do that!" at their age. Well-meaning loved ones overprotect, interpret the thoughts of older persons, expect them to accept the "facts of aging," and charge them with getting old if they cannot remember a name or forget where they placed their keys. The same actions of a younger person cause few if any reactions from the same family members. When younger persons express a legitimate distaste for life when circumstances are undesirable, friends may suggest counseling or offer empathy. When the person is older, the same behavior often results in a label of *cranky*.

Ageism is reflected in words, deeds, and actions. It is reflected in the things people do for older persons (e.g., speaking louder or slower than normal to be sure one is heard and/ or understood), their responses to older persons (e.g., becoming visibly frustrated when standing behind them in the grocery line, even though they may experience the same wait behind a mother with small children but not feel annoyed), and the things they fail to do with regard to older persons (e.g., consider them for paid tasks, not just volunteer work opportunities). Whenever people make choices and perform actions based on age, they may have succumbed to ageism.

A special note is necessary concerning the use of language to instill ageist attitudes, beliefs, and behaviors. This is a subtle and extremely pervasive means for the perpetuation of negative stereotypes about older persons. The most prominent example of the use of language in this manner is found in the frequently used term *the elderly*. The elderly implies that all persons who are elderly share some common characteristic or characteristics, usually with negative connotations as discussed earlier. The elderly are often seen as frail, ill, rigid, slow, boring, forgetful, and depressed. In actuality, there are more than 35 million Americans in this age category, and what they share in common is largely a function of chronological age. It could be said that the elderly population is composed of persons aged 65 and older, or aged 60 and older, or whatever chronological age, and that statement would be correct. Other statements concerning *the* elderly run the risk of being accurate for only a portion of the older population. Thus, use of the term *the elderly* functions to stereotype, label, categorize, and, in many instances, degrade the lives of older persons.

Johnson (1996) found the word *elderly* to be

> dangerous in the sense that armies of elders can ingest the word and start thinking of themselves as "the elderly" rather than as potent, respectful, and quite independent persons of worth . . . costly as well as dangerous . . . by relegating perfectly good elders to the ranks of something less than useful; dependent and generally incapable. Such imputations subvert one's sense of self and contribute to the flight toward a legitimate, but most dependent social role, the role of patient. (pp. 9, 13)

The good news is that in 2001 the American Psychological Association finally took a stand on this issue and observed in its popular style manual that "*Elderly* is not acceptable as a noun and is considered pejorative by some as an adjective" (p. 69). The power of language cannot be overemphasized. The point has been made that many negative attributes are associated with terms such as *aged, elderly,* and *old.* It is noteworthy that older persons who perceive themselves to be younger than their chronological age, either physically or mentally, report that they feel better and perceive their health status to be better than persons of the same age who self-identify as old. Chronological age is not the issue; rather, subjective age is what seems to correlate with positive mental health and wellness (Degges-White & Myers, 2006).

Ageism: Why?

Perhaps ageism simply results from human nature. People fear what they do not understand, and the processes of aging are not well understood. People also know more about older persons in institutional settings because those who are independent are far more difficult to access and to study. Those in institutional environments tend to be the most frail older persons and those who experience the most serious and disabling conditions. It should not be surprising that the association of aged and disabled results in fears of aging being equated with fears of disability. Thus, most studies of older persons reveal that fear of the loss of independence is the greatest fear associated with aging.

Furthermore, in the dominant Western culture, the principle of independence is highly valued, being part of the American mythos of rugged individualism. A society that prizes one's ability to make it on one's own would naturally devalue those who are unable to do so. This cultural predisposition toward youth emerges as ageism and can be even more damaging to older persons of minority groups that identify with different cultural norms (Sokolovsky, 1997). In addition, although death may be denied as a relatively remote prospect in the younger years, for older persons it increasingly becomes a reality. Fears of death contribute to fears of aging, the aging process, and being old.

Competition for resources and roles between persons of different ages or generations contributes to ageism. For example, the media frequently note that the Social Security system is running out of money, so younger persons who are paying Social Security taxes today are unlikely to benefit from this fund in their later years in terms of pensions. At the same time, the media note that today's older persons, who are living longer than was expected, are drawing a disproportionate share of Social Security funds. Younger persons reading this information cannot help but reflect on the implication that they are paying for the lifestyles of the older generation while facing an uncertain future with regard to funding their own later years. Yet such concerns are not unique to the United States. In early 2010, Greece's financial problems forced fellow European countries to bail them out economically. This was a hard sell in Germany and other nations, as the Greek retirement age of 61 is 6 years younger than the German norm of 67 years.

Predominant social values that place a high priority on full-time, paid employment also contribute to ageism. Retirement constitutes a loss of employment, and retired persons are viewed, often unconsciously, as unemployed. Thus, the retired role, although not well defined, is also not highly valued.

Tornstam (2006) outlined a typology of ageism and distinguished among its forms. He considered two dimensions: a positive (negative) attitude toward the old and knowledge (or lack thereof) about older persons. Ageism then is not merely an active or socialized prejudice but a passive, pervasive outlook that stems from an unawareness of the reality of aging and older persons. It is not merely chronological age that fuels ageist ideas but also ignorance, financial pressures, and a social system that equates employment and independence with prestige.

Nonageism: The Alternative

What alternatives does U.S. culture have to the current ageist state of affairs? There are other ways of being that value older persons and respect their wisdom and life experience (Edmondson & Kondratowitz, 2009). The dominant Western culture can grow by interacting with and acknowledging what other cultures have to offer with regard to older persons and aging. For example, deferential respect toward older persons is a significant behavior pattern in many Eastern cultures, including Korea (Sung, 2004). Older minority populations exhibit resiliency and have many strengths (Bahr, 1994; Strom, Collinsworth, Strom, & Griswold, 1992–1993). Americans can learn from other cultural heritages. As counselors, we aim to benefit all persons, young and old. Abraham Heschel (1996) argued that a true test of a people is how they behave toward the old. He said that it is easy to love children; even tyrants and dictators make a point of being fond of children. However, affection and care for the old, the incurable, and the helpless are the true gems of a culture.

Self-Fulfilling Prophecies: The Personal Impact of Ageism

Although it is important to understand the dynamics of negative social attitudes toward older persons, any discussion of ageism is incomplete without a consideration of the personal impact of social devaluation. A variety of authors (e.g., Lee, 1997; Sue & Sue, 1990) have explained in detail the processes of minority identity development. These authors have postulated that persons who belong to minority groups tend to internalize the predominant social perceptions of their group. Older persons are newfound members of a minority group. It is normal for them to have internalized the predominant societal views of aging for a lifetime before growing older. These negative thoughts directed at the self are manifest in self-doubt (Edmondson & Kondratowitz, 2009) and other thought patterns.

The consequences of internalizing negative attitudes include both a dislike of one's peers and lower self-esteem. Older persons may fail to develop relationships with their age peers and may become isolated because they prefer not to associate with "those old people." When they internalize negative societal beliefs about older persons, a sense of personal devaluation, vulnerability, and a decreased sense of self-efficacy are likely to result. When they begin to question their abilities, they may withdraw from normal activities and associations, which can further lower self-esteem. This process can become cyclical and devastating.

The social breakdown process, first described by Kuypers and Bengtson (1973), explains how ageism creates a climate in which older persons can be devalued and in which normal responses result in social and psychological withdrawal and decline. At the same time, this process implies a variety of interventions that have the potential to interrupt, halt, or even reverse this process. Prevention, undertaken from both individual and societal perspectives and across the life span, offers the potential for a better quality of life for older persons. All forms of prevention—primary (prevention of problems), secondary (early detection and remediation), tertiary (restoration of function), and quaternary (avoidance of the consequences of excessive institutional intervention)—are essential when addressing the needs of older adults.

Action Strategies for Counselors

Counselors are uniquely positioned to have a positive impact on the lives of older persons. As developmentalists, counselors recognize and support the possibility of positive growth across the life span. We also recognize and are able to respond to the needs of all individuals for assistance in coping with the normal circumstances of life, including career entry, career change, retirement, second careers, marriage, divorce, remarriage, parenting, and grandparenting. What is important is the arena in which we choose to apply these skills. Here we recommend a dual approach that includes both a macro or societal perspective that views the counselor as an agent for social change and an individual approach that views the counselor as a change agent on a personal level for others.

The Macro Perspective: Advocacy and Empowerment

Empowerment refers to actions intended to help people help themselves or to create personal power, whereas *advocacy,* as used here, refers to actions taken on behalf of others to ensure that empowerment does in fact occur. What is important in bringing these two actions together is the intended outcome: to create environments in which individuals are able to live their lives effectively and with a sense of well-being, in which they can choose to change themselves and/or their life circumstances to achieve their goals to live life more fully. Three aspects of environmental change that counselors can affect directly are policies, services, and accurate information.

Empowerment and Advocacy Through Policies

Laws and policies at all levels can affect the quality of life of older persons. Examples were provided earlier of mandatory retirement laws, elder abuse laws, and grandparent visitation laws. Numerous other examples could be provided. Counselors need to examine laws and policies in all settings with a consideration of the needs of persons across the life span. Where laws are restrictive, outdated, or nonexistent, advocacy for change is needed.

Working with policy makers and legislators must be a priority. Counselors can contribute to discussions on job sharing, second career training, phased retirement, older worker skills, and a variety of additional issues that affect quality of life and opportunities for older persons, but only if they make themselves part of the decision-making process. As they view the needs of older persons through a systemic lens, counselors must share with policy makers the institutional and pervasive problems of access and opportunity for older persons in general and minority elders in particular. The lack of recognition of the need for formal services for minority older persons must be addressed (Brotman, 2003). Counselors need to support legislation and policies that enhance the rights of older persons and help to defeat or replace policies that limit the rights of older persons. Those rights, first identified with the passage of the Older Americans Act (OAA) in 1965, are relevant today (see Appendix 11.1). That act continues to set national policy for older Americans. Counselors need to have a presence with lawmakers when the OAA is reauthorized. Although the OAA includes provisions for counseling, it only specifies legal counseling, nutrition counseling, and health counseling. Professional counseling can and should be added.

In 1977, the American Counseling Association introduced a set of proposed revisions to the OAA titled the "Older Persons Comprehensive Counseling Assistance Act of 1977." This act proposed many things, including a national clearinghouse of information on counseling services for older persons, the creation of state plans to provide counseling services, grants to states to provide counseling assistance, grants to train counselors to work with older people, and research to identify and develop effective services and programs to meet the mental health and counseling needs of older people. Though the act was never approved, the repeated introduction of this legislation served as a means of advocacy both for professional counselors and for the older population. Perhaps at some point this legislation may be in reintroduced with greater success. It is encouraging to note that the national climate for health care is changing, prevention and wellness have become national priorities, and 2008 saw the passage of legislation that places mental health on parity with physical health. Although this victory is vital for the counseling field, professional counselors must continue placing pressure on decision makers at all levels to include the needs of older persons in their deliberations.

Empowerment and Advocacy Through Services

If older persons are to experience the benefits of preventive and remedial mental health services, counselors need to be trained and available to work with them. In the absence of federal legislation mandating gerontological counselor training, it is up to *counselors* to ensure that their field is prepared to address the needs of this population.

Because training opportunities for counselors in gerontological issues are limited, counselors need to approach decision makers in the educational arena: counselor educators and educational administrators. Any time we as counselors get a chance to fill out a professional development needs assessment form or comment on the quality of education we received from our alma mater, we are presented with an opportunity to say we need more training to work with older persons.

Counselor educators are in a unique position to advocate for enhanced counselor training. Educators can revise existing curricula to include more courses and curricular units specific to life-span and later life issues. In addition, to promote the infusion model, counselor educators can take care in choosing texts for core courses that include aging issues. To do so will send messages to publishers and textbook authors that life-span concerns must be incorporated into effective counselor training (Myers, 1995).

Although it is important to both train counselors for work with older persons and encourage the accreditation of training programs for specialty training and certification of gerontological counselors, these measures will result in discouraged counselor education program graduates if the job market does not provide opportunities for employment commensurate with their training. Social services for older persons grew out of welfare programs for older and disabled persons. These programs traditionally were staffed by social workers. Hence, it is not surprising that many jobs in the aging network list social work training and credentials as prerequisites, and many of these positions are legislatively mandated or enabled. For example, each state has laws relating to long-term-care facilities, formerly known as *nursing homes*. These laws uniformly require that facilities employ social workers, not counselors.

Counselors, especially gerontological counselors, are relative newcomers to the field of services for older persons. They cannot expect automatic acceptance, especially when positions are legislatively controlled. Advocacy with legislators and employers in the community, such as community mental health centers, must take place to ensure that counselors are hired in positions earmarked for geriatric mental health providers. The crossover between training, credentialing, and advocacy is increasingly evident here: Counselors cannot present themselves as the best trained professionals for such positions in the absence of strong training programs, accreditation, and certification to document their claims.

Adequate training is a first step, but counselors must daily promote the rights and needs of older persons if they truly seek to advocate. Promoting agency for this population should be a major focus of counselors' work (Jolanki, 2009). How is the agency of older clients inhibited or promoted by their social or physical environment, health, and other people? To address these questions, counselors must view older adults' context with a systemic lens and respond through advocacy as they discover answers. They may even revisit the concept of agency as a cultural construct and reevaluate the current medical focus of the dialogue about older persons (Jolanki, 2009). They can be at the forefront of a new discourse, challenging societal and family systems for the benefit of their older clients. In addition, in order to provide effective mental health interventions for older persons and their families, counselors require a comprehensive knowledge base relative to this population (Myers, 1989, 1995).

Empowerment and Advocacy Through Accurate Information

The fact that all older persons are not alike has been established; but what *are* older persons like? Enough is known about this population to define at least three subsets of older persons—young-old, middle-old, and old-old—with some lifestyle and health issues marking the differences between the three groups. Ethnic and cultural differences within the older population are significant, and many of the problems of ageism are less apparent or not relevant for older minority individuals within the family and cultural environment. But these individuals are placed in a situation of double jeopardy, being subject simultaneously to the effects of isms related to age as well as race. The addition of disabling conditions, gender, and sexual orientation as factors increases the potential negative effects of discrimination.

Counseling practices must be informed with accurate information. Support for research on effective interventions and outcomes for older persons is essential. To the extent that older persons are like persons of other ages, counseling research will inform work with this population. However, there is some indication that strategies and techniques vary in their effectiveness with older people and that some interventions may be more effective at certain times and with certain older persons (see Myers & Harper, 2004, for a discussion of evidence-based practice with older persons). Outcome research studies are essential if counselors are to learn what works, when, with which older persons experiencing which conditions, and under what circumstances. Counselors also need to develop interventions that help older persons conceptualize and develop lifestyles oriented toward health and wellness in their later years.

Although the focus of this chapter is on living well, death and dying are a part of the aging process. Persons who are dying have unique needs. Byock (1997) stated that everyone needs to be loved, to be forgiven, and to have the opportunity to say goodbye. Other common needs are to have one's values and oneself respected or honored and to be treated with dignity. Those who are dying will also likely need to have special loved ones near, to have quality of life, and to experience a certain level of comfort. Furthermore, some of the needs of those who are dying are unique to the individual and are shaped by enculturation. Diversity and end of life is a new field of research; physicians and nurses in hospital contexts are educating themselves about different cultures and how they view the end of life so they can be more responsive (Doka & Tucci, 2009). Counselors must learn from and work with older persons.

The Micro Perspective: The Counselor as Change Agent

Someone has to implement the strategies for reducing the effects of ageism just discussed, and that someone could be a professional counselor. To be effective as advocates for social change, counselors must first determine their own needs for attitudinal change. Then, in addition to receiving training to prepare them for work with older individuals and groups, counselors may find opportunities to advocate on an individual basis for older persons.

Counselor: Know Thyself

As members of an ageist society, counselors are likely to hold negative views of older persons or negative perceptions of the potential of older clients for growth and change. It is imperative that they explore those attitudes prior to beginning work with older clients. Awareness training can be obtained at professional conferences as well as in graduate coursework. This training needs to include adequate opportunity for personal exploration and discussion in a safe environment, with group members available to gently challenge one another's mistaken beliefs and perceptions about older clients. Counselors also need to explore their own fears and feelings about the processes of growing older and death and dying. Again, this may occur in professional training settings or through individual or group counseling.

Everyone seeks to make meaning of their own lives, and as they grow older, these existential needs tend to come to the fore. Counselors must help older clients explore these questions, and in the process they must address them for themselves. Consider the opportunity for personal growth that accompanies working with clients who have accumulated a lifetime of life experience. In the continuous process of human development, people strive toward a meaningful life and an understanding of their past and future (Edmondson & Kondratowitz, 2009). There is the potential for a reciprocal exchange as counselors can learn from their older clients while they work with them on their own journey.

Those who work with older persons need to examine their motivations to ensure that their goal is to empower, not to patronize or to do for older people what they seemingly cannot accomplish for themselves. If we as counselors find that we feel sorry for our older clients, it will be hard to help them. If transference is an issue, in that many of our older clients remind us of an older relative or friend, then we are likely to be unable to accept our clients as individuals and to respect them enough to confront their issues caringly and challenge them to continue to grow. If we tend to treat all older persons alike, then we may be experiencing transference. If we think all older persons are like the ones we know best, then we are likely to be engaging in stereotyping and ageism—for better or for worse. As part of our professional development as counselors, we should meet, learn about, and work with a variety of older persons, those who are independent as well as those who are frail or ill. Finally, we need to examine our language when we speak with and about older persons. The words we use, the phrases we choose, and the intonations we unconsciously use reflect the real meaning behind what we say. We need to become more aware of what we say, how we say it, and what we truly mean. We should avoid words or phrases that demean (*old maid, old codger, old fool, over the hill, has-been*), patronize (*cute, sweet, dear, little*), or stereotype (*passive, dependent, nagging, shrewish, dirty old man, grumpy old woman, leech, deaf, dentured, fragile, frail, withered, doddering*). Some suggestions for revising our language so as to avoid stereotyping older persons are found in Table 11.1. These suggestions require and can result in significant attitudinal changes,

Table 11.1 • How to Say Things in a Nonageist Way

Ageist Statement	Nonageist Statement
At 72, she is confused, apathetic, withdrawn, taking no interest in anything.	All her life she has been confused, apathetic, withdrawn, taking no interest in anything. No wonder she's that way at 72.
What does an old man like that want with a sports car?	Now that his children are on their own, he can have that sports car he has always wanted.
That man she's with must be half her age!	Men of all ages find her attractive.
Ask my grandmother. I'm sure she'll do it. She always has plenty of time!	Ask my grandmother. She always tries to make time to help others.

Note. Adapted from *Truth About Aging: Guidelines for Publishers,* by the AARP, 1984, Washington, DC: Author.

thus helping to reduce ageist beliefs and attitudes for counselors and for those with whom we interact when speaking with and about older persons.

Advocacy: Daily Opportunities to Be an Agent for Change

Everyone has opportunities on a daily basis to be advocates for change. Counselors need to become more aware of these opportunities and take advantage of them on behalf of themselves and their older clients. When faced with recommending persons for positions—paid as well as volunteer—or recommending members of advisory and governing boards, counselors have a choice to recommend only those who are younger or to include those who are older. When they decide for older persons that they would not be interested, would not want to use their time in a particular manner, would not have the energy, or would not be able to present new and creative ideas, then they must catch themselves being ageist and take a different approach. Perhaps it is the older persons counselors know personally who are not appropriate choices. If so, the problem could be that they do not know enough older persons to make such choices. Counselors may need to broaden their social and professional networks and actively create opportunities to interact with a variety of older people. To do so will enrich their lives as well as the older adults' lives.

As we have argued, counselors can be more intentional in their outreach efforts by going into communities, offering services, and promoting the agency of older persons. And clinicians must capitalize on the research, resources, and programs already in place. But at a fundamental level, the youth-obsessed dominant culture needs to undergo a paradigm shift, and counselors have an opportunity to affect individuals as well as advance the field (Rollins, 2008). Such a collective realignment begins by counselors looking at themselves and their own assumptions, biases, and personal narratives about the aging process to develop genuine empathy, better understand the unique needs of the aging person, and engage in modeling. Instead of being stuck in the existing negative social mindset on aging, counselors should take a page from Edmondson and Kondratowitz (2009) and think in terms of *successful aging* and *active aging*. The following case demonstrates many of these concepts.

Working With an Older Client: A Case Study

Counselors have used psychodynamic, cognitive behavior, behavioral, family systems, and group counseling, among many other approaches, to work with older persons. Coping skills development, assertiveness training, career transition or retirement planning and preparation, early recollections (ERs), lifestyle assessment, and using pets or animals to foster connection are just a few techniques (Myers, 1989). Drawing an age-line helps people review significant points in their life stream and identify their challenges; it is a strengths-based technique that provides insight into clients' coping skills. Autoethnography is a narrative tool in which clients are given space to tell their life stories and explore what meaning they make of the whole. Some autoethnographical approaches even involve a cultural partner, which enables deeper understanding from shared cultural heritage (Douthit, Santiago, & Garrick, 2009). Although there are a myriad of ways to effectively work with older persons, here we focus on the use of the Adlerian lifestyle assessment (Sweeney, 2009) in conjunction with ERs (Clark, 2001, 2002).

In addition to fostering trust and building the counselor–client relationship, ERs invite older persons to talk openly about their childhood experiences. Frequently, older persons would rather spend time in the past than in their current emotional and psychological state. Recalling ERs is often perceived by older persons as an acknowledgement of their wisdom and an expression of interest in their well-being (Allers, White, & Hornbuckle, 1990;

Clark, 2001, 2002; Sweeney & Myers, 1986). Using ERs creates space to explore one's early memories, which gives direct insight into how one functions in daily life. Therefore, this case study depicts how to use ERs to understand the ways in which clients make meaning, which is an important beginning step in the counseling process. Helping clients understand and make meaning of their ERs is also a respectful (Mosak & Kopp, 1973) and culturally responsive way of understanding from the clients' perspective.

ERs are obtained by asking the client to relate his or her earliest memory of an event. This can be done in conjunction with an Adlerian lifestyle assessment; ERs are often elicited in this process and are used to explore the meaning clients make of childhood experiences. The counselor needs to retrieve at least three ERs so that he or she can identify patterns and main themes. Counselors also seek detail in the ERs, making sure to identify the emotions (felt at the time of the memory), persons present, colors, sounds, smells, and so on.

Description of the Client and the Adlerian Lifestyle Assessment

Elaine is a 60-year-old high-functioning kindergarten teacher. She has been married for 36 years and has one daughter. Elaine used to enjoy teaching; however, her students' emotional and behavioral needs have become increasingly more challenging, and support from the administration is nonexistent. Exceptional student education classes are no longer offered, and she no longer has a teacher's aide. Children who would otherwise attend exceptional student education classes stay in the classroom, and teachers do not have the specialized training to adequately respond to their needs. Resources (i.e., the computer lab, art, physical education, and music) have been cut to make room for new staff who frequently observe classrooms, providing critical evaluation. Elaine reports feeling "negativity" all around her. Her students have traditionally excelled, scoring several standard deviations above the mean for their grade level; Elaine has been identified as a master teacher and currently serves as a mentor to a new teacher with whom she coteaches every day. Elaine said, "Although I like working with her, it is an added stress, as I'm responsible for her progress." Although Elaine's skills have been identified as outstanding, she does not feel like she has a voice in her system.

Elaine finds the constant updating of standards and routine testing overwhelming. She said, "Over and over we have a whole new set of things to implement, color coding children's drawings, new ways of giving feedback, different ways to evaluate—it's ridiculous! I have to check this and check that, it's like the Gestapo. They take all the fun out of teaching! I've been teaching for over 30 years, I know how to teach, but I can't say anything. I feel like a sausage, they just keep stuffing in more and more and pretty soon I'm going to pop! I'm looking forward to retiring!"

In addition to the stress of her current context, Elaine's upbringing was painful, as her mother died when she was 16 after being sick for several years. When she was 3, Elaine went to live with her grandmother, then at age 6 she went to live with her brothers, sisters, and father while her mother was in a different town. Elaine had limited contact with her mother and reports that she took off work when raising her own daughter because she wanted her daughter to have the connections with her mother that she herself did not have. Elaine's father was a provider but was not involved. In fact, he was controlling and abusive toward her mother and others.

During the Adlerian lifestyle assessment, I (Laura R. Shannonhouse) began to understand how Elaine viewed herself in relation to her siblings (Patricia, Jenny, Todd, and Mack); she was the youngest of five. Elaine did what she was supposed to do, she wanted people to get along, and most of all she wanted to be included. She could entertain herself and found many things interesting. She did not view herself as particularly smart or pretty; she would say that she was "okay." Today Elaine struggles with her self-esteem and questions whether she is a good person. These themes are reflected in her ERs, of which we obtained nine (see Table 11.2). Understanding the meaning behind ERs requires looking for themes and patterns and metaphors for how the client views life, self, and others. These themes are then related to present-day issues.

As seen in her ERs, when Elaine is alone she feels lonely, deserted, not good enough, shocked, sad, chastised, and confused. Elaine's ERs with her brothers reflect feeling scared, afraid, guilty, and being in pain. She feels connected, warm, close, safe, and that she matters in the ERs that involve her sisters and her grandparents. Today Elaine hates being alone; one of her fears is that she will die alone. She struggles to trust men and people in general. In a follow-up session, we might explore these themes to further understand her private logic.

When thinking about what this lifestyle assessment was like for her, Elaine said, "I am okay, others are okay, and life is okay." After a minute or so, she began to cry, and when asked what feelings were coming up, she said sadness and pain. She said, "Life isn't fair." Things are not what she had imagined or had hoped for. Elaine has found ways to exist in the world at a highly functional rate; however, she struggles with self-esteem, self-concept, loneliness, and, from time to time, depression. Being separated from her nuclear family so early in life certainly impacts her today, and it should not be surprising that she struggles with separation and attachment in relationships.

Action Strategies to Help Elaine

Accurate information about older adults is readily available. Counselors willing to confront ageist stereotypes will find this information useful in working with any older individual. We encourage counselors to seek continuing education to learn more about older clients, to prepare for their own aging, and to prepare to help older persons and their families. A major finding will be that older adults are reluctant to seek counseling. Thus, Elaine is unlikely to reach out to counselors in her community. From an advocacy perspective, counselors need to reach out to her.

Earlier we stressed the need for advocacy and empowerment through services. Counseling services for older adults are notably lacking in most communities, and most counselors are unprepared to deal with the needs of older adult clients. Helping Elaine find a counselor who understands her needs and how best to work with her may be exceptionally difficult if not impossible. Is it necessary for a counselor to have training in gerontological issues to be able to intervene successfully in this instance? The answer has to be no, or the outlook will be bleak. Any counselor should be able to work with Elaine, as a woman, a teacher, a mother, a daughter, a sibling. Counselors who are uncertain about their ability to help such a client may find that group interventions in which older age peers are present can help clients like Elaine connect with others, experience a sense of support for shared experiences and challenges, and work together to overcome negative thought patterns and develop new coping strategies to use in their daily lives.

From a macro perspective, counselors need to consider how to help clients experience a sense of personal power. Elaine feels powerless in her current job and in her personal relationships. She may in fact not be empowered in the educational system. Educators as well as administrators are struggling to address the needs of younger persons today, as reflected in the high burnout rate among teachers. The National Commission on Teaching

Table 11.2 • Early Recollections From the Case Study of Elaine

Age	Recollection	Feelings	Alone or With Others
3[a]	I remember leaving my family to live with my grandmother. I wasn't happy about it, when it happened, and now all I was only around was an old lady and an old man.	Lonely, deserted, not good enough to be with my family	Alone
4	Patricia and Jenny dressed me up, took pictures of me.	Pretty, important, that I mattered	With others— sisters
3–5	I sat on B's [step-grandfather's] lap . . . he scraped the apple with a knife . . . and he took a bite, and then he scraped the apple again and give me a bite . . . he didn't have enough teeth.	Close, warm, and safe	With others— grandfather
3–5	B and I went into the woods every day to check the rabbit traps, we also searched for "bean poles" [straight sticks] . . . we put them in the wagon, and went downtown to sell the poles to the ladies for their string beans . . . so they would crawl up the pole, B gave me money from selling the bean poles and we went shopping . . .	Appreciated, it was interesting, I loved go- ing out and doing the rabbit traps	With others— grandfather
3–5	I remember the first time my grandmother killed a chicken, by wringing its neck, it walked around, the blood shooting out of its neck . . . I fed the chickens and talked to the chickens . . .	Shocked, it felt like losing a pet	Alone
7	Dad came home and was questioning Mother about Patricia, we were in the bed, when all this happened . . . my father became very angry with mother and we were all so scared that my brothers came in my bedroom and got me and we went outside and hid . . . there was a lot of screaming and loud noises, the next day we saw she had a split lip, black eye, broken teeth.. . .	Scared, guilty that we didn't do anything	With others— brothers
7 or 8	Mr. S's grandson came to visit and Mack and Todd just wouldn't stop teasing me, and so I picked up what I thought was a clod of dirt and threw it at them (as they were running away) . . . it split the back of the neighbor's head, there was blood . . . it was really meant for Todd . . . we ran back to our house and I hid behind the couch, because they were saying, "They are coming to get you" . . .	Terrified, afraid I was in trouble	With others— brothers
7	Todd told me to go to the other side of the water with the fish hook, so I was walking, being the good little girl, and the line became tighter and tighter and as soon as I let go, it went right into my finger, so we went home and my father pushed the hook through to the other side.	Pain, scary, not knowing	With others— brothers
8	One day on the playground, the bossiest girl in the class matched me up with the ugly boy, because I had freckles and he did to . . . she was matching people up with who she thought they should be matched with . . .	Hurt, sad, this isn't right that she is doing this, who does she think she is?	With others— classmates

[a]Earliest recollection.

and America's Future (2003) confirmed that teacher turnover has become a national crisis. Many respond to the stresses of teaching by leaving. Older teachers nearing retirement have fewer options. Even if unhappy, they cannot leave their jobs. Feeling trapped can lead to anxiety, depression, and decreased effectiveness in one's professional roles. Someone like Elaine who already has difficulty in relationships may be even more impaired.

From a policy perspective, a counselor might intervene with Elaine's school system to implement an employee assistance program in which teachers can feel free to discuss their struggles and connect with an internal advocate who can help create needed change. Perhaps this advocate can work with and on behalf of teachers, bringing their concerns to both the administration and the county. In addition to the myriad school reform models, some policies are being implemented in which teachers will be paid according to their children's progress and not the services provided. This policy places stress on the system: School counselors must be able to think systemically about these types of concerns and how they are impacting all of the stakeholders. It is hoped that school counselors can partner with administrative staff to give teachers a voice and to foster an encouraging and collaborative experience in which people feel that their voices are important and that they matter.

Counselors can offer personal counseling, group counseling, and psychoeducational services. Elaine may be reluctant to seek counseling but may willingly participate in a psychoeducational group designed to help teachers cope with changing generations of students and parents and changing requirements of the educational system. No doubt she would quickly find that other teachers share her concerns and challenges. Through positive reframing, perhaps she and her colleagues could reconnect with some of the joys of teaching and the reasons they were drawn to this work. Certainly all would experience some sense of shared perspective and social support. The importance of social support in relation to positive mental health cannot be overstated.

Elaine may benefit from both individual and group counseling to help her cope with her life circumstances, but in the absence of systemic intervention it is unlikely that her day-to-day stressors will change noticeably, and the overlap of aging and her lack of empowerment will continue to create challenges to adjusting to the changing circumstances of later life. The counselor can use Elaine's ERs to help her understand the significance of connected relationships in her life and help her find ways outside of her teaching roles to develop, sustain, and enjoy relationships with family and friends. This support will be essential during her final years of work and her transition to retirement.

Conclusion

The effects of ageism, or prejudice against older persons, are pervasive. Negative attitudes and stereotypes function to deny older persons the right to engage fully in the benefits of life in the United States, demeaning their sense of self-efficacy and resulting in a lower overall quality of life. Ageism is perpetuated by individuals as well as organizations.

Counselors have vital roles to play as change agents working both with and on behalf of older persons. They need to view themselves as advocates who can effect change in laws, policies, and society. At the same time, they can help older persons live more effective lives through the use of developmental interventions aimed at helping each person live life more fully throughout the life span. To be effective agents of change, counselors first need to examine their own personal beliefs and biases and develop healthy, respectful, positive, wellness-enhancing attitudes toward older persons. Because aging is a universal experience, all efforts to assist this population will result in significant personal as well as professional gains. Counselors will realize the ultimate benefits both vicariously as they watch their clients change and grow and personally as they themselves experience the joys and challenges of the processes of aging.

References

AARP. (1984). *Truth about aging: Guidelines for publishers.* Washington, DC: Author.

Administration on Aging. (2009a). *A profile of older Americans.* Retrieved from http://www.aoa.gov/prof/AoARoot/Aging_Statistics/Profile/2009/docs/2009profile_508.pdf

Administration on Aging. (2009b). *A statistical profile of Black older Americans aged 65+.* Retrieved from http://www.aoa.gov/AoARoot/Aging_Statistics/minority_aging/Facts-on-Black-Elderly2009-plain_format.aspx

Allers, C. T., White, J., & Hornbuckle, D. (1990). Early recollections: Detecting depression in the elderly. *Journal of Individual Psychology, 46*(1), 61–66.

American Psychological Association. (2001). *Publication manual of the American Psychological Association* (5th ed.). Washington, DC: Author.

Bahr, K. (1994). The strengths of Apache grandmothers: Observations on commitment, culture, and caretaking. *Journal of Comparative Family Studies, 25*(2), 233–248.

Brotman, S. (2003). The limits of multiculturalism in elder care services. *Journal of Aging Studies, 17,* 209–229.

Butler, R. (1975). *Why survive? Being old in America.* New York, NY: Harper & Row.

Byock, I. (1997). *Dying well, peace and possibilities at the end of life.* New York, NY: Berkeley.

Clark, A. (2001). Early recollections: A humanistic assessment in counseling. *Journal of Humanistic Counseling, Education and Development, 40,* 96–105.

Clark, A. J. (2002). *Early recollections: Theory and practice in counseling and psychotherapy.* New York, NY: Brunner-Routledge.

Costa, P. T. , & McCrae, R. R. (1964). Set like plaster? Evidence for the stability of adult personality. In T. F. Heatherton & J. L. Weinberger (Eds.). *Can personality change?* (pp. 21–40). Washington, DC: American Psychological Association.

Degges-White, S., & Myers, J. E. (2006). Transitions, wellness, and life satisfaction: Implications for counseling midlife women. *Journal of Mental Health Counseling, 28*(2), 133–150.

Doka, K. J., & Tucci, A. S. (Eds.). (2009). *Diversity and end-of-life care.* Washington, DC: Hospice Foundation of America.

Douthit, K. Z., Santiago, S., & Garrick, I. (2009, October). *Autoethnography as a transformative counseling research method for studying life stories of diverse older adults.* Presentation at the Association for Counselor Education and Supervision biannual conference, San Diego, CA.

Edmondson, R., & Kondratowitz, H. J. (2009). *Valuing older people: A humanist approach to ageing.* Bristol, England: Policy Press.

Heschel, A. J. (1996). *Moral grandeur and spiritual audacity.* New York, NY: Farrar, Straus & Giroux.

Johnson, R. (1996, Winter). Chronologically endowed vs. elderly: One gerontological counselor's pet peeve. *ADULTSPAN Journal,* pp. 9, 13.

Jolanki, O. H. (2009). Agency in talk about old age and health. *Journal of Aging Studies, 23,* 215–226.

Kuypers, J. A., & Bengtson, V. L. (1973). Competence and social breakdown: A social-psychological view of aging. *Human Development, 16,* 37–49.

Lee, C. C. (1997). *Multicultural issues in counseling* (2nd ed.). Alexandria, VA: American Counseling Association.

Mosak, H. H., & Kopp, R. R. (1973). The early recollections of Adler, Freud, and Jung. *Journal of Individual Psychology, 29*(2), 157–166.

Myers, J. E. (1989). *Infusing gerontological counseling into counselor preparation: Curriculum guide.* Alexandra, VA: American Association for Counseling and Development.

Myers, J. E. (1995). From "forgotten and ignored" to standards and certification: Gerontological counseling comes of age. *Journal of Counseling & Development, 74,* 143–149.

Myers, J. E., & Harper, M. (2004). Evidence-based effective practices with older adults: A review of the literature for counselors. *Journal of Counseling & Development, 82,* 207–218.

National Commission on Teaching and America's Future. (2003). *No dream denied: A pledge to America's children.* Washington, DC: Author.

Nelson, T. (2002). *Ageism: Stereotyping and prejudice against older persons.* Cambridge, MA: MIT Press.

Older Americans Act of 1965, PL 89-73, 42 U.S.C. §§ 3001 *et seq.*

Rollins, J. (2008, October). The graying of the baby boomers. *Counseling Today,* pp. 32–37.

Sokolovsky, J. (Ed.). (1997). *The cultural context of aging: Worldwide perspectives* (2nd ed.). Westport, CT: Bergin & Garvey.

Strom, R., Collinsworth, P., Strom, S., & Griswold, D. (1992–1993). Strengths and needs of Black grandparents. *International Journal of Aging and Human Development, 36*(4), 255–268.

Sue, D., & Sue, S. (1990). *Counseling the culturally diverse: Theory and practice* (4th ed.). New York, NY: Wiley.

Sung, K. (2004). Elder respect among young adults: A cross-cultural study of Americans and Koreans. *Journal of Aging Studies, 18*(2), 215–230.

Sweeney, T. J. (2009). *Adlerian counseling and psychotherapy: A practitioner's approach.* New York, NY: Taylor & Francis.

Sweeney, T. J., & Myers, J. E. (1986). Early recollections: An Adlerian technique with older people. *The Clinical Gerontologist, 4*(4), 3–12.

Tornstam, L. (2006). The complexity of ageism. *International Journal of Ageing and Later Life, 1*(1), 43–68.

United Nations. (2007). *World population ageing: 2007.* Retrieved from http://www.un.org/esa/population/publications/WPA2007/wpp2007.htm

Whitbourne, S. B. (2010). The intersection of physical and mental health in aging: Minding the gap. In J. C. Cavanaugh, C. K. Cavanaugh, S. Qualls, & L. McGuire (Eds.), *Aging in America: Vol. 2. Physical and mental health* (pp. 141–170). Santa Barbara, CA: Praeger.

Additional Resources

AARP
>	www.aarp.org

Administration on Aging
>	www.aoa.gov

Administration on Aging Data Resources
>	www.data.aoa.gov

Center for Health Improvement for Minority Elders
>	www.chime.ucla.edu

National Center on Elder Abuse
>	http://www.ncea.aoa.gov/ncearoot/Main_Site/index.aspx

Appendix 11.1 • Rights and Obligations of Older Americans:
1961 White House Conference on Aging

Rights of Senoir Citizens

Each of our senior citizens, regardless of race, color, or creed, is entitled to

1. The right to be useful
2. The right to obtain employment based on merit
3. The right to freedom from want in old age
4. The right to a fair share of the community's recreational, educational, and medical resources
5. The right to obtain decent housing suited to needs of later years
6. The right to the moral and financial support of one's family so far as is consistent with the best interest of the family
7. The right to live independently, as one chooses
8. The right to live and die with dignity
9. The right of access to all knowledge as available on how to improve the later years of life

Obligations of Older Adults

The aging, by availing themselves of educational opportunities, should endeavor to assume the following obligations to the best of their ability:

1. The obligation of each citizen to prepare himself or herself to become and resolve to remain active, alert, capable, self-supporting, and useful so long as health and circumstances permit and to plan for ultimate retirement
2. The obligation to learn and apply sound principles of physical and mental health
3. The obligation to seek and develop potential avenues of service in the years after retirement
4. The obligation to make available the benefits of his or her experience and knowledge
5. The obligation to endeavor to make himself or herself adaptable to the changes added years will bring
6. The obligation to attempt to maintain such relationships with family, neighbors, and friends as will make him or her a respected and valued counselor throughout his or her later years

Note. From *Toward a Declaration of Rights and Obligations of Older Americans,* by the Department of Health, Education, and Welfare, Office of Human Development, Administration of Aging, 1974, Washington, DC: Author.

Chapter
12

Counseling Gay Men

A. Michael Hutchins

To understand a man's attraction to another man is to understand a unique way of being in the world. As a counselor, one hopes to invite clients to explore themselves fully and to be one with themselves and the world around them—to live in harmony and to creatively transcend dissonance. For many clients who identify as homosexual or who are exploring their sexual identity, coming to live in harmony with themselves can mean experiencing dissonance in the community at large. Thus, counselors may need to assist clients in developing the skills necessary to make choices that may create internal harmony while helping them develop the strength to face adverse conditions in the world at large. In addition, counselors may have to take steps to create greater understanding and inclusion in the community at large.

Counselors can better understand the dissonance experienced by men coming to an understanding of their sexual orientation if this search for clarity about sexuality is framed as a developmental process. There are several models for understanding sexual identity development (Cass, 1979; Coleman, 1982; Troiden, 1979, 1989). All of these models have stages of awareness, dissonance, acceptance, and synthesis. Appleby (2001) recommended that in understanding a man's sexual orientation, the counselor understands the levels of development on five interconnected levels: (a) historical, (b) environmental-structural, (c) cultural, (d) family, and (e) individual. He suggested that it is the counselor's task "to assist . . . in the process of developing a positive self and group identity, to manage the information around the stigmatized identity, and to advocate for more nurturing (nondiscriminatory) environments" (p. 8). In this chapter, identity development is considered primarily from Cass's (1979) model, which integrates Appleby's recommendations.

While exploring the sexual identity of individual men, counselors must be aware of the environmental and cultural dynamics of the community in which that identity development is occurring (Hutchins, 2012). Some cultures and communities are supportive of the healthy development of alternative lifestyles. However, other communities may be less tolerant of diverse worldviews. This may create dissonance for a man developing a sexual identity. In terms of individual development, a potential developmental process in communities will be explored in this chapter.

In exploring personal identity development, it is important to acknowledge the communities in which the developing man lives. Each individual grows to maturity living in a community. Often the standards and norms one holds for oneself are different from those of the community in which one lives. As individual men come to a greater understanding and acceptance of their sexual orientation, they may experience less and less harmony with the community at large. In such cases, counselors may need to become involved in community education and advocacy. In other cases, the community norms may be more accepting and celebratory of an individual's sexual orientation—perhaps even more so than he himself is. In such cases, counselors may need to assist the client in becoming aware of the resources in the community in which he lives and in working with the community as advocates to become more inclusive for men in all stages of sexual identity exploration (Hutchins, 2010, 2012; Lewis, Arnold, House, & Toporek, 2002; Ratts, 2009; Ratts & Hutchins, 2009; Ratts, Lewis, & Toporek, 2010). Where one sees the dissonance in individuals and in communities, one sees the results of a society that is reflecting a history of homophobia and heterosexism (Chaney & Marszalek, 2009). It is incumbent on counselors to be aware of such dynamics and to work to create a more inclusive environment. When counselors are working with men who are members of communities that have already been marginalized, the task of addressing multiple arenas of discrimination becomes even more challenging.

Dynamics of the Cultural Context of Gay Men

Diversity

Much of the understanding of male sexuality development has historically come from attempts to understand the development of middle-class, English-speaking, Caucasian men (Tobias, 1998). For many men who do not fit into this group, additional developmental issues can be most significant. In this chapter, issues of diversity in the gay male community and in the community at large are addressed. A comprehensive exploration of such issues is beyond the scope of this chapter. The experience of men of color has often been quite different from the experience of most middle-class, English-speaking, Caucasian men (Appleby, 2001; Beam, 1986; Boykin, 1996; Chung & Szymanski, 2000, 2006; Hemphill & Beam, 1991; hooks, 2001; King, 2004; Longres, 1996; Nelson, 1993; Roscoe, 1988, 1995, 1998; Smith, 1983; Thompson, 1987; Williams, 1986; Wright, 2001). Different ethnic groups have different values and norms for sexual identity development within their communities (Appleby, 2001; Chung & Szymanski, 2000, 2006; King, 2004; Morales, 1992; Roscoe, 1988, 1995, 1998; Sears, 1994; Smith, 1983; Thompson, 1987). In addition, men of faith (de la Huerta, 1999; Fortunato, 1982, 1987; Lowenthal, 1997) may have unique experiences as they learn to integrate an understanding of sexual orientation into self-definitions that include membership in organized religious structures.

HIV/AIDS

A counselor cannot effectively work with gay men without having some understanding of the impact of HIV/AIDS on the gay population. For 30 years, HIV has been a reality in the gay community. At times it has been devastating, and men have had to confront issues of grief and loss as they have confronted their own mortality and witnessed the loss of lovers, friends, and family members. At other times it has hidden quietly, though formidably, in the background. For the past several years there has been a powerful resurgence in HIV-related diagnoses, particularly in the African American community and among younger men, as men have become less vigilant about practicing healthy sexual behavior and because symptom-reducing medications exist for those men and boys who have seroconverted. Where AIDS was once seen as a death sentence, it is now often perceived as a controllable chronic disease, except in those communities that do not have the fiscal and medical resources to provide comprehensive medical, social, and psychological services. The loss of peers from HIV/AIDS impacts the aging process of many older men. The perception that HIV-related illness has become less severe is being challenged daily in many communities, and advocates work diligently to educate at-risk groups, community members, decision makers, social service agencies, and others. With decreased funding for education and prevention programs, the challenges become greater.

Aging

In contemporary society, much emphasis is placed on youth. In gay society this emphasis is even stronger. Many young gay men experience discrimination and antigay bias in school, at work, and from friends and family (Russell, Clarke, & Clary, 2009; Russell, McGuire, Lee, Larriva, & Laub, 2008; Russell, Muraco, Subramaniam, & Laub, 2009). Bullying has become a part of the culture for many young men (Bauman, 2011; see also the antibullying group The Trevor Project [www.thetrevorproject.com]). In the adolescent community, the suicide risk is higher in young men struggling with sexual identity issues than it is in the community at large (Remafedi, 1994; www.suicidepreventionlifeline.org). In many areas within the young gay community, substance abuse and isolation are prevalent (Kus, 1990; Siegel & Lowe, 1994; Signorile, 1997). In this youth-oriented culture, counselors must explore ways to appropriately address changing cultural norms with clients and with organizations within the community at large.

A growing number of men are confronting the dynamics of aging within the gay world (see www.sageusa.org, a resource for lesbian, gay, bisexual, and transgender [LGBT] seniors). Single gay men report that they become "invisible" at earlier and earlier ages. Many single men report increased isolation and alienation. This is particularly true for men who have lost peers to HIV/AIDS. The emphasis on youth supports this perception of increasing invisibility. Senior residential communities are being formed in cities and towns with large sexual minority populations. The aging process, then, has some unique dynamics within the gay world (Gooch, 1999; Isay, 1989, 1996; Jackson, 1991, 1993; Kooden & Flowers, 2000; Siegel & Lowe, 1994).

Chemical Dependency and Substance Abuse

The center of the gay community has historically been gay bars. Although this may be changing in many communities, alcohol and the social scene surrounding bar life are still a reality for many gay men. In addition, many younger men are part of the circuit party set. In these venues alcohol and drugs are a significant part of life (Kominars & Kominars, 1996; Kus, 1990; Signorile, 1997). Often gay men present for counseling and report depression, isolation, and alienation that can temporarily be alleviated by drug and alcohol use (Hutchins, 2012). In addition, many men report that their incidence of at-risk sexual behavior increases when they are under the influence of drugs and alcohol. A growing number of men are meeting through online connection sites, hooking up, and using chemicals as part of the connection.

Technology

An increasingly important factor in the gay community and in the community at large is the role of the Internet. Since the mid-1990s, more and more men have been making connections with other men through the Internet, chat rooms, web pages, and other World Wide Web vehicles. Gay resources like *The Advocate* have established web pages (www. advocate.com). Additional resources that are available to gay men and those who work with them include PlanetOut (www.planetout.com) and Gay.com (www.gay.com). These and other resources open up the world for many men who have previously been isolated from other gay men and the greater gay world. A large social network (www.gaylife.about. com, www.match.com, www.perfectmatch.com, www.compatiblepartners.net) continues to evolve, and a greater number of men are meeting through these sites. For some emerging gay men, the Internet has opened up a new world within which they have begun to make connections with similarly searching men. For others, the Internet has helped to perpetuate isolation and alienation, as they become more reclusive and live more virtual lives. Many lonely and isolated men are in danger of compulsive or addictive use of the Internet, and counselors need to see the dangers as well as the resources in this emerging culture. Additional websites exist with information on domestic violence, bullying, substance abuse, hate crimes (www.gay.about.com, www.findlaw.com, www.matthewshepard.org), and other social issues.

Identity and Family

Within the gay community, ongoing discussions occur concerning acculturation, the loss of gay identity, and the importance of maintaining a unique community identity (Browning, 1994, 1998; Harris, 1997; Kooden & Flowers, 2000; Lowenthal, 1997; Siegel & Lowe, 1994; Signorile, 1997). Appleby (2001) saw this discussion as that of primarily a White, middle-class population, with members of other groups being more concerned with issues of marginalization and daily living. Some activists and other members of the gay community believe that as gay men, members of the gay community should not aspire to the norms of a White, middle-class, heterosexual and heterosexist society, whereas others work diligently for gay men to have domestic partner benefits, to be able to adopt children, and to have the same access to power that White heterosexual men have.

In addition, there is a debate within elements of the gay community that focuses on the nature of relationships. Are there healthy alternatives to being either single or in a committed monogamous relationship with another man? What is the nature of family, and can a family of origin be supplemented with, replaced by, or integrated with a family of choice? Should men be allowed to form legal contracts acknowledging their relationships? How can men work together and with the community at large to address discrimination in housing, employment, medical services, and other areas? How can a man ensure that he has hospital privileges when another man with whom he has shared his life is dying? What happens when a lover dies and there is a legal battle with members of the deceased lover's family of origin for the remains of a shared life? With changing state laws, gay marriages and domestic partnerships are a reality in some states, whereas other states have passed legislation prohibiting such unions. In some states men are openly adopting children and finding surrogate mothers to bring children into families. With the December 2010 passage of federal legislation repealing the U.S. military's Don't Ask, Don't Tell policy, changing dynamics will impact counselors who work with military men and their families. As gay men sort through such questions, counselors need to be asking about their beliefs and practices in these arenas.

Spirituality

With the maturing of the HIV epidemic, there is a growing interest in gay spirituality (de la Huerta, 1999; Johnson, 2000; Kooden & Flowers, 2000; Rosco, 1995; Stowe, 1999; Thompson, 1987, 1995, 1997; www.spiritjourneys.com). Some of the interest is woven into the relationships with some organized religious structures concerning the acceptability of homosexual behavior and the meaning of homosexuality. Many gay men choose to remain in the religious tradition in which they were raised and attempt to blend into such religious groups and behave as if the issues do not exist for them. Others choose to remain in such structures and work to bring about change in doctrine and practice. Many gay men choose to look elsewhere for spiritual support. For many of these men, the decision to move away from the religious structures within which they were raised leads to an exploration of spirituality that is not grounded in historical religious structures or that is grounded in a non-Judeo-Christian tradition. The role of spirituality is becoming increasingly important in the gay community, and many clients who come to counseling are exploring nontraditional expressions of spiritual growth.

The Cass Model of Homosexual Identity Formation

What follows is an exploration of some of the aforementioned dynamics in an attempt to further understand gay male identity development. The developmental stages of the Cass (1979) model of homosexual identity formation are presented along with case studies with a variety of intervention possibilities and several different ways of addressing the client and his issue. As with any developmental model, the stages are described as separate and well defined. The reality of development is that the stages are often much less clear and more ambiguous. Counselors must be cognizant of such lack of clarity and see the model as a framework from which to explore rather than as a box within which to fit individuals and communities.

In exploring the individual developmental stages, one can conjecture that there are developmental stages through which the community at large moves as well. The community at large may include simple organizations, professional associations, social groups, local municipalities, state or regional coalitions, or the nation as a whole. As American society examines ways to integrate sexuality, the complex issues of sexual orientation are a critical part of the examination and exploration of the evolution of the identity of a gay man. For this reason, the evolution of the community is examined in each case study.

Stage 1: Identity Confusion

The initial stage of the model, which Cass labels *Identity Confusion,* is marked by denial and confusion about sexual behavior, feelings of attraction, and sense of self. At this stage of development the individual may focus on sexual behavior and not make a distinction between sexual behavior and sexual orientation.

The Center for Substance Abuse Treatment (2001) defines *sexual orientation* as "the erotic and affectional (or loving) attraction to another person, including erotic fantasy, erotic activity or behavior, and affectional needs" (p. 4) and indicates that sexual behavior, or sexual activity, differs from sexual orientation and alone does not define someone as a (gay) individual. Any person may be capable of sexual behavior with the same or opposite sex, but an individual knows his . . . longings—erotic and affectional—and which sex is likely to satisfy those needs. (pp. 4–5)

In the Identity Confusion stage, the individual does not distinguish among the physical, erotic, emotional, and psychological aspects of sexuality and sexual orientation. He does recognize that information about homosexuality is somehow personally relevant and that the attraction cannot be ignored or denied completely. He experiences a sense of inconsistency and dissonance in his sense of self. He may privately begin to suspect that his thoughts, behaviors, or feelings could possibly be homosexual. He may appear to be heterosexual (or straight acting), or at least believe that he does, and he believes that others perceive him as heterosexual as well. Fear about homosexuality is a strong component of this emerging man, though he may deny any fear. When explored, fear of any kind of sexuality is often even more fundamental than fear of being attracted to someone of the same sex.

According to Cass, the individual does not find the definition of himself as homosexual to be desirable or acceptable. He may avoid getting information about homosexuality, may inhibit his sexual behavior, may deny any relevance of information about homosexuality, may actively engage in heterosexual behavior, may become asexual, may seek to be cured, and/or may become an antigay crusader.

On many levels the individual disowns feelings, thoughts, and actions that would be associated with same-sex attraction. When he fails to do this he may define his actions and rationalize his behavior (e.g., "I was just experimenting," "I was drunk," "It was an accident," "I just did it for the money"). For many men, this kind of behavior may continue, and they may not move beyond this stage.

Other men recognize that the information they are receiving does have meaning for them, and they begin to gather more information about same-sex attraction. In past generations, boys and men attempted to gather information (often furtively) from libraries, books, magazines, and others in whom they could trust. In contemporary society, men are using the Internet to gather information. Much of the information available is healthy and helpful. Other information may be confusing and may focus more on behavior or acting out (i.e., acting on same-sex attractions) rather than on the integration of all aspects of sexuality.

Many segments of the community at large may exhibit a corresponding set of norms for addressing homosexuality. In such communities, sexuality is understood as behavior, and there is little or no understanding of the more integrated nature of sexuality. Fear of sexuality may be prevalent, and the community may not even acknowledge that homosexuality could be a part of the community. Such communities may at times be labeled *homophobic.* In actuality, the underlying fear may be of any kind of sexual expression. If the community does look at the possibility that homosexuality can exist within its structure, it may focus on behavior; label such behavior as *sinful, immoral, unnatural,* or *sick;* and then develop ways to ostracize or punish individuals who engage in homosexual behavior. Such fear-based community norms can reinforce the individual man's struggle within himself. Such communities may take overt actions to search out and punish sexual minority members of their own and other communities.

For the emerging man, this stage of development can be tumultuous. He may seek counseling and report that he is depressed or anxious. Often he does not seek counseling of his own volition. He may be immersed in a culture that does not value counseling and may not seek assistance for many different reasons. At times younger men may seek assistance after having acted out, having been involved with drug-related activity, having felt alienated and depressed, or having begun to self-disclose issues related to sexual identity. Older men may act out and come into counseling when other parts of their lives begin to become problematic. Issues with dependence on alcohol or other chemicals may precipitate interventions or counseling. At times men are referred after experiencing legal difficulties. Even in such circumstances there may be a very high level of denial based on fears of others discovering their behavior and fears of sanctions.

Case Study: Tyrone

Tyrone is a 30-year-old African American man who is a captain in the U.S. Army stationed in rural Arizona. He was referred for counseling by his civilian attorney after charges were filed against him for attempted sodomy, indecent exposure, and driving while intoxicated.

Tyrone had regularly been chatting online with gay men in a local Internet chat room. One night, after he had been drinking at a local bar with fellow officers, he stopped at a rest area on the interstate and connected with an attractive man in the parking lot. He invited the man back to his apartment, and the man returned home with him. Tyrone reports that when they entered his apartment, the man made sexual advances toward him, and he responded. At that point the man identified himself as an undercover local police officer and arrested Tyrone.

Tyrone was charged with sexual offenses, and the information was forwarded to his commanding officer. The U.S. Army is investigating the incident to determine whether Tyrone should be discharged.

Tyrone does not identify as a gay man. He reports that, if forced to identify a sexual orientation, he "might call myself bisexual." He reports that he has not had sexual contact with a woman in "about 10 years" and that his only sexual contact with men has been when he has been drinking heavily or, occasionally, when he has been using cocaine.

He reports that he does spend from 2 to 4 hours daily in gay chat rooms and that "once in awhile" he will go online when he is in his office. He reports that he has made sexual contact "a few times" with the men with whom he has chatted online.

In sharing his sexual history, Tyrone acknowledges that he was introduced to being sexual by his football coach when he was 14. He reports that he felt ashamed of this contact, which lasted for several years, and that he would "get drunk" in order "to hide what was happening."

Throughout the first few counseling sessions Tyrone maintained that he is not homosexual, that his behavior only occurs when he is under the influence of drugs or alcohol, that his drinking "could possibly be a problem," and that he was "trapped" by the police officer.

According to Tyrone, when his case was brought before the local judge the judge reported that he wanted to "send a message to men like you" and "make sure the community is safe." His attorney had referred Tyrone to counseling in order to demonstrate to the court that Tyrone was remorseful for his actions and that he was seeking help. His military attorney told him that "the best you can hope for is a General Discharge." Changing military policy may impact the case.

Discussion. In this case, the counselor can work with Tyrone in several areas. Initially it is important for Tyrone to see that his behavior is problematic. It may be important to suspend any labels about sexuality and sexual orientation; to explore the loneliness and isolation he has experienced; and to look at the thinking, feeling, and behaving that led to his being in his current situation.

Much of the counseling at this point may involve providing information and teaching Tyrone some decision-making skills. The counselor may be called on to provide information about Tyrone's behavior and mental health in the court hearings. The initial sessions may need to focus on the immediacy of the court hearings and the military decisions. If Tyrone is placed on probation, he will need support and connections within the community. If he is discharged or voluntarily leaves the Army, he will need assistance in many areas of his life. If he remains in the military, additional clarification about his role in the military may be needed.

It is important to look at the role alcohol and drugs play in his life and how his decision making is affected by such use. In one session, Tyrone acknowledges that in his loneliness, and under the influence of drugs and alcohol, he has engaged in unsafe sexual practices. He refuses to be tested for HIV, reporting that he does not want to know his HIV status. At some point it is important to explore this decision and its implications.

According to Appleby (2001), it may be important to explore Tyrone's introduction to sexuality and the effects of that introduction. If Tyrone was introduced to sexuality by his football coach, it is important to explore the effects of sexual abuse on his sexual identity development. It is also possible that his coach is still in a position in which he can have contact with young men. If this is the case, the counselor may need to explore reporting the coach's behavior.

Tyrone grew up in a working-class African American family and community. He reports that his mother was the head of the household and that church was and continues to be an important part of the family's life. He reports that there is no acceptance of homosexuality in his family or church community. He has not yet told his family of his situation and may need to explore ways of doing that. He may find out that there are resources within his church community.

Tyrone's use of Internet chat rooms may stem from his loneliness and isolation and/or may be compulsive behavior. It may be important to explore the dynamics underlying this behavior. Because he lives in a rural community, he may find that the Internet is the most reasonable way to meet other men. However, it has many dangers, and Tyrone may need to explore these dangers.

The community in which Tyrone lives and the U.S. Army base on which he works have traditionally not been rich sources of support and, as can be witnessed by the judge's statements, may be quite hostile. It may be helpful for the counselor to develop a coalition of helping professionals who can provide education about sexual identity development for local organizations and leaders. In addition, it may be helpful to seek assistance from national organizations that address issues of discrimination on the basis of sexual orientation. A changing military culture may be able to provide a structure for support. All such activity would need to be sensitive to Tyrone and the situation in which he finds himself.

Stage 2: Identity Comparison

When a man begins to ask the question "Am I homosexual?" he has begun exploring in the Identity Comparison stage. This stage occurs when the emerging man accepts that he may be homosexual. In the first stage, Identity Confusion, the person struggles with self-alienation. In the Identity Comparison stage the focus is on exploring the social alienation that comes from feeling different from family, peers, and society at large.

During this stage, the individual becomes aware that many of the social expectations that have been a part of his culture no longer apply to him. He begins to realize that traditional life structures do not apply to him, and may experience a sense of loss and grief. Expressing this sense of loss in a healthy manner may help him to develop the resources needed to move through his life and integrate his sexual identity. When a man has no opportunity to work through grief, isolation and withdrawal and/or acting out with at-risk behaviors can become factors in his development.

Certain conditions have historically increased the sense of isolation for the emerging gay man. Geographic isolation has meant a lack of access to information and other men who are exploring their emerging sexual identity. With the advent of the Internet, many men are learning to explore resources and make connections that were unavailable in the not-too-distant past. If the individual is from a deeply religious background in which he has learned that homosexuality is sinful, he will often find the alienation even more devastating.

During this stage, the individual may accept the possibility of being different, though not explore this fully in his behavior. He may begin to grieve the loss of heterosexual expectations and ways of being in the world. Some men will accept being different and may creatively work through the feelings, thoughts, and behaviors of being different.

Others may attempt to pass as heterosexual. They may show up at social events with women or spend a great deal of time with women, though nothing romantic develops. At times they may shun any social events that require heterosexuality. A man may become acutely aware of his wardrobe and work to make certain that he doesn't "look" gay; he may further avoid any behavior that might be interpreted as gay. During this stage, a man may actively cultivate a masculine image. In some cultures this is even more highly valued, and an exaggerated sense of masculinity may be rewarded.

A man may recognize that he is attracted to other men at this stage and may seek ways to be connected with attractive men in ways that do not appear to be sexual. He may value a best friend and even fantasize about this man but never allow himself to fully accept the attraction. He integrates into his thinking and vocabulary such phrases as "If it weren't for this person, I wouldn't be gay," "I refuse to categorize myself; gender doesn't matter to me," "I could be heterosexual at any time," and "It's nobody's business what I do in bed."

This can be a time of great anxiety and preoccupation with sexuality. There is a high risk for alcohol and drug abuse during this stage of development and a growing conflict about social situations. Younger men may be more willing to explore during this stage, reporting that it is "fashionable" to be undefined. For older men, this can be more nonfactual. Men may remain married during this stage but have sexual liaisons outside of the marriage, justifying such encounters as not being unfaithful to their primary relationships because they are not socially and emotionally connected to the men with whom they are having contact. In addition, making anonymous connections through online chat rooms may become part of the exploration. Men at this stage of development may not seek counseling unless something happens in their lives to upset the carefully developed equilibrium.

In communities that are in a comparable stage of development, it is not safe to acknowledge homosexuality. Again, homosexuality in such communities may be understood in terms of acting out sexual behavior that may be labeled as *unnatural, sinful,* or *sick.* These communities may continue to deny that homosexuality exists within the community. However, these communities differ from communities in the Identity Confusion stage of development in that they are not likely to go witch hunting in search of deviants. Although there continues to be a sense of fear and shame around misunderstood sexuality, the same level of hostility may not be present. In this climate, it may still not be safe to discuss sexuality or sexual orientation. Persons living in such communities need to get their information from resources outside the main community support systems. Many online resources have emerged for this purpose, and the number of resources continues to grow. If the counselor is a member of the community, it can be very important for him or her to begin gathering support to provide education about sexuality and sexual orientation for the community at large. Again, in the age of Internet access, resources are increasingly more readily available.

Case Study: Henry

Henry is a 21-year-old male from the Navajo Nation who is working as an apprentice silver-smith in a small town in southern New Mexico. He grew up on the reservation in northern New Mexico until he graduated from high school, when he moved south to work with an artist who knows his family and who has always shown an interest in Henry. The artist is 15 years older than Henry, and, according to Henry, they have been lovers for 3 years.

Henry is not certain that he is gay because, he reports, he does not know what being gay means. He does know that he and his partner use drugs and alcohol and that at times they have gotten violent with each other. He and his partner have been arrested for domestic violence. Henry recently discovered that his partner is HIV positive. Afraid, Henry was tested and discovered that he too is HIV positive, although he is asymptomatic.

Henry was referred for counseling by the county public health department when he was given his test results. He reports that he does not want to talk about his situation and that, although he does not want to come to counseling, he does not know what else to do. During the initial session, Henry was very quiet, and there were long periods of silence. His appointment was scheduled as the last appointment of the day, and the counselor allowed the session to extend well beyond a 50-minute hour.

In the initial session, Henry was invited to share how he would address his life situation if he were on the reservation. He smiled and reported that he would probably get drunk. When asked to explore other options, he thought for a long time. When he spoke, he reported that he would probably get up very early in the morning and walk eastward to meet the sun; he would dance with the men in his village; he would draw his story and incorporate it in his silver work; and, finally, he would go to his grandmother, tell her his story, and listen to her advice. He also reported that he would read stories about being a gay man and that he would get more information about HIV/AIDS.

With assistance from the counselor, Henry found a local group of Navajo men who danced together regularly and who, Henry discovered, were related to him. In addition, he found an area along the Rio Grande River basin where he could run in the morning and pray. Henry agreed to create stories in pictures and share the stories with the counselor and with other men from his dance group, some of whom he suspected were gay. Henry agreed to read *Living the Spirit* and *Queer Spirits* (Roscoe, 1988, 1995) and to create some of his own drawings and paintings telling his stories.

Henry was referred to a physician who integrates Western medicine and traditional Navajo healing methods and who can work with him in developing a holistic health plan. Henry also agreed to see the counselor on a monthly basis to explore the role that substance abuse and domestic violence have played in his life.

Discussion. The initial contact with Henry established the scope of some of his concerns. He has questions about sexual orientation, but seeing a counselor and discussing issues of sexuality are not congruent with his cultural style of solving problems. He has sought out a counselor because he does not know what else to do. There appear to be problems of substance abuse, depression, violence, and spiritual connectedness. In addition, Henry's HIV status is of significant concern.

Henry can use information about what it means to be a gay man. He does not identify with the mainstream gay society and does not appear to have much if any information about sexual orientation in Native American communities. Henry had a connection to the spiritual healing traditions of the Navajo Nation while living on the reservation. Reconnecting with a Navajo community seems to be an important part of his growth. In addition, it may be very important for Henry to discover men from his own nation who understand issues of sexuality.

The referral to a physician who integrates different healing approaches is important. It speaks to the need for counselors to have knowledge about all aspects of the communities in which they live. There are different responses to homosexuality and HIV in different Native American communities, and Henry can benefit from connectedness with his own culture as he attempts to integrate his sexual identity into his greater identity.

Stage 3: Identity Tolerance

The Identity Tolerance stage occurs when the emerging man comes to accept the possibility that he may be homosexual and recognizes the sexual, social, and emotional needs that go along with being homosexual. He moves beyond the confusion and turmoil of earlier stages and has the energy to begin exploring what may be available in a community. He begins to see greater differences between himself and heterosexual peers and begins seeking out a gay subculture. As he does this, he begins to decrease his social isolation, looking for others who are more like him. The move toward a gay community helps him move toward a more positive gay identity. He may begin to find a more supportive and understanding support system, and this increases his potential for meeting a partner or partners. He may have greater access to positive role models and may have greater opportunity to practice being more at ease as a gay man.

If his contacts with the gay community are positive, he is likely to develop a more positive sense of himself. If they are more negative, his entry into the community may be more difficult and he may choose to remain outside the community.

As mentioned previously, the center of gay life has historically been the bar scene. A man who is not comfortable in such a scene may find entering into the community to be very difficult. If he is a member of other marginalized communities, his entry is even more difficult. If and when men of color and men of other ethnic and language groups attempt to enter mainstream gay culture, they may encounter racism and other forms of discrimination. Many more men are now making social connections through the Internet. As society changes, more options are open for the emerging gay man. In many communities, gyms and fitness centers are replacing bars as places for men to meet (Chaney, 2008). In communities that are emerging as more gay friendly, there are community centers; interest-based associations (hiking clubs, bowling leagues, photography clubs, theater groups, softball leagues, ski clubs, bridge clubs, discussion groups, 12-step meetings, dinner clubs, etc.); local publications; political organizations; HIV service organizations; religious groups; groups based on racial, language, and ethnic identities; and business and professional associations that operate on local, state, regional, and national levels. Many corporations have LGBT organizations.

For some men, there can be an emerging sense of spiritual dissonance during this stage of development. Many gay men have explored relationships with God through organized religious structures. During this stage of development, they may begin to explore more openly their relationship with organized religious thought or practice. If they become aware of religion-based, gay-supportive groups, they may seek support through these groups. In later stages of development, spirituality may take on different forms.

As a man enters the gay community, he has much from which to choose. However, many communities reflect histories of fear, shame, discrimination, and oppression. If the individual has poor social skills (as is often the case), or low self-esteem, or a strong fear of exposure, or fear of the unknown, he may find entering into the gay community to be more difficult. Often communities themselves are characterized by members who have the same concerns, issues, or characteristics. In addition, if he is already a member of a marginalized community, he may choose an option other than assimilation into a gay community.

If he encounters members of the greater gay community who themselves are struggling with early-stage concerns, he may have more difficulty. If he encounters men who are open and invite his participation in the community, his chances of integrating into the community are greater.

At this stage of a man's development, it is important for him to find a community. However, for the gay community it now becomes more important for the community at large to be more gay friendly. As a community enters a comparable stage of development, it begins to acknowledge gay members. Members of the community may speak about the need for community support for diverse populations, including those who are diverse because of sexual orientation. The fear that characterizes communities in earlier stages is lessened, though often still present. The denial about sexual orientation that is pervasive in previous developmental stages is not so pervasive here. Community members acknowledge that sexuality is about more than behavior, and the community begins to acknowledge the complexity of sexuality. In such emerging communities there is an increased awareness of the effects of discrimination and oppression. The emerging gay man may or may not recognize the inclusiveness of some of these communities. However, as he becomes more involved in a gay culture, he will begin to be more aware of access to power and issues of social oppression.

At this point in his development, the emerging gay man begins to recognize that more of his support system is gay identified. If this is a positive experience for him he may move on to the next stage. If it is negative, he may experience greater difficulty.

Case Study: Chuck

Chuck is a 52-year-old White male who works as a dispatcher for a large trucking company. He was referred for counseling by his employer because he was beginning to miss work on a regular basis, and when he was at work he appeared isolated and withdrawn.

In the initial session, Chuck admitted that he is an alcoholic in recovery and that he has remained sober by attending 12-step meetings and talking with his sponsor. He has not attended a meeting in "more than 3 months" and has not spoken to his sponsor in "more than a month." He believes that he is in danger of relapse.

Chuck grew up in Oklahoma and married at age 19. He married his high school sweetheart, and they had two children, a son, Tim, and a daughter, Carol, by the time Chuck was 22 years old. He reports that he and his ex-wife did not have much of a social life and that during his wife's second pregnancy he began having anonymous sexual encounters with other young men.

Chuck was trained as a long-distance trucker and began driving cross-country in his mid-20s. At this time he began to increase his drinking and began having "regular" men in different cities along his trucking route. He became "serious" about one man who told Chuck that he was "in love with me." When Chuck attempted to break off the relationship, the man contacted Chuck's wife and employer. Through a series of "rough times," Chuck was divorced, lost his job, and was denied custody of his children.

When he was 30, Chuck moved to Dallas, got sporadic employment, and began drinking and "partying" heavily. By the time he was 32 he had become a regular in the Dallas bar scene. He proudly reports, "Even when things were at their worst, I talked with my kids every week and never forgot their birthdays."

At age 33 Chuck met Tom, the manager of a trucking company, at a gay pride event in Dallas. They became lovers and moved in together. As their life together developed, they acknowledged that they "had drinking problems" and decided to "get sober together." They began attending 12-step meetings, and Chuck began working for Tom in his company. When he "got sober" Chuck was tested for HIV and discovered that he was HIV positive.

He became frightened, angry, and depressed. Tom was tested and was found to be HIV negative. Chuck was suspicious of the local AIDS service organization but agreed to get help. He has had several bouts with pneumocystis pneumonia but is currently in good health and takes a daily AIDS cocktail that includes steroids.

While Chuck was "trying to get healthy" his son was beginning to get into trouble. Chuck's former wife called him when Tim was 14 years old and asked whether he would take over parenting Tim. He agreed to do that, and Tim came to live with Chuck and Tom. For the next several years Chuck and Tom raised Tim until he graduated from high school. Chuck reports that though things were tough during these times, he was very happy and life was going well. Chuck and Tom had what Chuck calls a "pretty good" relationship when they were raising Tim. There was some difficulty within the gay community until they found some other gay parents, and the school sometimes asked questions about their family, which they chose to quietly avoid as best they could.

Chuck reports that "just when things were finally going smoothly" Tom came home and said that he had met a younger man and wanted to end his relationship with Chuck. Chuck was angry, hurt, and depressed when Tom left. They fought about possessions and Chuck changed jobs, going to work for a competitor. Chuck was successful at using his "12-step family" to get through this time.

As a single man, Chuck has discovered that he "hates dating" and that he has become "invisible" in the gay community. His old friends are no longer around, and he is not interested in the bar scene. He tends to be attracted to men his own age, and they tend to be attracted to much younger men. He began "surfing the Web" to meet men and discovered that he was able to meet "cyberfriends" online through local chat rooms. He had recently begun dating a man he met online and believed that things were "going okay" and that there was some possibility for the relationship.

About 3 months ago Chuck discovered that the man was dating other men. Chuck ended the relationship and has been feeling lonely, depressed, and angry since the breakup. He believes that he could easily return to drinking to "numb the pain." He agreed to come for counseling when his boss explained that he was in danger of losing his job and when his sponsor called him and told him that he had better do something soon.

Discussion. Chuck is facing a number of issues. As a man in his 50s, he has become invisible in a youth-oriented gay community. His strengths are that he has a supportive 12-step family and he lives in a city that has many resources for gay men. Chuck has a relationship with his son and, apparently, with his boss and sponsor. He has less contact with his daughter. Chuck is not likely to become voluntarily involved in insight-oriented psychotherapy but is likely to respond to action-oriented, practical interventions. He has some contact with the gay community and can begin to make use of that social community.

He describes himself as "interested in" church activities and is "willing to check out" some of the other non-bar-related social resources. He is also willing to do some volunteer work at the LGBT community center. He is currently asymptomatic in terms of his HIV status. He manages his health through a medical regime, diet and nutrition, and "almost compulsive" working out. Although he has participated in "some HIV support groups," he reports that "they're too depressing and 12-step groups are more helpful."

Chuck is willing to explore other kinds of community involvement. He reports that he "doesn't care who knows I'm gay." Though he is more private about his HIV status, he reports that he is "no activist" and "doesn't expect anyone else to help me work out my problems." He laughs and reports, "That's probably the addict in me." He is willing to explore ways to get support from the gay 12-step community.

Chuck acknowledges that if he were in a community with fewer resources, he could find 12-step meetings online, but those would not be as helpful and he could "get in trouble online." He also acknowledges that he can get support from the gay Christian community in Dallas and that such support would be difficult to get "back in Oklahoma." He reports that he "would never go back" to a community where he would need to hide his sexual orientation, "even though it is nobody else's business."

Stage 4: Identity Acceptance

According to Cass (1979), Identity Acceptance occurs when the person accepts, rather than tolerates, a homosexual self-image and there is increasing contact with a gay culture. The individual now has a positive identification with other gay people, and his worldview may be very much formed by the views of those around him. If they compartmentalize their own sexual orientations, he may choose to do so as well. To reduce stress he has less and less contact with a more overtly homophobic world, choosing to spend more of his time and energy with newly found gay friends. He does not escape the effects of homophobia, but homophobia takes different forms. He may be selective about sharing his life with nongay associates and seeks to filter information about his personal life as much as possible. In many ways his life is about fitting in and not making waves.

If his new associates celebrate their gay identities, he may easily accept a perception of himself as gay. Doing so may move him further from society at large but bring him closer to aspects of gay society. He begins to experience homophobic attitudes—his own and those of others—as offensive. He may continue in his own personal growth and become angrier at the inequities of society. If he is a man from another marginalized group, he may already be in touch with this anger about inequity and may have some cultural norms for addressing it. For men from other marginalized groups there is the task of integrating multiple identities. For some, such integration becomes easier, depending on their development. For others, this multiple integration is considerably more stressful. With the increase in anger at injustice, the individual may move on to the next stage of development.

Some communities at large are emerging into an acceptance stage. Community leaders and others may see that there are members of the community who make significant contributions and that these members are gay. They may be willing to discuss issues of sexuality, ways to integrate gay members into the community, and ways to address discrimination on the basis of sexual orientation. Community members are cognizant of their own homophobia and are willing to explore its effects. Attempts may be made, and at times may succeed, to have antidiscrimination measures passed and enforced. In such communities, there may be ordinances that prohibit discrimination in housing, employment, and other arenas. Yet although there may be official changes in policy, there may still be incidences of individual discrimination. These communities may at times be more inclusive in language and practice than the greater communities of which they are a part. Such communities may also explore how other forms of discrimination and oppression exist and are manifested in their culture. Although there may continue to be some misunderstanding about the nature of sexuality and sexual orientation, the community feels safe enough to explore issues and develop problem-solving strategies.

Case Study: Zhou

Zhou is a 50-year-old professional consultant who has lived in New York City for the past 20 years. Zhou is Chinese American and has been closely connected to his family all of his life. His family lived in California and Washington State for most of Zhou's adult life.

Since acknowledging his homosexuality as a young man, Zhou has lived in large metropolitan areas that are far from his family. As a result, he has never discussed his homosexuality with his family. Zhou has had a "boyfriend" for more than 15 years. They do not live together and are not monogamous in their relationship. They do, however, describe their relationship as "primary" and report that they truly love each other. Zhou's boyfriend is 20 years older than he is.

Zhou has been active in the gay community in Chelsea, a New York City neighborhood. He has been involved in the LGBT community center, having served on its board and on multiple committees. He is on the board of an AIDS service organization and is active in the LGBT organization in his company. He is also active in Asians and Friends (www.intlfriendship.org/history.htm), an organization for Asian gay men and the men attracted to them.

Zhou has entered counseling because he is experiencing dissonance in his life related to "keeping secrets" from his family. He reports feeling isolated and alienated. He reports that there is little tolerance for homosexuality in his family and in the Chinese American community in which he grew up. Although he has friends in the gay community at large, he reports that others do not fully understand the experiences of Asian gay men. He is angry about the racism in the gay community and about the homophobia in the Chinese community. He has considered moving to San Francisco, where he believes there is a more supportive, openly gay community. To do so would mean ending his long-term relationship with John, an Irish American, and leaving a career that is rewarding and nurturing for him. In addition, he would be living in a city in which he has siblings. Such a move would mean "coming out" to family members, and he believes that he is not ready to disclose his sexual orientation to his family at this time.

Zhou initially sought counseling for depression through his company's employee assistance program. He reported feeling frustrated and misunderstood and requested that he be referred to a gay-identified counselor who sees clients individually and in a group setting. Zhou is currently in a counseling group with seven other men from diverse backgrounds. They are able to discuss concerns about marginalization, cultural expectations, and problem solving. The group focuses on coming to a greater understanding of the diversity of life experiences and worldviews. Zhou reports that as a result of his participation in the group, his communication with his boyfriend John is improving. They are beginning to discuss the option of living together and perhaps marrying and the implications of this for their sexual lives and their medical, familial, and financial situations. John is beginning to have medical problems that he and Zhou are beginning to address regularly. Zhou has spoken with his older sister about his relationship with John, only to find out that the family has known of the relationship for most of the time the men have been together. They have laughed about Zhou's homophobia and have become closer as a result. They are discussing ways that Zhou can share the information with other family members.

Zhou has agreed to participate in an open discussion of racism at the LGBT community center and is exploring ways to mentor young gay Chinese American men through the community center. He acknowledges that his counseling group is a significant source of support for him and that he needs to find other sources of support within the community. Although he does not see himself "becoming an activist," he does acknowledge the need to channel his anger about homophobia and racism into avenues that can bring about some change.

Discussion. In this case, Zhou has begun exploring his gay identity in the gay community. He works in a gay-supportive, primarily heterosexual world and is exploring ways to bridge the gap between several identities. As a professional man, he has a commitment to a career. As a Chinese American man he has been integrating his identity in a Euro-centered,

English-speaking world. As a gay-identified man, he is working to integrate his ethnic identity with his sexual identity. He is acutely aware of the racism in the gay community and, with support, sees that he has the skills to address some of the issues. He is less certain about his ability to address the homophobia in the Chinese American community. With the assistance of the group, he shared some of his life with his sister and discovered that his homophobia was at play in relationships within his family.

Zhou is experiencing some of the anger encountered when individuals and groups are the target of oppression and discrimination. He has begun looking to the gay community for support and understanding. He voiced his lack of support with his initial counselor and was referred to a gay-identified counselor. At this point in his development, it may be important to work with a gay-identified professional. Although this may not be an issue in earlier stages of development, it is important at this stage.

Zhou is exploring some of his racial and cultural identity. He is confronting some of the issues of Chinese American gay men. As he uses the group to clarify some of these issues, he is making a commitment to use his skills as a more mature man to mentor younger Chinese American men within the gay community. He is also addressing the issues of racism by participating in the panel at the cultural center.

Zhou is addressing issues of growing older in the gay community. He has a vigorous workout program and brings up issues in his counseling group. He is also renegotiating his relationship with John. Changing laws have created new options for Zhou and John. The difference in their ages is now being discussed, as John has emerging health concerns. Issues of maintaining a primary relationship are discussed in the group, and Zhou is looking at different ways of participating in his primary relationship.

As a result of his work in the group, Zhou is continuing to take actions that are consistent with his sense of who he is and who he is becoming. He lives in a community that is large enough and sophisticated enough to provide support for his exploration. He acknowledges that he would have more difficulty finding support in a less cosmopolitan community.

Stage 5: Identity Pride

The next stage, Identity Pride, occurs when, accepting the philosophy of full legitimatization, the person becomes immersed in the gay subculture and has less and less to do with heterosexual others. The individual now divides his world into those who are gay and those who are not. As he becomes more identified with the gay community, he feels greater pride in its accomplishments. In his daily living he may still encounter the heterosexual world and homophobic responses, and these encounters can produce feelings of frustration and alienation. The combination of pride and anger may energize the individual, and, with encouragement from peers, he may become an activist, speaking out to address issues of inequity in a public forum.

If the emerging man chooses to confront the heterosexual establishment, he moves more and more into public view and abandons attempts to conceal his sexual orientation. As a result, he continues his coming out process. If he encounters resistance from heterosexual colleagues, he is confirmed in his beliefs in a we/they framework. When his colleagues are supportive of his emerging self, he may be encouraged to move to the final stage of development.

Some communities at large are also moving into a comparable stage of development. In such communities, sexual identity is supported and celebrated. Community leaders and supporters work for equity in all arenas of social development. There is a growing awareness of sexual and spiritual issues and a greater acceptance of diverse sexual and spiritual worldviews. When communities are in this stage of development, they may become increasingly aware of many different forms of discrimination and oppression. They are also increasingly aware of how they perpetuate such discrimination and oppression, thereby taking on the willingness to look within and create change in their own systems. In many gay-identified communities, discrimination on the basis of age, physical attractiveness, race, sex, gender, ethnicity, language, and other criteria exists. In this stage of development, communities are willing to explore how this discrimination and oppression inhibit the growth of all individuals and of the community at large. Anger about all forms of discrimination becomes increasingly evident, and individuals and community leaders become increasingly active socially. At times the dissonance in such communities is palpable as the communities struggle to develop coalition-building and collaboration skills.

Case Study: Javier

Javier is a 38-year-old Mexican American graduate student who was referred for counseling after having been arrested for participating in a demonstration after a friend had been assaulted and beaten up outside a gay bar. Javier is active in his LGBT community center and was instrumental in organizing a meeting with the local police department when leaders of the LGBT community were dissatisfied with how the police department handled this "hate crime."

Javier acknowledges that he is very angry about the way gays in his community are treated. He believes that the problem was not resolved satisfactorily because the man who was assaulted was not only gay but Mexican American as well.

Javier reports that his anger may be disproportionate to the specific incident, but he acknowledges that he carries with him a growing, chronic anger at the injustices experienced by the Mexican American community in his city. In addition, he is angry about the homophobia he experiences as a gay man in the Mexican American community and in the larger society.

He reports that he has been "openly gay" since he was in high school and that he had his first sexual experiences with his college roommate during his freshman year at the university. He reports that he has had several relationships, none lasting more than 2 years. He believes that he will eventually be involved in a monogamous relationship and that "when I am ready Mr. Right will come into my life."

He reports that when he "came out" to his family in high school at age 17 his mother said that she had always known that he was gay and his father "said nothing." He has since spoken openly with his father about his attraction to men, and though his father "doesn't understand" he is supportive and proud of Javier and they have a closer relationship now than they have ever had. He believes that this is because he has always been respectful of his father, and that is what is most important. He has a less open relationship with his brothers, whom he describes as "being caught up in being macho."

Javier does not believe that his counseling needs to focus on issues of sexual identity but rather on his anger and the injustice experienced by gay and Mexican American men. What he would like most from his counseling sessions is assistance and direction from the counselor as he develops the skills to creatively use his anger to address issues of social justice.

Discussion. In this case, Javier has identified the need to address his anger in a productive manner and to find ways to direct his experiences of injustice in a way that can bring about a change in his community. He can see the injustice clearly and understands that his anger about discrimination and oppression is appropriate. He does not like the way he expresses his anger, nor does he like the consequences of his behavior. At no time does he not accept responsibility for his anger. He does believe that the way he expresses his anger does not serve him or his community well.

He is in a position as a graduate student to have an impact on his community and to use resources to bring about greater awareness of oppression. In addition, he can work with other activists in his community to build coalitions to address issues of injustice.

Javier's family members are supportive of him, and, as he describes the dynamics, if he is respectful and engaged in the family, they will continue to be supportive. He is the first family member to go to school beyond high school, and the family is proud of his accomplishments. He reports that he learned much of his commitment to social action from his father, who has been an activist for Mexican American migrant workers, and from his mother, who has been a union organizer.

The counselor in this case can support Javier in channeling his anger in ways that are life enhancing for him and the community in which he lives. The counselor can help Javier to develop decision-making, problem-solving, and coalition-building skills. It is important for Javier, at this stage of his development, to have a counselor who is familiar with the pride stage of development and aware of and sensitive to issues of discrimination in the community within which he lives.

Stage 6: Identity Synthesis

The final stage of identity development, Identity Synthesis, occurs when a person develops an awareness that the us/them philosophy, in which all heterosexuals are viewed negatively and all homosexuals positively, no longer holds true. The emerging man recognizes and accepts that there are nongay people who can be active allies, who will support his developing gay identity, and who will work collaboratively to address issues of discrimination and oppression based on sexual orientation. The anger that the individual experienced in previous stages does not cease to exist, but its intensity decreases and the anger may be used to enhance the man's developing sense of self rather than inhibit it. Heterosexuals are not viewed in as hostile a manner, and the gay man becomes increasingly aware of coalition-building and ally relationships with people in the community at large. As a result, he begins to regain trust in selected segments of the community at large, and it is no longer necessary to see the world from an us/them framework. With the decrease in the need to dichotomize, the emerging man can now integrate his sexual identity will all other aspects of himself.

With the emergence of identity synthesis, spirituality can become an ever-increasing aspect of the man's life. He may continue to seek spiritual integration and sees his sexual self as deeply woven together with his spiritual self. He may work to integrate a spiritual tradition that reflects his earlier religious upbringing, or he may seek out alternative spiritual modalities. Whatever the case, he continues to see the integration of spirituality and sexuality as essential in his life.

In communities that are moving into the synthesis stage, community members and leaders are aware of the sexual diversity within the community and are willing to openly discuss such diversity. The fear of differences is less pronounced, and different sexual identities are not seen as a danger to the community. When discrimination on the basis of sexual orientation exists, it can be brought to the table for discussion and resolved. At times the community experiences the stress and dissonance of working through diverse issues. However, the community is not afraid to take on such issues, for there is a respect for diversity, even when some dynamics are not understood and some skills for resolving conflict have not been identified. Other forms of discrimination and oppression may also exist within the community, and, when recognized, such discrimination and oppression are openly brought to the table and resolved. Legislation and other forms of public actions work to make the communities safer for all members. These communities may also speak up to defend their position when they are confronted by more powerful forces in the yet-larger community. Members of the community feel safe enough to address the issues and comfortable enough to celebrate the diversity. The need for all members of the community to share the same worldview is not present, and community members and leaders invite strength through diversity. An underlying sense of spiritual, social, emotional, and psychological harmony and safety is characteristic of the community at its members.

Case Study: Patrick

Patrick is a 45-year-old Irish American man who grew up in a traditional Roman Catholic family. He graduated from Catholic schools and a Jesuit university. While in college he met a Catholic priest, Sean, with whom he became lovers. Eventually Sean left the priesthood and they remained partners for 15 years. During that time, Patrick was actively involved in Dignity, an organization for gay Catholics.

Patrick and Sean separated after 15 years when Sean's alcoholism became serious and Patrick was no longer willing to support Sean's alcohol use and the resulting dissonance in their relationship. After the separation Patrick moved to San Francisco and became actively involved in the gay community in the city.

For a while Patrick became involved in the "party scene," taking designer drugs and exploring many forms of sexuality. During this time many of his friends and acquaintances were diagnosed with HIV and died from HIV-related illnesses. Patrick reports that "it is a miracle that I have not seroconverted." Afraid, Patrick decided not to have any sexual contact and remained celibate for 3 years.

Patrick has a wide circle of friends professionally and personally. He is not currently in a long-term relationship and reports that he believes that a relationship will happen when he is ready for it to happen.

Patrick has entered counseling because he is feeling the "loss of a spiritual life." He no longer feels connected to Roman Catholicism and has attended services at other Christian denominations, reporting that he feels "disconnected" in these services. He reports that the churches "accept my homosexuality, but they don't really seem to understand it." He reports that he seeks balance in his life and that he works out physically, eats a healthy diet, enjoys physical activities, has a well-rounded circle of friends, is involved in the community, attends cultural events regularly, likes his job, and sees opportunities for career advancement.

After several individual counseling sessions, Patrick was referred to a group for gay men. The men in the group meet weekly to discuss issues related to gay spirituality. They frequently read excerpts from such books as *Coming Out Spiritually* (de la Huerta, 1999) and *Gay Soul* (Thompson, 1995). Several of the men have attended retreats sponsored by Spirit Journeys (http://www.spiritjourneys.com/gay-spirituality-resources), and the group facilitator is trained in Jungian psychology. The men in the group are all interested in exploring the spiritual dynamics related to sexual orientation, and they come from diverse racial, ethnic, and spiritual backgrounds. Patrick seems to have found an arena for his exploration. Along with the group, Patrick marched in the Pride parade and is working with his peers to develop a series of retreats for younger gay men who have been diagnosed as HIV positive.

Discussion. In this case, Patrick has moved into the gay community and into the community at large. As a younger man he was involved in a religious tradition that was important to him. In his relationship with Sean, Patrick was able to continue his religious and spiritual exploration. When the relationship ended, Patrick was able to move on in many aspects of his life. He acknowledges that his spiritual growth got lost as he attended to other aspects of his life. He further acknowledges that he was not able to find a spiritual connection but continued to explore. As a result of his involvement with the counseling group, Patrick connected with other men from a variety of spiritual traditions. He became involved in a variety of experiences and has decided to share his experiences with others as part of his spiritual growth. He is also living in a community that supports, encourages, and celebrates the kind of growth he seeks.

Conclusion

When counseling a gay man, the counselor must be prepared to meet the man where he is in his own development. This means that the counselor must be aware of the individual's personal growth, his connection to his family, and the family's approach to sexual identity development. Often family-of-origin dynamics have a strong influence on the developing gay man's sense of who he is and who he wishes to become. In addition, it is important to have a working understanding of the culture within which the emerging man lives. At times his culture will be supportive of his emerging self. More often, cultural dynamics may impede development.

If the counselor is to be most helpful to the emerging gay man, he or she must be familiar with community resources. As the client evolves, he will need to become increasingly involved in the gay community. For many emerging gay men, the only community with which they are familiar is the bar community. In contemporary American society, many other options exist. The counselor must know his or her community and must be able to provide appropriate referrals for the emerging gay man. In some communities, this means that counselors may be on community boards, be active in providing services to many different community members, run for elected office in order to encourage legislative change, or serve in other capacities in their communities.

Often the emerging gay man may need allies as he confronts discrimination in the community. Counselors may need to be prepared to become involved in fighting-oppression workshops or other activities that help to bring about social change. Counselors can become actively involved as advocates in community organizations and on decision-making or advisory commissions. They can also work to change laws and policies in larger organizations and in the community at large. As Appleby (2001) has identified, counselors must be prepared to address the concerns of the emerging gay man in his emerging community on the historical, environmental-structural, cultural, familial, and individual levels. For many counselors, this becomes an opportunity for personal growth and development.

References

Appleby, G. (Ed.). (2001). *Working class gay and bisexual men.* New York, NY: Harrington Park Press.

Bauman, S. (2011). *Cyberbullying: What counselors need to know.* Alexandria, VA: American Counseling Association.

Beam, J. (Ed.). (1986). *In the life: A Black gay anthology.* Boston, MA: Alyson.

Boykin, K. (1996). *One more river to cross: Black and gay in America.* New York, NY: Anchor Books.

Browning, F. (1994). *The culture of desire: Paradox and perversity in gay lives today.* New York, NY: Vintage Books.

Browning, F. (1998). *A queer geography: Journeys toward a sexual self.* New York, NY: Noonday Press.

Cass, V. C. (1979). Homosexual identity formation: A theoretical model. *Journal of Homosexuality, 4,* 219–235.

Center for Substance Abuse Treatment. (2001). *A provider's introduction to substance abuse treatment for lesbian, gay, bisexual, and transgender individuals.* Rockville, MD: U.S. Department of Health and Human Services, Substance Abuse and Mental Health Services Administration.

Chaney, M. P. (2008). Muscle dysmorphia, self-esteem, and loneliness among gay and bisexual men. *International Journal of Men's Health, 7,* 157–170.

Chaney, M. P., & Marszalek, J. (2009). Sexual orientation and heterosexism. In D. G. Hays & B. T. Erford (Eds.). *Handbook for developing multicultural counseling competency: A systems approach* (pp. 13–14). Upper Saddle River, NJ: Prentice Hall.

Chung, Y. B., & Szymanski, D. M. (2000, August). *Multiple identities of Asian American gay men: A qualitative study.* Paper presented at the Annual Convention of the American Psychological Association, Washington, DC.

Chung, Y. B., & Szymanski, D. M. (2006). Racial and sexual identities of Asian American gay men. *Journal of LGBT Issues in Counseling, 1*(2), 67–93.

Coleman, E. (1982). Developmental stages of the coming out process. *Journal of Homosexuality, 7*(2–3), 31–43.

de la Huerta, C. (1999). *Coming out spiritually: The next step.* New York, NY: Tarcher/Putnam.

Fortunato, J. (1982). *Embracing the exile: Healing journeys of gay Christians.* San Francisco, CA: Harper & Row.

Fortunato, J. (1987). *AIDS: The spiritual dilemma.* San Francisco, CA: Harper & Row.

Gooch, B. (1999). *Finding the boyfriend within: A practical guide for tapping into your own source of love, happiness, and respect.* New York, NY: Simon & Schuster.

Harris, D. (1997). *The rise and fall of gay culture.* New York, NY: Hyperion.

Hemphill, E., & Beam, J. (1991). *Brother to brother: New writings by Black gay men.* Boston, MA: Alyson.

hooks, b. (2001). *Salvation: Black people and love.* New York, NY: Morrow.

Hutchins, A. M. (2010). Advocacy and the private practice counselor. In M. Ratts, R. Toporek, & J. Lewis (Eds.), *ACA advocacy competencies: A social justice framework for counselors* (pp. 125–138). Alexandria, VA: American Counseling Association.

Hutchins, A. M. (2012). Moving through the void: Counseling gay men with histories of chemical abuse and dependency. In S. H. Dworkin & M. Pope (Eds.), *Casebook for counseling lesbian, gay, bisexual, and transgender persons and their families* (pp. 281–288). Alexandria, VA: American Counseling Association.

Isay, R. (1989). *Being homosexual: Gay men and their development.* New York, NY: Farrar, Straus & Giroux.

Isay, R. (1996). *Becoming gay: The journey to self-acceptance.* New York, NY: Holt.

Jackson, G. (1991). *The secret lore of gardening: Patterns of male intimacy, Book 1.* Toronto, Ontario, Canada: Inner City Books.

Jackson, G. (1993). *The living room mysteries: Patterns of male intimacy, Book 2.* Toronto, Ontario, Canada: Inner City Books.

Johnson, T. (2000). *Gay spirituality: The role of gay identity in the transformation of human consciousness.* Los Angeles, CA: Alyson Books.

King, J. L. (2004). *On the down low: A journey into the lives of "straight" Black men who sleep with men.* New York, NY: Broadway Books.

Kominars, S., & Kominars, K. (1996). *Accepting ourselves and others: A journey into recovery from addiction and compulsive behaviors for gays, lesbians, and bisexuals.* Center City, MN: Hazelden.

Kooden, H., & Flowers, C. (2000). *Golden men: The power of gay midlife.* New York, NY: Avon Books.

Kus, R. (1990). *Keys to caring: Assisting your gay and lesbian clients.* Boston, MA: Alyson.

Lewis, J. A., Arnold, M. S., House, R., & Toporek, R. L. (2002). *ACA advocacy competencies.* Retrieved from http:/www.counseling.org/resources/competencies/advocacy_competencies.pdf

Longres, J. (Ed.). (1996). *Men of color: A context for service to homosexually active men.* New York, NY: Harrington Park Press.

Lowenthal, M. (Ed.). (1997). *Gay men at the millennium: Sex, spirit, community.* New York, NY: Tarcher/Putnam.

Morales, E. S. (1992). Counseling Latino gays and Latina lesbians. In S. Dworkin & J. Gutierrez (Eds.), *Counseling gay men and lesbians: Journey to the end of the rainbow* (pp. 125–139). Alexandria, VA: American Association for Counseling and Development.

Nelson, E. (Ed.). (1993). *Critical essays: Gay and lesbian writers of color.* New York, NY: Harrington Park Press.

Ratts, M. J. (2009). Social justice counseling: Toward the development of a "fifth force" among counseling paradigms. *Journal of Humanistic Counseling, Education and Development, 48,* 28–30.

Ratts, M. J., & Hutchins, A. M. (2009). ACA advocacy competencies: Social justice advocacy at the client/student level. *Journal of Counseling & Development, 87,* 269–275.

Ratts, M. J., Lewis, J. A., & Toporek, R. L. (2010). Advocacy and social justice: A helping paradigm for the 21st century. In M. J. Ratts, R. L. Toporek, & J. A. Lewis (Eds.), *ACA advocacy competencies: A social justice framework for counselors* (pp. 3–10). Alexandria, VA: American Counseling Association.

Remafedi, G. (Ed.). (1994). *Death by denial: Studies of suicide in gay and lesbian teenagers.* Boston, MA: Alyson.

Roscoe, W. (Ed.). (1988). *Living the spirit: A gay American Indian anthology.* New York, NY: St. Martin's Press.

Roscoe, W. (1995). *Queer spirits: A gay men's myth book.* Boston, MA: Beacon Press.

Roscoe, W. (1998). *Changing ones: Third and fourth genders in native North America.* New York, NY: St. Martin's Press.

Russell, S. T., Clarke, T. J., & Clary, J. (2009). Are teens "post-gay"? Contemporary adolescents' sexual identity labels. *Journal of Youth and Adolescence, 38,* 884–890.

Russell, S. T., McGuire, J. K., Lee, S., Larriva, J. C., & Laub, C. (2008). Adolescent perceptions of school safety for students with lesbian, gay, bisexual, and transgender parents. *Journal of Gay and Lesbian Issues in Education, 5,* 11–27.

Russell, S. T., Muraco, A., Subramaniam, A., & Laub, C. (2009). Youth empowerment and high school gay-straight alliances. *Journal of Youth and Adolescence, 38,* 891–903.

Sears, J. (Ed.). (1994). *Bound by diversity: Unity emerges from a chorus of voices. Contributions by members of the lesbian, gay, bisexual and transgender communities.* Columbia, SC: Sebastian Press.

Siegel, S., & Lowe, E. (1994). *Uncharted lives: Understanding the life passages of gay men.* New York, NY: Dutton.

Signorile, M. (1997). *Life outside: The Signorile report on gay men: Sex, drugs, muscles, and the passages of life.* New York, NY: HarperCollins.

Smith, M. (Ed.). (1983). *Black men/White men.* San Francisco, CA: Gay Sunshine Press.

Stowe, J. (1999). *Gay spirit warrior: An empowerment workbook for men who love men.* Tallahassee, FL: Findhorn Press.

Thompson, M. (Ed.). (1987). *Gay spirit: Myth and meaning.* New York, NY: St. Martin's Press.

Thompson, M. (Ed.). (1995). *Gay soul: Finding the heart of gay spirit and nature.* San Francisco, CA: HarperCollins.

Thompson, M. (1997). *Gay body: A journey through shadow to self.* New York, NY: St. Martin's Press.

Tobias, A. (1998). *The best little boy in the world grows up.* New York, NY: Random House.

Troiden, R. R. (1979). Becoming homosexual: A model for gay identity acquisition. *Psychiatry, 42,* 362–373.

Troiden, R. R. (1989). The formation of homosexual identities. *Journal of Homosexuality, 17,* 43–74.

Williams, W. (1986). *The spirit and the flesh: Sexual diversity in American Indian culture.* Boston, MA: Beacon Press.

Wright, E. (2001). *Cultural issues in working with lesbian, gay, bisexual, and transgender individuals. A provider's introduction to substance abuse treatment for lesbian, gay, bisexual, and transgender individuals.* Rockville, MD: U.S. Department of Health and Human Services, Substance Abuse and Mental Health Services Administration.

Additional Resources

About.com: Gay Life
    www.gaylife.about.com

The Advocate
    www.advocate.com

Asians and Friends
    www.intlfriendship.org/history.htm

Compatible Partners
    www.compatiblepartners.net

FindLaw
    www.findlaw.com

Gay.com
    www.gay.com

Gay Men's Health Summit discussion group
    http://groups.yahoo.com/group/GayMensHealthSummit/

Match.com
    www.match.com

Matthew Shepard Foundation
    www.matthewshepard.org

National Suicide Prevention Lifeline
    www.suicidepreventionlifeline.org

PerfectMatch.com
    www.perfectmatch.com

PlanetOut
    www.planetout.com

Services and Advocacy for Gay, Lesbian, Bisexual, and Transgender Elders
    www.sageusa.org

Spirit Journeys
    www.spiritjourneys.com

The Trevor Project
    www.thetrevorproject.com

Chapter 13

Counseling Lesbian, Bisexual, Queer, Questioning, and Transgender Women

Anneliese A. Singh and Kirstyn Yuk Sim Chun

Counseling lesbian, bisexual, queer, questioning, and transgender (LBQQT) women requires that counselors have special awareness, knowledge, and skills. The experiences of societal prejudice and discrimination that LBQQT women must navigate influence their well-being. However, this group also has daily lived experiences of individual resilience and coping with this societal oppression that counselors should be aware of and support. In addition, like many historically marginalized communities, LBQQT women often develop collective resilience within their communities as they seek to fulfill their human potential and live authentically.

Although there are no accurate statistics on the number of LBQQT women in the United States, it is estimated that this group makes up 10% of the U.S. population. Accurate statistics are difficult to collect because of societal heterosexism that contributes to LBQQT women not feeling safe disclosing their sexual orientation and/or gender identity. Yet counselors should feel prepared to work with this group, as it is likely that they will counsel LBQQT women and/or work with important individuals in their lives. This chapter introduces terminology important for counselors to know and use when working with LBQQT women. The chapter also discusses common counseling concerns, helpful counseling interventions, typical counselor advocacy, and community resources for working with this group.

Knowing the Queer Terminology

A good first step in obtaining the necessary knowledge to work with LBQQT women is to understand the language the members of this group use to describe themselves. *Queer* is a word that people often have difficulty understanding and feel uncomfortable using. However, it is important for counselors not only to be able to say this word but to understand its history and meaning. People feel uncomfortable using this word because it has a history of being used to pathologize and denigrate LBQQT women. Recently, the word *queer* was reclaimed by youth and other individuals with a politicized view of gender and sexuality. This politicized view includes challenging the binary gender assignment and role system that asserts that there are two genders: male and female. In addition, *queer* is used as an umbrella term for sexual orientations that are not heteronormative or "straight." So, a queer woman may challenge traditional norms and roles in terms of both gender identity and sexual orientation.

Lesbian is a sexual orientation that describes women who feel attractions to other women, whereas *bisexual* is used to describe women who experience attractions to both women and men. *Questioning* is used to describe women who are exploring their attractions to women and men. Questioning women may or may not express confusion about their sexuality. Both bisexual and questioning women may experience misunderstanding and even prejudice from people both within and outside of the queer community.

Like *queer*, the word *transgender* is often used as an umbrella term. However, *transgender* refers to gender identities and expressions that are outside of the traditional binary genders of male and female. Transgender women may not identify with the sex (i.e., anatomy) they were assigned at birth if it is not congruent with their internal sense of gender (e.g., identity as man, woman, neither, or something else). *Transsexual* women are those who select hormonal and/or medical treatment to align their sex with their gender (see Lambda Legal, 2008, for a full discussion). Counselors should also be aware that people assigned female at birth may identify with terms such as *genderqueer, genderfluid,* or *bigender* (terms similar to *queer* but that may also include a disidentification with gender labels or a fluid sense of gender). To familiarize themselves with these terms, counselors should consult the Additional Resources section and Appendix 13.1.

Feminist, Multicultural, and Social Justice Issues in Counseling LBQQT Women

Because LBQQT women continue to face societal discrimination, counselors should be familiar with feminist, multicultural, and social justice issues in working with this group. *Feminism,* a theoretical framework for working with clients who experience systemic oppression, focuses on client empowerment. Worell and Remer (2003) identified four tenets of feminism in working with women clients: (a) valuing women's lived experiences, (b) recognizing the intersections of women's identities within sociopolitical and sociohistorical contexts, (c) holding egalitarian relationships, and (d) understanding that the "personal is political" (p. 65; i.e., understanding the connection between individual experiences of oppression and systemic oppression and vice versa).

It is also important for counselors to understand multicultural issues in counseling LBQQT women. LBQQT women have multiple identities (in terms of race/ethnicity, ability status, social class, religious/spiritual affiliation, etc.) that intersect with their sexual orientation, gender identity, and expression. For instance, a transgender women of color who is Muslim may have distinctly different counseling needs than a woman who identifies as White, Christian, and lesbian. There is not one simple approach to understanding clients' experiences as their multiple identities intersect, as this is a very complex process. However, counselors should have facility in using the Association for Multicultural Counseling and Development's Multicultural Counseling Competencies (see Sue, Arredondo, & McDavis, 1992) as a framework for working with LBQQT women. Counselors can add a perspective of intersectionality by asking the following questions: (a) What is the awareness I need to have in working with the intersection of LBQQT women's identities? (b) What is the knowledge I need to have in working with the intersection of LBQQT women's identities? and (c) What are the skills I need to have in working with the intersection of LBQQT women's identities?

Among the social justice issues counselors should understand prior to engaging in counseling practice with LBQQT women is heterosexism. *Heterosexism* is a system of societal oppression that privileges heterosexual identities, practices, and worldviews while devaluing those that are nonheteronormative. Because of heterosexism, LBQQT women may experience *homoprejudice* (discrimination against LBQQ women) or *transprejudice* (discrimination against transgender women). Homoprejudice and transprejudice influence LBQQT women's well-being and can manifest in internalized oppression (i.e., negative attitudes about being an LBQQT woman). Therefore, counselors may use a social justice approach as an overall framework for intervening with this group.

Common Counseling Concerns

LBQQT women are likely to experience heterosexism as they come to terms with their identities and begin to share these identities with others. This process of identity development and coming out may be further complicated when LBQQT women experience multiple forms of marginalization through their identification with multiple groups traditionally marginalized by U.S. society. In spite of these challenges, LBQQT women have demonstrated remarkable resilience in learning to thrive as sexual minorities, integrate multiple minority experiences, and communicate and connect with the communities that surround them.

Effects of Heterosexism on LBQQT Women

There have been several recent legal, political, and social advances in lesbian, gay, bisexual, and transgender (LGBT) rights, for instance, decriminalization of same-sex sexual behavior in *Lawrence et al. v. Texas* (U.S. Supreme Court, 2003), some protection for same-sex relationships, and the passage of LGBT-inclusive hate crimes legislation. However, heterosexism remains a reality for LBQQT women coming to terms with minority sexual and gender identities. When positive advances are derailed by shifts in anti-LGBT political movements (e.g., the passage of Proposition 8 in California overturning marriage rights for same-sex couples; the proposal of the Employment Non-Discrimination Act, which did not include transgender individuals), sexual and gender minorities may experience psychological distress (Russell, 2004; Russell & Richards, 2003).

Herek (1986) defined *heterosexism* as "a world-view, a value-system that prizes heterosexuality, assumes it as the only appropriate manifestation of love and sexuality, and devalues homosexuality and all that is not heterosexual" (p. 925). In addition to political influences, heterosexism may be fueled by popular opinion; media; stereotypes; and correlates of heterosexism, such as conservative attitudes, fear of being LGBT, male attitudes, peer attitudes and personal contact, demographics, and religious beliefs (Badgett, Lau, Sears, & Ho, 2007; Ritter & Terndrup, 2002). *Transphobia* is discrimination and prejudicial attitudes against transgender people.

Ongoing exposure to these influences and other forms of heterosexism may result in significant psychological challenges for LBQQT women. When homoprejudice, transprejudice, and sexism fuel violence and other forms of victimization against LBQQT women, even greater levels of psychological distress and impairment may be experienced (Garnets, Herek, & Levy, 2003). For example, LBQQT women may exhibit social withdrawal and passivity; anxiety, suspicion, and insecurity; and denial of minority group membership in response to sexual and gender prejudice (Ritter & Terndrup, 2002). Even when LBQQT women remain physically unscathed by their immediate surroundings, they may experience internalized homoprejudice or internalized transprejudice as they personalize negative societal attitudes toward sexual and gender minorities and begin to devalue themselves and other LBQQT women (Ritter & Terndrup, 2002).

Identity Development and Coming Out Issues for LBQQT Women

The mental health consequences of sexual and gender prejudice often include negative effects on the identity development and coming out processes of LBQQT women. Many of the sexual and gender minority identity development models (e.g., Cass, 1979; Coleman, 1982; Grace, 1992; Lev, 2004; Troiden, 1989; Weinberg, Williams, & Pryor, 1994) conceptualize identity development in terms of stages through which individuals often, but not exclusively, move in succession from limited awareness to full acceptance of LBQQT identities.

Progression through these stages of identity development is often mediated by psychosocial stressors such as heterosexism, transphobia, and other forms of prejudice (Fassinger & Richie, 1997; Gonsiorek & Rudolph, 1991). For example, individuals who face significant sexual and gender identity prejudice may be hindered in their ability to fully embrace their identities and live open and productive lives as LBQQT women. Conversely, individuals who receive support and acceptance from their family and friends may progress more quickly toward the development of healthy LBQQT identities (Hom, 2003).

The process of coming out as LBQQT is often similarly mediated by homoprejudice, transprejudice, and other forms of prejudice. Although Reynolds and Hanjorgiris (2000) included sexual minority identity development in their definition of coming out, others have typically defined coming out as a lifelong process through which LBQQT and other sexual and gender minority individuals disclose their identities to others (e.g., Herek, 2003). When heterosexism is present, LBQQT women may experience emotional distress as they publicly identify with a "socially denigrated nonheterosexual LGB identity" (Dworkin, 2000, p. 165). Indeed, the mental health consequences of coming out in the midst of sexual and gender identity prejudice may include mood disorders, substance abuse, eating disorders, somatic concerns, and even suicide (Caitlin & Futterman, 1997; Gonsiorek, 1995).

Coming out as bisexual or sexually fluid may pose unique challenges for LBQQT women, as these women may concurrently encounter heterosexism from heterosexuals and biphobia (i.e., discrimination against bisexual people) from lesbians and other sexual minorities (Dworkin, 2000; Firestein, 2007). Because their sexual identities are often assumed to be dependent on the gender of their current partners, sexually fluid LBQQT individuals may struggle to assert a stable bisexual identity over time regardless of their current relationship status (Dworkin, 1996; Fox, 1995; Matteson, 1996). Perhaps most challenging of all, most bisexual women struggle to find heterosexual or lesbian/gay communities in which they feel truly accepted. Communities composed entirely of sexually fluid individuals are difficult to locate, even in major metropolitan areas, given the ongoing invisibility and stigma attached to bisexuality (Firestein, 2007).

The identity development and coming out processes of LBQQT individuals who identify as transgender may be mediated by both transprejudice and possibly homoprejudice, depending on their sexual identities. The identity development of gender-variant LBQQT individuals may also be complicated by the medical model of diagnosis and approval for those seeking medical treatment (Hausman, 1995; Lev, 2004). For example, transgender LBQQT individuals may be "forced to lie and create false narratives" to qualify for medical treatments needed to complete "self-actualization" and render their gender identity and gender expression consistent (Lev, 2007, p. 153).

Like their sexual minority counterparts, but perhaps even more so in some situations, transgender individuals remain unprotected by federal and state laws in a variety of domains. In 2009, for example, it was still legal in 38 states to terminate employment solely on the basis of gender identity and expression (Human Rights Campaign, 2009). In a review of more than 50 studies over the past decade, the Williams Institute (Badgett et al., 2007) found that gender identity discrimination was a "common occurrence" (Executive Summary, p. 2) in many occupational settings nationwide. Specifically, the Williams Institute's review of existing research revealed "consistent and compelling evidence" (Badgett et al., 2007, p. 21) of discrimination against transgender and other LBQQT individuals with regard to wages, employment, and workplace environment. The report concluded, "Lower incomes and difficulty in getting or keeping a job create direct disadvantages for LGBT people who have experienced discrimination in the workplace" (p. 21).

Intersections of Identity Among LBQQT Women

In addition to being influenced by heterosexism and other forms of prejudice, identity development and coming out processes among LBQQT women are mediated by demographic factors such as race/ethnicity, ability, religious affiliation, age, and other aspects of identity (Dworkin, 2000; Singh & Chun, 2012). Early stage models of sexual minority identity development (e.g., Cass, 1979) emphasized disclosure as a necessary component of identity acceptance and depicted limited disclosure as unhealthy (Smith, 1997). However, subsequent writings have criticized this interpretation as culturally biased in that it values individuation over collective loyalty to one's family and cultural background (Trujillo, 1997).

A rigid interpretation of the stage models regarding sexual and gender identity development also ignores the cultural complexity and layers of marginalization often experienced by LBQQT women of color (Fukuyama & Ferguson, 2000). LBQQT women who experience multiple forms of marginalization may experience *multiple minority stress,* in which emotional distress multiplies in direct proportion to an increase in exposure to multiple forms of prejudice (Bowleg, Huang, Brooks, Black, & Burkholder, 2003; Chung & Katayama, 1998; Fukuyama & Ferguson, 2000; Liddle, 2007; I. H. Meyer, 2003; Rosario, Schrimshaw, & Hunter, 2004, 2008). Indeed, Greene (1995) used the term *triple jeopardy* to describe the experiences of Black lesbians and other LBQQT women of color as they struggle with a combination of racism, sexism, and heterosexism.

This exposure to multiple forms of discrimination on different fronts often requires a more nuanced approach to coming out for LBQQT women of color (e.g., Greene, 1994; Nakamura, Flojo, & Dittrich, 2009; Rice & Nakamura, 2009). LBQQT women of color who experience racism, for example, require support and affirmation from their families and cultural communities regarding their racial identities in a way that White LBQQT individuals who experience racial privilege do not (Greene, 1994; Liddle, 2007). LBQQT women of color who are also immigrants may find themselves even more dependent on their cultural communities for assistance with language and access to the dominant culture. This dependency may be especially pronounced for undocumented individuals, whose immigration status could be significantly jeopardized by rejection from the family and cultural community (Greene, 1994).

It is unfortunate that despite the extent to which LBQQT women of color rely on their families, they may still experience a degree of isolation from their cultural communities with regard to their relationships and friendships (Chan, 1989; Greene, 1997; Jackson & Brown, 1996; Singh & Chun, 2012). There is also some risk that internal conflicts among one's sexual, gender, and racial/ethnic identities could hinder the development of an integrated sense of identity for LBQQT women of color (Chan, 1997; Greene, 1997). Additional research regarding intersections among sexual orientation, gender identity, and race/ethnicity is needed to more fully understand the experiences of LBQQT women of color (DeBlaere, Brewster, Sarkees, & Moradi, 2010; Harper, Jernewall, & Zea, 2004; Moradi, DeBlaere, & Huang, 2010).

Connecting with LBQQT-affirmative communities may also be an issue for LBQQT women with disabilities. Individuals with mobility impairments, for example, may encounter problems physically accessing community events, especially if they depend on family members for transportation (Greene, 2003). This reliance on others for assistance may also hinder the disclosure of one's LBQQT identity among individuals with disabilities (Caitlin & Futterman, 1997). In general, more research regarding LBQQT individuals with disabilities is needed to provide additional information about this population (Dworkin, 2000; Liddle, 2007).

LBQQT individuals who identify with traditional religious communities may also experience feelings of alienation and isolation, depending on the degree to which their religious community accepts sexual and gender identity minorities. Dworkin (1997), for example, discussed the challenges lesbian Jews face in navigating multiple forms of marginalization, such as sexism, heterosexism, and anti-Semitism. Greek Orthodox LBQQT individuals may experience similar struggles in attempting to integrate their identities and find communities that affirm all aspects of themselves (Fygetakis, 1997).

In these and other instances in which religion is closely linked with cultural experiences and identities, for example, in African American Christian communities (Folayan, 1992) or among Latin American Catholics (Davidson, 2000), LBQQT women who struggle with decisions about whether to remain within their faith communities may find themselves contemplating the loss of their cultural communities as well (Folayan, 1992; Gock, 1992). It should be noted that significant within-group as well as between-group differences may be found among religious communities.

It is also important to note that these intersections of identity among race/ethnicity, ability, religious affiliation, and LBQQT identity may vary significantly according to generational cohort. LBQQT women who came of age prior to the Stonewall riots of 1969 may not even refer to themselves as "LBQQT," preferring instead terms like *lesbian, butch,* and *femme.* Conversely, current youth who believe they live in a postgay society may reclaim former epithets like *queer* or eschew labels for sexual orientation and gender identity entirely (Savin-Williams, 2005).

Another way in which age may influence the sexual identity development and coming out processes of LBQQT women is in the degree to which it may restrict access to LBQQT events and resources (Liddle, 2007). For example, sexual and gender identity minority youth may not have access to bars or other events that require them to be of majority age (Safren & Pantalone, 2006). As minors with limited options, they may also be especially dependent on family and school personnel who wish to limit their participation in LBQQT community activities (Sanders & Kroll, 2000; Scourfield, Roen, & McDermott, 2008).

Older LBQQT women may in turn worry about maintaining their connections to the local LBQQT community if they must move to retirement communities. Concerns about preserving and protecting same-sex relationships may also arise as issues regarding advance health care directives and rights of survivorship become more relevant (Barón & Cramer, 2000).

Resilience and Coping in LBQQT Women

In spite of challenges regarding heterosexism, identity development, coming out, and intersecting identities, LBQQT women demonstrate the capacity for tremendous resilience and adaptation to adversity (Bowleg et al., 2003; Connolly, 2005, 2006; Greene, 1995; Stepakoff & Bowleg, 1998). Masten, Best, and Garmezy (1990) defined *resilience* as "a process, capacity, or outcome of successful adaptation despite challenges or threatening circumstances" (p. 426). Greene (1994) has speculated that individuals confronted with multiple forms of marginalization may be able to access coping strategies and resources developed in response to prior experiences with oppression.

I. Meyer (2010) expanded on this idea by describing resilience as a protective factor that reduces stress levels during the onset of the stressor, inoculates lesbian, gay, and bisexual individuals against high levels of stress even after the onset of the stressor, and directly improves the health outcomes of sexual minorities. Specifically, I. H. Meyer (2003) suggested that sexual minorities utilize both personal and group resources. Accordingly, LBQQT women may cope with minority stress by utilizing resources at both the individual and group level. Affiliation with other sexual and gender minorities provides support in environments that are affirming of LBQQT identities (Jones et al., 1984). In addition, membership in LBQQT groups may yield opportunities for in-group "reappraisal of the stressful condition, yielding it less injurious to psychological well-being" (I. H. Meyer, 2003, p. 677).

Case Studies of LBQQT Women

In this section we present two case studies that illustrate the diversity inherent in LBQQT women's communities. Each case study is followed by discussion questions to facilitate the application of theory to a clinical case.

The Case of Thu: Sexual Fluidity and Coming Out in Familial and Cultural Contexts

Thu is a 28-year-old single Vietnamese and Chinese American woman who is unsure about how to label her sexual identity. She and her family emigrated as refugees from Vietnam when she was 11 years old. Although both of her parents were born in Vietnam, her father is ethnically Vietnamese and her mother is ethnically Vietnamese and Chinese. Thu is the oldest of five siblings, and her youngest two siblings were born in the United States after the family immigrated. Thu learned English in middle school and is now bilingual. Raised Catholic by her parents, she has not practiced the religion since she began her undergraduate studies. Though she still lives at home, Thu is a fourth-year graduate student pursuing her PhD in chemistry at a local university.

She presents for counseling with concerns about her sexual identity and the prospect of disclosing her 2-year romantic relationship with a female lab partner. This is Thu's first same-sex relationship, and she reports that it "just happened, just came out of the blue . . . totally unexpected." Prior to this relationship, Thu had only had romantic and sexual relationships with men. She reports enjoying these experiences and therefore remembers feeling "really confused" when she first started having feelings for her lab partner, Jillian: "All I wanted to do was be around her, all the time . . . when I couldn't see her, it ached inside. I didn't know why at first." Since then, Thu and Jillian have developed a loving and supportive intimate partner relationship. Jillian, a fourth-generation Euro-American woman, has more experience dating women and identifies as lesbian. In spite of their differences, Thu describes her girlfriend as "really patient, really accepting" about Thu's process of discovering her identity and her feelings for Jillian.

Recently, Jillian has begun to ask Thu about the possibility of them living together. Although Thu knows that she is not yet ready to move out of her parents' home and take this step, the conversations between them have prompted Thu to consider moving toward explaining to her parents that Jillian is "more than a friend." However, Thu presents in therapy with confusion and concern about whether and how to do this. "I don't even know what to call myself . . . how can I come out to my parents when I don't know what I am? They are *so* Catholic and *so* Asian, I just know they would *die* if I told them the truth about Jillian." Thu explains, "We don't even talk about *straight* sex in our culture. There's no *way* I want them thinking about me having gay sex with my girlfriend." She wonders aloud whether Jillian would mind continuing on as they have for the past 2 years: "I mean, my parents are really nice to Jillian . . . they call her my 'special friend' and cook for her . . . maybe that could be enough for now?"

Counseling Considerations With Thu

Multiculturally responsive counseling with Thu should be grounded in an approach that affirms the struggle Thu has between her sexual orientation and her racial/ethnic identity and cultural background. Initially the counselor should seek to understand more about Thu's values related to her various identities. The counselor should also know that many LBQQT environments in the United States are predominantly White and Western in their perspective. Therefore, understanding how Thu experiences her partner's White-ness and the extent to which Thu is connected with an Asian American/Pacific Islander LBQQT community or online resources is also important. If Thu is feeling pressured to choose her partner over her family or vice versa, the counselor can provide an environment in which to explore the potential influences that either route might have on her life. Because many Asian American/Pacific Islander cultures express their experiences of stress somatically in the body, the counselor can also assess the degree to which Thu is experiencing somatic complaints and explore how these might be related to the stress she feels about her various identities.

A large portion of cultural competence with Thu is being mindful that disclosing one's sexual orientation and/or gender identity and expression is emphasized in White, Western LBQQT cultures. However, many LBQQT people of color may experience more stress being disconnected from their families as a result of coming out. So, working with Thu includes staying close to her values and exploring ways in which she can negotiate the stressors of *both* her sexual orientation and cultural background as opposed to framing these stressors as choices she has to make. Providing Thu with readings and online resources about Asian American/Pacific Islander LBQQT people with similar stories may also help ameliorate some of the isolation Thu may be experiencing. These stories should also include some reference to or exploration of religious identity, as this may be a salient aspect of Thu's struggle. Lastly, throughout the counseling process, the counselor should self-assess his or her own biases, assumptions, and stereotypes about sexual orientation, race/ethnicity, and religion—in addition to how these identities intersect with one another from the counselor's perspective—in order to center Thu's particular concerns and intersections of identities.

The Case of C.J.: Gender Identity Development and Coming Out to Partners

C.J. is a 47-year-old same-gender-loving individual of African descent who is in a committed relationship with his partner, Angela. They have lived together for the past 14 years, and together they are raising Angela's 15-year old son Darren from her previous marriage to a man. C.J. has worked as a real estate agent for the past 21 years and reports enjoying his job. Angela, who is of African American and Latina heritage, is a radiology technician at a local hospital.

Until he was in his early 40s, C.J. (who now uses masculine pronouns) had always identified as butch. His prior female masculinity had been an attribute to which Angela (who tends to express her gender identity as femme) had been very attracted. Though both partners were emotionally supportive of and expressive to each other, C.J. had enjoyed playing the more butch role in their relationship. It was he who had always handled home repairs, finances, and athletic activities with Darren.

In spite of this apparent fit between C.J.'s prior butch identity, gender expression, and role in the family, he presents in counseling with concerns that "something has always been not right with my body." He speaks of feeling overwhelmingly uncomfortable with his body parts, whispering quietly that "not even binding my chest or 'packing' makes it right . . . it's still all wrong." C.J. reveals having struggled since high school to feel comfortable in his body, as back then he could not bear to look at his naked body in a mirror and thought constantly of ways to "make it all go away." He shares that his apparent identification as a "same-gender-loving" butch in his 20s allowed him to wear men's clothing that had at least allowed him to be "read" as male most of the time.

However, the feelings of discomfort and shame about his body "never really went away . . . just kept coming at me over and over." After watching a documentary on the news about transgender youth who are beginning to take therapeutic doses of testosterone, C.J. apparently asked Angela what she thought about him receiving hormone therapy too ("Just the hormones for now, I'm not sure about all that other stuff. Maybe the chest surgery someday, but that's it"). C.J. reports having felt angry and hurt when Angela quickly laughed and remarked, "Oh baby, come on, you're too old for that." When she realized C.J. was serious, Angela reportedly looked worried, saying, "Now why do you have to do a crazy thing like that? I mean, you already look like a man. Why do you have to have the parts too? If I wanted a real man, I would have stayed with my ex-husband. Girl, you know I'm gay . . . I can't go back to being straight."

Counseling Considerations With C.J.

In order to work with C.J. in a culturally responsive manner, the counselor first should assess his or her general assumptions about gender identity and/or expression. What are the stereotypes the counselor holds about transgender people? For instance, it is common for transgender people to identify with a lesbian, gay, or bisexual sexual orientation before they are able to embrace their gender-variant identity. However, the counselor should not make assumptions that because clients are gender nonconforming that they are also then lesbian, gay, or bisexual. This indeed *might* be the case, and the counselor may explore how the client's gender identity and expression intersects with his or her sexual orientation if these are salient concerns for the client. For C.J. in particular, his partner is challenging the notion that C.J. might be transgender. His partner may not have information about transgender people and therefore may not also know that there are significant differences between identifying as "gay," as she noted, and identifying as transgender. If one were to work with C.J. and Angela in couples counseling, the focus of interventions may include supporting both partners in their growing understanding of the differences between sexual orientation and gender identity and expression. Couples work may also involve exploring how C.J.'s evolving identity has influenced the relationship and what both partners need in terms of exploring their current relationship. It would also be important for the counselor to validate C.J.'s gender identity and expression, especially because many transgender and gender-nonconforming people are viewed as having something wrong with them, when actually their gender identity and expression are very natural parts of how they are that must be valued by the people in their lives.

Individual counseling with C.J. should also include validation of his thoughts and feelings about his gender. The counselor who aspires to provide multiculturally relevant counseling works from the perspective that clients have the best information on their identities and expressions. The counselor should demonstrate respect by using the pronouns and name that the client uses and should not think of these terms as mere preferences. Counselors should also validate the fact that many transgender people feel some discomfort about the fact that their assigned sex at birth does not align with their current gender identity and expression. Similarly, the counselor can affirm that transgender people may select to undergo medical and surgical interventions—or select not to do so. Above all, the counselor's role is to support C.J. in understanding how he would feel most comfortable in terms of his gender identity and expression. In addition, the counselor should pay attention to the ways in which C.J.'s gender identity and expression intersect with his racial/ethnic identity and any other identities that may be salient to him. For instance, if C.J. ascribes to a religious and/or spiritual faith, the counselor can share the history of transgender people in sacred positions in cultures and religions around the world. Also, as an African American transgender man, C.J. may or may not feel connected to a similar community; thus, the counselor may share community and online resources for African American transgender individuals. A more thorough discussion of the competencies involved in working with transgender people may be found in the Competencies for Counseling With Transgender Clients (Association for Lesbian, Gay, Bisexual, and Transgender Issues in Counseling, 2009).

Helpful Counseling Interventions

Although there are several unique considerations in working with LBQQT women, as we discussed earlier, counselors should remember that there remain universal approaches to building a strong therapeutic relationship. In this section we discuss these universal considerations. Then we review the phenomenon of internalized heterosexism and discuss related assessment tools counselors may use with LBQQT women. We also describe community resources counselors should be aware of and share with LBQQT clients.

Building a Strong Therapeutic Relationship With LBQQT Women

Counselors should be aware that LBQQT clients may not present with their gender and/or sexual orientation identities as the main focus or goal for exploration in counseling. However, because of societal heterosexism and individual homoprejudice and transprejudice, LBQQT clients deserve a counseling environment that is respectful of their multiple identities. Rogers (1961) discussed three core conditions of the therapeutic relationship that have particular application to LBQQT women.

The first condition Rogers (1961) discussed is unconditional positive regard on the part of counselors toward LBQQT women. Such regard helps develop and strengthen the counseling relationship. Unconditional positive regard should not come about in a passive or happenstance manner. Often LBQQT clients will look for cues that a counselor is friendly toward their concerns. These cues, which are simple for counselors to integrate into the beginning of the counseling relationship, may include the following:

- Having a rainbow safe zone sticker in the counseling waiting room and office.
- Including a space on intake paperwork (offline and online) where LBQQT clients can write in their gender as opposed to selecting between only "male" and "female."
- Using *partner status* as opposed to *marital status* on paperwork to acknowledge that not all people have the right to marry.
- Displaying books, DVDs, brochures, and other media materials geared toward LBQQT women (Singh, 2010).

Empathy is the second core condition of the therapeutic relationship that supports client change. Counselors may or may not have had similar experiences of both oppression and resilience as LBQQT clients, however demonstrating empathy for their clients' concerns communicates a nonjudgmental stance. Just as unconditional positive regard should be action focused, empathy is demonstrated through the words and actions of the counselor. It is not enough for counselors to attempt to walk in a client's shoes. Rather, counselors working with LBQQT women should demonstrate empathy by attempting to see the world as LBQQT women see and experience it.

Finally, Rogers (1961) discussed congruence as the third core condition important to the counselor–client relationship. *Counselor congruence* refers to counselors being authentic with clients about their thoughts and feelings in the therapeutic relationship. This core condition should remind the counselor to reference multicultural competencies (Sue et al., 1992). Counselors should actively seek ongoing professional development and personal experiences with LBQQT women in order to increase their awareness, knowledge, and skill set with this group. It is not ethical to purport having a supportive stance toward LBQQT women's gender and sexual orientation identities and then engage in conversion or reparative therapy efforts with this group (American Psychological Association, 2009; Whitman, Glosoff, Kocet, & Tavydas, 2006). It is also not best practice to halfway support LBQQT women in their gender and sexual orientation identities (e.g., "I support your expression of sexual orientation or gender identity except . . .").

Collaboratively Identifying Internalized Heterosexism in LBQQT Women

In addition to showing unconditional positive regard, empathy, and congruence (Rogers, 1961), counselors should be able to proactively and collaboratively assess potential internalized heterosexism in LBQQT clients and how this may impinge on client functioning and well-being. Croteau (2008) asserted that it is critical to address internalized heterosexism in counseling because queer people have "suffered deeply from the internalized heterosexism that attacks such a central part of what it is to be human, the capacities for eroticism, passion, and love" (p. 645). He also reminded counselors that much clinical and research-based knowledge is based on the experiences of predominantly White queer individuals.

Brown (2008) echoed this sentiment and added that internalized heterosexism is "likely to have a psychic price" (p. 640). She urged counselors to explore the resilience LBQQT women have despite internalized heterosexism.

Kashubeck-West, Szymanski, and Meyer (2008) detailed several clinical implications for practice based on the research on internalized heterosexism that are helpful in working with LBQQT women. The following is a list of topics counselors should explore with their LBQQT clients:

- Coming-out stories
- Thoughts and feeling about being LBQQT women
- Experiences with heterosexism in school, family, work, and religious institutions
- Interaction with other LBQQT women
- Support and resources available to clients
- Sexual identity disclosure to others
- Stereotypes and attitudes about LBQQT women clients have learned
- Clients' acceptance of their status as sexual minorities and their gender identity
- Clients' experiences of shame or embarrassment about their sexual orientation and gender identity and expression
- Clients' experiences of pride related to their sexual orientation and gender identity and expression
- Clients' experiences with homophobia, biphobia, and transphobia

In addition to exploring internalized heterosexism, counselors should explore how internalized heterosexism may intersect with LBQQT women's multiple identities. For example, Moradi, Wiseman, et al. (2010) studied differences in internalized homophobia (i.e., heterosexism), heterosexist stigma, and "outness," finding that LGB people of color demonstrated less "outness" than White LGB people and weaker relationships between internalized homophobia and heterosexist stigma. The authors suggested that one of the reasons for these findings might be that LGB people of color find less support in "out" contexts such as queer communities than in their racial/ethnic communities. Moradi et al. stated that one of the clinical implications of this study is the need for counselors to carefully assess the salience and intersection of the multiple identities of LGB people of color.

Using Transgender-Affirmative Interventions

Counselors working with transgender women should have extensive knowledge of and experience with the important concerns of this group. Transgender women may present with general mental health concerns. In these cases, counselors should be aware of societal transprejudice and internalized transprejudice that may influence client well-being and functioning.

Other times, transgender women will present with counseling goals of making a transition. It is important for counselors to know that the word *transition* can be vague and can have different meanings for different people. Counselors may explore, assess, and specify collaboratively with clients whether they are referring to a social transition or a medical transition. Social transitions may involve name changes, the use of pronouns appropriate for clients' self-identified gender (not pronouns related to their sex assigned at birth), and interpersonal interactions. Transgender women who make a social transition may or may not elect to have medical interventions such as hormone therapy and/or surgery (medical transition).

When clients' goals center around social and/or medical transitions, counselors should ensure that they themselves have the knowledge, skills, and awareness (Sue et al., 1992) to work with transgender clients. The World Professional Association for Transgender Health Standards of Care (formerly the Harry Benjamin Standards of Care; W. Meyer et al., 2001; see www.wpath. org) guide counselors and other helping professionals in working with transgender women and girls. These guidelines have been found to be both helpful and controversial, depending on the point of view helping professionals have about counseling transgender people. Those who have found the standards to be helpful tend to see the usefulness of including gender identity disorder in the *Diagnostic and Statistical Manual of Mental Disorders*. This would enable transgender clients who want to make a social and/or medical transition to access necessary psychological and medical interventions using health insurance and would communicate to employers and loved ones of transgender women that being transgender is a real experience. Those who find the standards to be controversial tend to be transgender activists and their allies who believe that helping professionals should not be able to assess the psychological readiness of transgender women to make a social and/or medical transition, especially the requirement of a "Real Life Experience." This Real Life Experience includes expressing one's gender in a way that is congruent to the client and not related to sex assigned at birth. Those with concerns about this Real Life Experience cite the high incidence of hate crimes and safety issues related to transgender women undergoing what may seem like a gender test in addition to sexist notions grounded in binary conceptions of what being a man or a woman is or is not.

In addition to being familiar with the World Professional Association for Transgender Health Standards of Care, counselors should be aware that the American Counseling Association (ACA) has endorsed the Competencies for Counseling With Transgender Clients (Association for Lesbian, Gay, Bisexual, and Transgender Issues in Counseling, 2009). These competencies are organized around the nine Council for Accreditation of Counseling and Related Educational Programs domains of training for counselors (e.g., helping relationships, social and cultural foundations, group work) and referenced the ACA Advocacy Competencies (Lewis, Arnold, House, & Toporek, 2002) and the Multicultural Counseling Competencies (Sue et al., 1992) in their development. The competencies recommend that counselors integrate six themes into their practice with transgender clients (Singh et al., 2010). A brief description of these themes follows, but counselors are encouraged to read and be familiar with the entire document:

- *Reflection and self-awareness.* Counselors are aware of their own biases and definitions of sex and gender.
- *Resilience and strengths-based framework.* Counselors recognize the strengths and resilience of transgender women despite oppressive societal conditions and do not pathologize transgender clients based on their sex, gender, or other intersecting identities.
- *Feminist approach and perspective.* Counselors are familiar with feminism and its challenge to socially constructed and prescribed gender roles according to the binary of male and female across cultural groups. They recognize feminists exist in every culture and that sexist beliefs systems have been challenged in every culture throughout history.
- *Intersectionality and sociocultural perspectives.* Counselors recognize that transgender women may not present with their gender identity and/or expression as the focus of counseling and may have multiple salient intersecting identities that are influenced by a variety of sociocultural contexts.
- *Social justice and human rights perspective.* Counselors are aware that transgender women have existed in every culture in the world and that advocacy and activism are integral aspects of the counselor role in working with transgender clients because of the hate crimes and extensive societal prejudice and discrimination they face.
- *Collaboration, supervision, and consultation.* Counselors recognize that the research, practice, and advocacy needs of transgender women are constantly changing. They recognize that counselors should proactively seek to collaborate with clients on their counseling goals and should constantly seek supervision and consultation with other experts in transgender counseling.

Identifying Community Resources

Although prejudicial and oppressive attitudes and actions continue to be targeted toward LBQQT women, tremendous strides have been made in societal acceptance, validation, recognition, and support of this group. Counselors can further support LBQQT clients by having knowledge of the resources available to this group both offline and online.

Offline resources for LBQQT women typically take the form of support groups. If a counselor is working in a major city or urban area, there are likely to be monthly support group meetings for LBQQT women. Sometimes these groups may focus solely on sexual orientation or gender identities, so counselors should be aware of these distinctions. Support groups for LBQQT women may focus more on issues of coming out (i.e., to family, friends, and work colleagues), dating and relationship issues, the development of support systems around being LBQQT, and issues of internalized heterosexism. In contrast, support groups for transgender women may focus more on making a social and/or medical transition, developing support systems around being transgender, negotiating societal transprejudice, and accessing transgender-positive health care and employment.

Support groups may also center on supporting LBQQT women with families (see the MEGA Family Project, www.megafamilyproject.org), the families and friends of LBQQT women (see Parents, Families, and Friends of Lesbians and Gays, www.pflag.org; and TransYouth Family Allies, www.imatyfa.org), or the children of LBQQT women (see Colage, www.colage.org). Some support groups focus on a certain mental health concern, such as substance abuse (e.g., Alcoholics Anonymous), codependency (e.g., Emotions Anonymous), mental illness (e.g., state and local chapters of the National Alliance on Mental Illness), or intimate partner violence. Other support groups may focus on issues of disability, youth (e.g., YouthPride, www.youthpride.org), race/ethnicity (e.g., Trikone, www.trikone.org), physical health (e.g., the Mautner Project of the National Lesbian Health Organization, www.mautnerproject.org), or even recreation (e.g., travel, socializing) and human rights/activism.

Many LBQQT women may live in suburban or rural areas that have fewer offline resources and may or may not be able to travel to cities where these resources do exist. If a client has the financial means and/or transportation to do so, it may be advisable that she attend a one-time or monthly support group to connect with other LBQQT women. It may also be helpful for clients to know about or attend LBQQT Pride festivals and celebrations throughout the United States and abroad (see InterPride, www.interpride.org).

No matter where LBQQT women live and are able to access resources, keep in mind the following important considerations when sharing resources with these women (see also the list of national online resources in "Additional Resources").

- Explore with clients how much they know about online and offline resources.
- Seek to understand whether clients think they would benefit from particular types and focuses of online and offline resources.
- Ensure that online resources contain updated and accurate information.
- Address any potential myths, stereotypes, fears, and confidentiality issues clients may have about attending a support group.
- Identify how clients will know whether a support group is the right one for their needs.
- Assess how to follow up with clients about their experiences accessing resources.

Using the ACA Advocacy Competencies With LBQQT Women

Previously, we discussed the importance of using the Association for Multicultural Counseling and Development's Multicultural Counseling Competencies in working with LBQQT women (Sue et al., 1992). However, having knowledge, skills, and awareness of best practices with this group is not sufficient preparation for competent counseling with LBQQT clients (see Singh, 2010, for a full discussion). Counselors may use the ACA Advocacy Competencies (Lewis et al., 2002) to empower LBQQT women and address societal oppression.

These competencies are organized around three domains: microlevel (client/student), mesolevel (community/school), and macrolevel (public arena). Also, the competencies are structured around interventions counselors may use in *acting with* clients or in *acting on behalf of* clients. Acting with clients focuses on collaborative empowerment, whereas acting on behalf of clients describes interventions that should take place when clients may not have access to resources and the power to advocate for themselves.

At the microlevel, counselors may work with LBQQT women to identify barriers to their resilience and needs they have to increase their well-being. For instance, counselors may collaboratively explore the needs of LBQQT women who have children (e.g., day care, social support) and support clients in either developing means to create these supports or advocating for these needs. At the mesolevel, depending on the setting (e.g., community, school), counselors may examine institutional barriers and needs for LBQQT women. For instance, a school counselor may identify the need for a gay/straight alliance for LBQQT girls and seek out a teacher or administrator who can become an advisor for such a group (in some states and schools, school counselors are not able to directly sponsor school clubs such as gay/straight alliances). At the macrolevel, counselors may engage in legislative advocacy and/or develop LBQQT-affirmative media to create a more affirming, positive environment for LBQQT women (see Singh, 2010, for an extensive discussion of applying the ACA Advocacy Competencies to counseling and advocacy with and on behalf of queer clients).

Conclusion

In this chapter we provided an overview of the salient issues involved in working with LBQQT women. This overview included a discussion of important terminology counselors should be able to use with clients and a counselor assessment of biases related to LBQQT women. We also detailed helpful counseling interventions, including a focus on addressing internalized oppression and societal prejudice. Finally, we reviewed strategies for advocacy with this group using the ACA Advocacy Competencies as a framework.

References

American Psychological Association. (2009). *Report of the APA Task Force on the appropriate response to sexual orientation change efforts.* Washington, DC: Author.

Association for Lesbian, Gay, Bisexual, and Transgender Issues in Counseling. (2009). *Competencies for counseling with transgender clients.* Alexandria, VA: Author.

Badgett, M. V. L., Lau, H., Sears, B., & Ho, D. (2007). *Bias in the workplace: Consistent evidence of sexual orientation and gender identity discrimination.* Retrieved from http://escholarship.org/uc/item/5h3731xr

Barón, A., & Cramer, D. W. (2000). Potential counseling concerns of aging lesbian, gay, and bisexual clients. In R. M. Perez, K. A. DeBord, & K. J. Bieschke (Eds.), *Handbook of counseling and psychotherapy with lesbian, gay, and bisexual clients* (pp. 207–223). Washington, DC: American Psychological Association.

Bowleg, L., Huang, J., Brooks, K., Black, A., & Burkholder, G. (2003). Triple jeopardy and beyond: Multiple minority stress and resilience among Black lesbians. *Journal of Lesbian Studies, 7*(4), 87–108.

Brown, L. S. (2008). Reflections on Kashubeck-West, Szymanski, and Meyer's major contribution. *The Counseling Psychologist, 36,* 639–644.

Caitlin, R., & Futterman, D. (1997). *Lesbian and gay youth: Care and counseling.* Philadelphia, PA: Hanley & Belfus.

Cass, V. C. (1979). Homosexual identity formation: A theoretical model. *Journal of Homosexuality, 4,* 219–235.

Chan, C. S. (1989). Issues of identity development among Asian-American lesbians and gay men. *Journal of Counseling & Development, 68,* 16–21.

Chan, C. S. (1997). Don't ask, don't tell, don't know: The formation of a homosexual identity and sexual expression among Asian American lesbians. In B. Greene (Ed.), *Psychological perspectives on lesbian and gay issues: Ethnic and cultural diversity among lesbians and gay men* (Vol. 3, pp. 240–248). Thousand Oaks, CA: Sage.

Chung, B. Y., & Katayama, M. (1998). Ethnic and sexual identity development of Asian-American lesbian and gay adolescents. *Professional School Counseling, 1*(3), 21–25.

Coleman, E. (1982). Developmental stages of the coming out process. *Journal of Homosexuality, 7*(2–3), 31–43.

Connolly, C. M. (2005). A qualitative exploration of resilience in long-term lesbian couples. *The Family Journal, 13*(3), 266–280. doi:10.1177/1066480704273681

Connolly, C. M. (2006). A feminist perspective of resilience in lesbian couples. *Journal of Feminist Family Therapy, 18*(1), 137–162. doi:10.1300/J086v18n01_06

Croteau, J. M. (2008). Reflections on understanding and ameliorating internalized heterosexism. *The Counseling Psychologist, 36,* 645–653.

Davidson, M. G. (2000). Religion and spirituality. In R. M. Perez, K. A. DeBord, & K. J. Bieschke (Eds.), *Handbook of counseling and psychotherapy with lesbian, gay, and bisexual clients* (pp. 409–433). Washington, DC: American Psychological Association.

DeBlaere, C., Brewster, M. E., Sarkees, A., & Moradi, B. (2010). Conducting research with LGB people of color: Methodological challenges and strategies. *The Counseling Psychologist, 38,* 331–362. doi:10.1177/0011000009335257

Dworkin, S. H. (1996, August). *Bisexual women, understanding sexual identity: Research in progress.* Paper presented at the 104th Annual Convention of the American Psychological Association, Toronto, Ontario, Canada.

Dworkin, S. H. (1997). Female, lesbian, and Jewish: Complex and invisible. In B. Greene (Ed.), *Psychological perspectives on lesbian and gay issues: Ethnic and cultural diversity among lesbians and gay men* (Vol. 3, pp. 63–87). Thousand Oaks, CA: Sage.

Dworkin, S. H. (2000). Individual therapy with lesbian, gay, and bisexual clients. In R. M. Perez, K. A. DeBord, & K. J. Bieschke (Eds.), *Handbook of counseling and psychotherapy with lesbian, gay, and bisexual clients* (pp. 157–181). Washington, DC: American Psychological Association.

Fassinger, R. E., & Richie, B. S. (1997). Sex matters: Gender and sexual orientation in training for multicultural counseling competency. In D. B. Pope-Davis & H. L. K. Coleman (Eds.), *Multicultural counseling competencies: Assessment, education, training, and supervision* (pp. 83–110). Thousand Oaks, CA: Sage.

Firestein, B. A. (2007). Cultural and relational contexts of bisexual women: Implications for therapy. In K. J. Bieschke, R. M. Perez, & K. A. DeBord (Eds.), *Handbook of counseling and psychotherapy with lesbian, gay, bisexual, and transgender clients* (2nd ed., pp. 91–117). Washington, DC: American Psychological Association.

Folayan, A. (1992). African-American issues: The soul of it. In B. Berzon (Ed.), *Positively gay: New approaches to gay and lesbian life* (pp. 235–239). Berkeley, CA: Celestial Arts.

Fox, R. C. (1995). Bisexual identities. In A. R. D'Augelli & C. J. Patterson (Eds.), *Lesbian, gay, and bisexual identities over the lifespan* (pp. 48–86). New York, NY: Oxford University Press.

Fukuyama, M. A., & Ferguson, A. D. (2000). Lesbian, gay, and bisexual people of color: Understanding cultural complexity and managing multiple oppressions. In R. M. Perez, K. A. DeBord, & K. J. Bieschke (Eds.), *Handbook of counseling and psychotherapy with lesbian, gay, and bisexual clients* (pp. 81–105). Washington, DC: American Psychological Association.

Fygetakis, L. M. (1997). Greek American lesbians: Identity odysseys of honorable good girls. In B. Greene (Ed.), *Psychological perspectives on lesbian and gay issues: Ethnic and cultural diversity among lesbians and gay men* (Vol. 3, pp. 152–190). Thousand Oaks, CA: Sage.

Garnets, L. D., Herek, G. M., & Levy, B. (2003). Violence and victimization of lesbians and gay men: Mental health consequences. In L. D. Garnets & D. C. Kimmel (Eds.), *Psychological perspectives of lesbian, gay, and bisexual experiences* (2nd ed., pp. 188–206). New York, NY: Columbia University Press.

Gock, T. (1992). Asian-Pacific Islander issues: Identity integration and pride. In B. Berzon (Ed.), *Positively gay: New approaches to gay and lesbian life* (pp. 247–252). Berkeley, CA: Celestial Arts.

Gonsiorck, J. C. (1995). Gay male identities: Concepts and issues. In A. R. D'Augelli & C. J. Patterson (Eds.), *Lesbian, gay, and bisexual identities over the lifespan* (pp. 24–47). New York, NY: Oxford University Press.

Gonsiorek, J. C., & Rudolph, J. R. (1991). Homosexual identity: Coming out and other developmental events. In J. C. Gonsiorek & J. D. Weinrich (Eds.), *Homosexuality: Research implications for public policy* (pp. 161–175). Newbury Park, CA: Sage.

Grace, J. (1992). Affirming gay and lesbian adulthood. In N. J. Woodman (Ed.), *Lesbian and gay lifestyles: A guide for counseling and education* (pp. 33–47). New York, NY: Irvington.

Greene, B. (1994). Ethnic-minority lesbians and gay men: Mental health and treatment issues. *Journal of Consulting and Clinical Psychology, 62,* 243–251. doi:10.1037/0022-006X.62.2.243

Greene, B. (1995). Lesbian women of color: Triple jeopardy. In B. Greene (Ed.), *Women of color: Integrating ethnic and gender identities in psychotherapy* (pp. 389–427). New York, NY: Guilford Press.

Greene, B. (1997). Ethnic minority lesbians and gay men: Mental health and treatment issues. In B. Greene (Ed.), *Psychological perspectives on lesbian and gay issues: Ethnic and cultural diversity among lesbians and gay men* (Vol. 3, pp. 216–239). Thousand Oaks, CA: Sage.

Greene, B. (2003). Beyond heterosexism and across the cultural divide—Developing an inclusive lesbian, gay, and bisexual psychology: A look to the future. In L. D. Garnets & D. C. Kimmel (Eds.), *Psychological perspectives of lesbian, gay, and bisexual experiences* (2nd ed., pp. 357–400). New York, NY: Columbia University Press.

Harper, G. W., Jernewall, N., & Zea, M. C. (2004). Giving voice to emerging science and theory for lesbian, gay, and bisexual people of color. *Cultural Diversity and Ethnic Minority Psychology, 10*(3), 187–199.

Hausman, B. L. (1995). *Changing sex: Transsexualism, technology, and idea of gender.* Durham, NC: Duke University Press.

Herek, G. M. (1986). The social psychology of homophobia: Toward a practical theory. *Review of Law and Social Change, 14,* 923–934.

Herek, G. M. (2003). Why tell if you're not asked? Self-disclosure, intergroup contact, and heterosexuals' attitudes toward lesbians and gay men. In L. D. Garnets & D. C. Kimmel (Eds.), *Psychological perspectives of lesbian, gay, and bisexual experiences* (2nd ed., pp. 270–298). New York, NY: Columbia University Press.

Hom, A. Y. (2003). Stories from the homefront: Perspectives of Asian-American perspectives with lesbian daughters and gay sons. In L. D. Garnets & D. C. Kimmel (Eds.), *Psychological perspectives of lesbian, gay, and bisexual experiences* (2nd ed., pp. 549–562). New York, NY: Columbia University Press.

Human Rights Campaign Foundation's Workplace Project. (2009). *State of the workplace.* Retrieved from http://www.hrc.org/about_us/7061.htm

Jackson, K., & Brown, L. B. (1996). Lesbians of African heritage: Coming out in the straight community. *Journal of Gay and Lesbian Social Services, 5*(4), 53–67.

Jones, E. E., Farina, A., Hestrof, A. H., Markus, H., Miller, D. T., & Scott, R. A. (1984). *Social stigma: The psychology of marked relationships.* New York, NY: Freeman.

Kashubeck-West, S., Szymanski, D., & Meyer, J. (2008). Internalized heterosexism: Clinical implications and training considerations. *The Counseling Psychologist, 36,* 615–630.

Lambda Legal. (2008). *Bending the mold: An action toolkit for transgender youth.* Retrieved from www.lambdalegal.org/publications/bending-the-mold

Lewis, J. A., Arnold, M. S., House, R., & Toporek, R. L. (2002). *ACA advocacy competencies.* Retrieved from http://www.counseling.org/Resources/Competencies/Advocacy_Competencies.pdf

Lev, A. I. (2004). *Transgender emergence: Therapeutic guidelines for working for gender-variant people and their families.* Binghamton, NY: Haworth Press.

Lev, A. I. (2007). Transgender communities: Developing identity through connection. In K. J. Bieschke, R. M. Perez, & K. A. DeBord (Eds.), *Handbook of counseling and psychotherapy with lesbian, gay, bisexual, and transgender clients* (2nd ed., pp. 147–175). Washington, DC: American Psychological Association.

Liddle, B. J. (2007). Mutual bonds: Lesbian women's lives and communities. In K. J. Bieschke, R. M. Perez, & K. A. DeBord (Eds.), *Handbook of counseling and psychotherapy with lesbian, gay, bisexual, and transgender clients* (2nd ed., pp. 51–69). Washington, DC: American Psychological Association.

Masten, A. S., Best, K. M., & Garmezy, N. (1990). Resilience and development: Contributions from the study of children who overcome adversity. *Development and Psychopathology, 2,* 425–444. doi:10.1017/S0954579400005812

Matteson, D. R. (1996). Counseling and psychotherapy with bisexual and exploring clients. In B. A. Firestein (Ed.), *Bisexuality: The psychology and politics of an invisible minority* (pp. 185–213). Newbury Park, CA: Sage.

Meyer, I. H. (2003). Prejudice, social stress, and mental health in lesbian, gay, and bisexual populations: Conceptual issues and research evidence. *Psychological Bulletin, 129,* 674–697. doi:10.1037/0033-2909.129.5.674

Meyer, I. (2010). Identity, stress, and resilience in lesbians, gay men, and bisexuals of color. *The Counseling Psychologist, 38,* 442–454. doi:10.1177/0011000009351601

Meyer, W., III, Bockting, W. O., Cohen-Kettenis, P., Coleman, E., DiCeglie, D., Devor, H., . . . Wheeler, C. C. (2001). *The Harry Benjamin International Gender Dysphoria Association's standards of care for gender identity disorders, sixth version.* Retrieved from http://wpath.org/Documents2/socv6.pdf

Moradi, B., DeBlaere, C., & Huang, Y. P. (2010). Centralizing the experiences of LGB people of color in counseling psychology. *The Counseling Psychologist, 38,* 322–330. doi:10.1177/0011000008330832

Moradi, B., Wiseman, M. C., DeBlaere, C., Goodman, M. G., Sarkees, A., & Brewster, M. E. (2010). LGB of color and White individuals' perceptions of heterosexist stigma, internalize homophobia, and outness: Comparison of levels and links. *The Counseling Psychologist, 38,* 397–424.

Nakamura, N., Flojo, J. R., & Dittrich, M. L. (2009). Lesbian, gay, and bisexual Asian Americans: Coming out in context. In J. L. Chin (Ed.), *Diversity in mind and in action: Multiple faces of identity* (Vol. 1, pp. 33–45). Santa Barbara, CA: Praeger/ABC-CLIO.

Reynolds, A. L., & Hanjorgiris, W. F. (2000). Coming out: Lesbian, gay, and bisexual identity development. In R. M. Perez, K. A. DeBord, & K. J. Bieschke (Eds.), *Handbook of counseling and psychotherapy with lesbian, gay, and bisexual clients* (pp. 35–56). Washington, DC: American Psychological Association.

Rice, T., & Nakamura, N. (2009). Bridging the margins: Exploring sexual orientation and multiple heritage identities. In R. C. Henriksen & D. A. Paladino (Eds.), *Counseling multiple heritage individuals, couples, and families* (pp. 157–177). Alexandria, VA: American Counseling Association.

Ritter, K. Y., & Terndrup, A. I. (2002). *Handbook of affirmative psychotherapy with lesbians and gay men.* New York, NY: Guilford Press.

Rogers, C. (1961). *On becoming a person: A therapist's view of psychotherapy.* London, England: Constable & Robinson.

Rosario, M., Schrimshaw, E. W., & Hunter, J. (2004). Ethnic/racial differences in the coming-out process of lesbian, gay, and bisexual youths: A comparison of sexual identity development over time. *Cultural Diversity and Ethnic Minority Psychology, 10*(3), 215–228.

Rosario, M., Schrimshaw, E. W., & Hunter, J. (2008). Ethnic/racial disparities in gay-related stress and health among lesbian, gay, and bisexual youths: Examining a prevalent hypothesis. In B. C. Wallace (Ed.), *Toward equity in health: A new global approach to health disparities* (pp. 427–446). New York, NY: Springer.

Russell, G. M. (2004). Surviving and thriving in the midst of anti-gay politics. *Policy Journal of the Institute for Gay and Lesbian Strategic Studies, 7*(2), 1–7.

Russell, G. M., & Richards, J. A. (2003). Stressor and resilience factors for lesbians, gay men, and bisexuals confronting antigay politics. *American Journal of Community Psychology, 31,* 313–328. doi:0091-0562/03/0600-0313/0

Safren, S. A., & Pantalone, D. W. (2006). Social anxiety and barriers to resilience among lesbian, gay, and bisexual adolescents. In A. M. Omoto & H. S. Kurtzman (Eds.), *Sexual orientation and mental health: Examining identity and development in lesbian, gay, and bisexual people* (pp. 55–71). Washington, DC: American Psychological Association.

Sanders, G. L., & Kroll, I. T. (2000). Generating stories of resilience: Helping gay and lesbian youth and their families. *Journal of Marital and Family Therapy, 26,* 433–442. doi:10.1111/j.1752-0606.2000.tb00314.x

Savin-Williams, R. C. (2005). *The new gay teenager.* Cambridge, MA: Harvard University Press.

Scourfield, J., Roen, K., & McDermott, L. (2008). Lesbian, gay, bisexual, and transgender young people's experiences of distress: Resilience, ambivalence, and self-destructive behavior. *Health and Social Care in the Community, 16*(3), 329–336. doi:10.1111/j.1365-2524.2008.00769.x

Singh, A. A. (2010). It takes more than a rainbow sticker! Advocacy on queer issues in counseling. In M. J. Ratts, J. A. Lewis, & R. L. Toporek (Eds.), *ACA advocacy competencies: A social justice framework for counselors* (pp. 29–41). Alexandria, VA: American Counseling Association.

Singh, A. A., Burnes, T. R., Harper, A., Harper, B., Moundas, S., Maxon, W., . . . Scofield, T. (2010, March). *Introducing the ALGBTIC transgender counseling competencies.* Paper presented at the Annual Conference & Exposition of the American Counseling Association, Pittsburgh, PA.

Singh, A. A., & Chun, K. Y. S. (2012). Multiracial/multiethnic queer and transgender clients: Intersections of identity and resilience. In S. H. Dworkin & M. S. Pope (Eds.), *Casebook for counseling lesbian, gay, bisexual, and transgender persons and their families* (pp. 197–209). Alexandria, VA: American Counseling Association.

Smith, A. (1997). Cultural diversity and the coming out process: Implications for therapy practice. In B. Greene (Ed.), *Ethnic and cultural diversity among lesbians and gay men* (pp. 279–300). Newbury Park, CA: Sage.

Stepakoff, S., & Bowleg, L. (1998). Sexual identity in sociocultural context: Clinical implications of multiple marginalizations. In W. G. Herron (Ed.), *Mental health, mental illness, and personality development in a diverse society: A source book* (pp. 618–653). Northvale, NJ: Jason Aronson.

Sue, D. W., Arredondo, P., & McDavis, R. J. (1992). Multicultural counseling competencies and standards: A call to the profession. *Journal of Counseling & Development, 70,* 477–486.

Troiden, R. R. (1989). The formation of homosexual identities. *Journal of Homosexuality, 17*(1–2), 43–73.

Trujillo, C. M. (1997). Sexual identity and the discontents of difference. In B. Greene (Ed.), *Ethnic and cultural diversity among lesbians and gay men* (pp. 266–278). Newbury Park, CA: Sage.

U.S. Supreme Court. (2003). *Lawrence et al. v. Texas Certiorari to the Court of Appeals of Texas, Fourteenth District* (Syllabus No. 02-102). Retrieved from http://data.lambdalegal.org/pdf/236.pdf

Weinberg, M. S., Williams, C. J., & Pryor, D. W. (1994). *Dual attraction: Understanding bisexuality.* New York, NY: Oxford University Press.

Whitman, J. S., Glosoff, H. L., Kocet, M. M., & Tavydas, V. (2006). *Exploring ethical issues related to conversion or reparative therapy.* Retrieved from http://www.counseling.org/PressRoom/NewsReleases.aspx?AGuid=b68aba97-2f08-40c2-a400-0630765f72f4

Worell, J., & Remer, P. (2003). *Feminist perspectives in therapy: Empowering diverse women* (2nd ed.). Hoboken, NJ: Wiley.

Additional Resources

Counselors may use the following list of affirmative media resources to increase their own learning about LBQQT issues and to provide resources for LBQQT women.

Books

Bi Lives: Bisexual Women Tell Their Stories by Kata Orndorff (Ed.)

Gender Outlaws: On Men, Women and the Rest of Us by Kate Bornstein

The Lesbian Health Book: Caring for Ourselves by Jocelyn White and Marissa C. Martinez (Eds.)

Plural Desires: Writing Bisexual Women's Realities by The Bisexual Anthology Collective (Ed.)

Whipping Girl: A Transsexual Woman on Sexism and the Scapegoating of Femininity by Julia Serano

The Whole Lesbian Sex Book: A Passionate Guide for All of Us by Felice Newman

Films

Chutney Popcorn (South Asian LBQQ)
Fire (South Asian LBQQ)
The Incredibly True Adventures of Two Girls in Love (White LBQQ)
The Journey (South Asian LBQQ)
La Vie en Rose (French transgender youth)
Normal (White transgender)
Saving Face (Asian American/Pacific Islander LBQQ)
TransAmerica (White transgender)

Websites

Gay, Lesbian, & Straight Education Network
    www.glsen.org
Gay-Straight Alliance Network
    www.gsanetwork.org
National Center for Transgender Equality
    www.transequality.org
National Gay and Lesbian Task Force
    www.ngltf.org
Parents, Families, and Friends of Lesbians and Gays
    www.pflag.org
PINKessence Transgender Social Network (similar to Facebook)
    www.pinkessence.com
TransQueer Nation (similar to Facebook)
    www.transqueernation.com
TransYouth Family Allies
    www.imatyfa.org
Trikone (South Asian Queer and Transgender Support)
    www.trikone.org

Appendix 13.1 • Important Terminology for Use With Transgender Women

Ag/aggressive/stud: Synonymous with a butch lesbian identity; more often these terms are used to describe a Black or Latina lesbian with a very masculine gender presentation. Though they are often read as boys or men, they do not usually identify as male.

Biological sex, sex: A term used historically and within the medical field to refer to the chromosomal, hormonal and anatomical characteristics that are used to classify an individual as female or male.

Bisexual: Emotionally and sexually attracted to some people of other [typically stated as "both"] genders. Does not presume nonmonogamy or any sexual activity, necessarily. Some people self-identify as bi, rather than bisexual.

Coming out: The process of first recognizing and acknowledging nonheterosexual orientation or transgender identity to oneself and then sharing it with others. Developmentally, many sexual minority youth will initially erect emotional barriers with acquaintances, friends and family by pretending (actively or through silence) to be heterosexual and congruent. Coming out means dropping the secrecy and pretense and becoming more emotionally integrated. This usually occurs in stages and is a nonlinear, lifelong process.

Drag king/drag queen: A performer who wears the clothing associated with another sex, often involving the presentation of exaggerated, stereotypical gender characteristics. The performance of gender by drag queens (males in drag) or drag kings (females in drag) may be art, entertainment and/or parody.

FTM (female to male), transgender man: Terms used to identify a person who was assigned the female sex at birth but who identifies as male.

Gender: A set of social, psychological and emotional traits, often influenced by societal expectations, that classify an individual as feminine, masculine, androgynous or other.

Gender affirmation surgery: Any one of a variety of surgeries involved in the process of transition from one gender to another. Many transgender people will not undergo SRS for health or financial reasons, or because it is not medically necessary for them.

Gender binary: The concept that everyone must be one of two genders: man or woman.

Gender dysphoria: An intense, persistent discomfort resulting from the awareness that the sex assigned at birth and the resulting gender role expectations are inappropriate. Some consider gender dysphoria to be a symptom of Gender Identity Disorder, a health condition recognized by the American Psychiatric Association. Many transgender people do not experience gender dysphoria.

Gender expression: The outward manifestation of internal gender identity, through clothing, hairstyle, mannerisms and other characteristics.

Gender identity: The inner sense of being a man, a woman, both or neither. Gender identity usually aligns with a person's sex, but sometimes does not.

Gender-nonconforming: Behaving in a way that does not match social stereotypes about female or male gender, usually through dress or physical appearance.

Gender role: The social expectation of how an individual should act, think and feel, based upon the sex assigned at birth.

Gender transition: The social, psychological and medical process of transitioning from one gender to another. Gender transition is an individualized process and does not involve the same steps for everyone. After gender transition, some people identify simply as men or women.

Genderqueer: A term used by some people who may or may not identify as transgender, but who identify their gender as somewhere on the continuum beyond the binary male/female gender system.

Appendix 13.1 • Important Terminology for Use With Transgender Women
(*Continued*)

Heterosexism: The individual person, group, or institutional norms and behaviors that result from the assumption that all people are heterosexual. The system of oppression, which assumes that heterosexuality is inherently normal and superior, negates LBGT peoples' lives and relationships.

Heterosexual: Clinical synonym for straight.

Homophobia: Originally coined to mean, in classic psychological terms, irrational fear of homosexuality. Now refers usually to bias against or dislike of gay, lesbian, bisexual and transgender people or of stereotypically gay/lesbian behavior, or discomfort with one's own same-sex attractions, or of being perceived as gay or lesbian. A less inflammatory term is antigay (as in antigay harassment).

Homosexual: Dated term; use "gay" instead.

Homosexual: Avoid this term; it is clinical, distancing and archaic. Sometimes appropriate in referring to behavior (although same-sex is the preferred adj.). When referring to people, as opposed to behavior, homosexual is considered derogatory and the terms gay and lesbian are preferred, at least in the Northwest.

Hormone therapy: Administration of hormones and hormonal agents to develop characteristics of a different gender or to block the development of unwanted gender characteristics. Hormone therapy is part of many people's gender transitions and is safest when prescribed and monitored by a health care professional.

Lesbian: Preferred term for gay women. Many lesbians feel invisible when the term gay is used to refer to men and women.

Lifestyle: An inaccurate term sometimes used to describe the lives of gays, lesbians and bisexuals. Implies that the homes, careers, and relationships of all sexual minorities are identical. There is a GLBT culture, with its own performing arts and body of literature. There is a GLBT community, with gay- and lesbian-identified businesses, publications and holidays. But the degree to which people who identify as gay, lesbian, bisexual or transgender take part in this culture and community varies from not at all to almost exclusively. There is no gay lifestyle, just as there is no straight lifestyle.

MTF (male to female), transgender woman: Terms used to identify a person who was assigned the male sex at birth but who identifies as female.

Openly gay/lesbian: Preferred over self-avowed or practicing. For example: He is an openly gay principal.

Oppression: The acts and effects of domination of certain groups in society over others, caused by the combination of prejudice and power. Systems of oppression include racism, sexism, homophobia and transphobia.

Outing: Publicly revealing the sexual orientation or gender identity of someone who has chosen not to share it.

Pink triangle: A symbol originally used by the Nazis, who forced gay men to wear pink triangles on their clothing, imprisoned them in concentration camps, and put many thousands of gay men to death. Now, the downward-pointing, equilateral, pink triangle is a symbol of GLBT pride and the struggle for equal rights.

Post-op, pre-op, non-op: Terms used to identify a transgender person's surgical status. Use of these terms is often considered insulting and offensive. Surgical status is almost never relevant information for anyone except a transgender person's medical providers.

Privilege: Social and institutional advantages that dominant groups receive and others do not. Privilege is often invisible to those who have it.

Appendix 13.1 • Important Terminology for Use With Transgender Women
(*Continued*)

Queer: Originally a derogatory slur, it has recently been reclaimed by some to be an inclusive word for all of those within the sexual minority community. Because of the original derogatory nature of the word, it is not necessarily accepted by all.

Racism: A system of institutionalized practices and individual actions that benefits White people over people of color.

Rainbow flag: A flag of six equal horizontal stripes (red, orange, yellow, green, blue and lavender or violet) adopted to signify the diversity of the lesbian, gay, bisexual, transgender community.

Safe zone sticker: Designed as a proactive and visible sign of support for LGBTQQA persons who deserve to feel safe at school. The sticker is recommended for use as a reminder to both show respect for students and to expect reinforcement from school personnel. Ultimately, the stickers would be best placed throughout the school, following a related in-service, which teaches adults proper enforcement of safe zones as related to LGBT, and among intersecting oppressions. [Sexism, racism, ableism, etc.]

Sexism: A system of institutionalized practices and individual actions that benefits men over women.

Sexual minorities: Gay, lesbian, bisexual and transgender people.

Sexual orientation: One's core sense of the gender(s) of people toward whom one feels romantically and sexually attracted. The inclination or capacity to develop intimate emotional and sexual relationships with people of the same gender, a different gender or more than one gender. Doesn't presume sexual experience/activity (i.e., sexual minority people are as capable as heterosexual people of choosing to abstain). To some degree, the qualities one finds attractive may be learned, probably in the first few years of life. There is growing evidence that people may be, however, biologically (hormonally, genetically) predisposed to be more attracted to one gender or another or to people of more than one gender. In all instances, use this term instead of sexual preference or other misleading terminology.

Sexual preference: Avoid this term; it implies a casual choice, which is rarely if ever the case. Sexual orientation is the correct term.

Stonewall: The Stonewall Inn tavern in New York City's Greenwich Village was the site of several nights of rioting/rebellion following a police raid on June 28, 1969. Although not the nation's first gay-rights demonstration, Stonewall is now regarded as the birth of the modern gay-rights movement.

Straight: Heterosexual; nongay. Term preferred by some straight people as less clinical and formal than heterosexual, but some dislike it because it gets confused with not using drugs or with being a rigid person. Some GLBT people object to it as implying that they must be, in contrast, bent.

Transgender or trans: An umbrella term used to describe those who challenge social gender norms, including genderqueer people, gender-nonconforming people, transsexuals, cross-dressers and so on. People must self-identify as transgender in order for the term to be appropriately used to describe them.

Transition: Not a single event—a lifelong process, most often refers to the period of time when a transgender person begins to assert their gender, which may include any combination of the following: alterations to dress, name changes, changing pronouns, hormone therapy or sex reassignment surgeries. Not all trans people want or have access to hormone therapy or sex reassignment surgery. Some transgender people identify only as a man or as a woman—having had transgender experience.

Appendix 13.1 • Important Terminology for Use With Transgender Women
(Continued)

Transphobia: The irrational fear of those who challenge gender stereotypes, often expressed as discrimination, harassment and violence.

Transsexual: A person who experiences intense, persistent, long-term discomfort with their body and self-image due to the awareness that their assigned sex is inappropriate. Transsexuals may take steps to change their body, gender role and gender expression to align them with their gender identity.

Note. LBGT, GLBT, LGBT, and LGBTQQA all refer to members of the lesbian, gay, bisexual, transgender, queer, questioning, and/or allied populations. Reprinted with permission of the Georgia Safe Schools Coalition (www.georgiasafeschoolscoalition.org).

Counseling Individuals With Physical, Cognitive, and Psychiatric Disabilities

Julie F. Smart

Why include a chapter on counseling individuals with disabilities in a book titled *Multicultural Issues in Counseling: New Approaches to Diversity*? For many readers, at first glance, the inclusion of this chapter will appear to be out of place. Often it is believed, although falsely, that people with disabilities (PWDs) are served primarily by rehabilitation counselors and allied health professionals. Also false is the notion that society serves PWDs by giving them charity; giving them disability benefits; segregating them; and making them subjects of inspiring posters, movies, and telethons. PWDs do not want charity or to be seen as inspiring. Instead, they want basic civil rights and full social integration (Fleischer & Zames, 2001). Indeed, PWDs who are younger than 20 years old are termed the *ADA Generation,* meaning that they grew up after the passage of the Americans With Disabilities Act of 1990 and therefore understand and expect their rights to full inclusion and equal opportunity (Scotch, 1984, 1988). PWDs also view themselves as more than a disability and want the same types of counseling services as anyone else.

This chapter provides direction for counseling PWDs. It begins with an exploration of the three broad categories of disability. Next models of disability are examined. These are followed by a set of guidelines for counselors to consider when working with PWDs. A case study is offered to illustrate aspects of culturally competent counseling with PWDs.

Disabilities are conceptualized in three broad categories, categories that were developed according to *symptoms* of the disabilities. Therefore, categories of disabilities are rarely based on *cause,* simply because there are physical causes of all types of disability (Smart, 2001, 2008, 2009). The three broad categories are (a) physical disabilities, (b) cognitive disabilities, and (c) psychiatric disabilities. Physical disabilities include sensory loss (blindness, deafness, deaf-blindness), orthopedic impairments, congenital limb deficiencies, amputations, and chronic illness. Cognitive disabilities include intellectual, learning, and developmental disabilities. Psychiatric disabilities include mental illness, alcohol abuse/dependence, and substance abuse/dependence. Of course, individuals often have more than one disability.

These three broad categories of disabilities—physical, cognitive, and psychiatric—reflect the hierarchy of stigma directed toward individuals. Generally speaking, there is less stigma and prejudice toward individuals with physical disabilities, there is more stigma toward individuals with cognitive disabilities, and the most stigma is directed toward those with psychiatric disabilities. Although the hierarchy of stigma may be somewhat abstract, this hierarchy does affect the daily lives of individuals with disabilities. Laws, policies, insurance plans, and a broad array of services are based on this hierarchy of stigma. More services, benefits, and resources are provided to individuals with physical disabilities than those with cognitive or psychiatric disabilities. Of course, other characteristics of the individual and factors of the disability influence both the way in which services are provided and the number of available services. For example, military veterans receive more benefits than nonveterans with the same disability, and in general men receive more services and benefits than women with the same disability.

The experience and counseling needs of PWDs should be included in books on multicultural counseling for the following reasons:

1. According to the U.S. Census, nearly one fifth (19%) of all Americans experience a disability (Brault, 2008); therefore, disability is very common, ordinary, and typical. It might be said that disability is very normal.

2. Disability has long been considered to be deviance rather than a strengthening and enriching diversity that could benefit everyone—with or without a disability (Anspach, 1979). In the same way that racial and ethnic minority groups have enriched the broader American culture, PWDs would like their experiences, histories, and viewpoints incorporated into American society. In the past, the general public has not been interested in the disability experience, except for a few celebrities and individuals who have accomplished remarkable goals (for anyone with or without disabilities). However, if people without disabilities (PWODs) would acknowledge and understand the disability experience, they would gain a more accurate picture of the experience of living with a disability.

3. PWDs have experienced prejudice, discrimination, marginalization, reduced opportunities, segregation, and lowered expectations in much the same way as some American ethnic groups have. The prejudice and discrimination toward PWDs has been termed *handicapism* or *ableism* (McCarthy, 2003).

4. Much like racism, heterosexism, and sexism, handicapism is not recognized; indeed, most PWODs are not aware of the unequal, undeserved, inferior treatment that PWDs, a large segment of the population, receive. In much the same way that White people often do not recognize White privilege, PWODs do not understand that the world (including attitudes, laws, the job market, and the physical environment) is designed for those without disabilities. In fact, most PWODs do not think of themselves as "people without disabilities," although PWDs use many humorous in-group terms to describe PWODs, such as *normies, CRABs* (currently regarded as able-bodied), and *TABs* (temporarily able-bodied; Smart, 2008).

5. PWDs are the only open minority group simply because anyone at any time can acquire (or be diagnosed with) a disability. Thus, prejudicial attitudes can become self-identifiers when an individual acquires a disability (Smart, 2001, 2005a). Zola (1982)

uses a wheelchair because he contracted polio at age 15 and was in an auto accident when he was 19. He described the way in which PWODs internalize the prejudices against PWDs.

> Born for the most part into normal families, we are socialized into that world. The world of sickness is one we enter only later, poorly prepared and with all the prejudices of the normal. The very vocabulary we use to describe ourselves is borrowed from society. We are de-formed, dis-eased, disorderd, ab-normal. (p. 206)

6. American society often views disability as inferiority and ambiguity that resides totally within the individual. Because of the influence of the biomedical model of disability, society has viewed disability as the problem of the individual rather than seeing that many of the causes of disability involve environmental factors, such as lack of insurance coverage, employment in physically demanding and dangerous work, and lack of prenatal care for pregnant women. These factors are related to sociopolitical conditions and therefore are able to be changed.

7. If counselors and the counseling profession fail to recognize the status quo of separate and unequal treatment of PWDs, they participate in the continuation of this oppression.

8. Finally, after medical stabilization, or the point when the patient has been released from the hospital and rehabilitation center and his or her medications have been stabilized, most PWDs have multiple identities, roles, functions, and assets. Therefore, PWDs will require the services of counselors in all specialty areas: aging and adult development; community mental health; school counseling; lesbian, gay, bisexual, and transsexual issues; group counseling; marriage and family counseling, career counseling; university counseling; and spiritual, ethical, and religious values (Smart & Smart, 2006).

Disability Is Both Common and Natural

Everyone will work with colleagues who have disabilities, attend school with students with disabilities, marry someone with a disability, or have a child with a disability. PWDs want to be considered as typical, ordinary people with normal needs and motivations. Stated differently, PWDs want to be viewed as individuals rather than a disability category.

The disability experience is growing more common as a larger proportion of the population and greater numbers of individuals experience some type of disability (Linton, 2004). Furthermore, these increases are viewed as societal progress. There are more disabilities because of advances in medicine (such as neonatal medicine and emergency medicine) and the longer life spans of both PWODs and PWDs. Because of these advances, people who in the past would have died now survive with a disability. Innovations in neonatal medicine have produced more *congenital disabilities,* or disabilities that are present at birth. For example, there were no children with spina bifida before 1957. (Spina bifida is a congenital disorder of the spinal column in which one or more vertebrae are left open.) In 1957, a shunt to drain excess fluid from the brain was developed, thus saving the lives of thousands of newborn infants with spina bifida. Of course, before 1957, infants were *born* with spina bifida; however, these infants died within a few days of their birth. According to the Centers for Disease Control and Prevention (2006), 1 in every 33 babies born in the United States has a congenital disability. Infants who earlier would have died now survive with a disability. As the rate of congenital disability increases, the rate of infant mortality decreases. These increases in congenital disability will place demands on counselors who specialize in family and marriage counseling. How does the birth of a child with a disability impact the family? What is the impact on the marriage?

Emergency medical professionals treat trauma and injury victims at the scene of the accident, and therefore survival rates have increased dramatically. Now, rather than dying at the scene of an accident, an individual survives, sometimes with a spinal cord injury or a traumatic brain injury. Survival rates have also increased in war. In the Iraq war, 16 soldiers were wounded and injured for every 1 soldier who died, compared to World War II, in which 3 soldiers were wounded and injured for every 1 solider who died. Amputations, traumatic brain injuries, and a host of other disabilities are increasing while the death rate due to combat declines.

Medical and scientific innovations have increased the life spans of both PWDs and PWODs (Trieschmann, 1987). Before the advent of antibiotics, many individuals with Down syndrome died before they reached adulthood from secondary infections such as pneumonia. In 2007 the average life span of someone with Down syndrome was 56 years, whereas in 1983 it was only 25 years (Smart, 2001, 2008). Young adults with Down syndrome now express a desire to marry, something that was rare in the past simply because these individuals did not live long enough to consider marriage. More than 90% of all children with any type of disability now survive to adulthood (White, 2002). Because of these longer life spans, many adult counseling services, such as premarital and marital counseling and counseling on aging, are required for PWDs.

Statistical factors, such as more accurate and complete reporting of disability, have also increased the number of PWDs. As more people report their disabilities, they will be able to access professional services. Also, expanding and liberalizing the definition of disability to include such conditions as learning disabilities, alcohol and substance abuse, and mental illness has resulted in better services and decreased stigma toward the individuals who experience these conditions. Individuals with those disabilities that were once considered to be moral failings, such as learning disabilities, often internalized society's judgmental and negative viewpoints into their self-identities. For example, schoolteachers often considered children with learning disabilities to be lazy and stupid, and many times these children believed those teachers' judgments.

A careful examination of each of these factors and their alternatives (death or lack of services) shows that the greater numbers of disabilities in fact reflect progress. Indeed, an increase in the number of disabilities is expected under President Barack Obama's new federal health care plan because Americans with chronic, long-term disabilities will receive better and more consistent care. Moreover, when prenatal and neonatal care are extended to greater numbers of women and infants, there will be an increase in the number of congenital disabilities and a corresponding decline in maternal and infant mortality. When all Americans have access to health care, more disabilities will be diagnosed and more PWDs will receive services.

Finally, individuals with disabilities are becoming more visible as they strive to gain their basic civil rights as Americans. Long segregated in institutions and special schools, PWDs are uniting and finding their voice. Some PWDs no longer wish to hide or minimize their disability in order to make PWODs comfortable. These individuals are proud of their mastery of their disability and know that there is nothing about themselves or their disability that warrants such fear and distress in those who do not have disabilities. Many in the disability rights movement learned from the African American civil rights movement of the 1960s, and indeed the Americans With Disabilities Act of 1990 was modeled on the Civil Rights Act of 1964.

Models of Disability

In order to meet minimum standards of practice, counselors will be required to become knowledgeable about and proficient in the disability experience. A lack of training (Bauman & Drake, 1997; Bluestone, Stokes, & Kuba, 1996; Hogben & Waterman, 1997) and the resulting failure to provide services may be due to the powerful influence of models of disability, as these models determine which academic disciplines study and teach the experience of disability. A growing interest in models of disability has emerged in recent years. Examining these models can assist counselors, as a profession and as individual practitioners, to reorient how they provide services. Counselor educators and practitioners should recognize that disability is never entirely an objective, standardized, and universal experience. Nor is disability a completely personal, subjective, and idiosyncratic experience. The conceptualization of disability as an attribute located solely within the individual is changing to a paradigm in which disability is thought to be an interaction between the individual, the disability, and the environment (both social and physical). The disability is typically not the single defining characteristic of the individual who has the disability; rather, it is an important part of the individual's self-identity (Smart, 2008). When counselors dismiss or ignore the disability, they may overemphasize the salience of the disability and automatically assume that the disability is the presenting problem. Indeed, the "roadblocks . . . imposed by counselors" may be due to a lack of professional training (Humes, Szymanski, & Hohenshil, 1989, p. 145).

A model (or paradigm) is simply a human-made tool for understanding the nature of phenomena or the human experience. Smart (2001) stated, "A model is a set of guiding assumptions, concerns, and propositions.. . . In short, models provide a window to our understanding of disability" (p. 33). Because models of disability are made by humans, they are capable of change and modification. Indeed, at this point of conceptual development, no one model can represent the totality of the experience of having a disability. Although these models are abstractions, they influence the daily lives of PWDs: where they live, which services they receive, and the degree of equal status social integration. In order to provide sensitive and effective services, it is important that counselors understand these models and their basic assumptions. Finally, each of these models influences the way in which everyone (with or without a disability) views his or her body.

Biomedical Model of Disability

The biomedical model defines disability in the language of medicine and science, giving this model strong explanatory power and the power and prestige of the medical profession (Kiesler, 1999). Indeed, of all the models, the biomedical model, with its scientific rigor, has the strongest explanatory power that society can understand, which gives the biomedical model great power and strength (Smart, 2004, 2005b).

Medical diagnoses are based on assumptions of clinical neutrality and standardization and the underlying idea that normality is the standard of evaluation (Eisenberg, 1996; Stone, 1984). According to the biomedical model, disability is defined as pathology, defect, dysfunction, abnormality, deficiency, and inferiority, all of which are found in an individual. Rarely is it considered that many diagnoses and labels are both value laden and stigmatizing (Wright, 1991). In this model, disability is a private concern, and all of the needs of the individual are medical. When taken to an extreme, the social and emotional needs of the individual with the disability are ignored. In addition, because pathology is assumed to be present and the measurements are considered to be objective (Conrad, 2004), it is possible to objectify diagnoses, thinking that diagnoses are objective conditions that exist in and of themselves. When diagnoses are objectified, it is possible to dehumanize the individual who carries the diagnosis.

Diagnoses are often stigmatizing, and they place individuals into categorizes, allowing the general public to view them as their disability—"the blind," "quads," "the mentally ill" (Wright, 1991). Regardless of the category, categorized people are viewed as the category and not as individuals. Occasionally, individuals with disabilities, especially severe and multiple disabilities, are considered only as their economic worth in terms of the work they perform or the resources they consume (e.g., they are defined as "luxuries we can ill afford," "drains," or "burdens").

Disability is thus individualized and medicalized. Therefore, the biomedical model is not considered to be an interactional model, because the definition of the problem and the treatment of the disability are considered to lie wholly within the individual with the disability. Thus, collaboration with nonmedical professions, such as counseling, rarely occurs.

A Canadian disability scholar summarized the biomedical model as follows:

> The most commonly held belief about (this model) of disablement is that it involves a defect, deficiency, dysfunction, abnormality, failing or medical "problem" that is located solely within the individual. We think it is so obvious as to be beyond serious dispute that the disablement is a characteristic of a *defective person,* someone who is functionally limited or anatomically abnormal, diseased, pathoanatomical, someone who is neither whole nor healthy, fit or flourishing, someone who is biologically inferior or subnormal. This essence of disablement, in this view, is that there is something *wrong* with people with disabilities. (Bickenbach, 1993, p. 61, emphasis in the original)

The biomedical model has remained silent on issues of social justice and has helped to relieve society of any responsibility to accord civil rights to individuals. The general public considers disability a personal tragedy and believes that only medical professionals should provide services. Therefore, after medical stabilization, society often communicates, "This is how the world is. Take it or leave it. Don't make any demands on society." The biomedical model legitimizes prejudice and discrimination; moreover, to the general public the treatment of PWDs often does not appear to be prejudicial or discriminating.

Because medical professionals originally worked with patients with acute conditions, who either were completely cured or died, the biomedical model is better suited to explaining acute conditions rather than chronic, long-term disability. The medical treatment of disabilities focuses on care, not cure. The biomedical model is also better suited to explaining physical disabilities rather than cognitive and psychiatric disabilities, and it does not take into account an individual's culture, ethnicity, or roles and functions. In its most extreme form, the biomedical model views the individual patient as a malfunctioning machine.

In spite of these shortcomings, no one suggests totally abandoning the biomedical model, because there are biological realities to all disabilities. Medical care is necessary but not sufficient treatment for PWDs. In addition, the success of medicine has increased the number of PWDs. No one suggests any intentional harm on the part of the medical professions. After all, the broader society has given the field of medicine its mandate concerning the way the profession should be practiced. Finally, it is safe to state that today many medical professionals incorporate into their practice many of the underlying philosophies of the interactional models of disability discussed below.

Functional Model of Disability

The functional model of disability is an interactional (or ecological) model, because disability is defined in relation to an individual's functioning. For example, the loss of a single finger would not be considered a disability unless the individual had spent years training to be a concert pianist. Sometimes this model defines disability as role failure. The overriding treatment or solution for disability is not rehabilitating the individual but rather providing accommodations and adaptations. Assistive technology, such as computerized wheelchairs, hearing aids, and communication boards, are important in this model. For example, there were no wheelchair sports until the 1980s because the sports wheelchair had not been developed. It is the functions the PWD chooses, rather than the individual, that are changed. This model has the capacity to focus on the individual's strengths and assets, values and interests, cultural identification, and functional requirements. In addition, as the individual changes (such as by gaining more education or acquiring a secondary disability) his or her functions change, and accordingly the definition of the disability changes. The biomedical model focuses on rehabilitating the individual; the functional model focuses on providing accommodations in the environment.

Environmental Model of Disability

The environmental model of disability is also an interactional model because disability is defined as an interaction between the individual, the disability, and the environment. The environment, both physical and social, can cause, define, or exaggerate disability. Disability is viewed as a product of a disabling, unresponsive, or insensitive environment. Environments can limit physical access, educational opportunities, social integration, and work opportunities. Certainly, an individual with paraplegia who does not have a wheelchair experiences a more severe disability than an individual with paraplegia who does have a wheelchair.

Obviously, the physical environment has been designed on the false assumption that everyone can see, walk, and hear. Furthermore, most of the general public does not recognize the lack of physical accommodations or notice the absence of PWDs in the environment.

Many environmental factors have changed the definition of disability, including psychotropic medications, which allow many individuals with mental illnesses to control their symptoms. Of course, these medications do not work for everyone, and often their use has very serious side effects. However, it is well understood that these drugs contributed to the deinstitutionalization movement, and moreover nothing changed in the disability (mental illness) or in the individual with the mental illness. The medications were an environmental change. Services, such as supported employment and supported living, are often provided to individuals with intellectual disabilities and psychiatric disabilities. These environmental changes have resulted in a substantially higher quality of life for PWDs.

More difficult than understanding changes in the physical environment is understanding the relationship between the social environment and disability. Prejudice and discrimination are not an inherent part of disability; instead, they are part of the environment, and it is possible to change the environment. Laws, such as the Americans With Disabilities Act and its amendments, are environmental changes that have improved the experience of disability. Wars can cause disability, but they can also provide opportunities for PWDs. World War II is termed the *Golden Age of Employment* for PWDs (Yelin, 1992). Because of the shortage of workers, Americans who had previously been disenfranchised in the labor market, such as racial and ethnic minorities, women, and PWDs, were needed. PWDs experienced their highest rate of employment, and succeeded in their work, during World War II.

Less prejudice and discrimination result from interactional models than from the non-interactional biomedical model because the disability is not conceptualized as being located only in the individual. There are handicapping situations in the environment, such as a lack of physical accessibility. Nonetheless, in both the functional model and the environmental model, prejudice and discrimination result because a deficit orientation is implied. For example, it is better to function than not to function.

Sociopolitical Model of Disability

The newest model of disability and the most difficult one for the general public to understand is the sociopolitical model. This model defines disability as a societal concern rather than a private concern. As would be expected, the sociopolitical model (sometimes termed the *independent living model*) is a response to the biomedical model and its emphasis on individualized inferiority (Longmore, 1995). For the first time, a group identity is being formed that includes individuals with all types of disability, and PWDs are finding their voice to advocate for their rights as Americans. PWDs want their civil rights rather than charity or pity.

According to the sociopolitical model, disability is caused by society, and many of the difficulties experienced by PWDs are the result of societal policies and practices (Fleischer & Zames, 2001). This makes sense because, after medical stabilization, many PWDs state that their most difficult problems are a lack of physical accessibility and the prejudice and discrimination found among the general public. PWDs become skilled at managing their disability; however, society creates the most difficulties for them. The sociopolitical model recognizes that there are biological components to all disabilities but also holds that inferiority is conferred on PWDs by society.

The Biomedical Model and Counselors

Those counselors (with the exception of rehabilitation counselors) who have received training in disability may have received training that is based on the biomedical model of disability, which considers disability to be a pathological attribute located solely within the individual. Counselors may avoid dealing with disability issues, or they may have restrictive ideas about the roles of PWDs. Therefore, counselors may not expand the range of roles and behaviors available to their clients with disabilities. Many of the assumptions about the disability experience and about individuals who have disabilities, although ostensibly based on kindness and good intentions, are inaccurate and may impede the counseling process. Inaccurate assumptions will lead to faulty case conceptualizations and problem formulation.

The biomedical model is being challenged and questioned, and furthermore, other models shape the self-identity and more accurately reflect the daily lives of PWDs. These newer models conceptualize disabilities as interactions among the individual and the environment, both physical and social. Disability is no longer thought to be a private misfortune (deviance) but rather a societal concern (diversity).

General Guidelines for Counselors

1. Counselors should engage in an ongoing examination of their own feelings and conceptualization of disability. If counselors view disability as a tragic inferiority, they may (unconsciously) limit the range of choices available to their clients.
2. The client's disability may arouse feelings of existential questioning, anxiety, and defensiveness in the counselor. Feelings such as "This could me!" could be stress inducing to the counselor. Many PWODs, including counselors, "harbor unspoken anxieties about the possibility of disablement, to us or someone close to us" (Longmore, 2003, p. 132). If counselors are able to accept their own vulnerability to disability,

   > it will be less likely that they will experience a negative, emotional response to a client with a disability. Countertransference, and other emotional reactions to the disability of the client, may prevent the counselor from fully understanding the client and therefore negatively affect the counseling relationship. (Smart & Smart, 2006, p. 37)

3. Counselors should recognize that most PWDs do not accept the basic tenets of the biomedical model, with its emphasis on inferiority, pathology, and deviance. Rather, PWDs view their disability as a valued part of their identity, are proud of their mastery and management of the disability, and see positive aspects and experiences in the disability. Rejecting the disability *role* of social devaluation and deviance does not mean that the individual is in denial about having a disability.

4. Counselors should understand that being a PWD is a normative role imposed by people with power: those who do not have disabilities. These rules, although unwritten, are widely held, and, as can be expected, PWDs typically do not accept them. These rules include complying with all treatment, making others comfortable with their disability, always being cheerful, never expressing anger or other seemingly negative emotions, keeping their aspirations and needs at an appropriately modest level, and always being grateful for accommodations and services. Most important is the socially imposed criterion of appearing normal. This can be engaging in gait training for individuals with mobility impairments in order to make their walking appear more normal, or wearing prostheses that are uncomfortable and have little functioning capability. These social expectations are exhausting burdens for PWDs. If the individual chooses not to comply with these externally imposed roles, he or she may be considered to have on chip on his or her shoulder or not to have accepted the disability. There are times when the individual capitulates to these rules in order to receive services and benefits, or simply because it is an easier course of action. Nonetheless, counselors should recognize that the PWD is the expert on his or her disability and its management.

5. Counselors should seek to understand the following experiences: overobservation, which includes the stares and intrusive questions of strangers; lack of privacy, which includes the use of sign language interpreters and personal care attendants; role entrapment, both social and vocational; solo status, which includes being the only PWD in certain settings; experiencing paternalism and infantilization, which involve considering the PWD as an eternal child; and experiencing stereotyping, which includes being considered not an individual but rather a disability category.

6. Counselors should obtain a deep and complete understanding of the client, including his or her varied functions, roles, and environments. Although the disability is an important and valued aspect of the client's self-identity, it is the total identity. The disability and its management is not the motivator of every decision of the client. In addition, one's disability identity undergoes continual changes, as all identities do. Like most people, individuals with disabilities consider their family life, work life, and community activity to be important parts of their self-identity (Smart, 2012).

7. Counselors should understand disability exhaustion. Disability exhaustion results when one is dealing with the disability bureaucracy and the prejudice and discrimination of the general public. Disability exhaustion can occur when environments are not accessible and accommodations are not in place. Inaccessible environments send a clear message to PWDs: You are not wanted.

8. Counselors should help their clients become empowered. Barnes, Mercer, and Shakespeare (1999) stated, "Their lives [the lives of PWDs] are saturated with unequal encounters with professionals" (p. 82). Obviously, most PWDs are required to meet with a large number of medical professionals, especially during the medical stabilization phase of their disability. PWDs report that they frequently are not permitted to ask questions, challenge diagnoses, or exercise choice in their treatments and services. However, counselors have the opportunity to empower their clients by assuring them that they are the decision makers in counseling sessions.

The following case study is fictional; however, it does show the importance of viewing the client as more than his or her disability. As you consider Jeff's career choice, you will quickly be able to see that his career choices have little if anything to do with his spinal cord injury. Therefore, the functional model of disability offers the best understanding of his disability and the ways in which to develop a case conceptualization.

Case Study

Jeff is an 18-year-old, second-semester freshman at a large state university. He has not declared a major but has adjusted successfully to life at the university and is doing well in his general education classes. He achieved excellent grades in high school and has continued in college with good study habits. He has recently begun to feel more pressure to choose a major. His chief concern about choosing a major was sparked by recent conversations with other students in the residence hall who are also concerned about choosing a major and a career. Clinically speaking, Jeff presents with self-doubt, a magical notion that there is one right answer, and the fear that he is inadequate in making this choice.

Jeff uses a wheelchair and is paraplegic because of a Thoracic 5 lesion caused by an auto accident when he was 12 years old. His older brother, who was driving the car, died in the accident. Jeff refers to himself as a "hick crip" because he is from a small farming community.

Jeff has the impression that he might be successful as either a counselor or a lawyer. These choices, however, have remained somewhat vague. Drawing him toward a career as a counselor has been his experience with counselors who have counseled him in the past, but he is concerned that he would not be as impactful as those who have helped him. In particular, he remembers Mr. Johnson, a counselor who seemed to be able to clearly understand Jeff's needs and always helped Jeff find answers to problems. Jeff goes so far as to say that Mr. Johnson understood his inability to relate to others. Jeff has doubts that he can be as impactful and caring as Mr. Johnson and is worried that his attempts to help others might fall short of his desire to help.

Jeff sees a career as a lawyer as another possibility, and his parents have encouraged this line of thought. They have pointed out to Jeff that he has a logical and analytical mind and that he is "good with words." They also believe that a career in law has better potential to earn a higher income, an important consideration because Jeff realizes that, as he ages, his disability-related expenses will increase. Regardless of Jeff's career choice, his parents want him to find work in their small, isolated, rural town so they can assist in Jeff's daily care. Jeff's parents are concerned that paid personal care attendants are often "crazed drug addicts who will abuse and neglect our son."

With this quandary of career choice in mind, Jeff has decided to seek help at the university counseling center. He has focused much of the same caring attitude in his current counseling experience, and he has hopes that his counselor will be able to quickly and accurately pinpoint the problem and come up with the "right" answer.

His current counselor listens well, and Jeff has begun to trust her and trust that although his counselor may not be able to come up with the one right answer, together they are building a good plan for Jeff's future. The counselor has suggested that Jeff work toward both careers at this point and that he continue to evaluate his progress with each alternative. Because law schools do not require any particular undergraduate major, Jeff would be free to major in psychology as a basis for a career as a counselor. At the same time, he would be able to work as a resident assistant and volunteer in a community social service agency or similar setting as a way to learn about helping others and evaluate his motivation and skill in his role as a helper. He could also visit the Prelaw Advising Office and arrange for an opportunity to shadow a practicing attorney.

Throughout these learning experiences, Jeff would also continue to evaluate the idea that he must be "charismatic" in order to be successful. The counselor has urged Jeff to explore his need to be boldly and unerringly helpful and has reassured Jeff that they can continue to explore this idea of success as they continue counseling.

In addition, the counselor has suggested that Jeff might find it helpful to take career interest inventories, go online or access printed material to read more about the details of each career, or enroll in a career exploration class. Jeff feels reassured that he has begun to develop a plan that is pointing the way toward declaring a major. He feels reassured that he does not have to immediately and unerringly make the "perfect" choice. He continues to evaluate his interests and skills and work toward decisions that are reasonable and seem to fit his personality. The pressure to be "bold" and "charismatic" and make the one perfect career decision has now faded, and Jeff feels reassured as he arranges the pieces of life's puzzles in a more step-by-step process and is less anxiety ridden.

Suggested Approaches

1. Clearly, this is case requires both vocational/career exploration and academic advising. The client's disability presents little or no functional limitations to either of his career choices. It may be necessary to explore and discuss the client's stated need to be "bold" and "charismatic." Taking sequential steps and pacing his decision making will allow the client to feel more in control.

2. Because of the client's successful transition from high school to university study, it appears that he has established an image of academic self-efficacy. In addition, the client has demonstrated a successful transition from the parental home in a small, remote, rural town to life in a large state university. For someone with a physical disability, leaving the parental home is a more complex undertaking than it is for most 18-year-olds. The successful completion of this transition shows resourcefulness and resilience.

3. Assisting the client in accessing various advising offices and vocational/career testing centers on campus will provide both information and experience. More important, these experiences will assist the client in developing a positive career-related self-efficacy expectation.

4. Disability considerations include ensuring that both the reception area and the counselor's office are physically accessible for wheelchairs. Appropriate table heights, door widths, and ramps into the building are necessary.

5. The counselor should learn more about paraplegia and what a Thoracic 5 lesion involves. It will be necessary to ask the client whether he will require repositioning during the 50-minute counseling sessions. (Individuals with spinal cord injuries do not feel pressure below the level of the injury, and therefore they are unable to shift their weight to relieve pressure.) Also, the counselor should ask the client whether the temperature of the room is satisfactory. (Many individuals with spinal cord injuries may experience excessive sweating and headaches due to a sudden rise in blood pressure caused by neural discharge from the autonomic nervous system.)

6. The counselor should understand that Jeff, like most PWDs, probably has had many experiences with professionals since acquiring his disability at age 12. PWDs require services and treatments from a wide array of professionals, and often PWDs are not allowed to give input into their treatment, are not permitted to ask questions, and are not

given direct and clear answers to their questions. Moreover, some of these professionals are gatekeepers to obtaining services and resources, and therefore PWDs submit to professional dominance and paternalism because they need the services and benefits. Counselors can help to empower clients with disabilities by listening and supporting them and not assuming that they themselves know about the experience of living with a disability or know what is best for their clients. In Jeff's case, the counselor has allowed Jeff to move at his own pace toward goals that Jeff himself has determined.

7. The counselor should consciously guard against imposing sympathy and lowered expectations with this client. Sympathy and lowered expectations most often arise from kindness; however, these attitudes can be stigmatizing and prejudicial, and they eventually limit clients' range of opportunities, foster dependence and passivity, and communicate to clients with disabilities that they are not perceived as capable.

8. Although it is necessary for the counselor to learn more about the medical diagnosis of the client in order to provide accommodations, the counselor should guard against making generalizations and categorizations. Recognize that Jeff is not his spinal cord injury. Nor is the spinal cord injury the motivator of all of Jeff's behaviors, attitudes, and decisions. Jeff has multiple identities, roles, and functions. The spinal cord injury is an important part of Jeff's self-identity; however, it is only one part of a complex identity.

9. The client may neither wish nor require any further accommodations or discussion about his disability. However, if the client does introduce the topic of his disability, it may be necessary for the counselor to listen to his or her experiences of prejudice and discrimination. In this case, Jeff may wish to discuss his experiences dealing with paternalism; being a forced representative; or being objectified, infantilized, sexualized, pathologized, or exoticized.

Conclusion

PWDs today are experiencing more social, educational, and vocational integration than ever before. They are becoming advocates for themselves, asserting their rights to professional counseling services in all specialty areas and in practice settings from counselors of all theoretical orientations. These advances require counselors to gain more training in disability issues in order to serve these individuals and practice within the scope of their training and competence. Most counselors have not taken a course in disabilities, and the little disability training they have received has been based on the biomedical model of disability. More information about disabilities can be obtained from the U.S. Department of Justice (*A Guide to Disability Rights Laws;* http://www.usdoj.gov/crt/ada/cguide.htm) or from the U.S. Census Bureau (http://www.census.gov/prod/2006pubs/p70-107.pdf).

References

Americans With Disabilities Act of 1990, PL 101-336, 42 U.S.C. §§ 12101 *et seq.*

Anspach, R. R. (1979). From stigma to identity politics: Political activism among the physically disabled and former mental patients. *Social Science & Medicine, 13A,* 765–773.

Barnes, C., Mercer, G., & Shakespeare, T. (1999). *Exploring disability: A sociological introduction.* Cambridge, England: Polity.

Bauman, H. D. L., & Drake, J. (1997). Silence is not without voice: Including deaf culture within the multicultural curricula. In L. J. Davis (Ed.), *Disability studies reader* (pp. 307–314). New York, NY: Routledge.

Bickenbach, J. E. (1993). *Physical disability and social policy.* Toronto, Ontario, Canada: University of Toronto.

Bluestone, H. H., Stokes, A., & Kuba, S. A. (1996). Toward an integrated program design: Evaluating the status of diversity training in a graduate school curriculum. *Professional Psychology: Research and Practice, 27,* 394–400.

Brault, M. (2008, December). *Americans with disabilities: 2005* (Current Population Reports No. P70-117). Washington, DC: U.S. Census Bureau.

Centers for Disease Control and Prevention. (2006). Improved national prevalence estimates for 18 selected birth defects—United States, 1999-2011. *Morbidity and Mortality Weekly Report, 54,* 1301–1305.

Conrad, P. (2004). The discovery of hyperkinesis: Notes on the medicalization of deviant behavior. In S. Danforth & S. D. Taff (Eds.), *Crucial readings in special education* (pp. 18–24). Upper Saddle River, NJ: Prentice Hall.

Eisenberg, L. (1996). Foreword. In J. E. Mezzich, A. Kleinman, H. Fabrega, Jr., & D. L. Parron (Eds.), *Culture and psychiatric diagnosis: A* DSM-IV *perspective* (pp. xii–xv). Washington, DC: American Psychiatric Association.

Fleischer, D., & Zames, F. (2001). *The disability rights movement: From charity to compensation.* Philadelphia, PA: Temple University.

Hogben, M., & Waterman, C. K. (1997). Are all of your students represented in their textbooks? A content analysis of coverage of diversity issues in introductory psychology textbooks. *Teaching of Psychology, 24,* 95–100.

Humes, C. W., Szymanski, E. M., & Hohenshil, T. H. (1989). Roses of counseling in enabling persons with disabilities. *Journal of Counseling & Development, 68,* 145–150.

Kiesler, D. J. (1999). *Beyond the disease model of mental disorders.* Westport, CT: Praeger.

Linton, S. (2004). Divided society. In S. Danforth & S. D. Taff (Eds.), *Crucial readings in special education* (pp. 138–147). Upper Saddle River, NJ: Prentice Hall.

Longmore, P. K. (1995). Medical decision making and people with disabilities: A clash of cultures. *Journal of Law, Medicine and Ethics, 23,* 82–87.

Longmore, P. K. (2003). *Why I burned my book and other essays on disability.* Philadelphia, PA: Temple University.

McCarthy, H. (2003). The disability rights movement: Experiences and perspectives of selected leaders in the disability community. *Rehabilitation Counseling Bulletin, 46,* 209–223.

Scotch, R. K. (1984). *From good will to civil rights: Transforming federal disability policy.* Philadelphia, PA: Temple University.

Scotch, R. K. (1988). Disability as a basis for a social movement: Advocacy and the politics of definition. *Journal of Social Issues, 44,* 159–172.

Smart, J. F. (2001). *Disability, society and the individual.* Austin, TX: PRO-ED.

Smart, J. F. (2004). Models of disability: the juxtaposition of biology and social construction. In T. F. Rigger & D. R. Maki (Eds.), *Handbook of rehabilitation counseling* (pp. 25–49). New York, NY: Springer.

Smart, J. F. (2005a). Challenges to the biomedical model of disability: Changes to the practice of rehabilitation counseling. *Directions in Rehabilitation Counseling, 16*(4), 33–43.

Smart, J. F. (2005b). The promise of the International Classification of Functioning, Disability, and Health (ICF). *Rehabilitation Education, 19,* 191–199.

Smart, J. F. (2008). The power of models of disability. *Journal of Rehabilitation, 75,* 3–11.

Smart, J. F. (2009). *Disability, society and the individual* (2nd ed.). Austin, TX: PRO-ED.

Smart, J. F., & Smart, D. W. (2006). Models of disability: Implications for the counseling profession. *Journal of Counseling & Development, 84,* 29–40.

Smart, J. F. (2012). *Disability across the developmental lifespan.* New York, NY: Springer.

Stone, D. A. (1984). *The disabled state.* Philadelphia, PA: Temple University.

Trieschmann, R. (1987). *Aging with a disability.* New York, NY: Demos.

White, P. H. (2002). Access to healthcare: Health insurance considerations for young adults with special health care needs/disabilities. *Pediatrics, 110,* 1328–1336.

Wright, B. A. (1991). Labeling: The need for greater person-environment individuation. In C. R. Snyder & D. R. Forsythe (Eds.), *Handbook of social and clinical psychology* (pp. 469–487). Elmsford, NY: Pergamon.

Yelin, E. H. (1992). *Disability and the displaced worker.* New Brunswick, NJ: Rutgers University.

Zola, I. K. (1982). *Missing pieces: A chronicle of living with a disability.* Philadelphia, PA: Temple University Press.

Multicultural Deaf Children and Their Hearing Families: Working With a Constellation of Diversities

Cheryl L. Wu and Nancy C. Grant

Before we begin, we encourage you the reader to explore your own starting point. When you see "multicultural deaf children and their hearing families," what are your feelings and thoughts in response to this brief description? What do you visualize? What are your assumptions? Your biases? As a counselor, what is your first reaction to this situation?

Multicultural families with deaf children contain multiple intersections of diversity within each family's unique environmental context. Sue's (2001) tripartite model of identity helps to illustrate the complexities of individual, group, and universal levels of identity and relationships. At the *individual* level, the deaf child's uniqueness in terms of genetic endowment and non-shared experiences (with family, especially) is significant. His or her *group*-level similarities and differences include deafness in addition to gender, ethnicity, race, and all of the other groups to which he or she may belong. Although the *universal* level applies to all humans, the deaf child's perception of common life experiences and the family's and (deaf and hearing) communities' perceptions and interactions with his or her basic humanity are shaped by this complex mix.

The diversity among deaf people and communities is increasing rapidly in terms of race, ethnicity, and mix (see Table 15.1). There is significant diversity in how individuals experience being deaf or hard of hearing and how they live. Factors include the circumstances and degree of deafness, what language(s) they have access to, what medical and audiological technologies they have (or do not have) access to and choose (or do not choose) to use, and what educational options they have. These all impact their identity along the deaf/hearing spectrum. There are, of course, the additional dimensions of sexual identity, disability, class, age, and so on. This chapter gives an overview of diversity within the deaf population, systems affecting deaf children and families, and counselor roles. It then focuses on deaf children born into hearing families, with an emphasis on immigrants, families of color, and deaf children with disabilities.

Table 15.1 • 2009–2010 Regional and National Summary of Data From the Annual Survey of Deaf and Hard of Hearing Children and Youth

Variable	%
Students of color	53
White students	47
Students who have had a cochlear implant	15
Students who have not had a cochlear implant	85
Students who have hearing aids for instruction	58
Students who have hearing parents	77
Students who have deaf or hard of hearing parents	9
English used regularly in the home	82
Spoken languages other than English used regularly in home	47
American Sign Language used regularly in the home	6
Homes in which the family does not sign regularly	72
Homes in which the family uses some form of signed language regularly	23
Students who are deaf or hard of hearing with one or more disability conditions	39
Students who are deaf or hard of hearing with no disability conditions	61

Note. Data are from *Regional and National Summary Report of Deaf From the 2009–2010 Annual Survey of Deaf and Hard of Hearing Children and Youth*, by Gallaudet Research Institute, 2011, Washington, DC: Author.

Demographics

American deaf students are increasingly diverse in terms of their deaf-related-identity, race/ethnicity, immigration (including international adoption), sexual identity, disabilities, socioeconomic status, and religion. Diversity impacts the makeup of the deaf population overall, the education of deaf children, and the character and characteristics of the deaf community. These deaf students are the future generations and leaders—and issues of diversity within the deaf world have an impact on deaf and hearing parents of deaf children. The following sociodemographic profile of deaf and hard of hearing students ages 0 to 22 from a November 2009 annual survey (Gallaudet Research Institute, 2011) highlights the diversity of students in deaf educational settings, including residential schools for the deaf and a range of educational settings in private and public schools.

Decreasing numbers overall have a disproportionate impact on any low-incidence group, particularly on the even smaller subgroups within. For the American Deaf community, residential schools for deaf children have functioned as the core deaf cultural enclave, the place where there are relatively large numbers of deaf people of all ages, in all positions, and where American Sign Language (ASL) is the norm. Like Deaf multigenerational families, residential schools are the places where people who identify as culturally Deaf learn and pass along their language, culture, traditions. Fewer deaf children are born now because of decreases in the incidence of rubella and other conditions that can cause deafness (Holt, Hotto, & Cole, 1994). Decreasing overall numbers of deaf children have led to the closure of many deaf schools. The increase in the use of cochlear implants and other medical technology has had a profound impact on the school population, focusing on rehabilitation as hearing rather than identity and culture as deaf.

As counselors explore the communities and resources for deaf children and their families, it is important that they keep in mind the diversity within the deaf community as well as the relationship between the deaf and hearing worlds. Simms, Rusher, Andrews, and Coryell's (2008) survey of 3,227 professionals in 313 deaf education programs found that

22.0% of teachers and 14.5% of administrators were deaf—a less than 10% increase in the number of deaf professionals since 1993. In addition, 21.7% of teachers and 6.1% of administrators were professionals of color. Of minority teachers, only 2.5% were deaf persons of color. Only three deaf administrators of color were identified. There is a clear need for education to diversify its professional force in order to utilize the intellectual, linguistic, and multicultural proficiencies of hearing teachers of color, deaf teachers, and deaf teachers of color. There are no similar studies on counselors of deaf children, adults, and families, but anecdotally speaking we are seeing a gradual increase in the number of deaf counselors, although the majority are still White and hearing. This counters the present image of school populations in which racial/ethnic minority deaf students make up more than 50% of the population and growing. There needs to be encouragement of multicultural representation as well as deaf and racial/ethnic competency among counselors.

We are primarily addressing hearing counselors—those from the majority group of people who can hear without difficulty, for whom hearing is assumed to be normal, who have limited experience with deaf and hard of hearing people, and who have limited engagement with the American Deaf community.

Working with a profoundly deaf person can be a shock to a hearing counselor, with potential dangers of romanticizing or demonizing deaf language and culture and viewing deaf people as one homogenous group. The dimensionality of deafness and tensions between deaf and hearing are well documented and discussed in the literature on deaf culture, most recently in the deafhood movement (Bauman, 2008; Ladd, 2003; Leigh, 2009).

Understanding the experiences of hard of hearing or deafened people (those who have lost their hearing after acquisition of spoken/heard language) requires mindful attention. Counselors (and families) may not believe that a client does not hear, especially if he or she has understandable speech. Learning and remembering to use skills related to communication can be challenging for hearing people. For hard of hearing, deaf, and deafened people, their emotional and physical state, as well as the environment (lighting, background noise levels, etc.), can have a profound impact on their capacity to "listen" (to lipread) and make sense of the words or syllables they do actually "hear" (or see).

Many Ways to Be Deaf

Along the cultural dimension of deaf experience, there is a wide spectrum of individual and collective experience. Some deaf people move easily among different ways of being deaf, of relating to and communicating with deaf and hearing people. Others are strongly identified with one part of the spectrum.

In the remainder of this chapter, we use lowercase *deaf* to refer to the whole spectrum of deafness as described previously. *Deaf* with a capital *D* is used to refer specifically to culturally Deaf people.

A culturally Deaf American comes from at least one generation of Deaf parents, uses ASL as a native language, and often is educated at a residential school for the deaf (where there is a community of people of multiple ages and adult role models). Being Deaf is a source of belonging and pride. Deaf culture ranges from ASL jokes, poetry, dance, drama, and sports; to ways of shaping the environment to be visually accessible; to criteria establishing credibility as a community member; to Deaf social organizations, schools, businesses, and formal and informal networks and systems. Deafness is not associated with hearing loss, impairment, or disability. Culturally Deaf parents can identify positively with their child's experience of being deaf and teach their own language and culture to their child from day one. Only about 5% of deaf children are born to culturally Deaf parents (Mitchell & Karchmer, 2002). The majority are White. These Deaf of Deaf children tend to become the core of the next generation of the Deaf community, often growing into leadership roles. Deaf parents also transmit what they have experienced in relation to hearing individuals and the hearing world. Experiences of oppression, discrimination, misunderstanding, and ignorance at the individual, family, group, and systems levels are common. In relation to the hearing world, the Deaf community emphasizes educating hearing people about the deaf experience and advocating for equal rights via access to communication, information, services, education, and employment. In recent years, the Deafhood (Ladd, 2003) and deaf studies (Bauman, 2008) movements have provided a framework for the American Deaf community to see its own history, oppression, and potential future.

About 95% of deaf children are born to hearing parents, most of whom who have had little contact with deaf people and community and have little awareness, knowledge, or skills related to being with a deaf person, much less raising a deaf child. At least at first, these parents tend to understand deafness in relation to their own experience of being hearing: that is, they often see deafness as a loss, impairment, or disability, not as a cultural difference. They need to work with their own feelings and cultural beliefs about the meaning of deafness and disability and develop their own deaf-related competencies, supports, resources, and networks (Lucas & Schatz, 2003; Lynch & Hanson, 2004).

Many deaf people have been raised with an emphasis on speech and hearing, and their goal is to engage successfully with the hearing world, to be as hearing as possible. This often involves undergoing medical and technological interventions and significant individual speech and hearing training. There are groups and organizations of oral deaf people, though not with the generations of community and culture of the American Deaf community. These individuals may identify as deaf, hard of hearing, hearing impaired, or having a hearing loss.

Some people have partial hearing/partial deafness and may identify as hard of hearing. Some start their lives with full hearing and, through injury, illness, or aging, lose their ability to hear or to process sound. Their actual physical ability to hear may fluctuate or may decrease progressively. Having lost a sense they started out with, they often identify as having a hearing loss or hearing impairment. Hard of hearing people are neither fully hearing nor fully deaf and may experience being caught between these two worlds (Grushkin, 2003).

Increasing numbers of deaf infants, children, youth, and adults are receiving cochlear implants, a medical and technological intervention that removes part of the natural mechanism of the ear and electronically connects auditory stimuli to the brain. Significant training and fine-tuning of the technology are required for someone with an implant to perceive and interpret these stimuli. Cochlear implants are very successful in some cases and not at all successful in others, so an appropriate assessment of both medical and psychosocial factors is critical. The procedure destroys whatever natural hearing is left, so a person with an implant is completely deaf when the mechanism is turned off.

What Does It Mean to Be Hearing?

Most hearing people tend to take their hearing for granted. It is just the way things are, they are. They do not think much about it or about the advantages and privileges it affords them simply because it is assumed to be the norm. Most environments are designed with hearing people in mind. We encourage you to think about what it means to be hearing, just as many multicultural educators and leaders ask people to think about what it means to be White (Sue, 2003, 2006; Sue & Sue, 2008; Ponterotto, Utsey, & Pedersen, 2006). What does being hearing mean to you as an individual? To the majority group of hearing people? To members of your cultural or ethnic group? How does that shape your understanding of and relationship to deaf and hard of hearing people? Being hearing is not something hearing people tend to consider, unless they are faced with a deaf person; even then the attention tends to be on the deaf person as other, different, or "less than." It is important to reflect on this for yourself. Also, think about your practice as a counselor. How well does your practice consider and include deaf people? What awareness, knowledge, skills, and encounters do you have that relate to deaf people?

Working with a deaf person is *not only* about deaf/hearing (or not deaf/not hearing). Counselors need to incorporate the breadth and depth of their multicultural training and experience and apply and integrate it with the additional dimension of deafness. The deaf/hearing context and its bridges and barriers are important to understand, and it is *also* important to remember that deaf people are more than just their deafness. The deaf world is changing rapidly along dimensions of race, ethnicity, and culture. It is also changing with regard to how people are deaf, something that is profoundly impacted by parental understanding, opportunities, and choices made early in a child's development. Deaf people may experience changes in their identity over their life span depending on a host of helpful and hurtful influences. It is important to consider deaf individuals from the perspective of the deaf world and explore where they fit within that world. It is also important to consider the worldviews of their families and communities and explore their identities within those contexts (Corbett, 2002). When a deaf child has disabilities (and the number of such children is increasing), there is yet another layer of potential inclusion and/or marginalization to consider (Edwards & Crocker, 2008). Immigration issues can be significant for documented and undocumented families with a deaf child or for an immigrant deaf person. Socioeconomic class affects access to health care, services, education, and other supports. All intersections of diversity affect deaf people (Christensen, 2000; Leigh, 2009, 2010, 2012; Leigh & Maxwell-McCaw, 2001).

How Counselors Can Help?

Counselors can provide multiculturally competent support to the deaf child, his or her family, communities the child and family belong to, and the school by being a cultural mediator (Portman, 2009), helping to engage all stakeholders. Our interpretation of positive mental health/wellness focuses on the whole child, recognizing the child's potential multidimensionality of identity. This naturally includes healthy deaf identity but is not restricted to deaf pride at the expense of other aspects of self and heritage. *Health* is a term that is culturally bound. It is important to explore what deafness and health might mean to the individual client, to parents, and to educators and counselors. It is helpful for the client to have access and connection to their communities; language and understanding to understand their environments and how they fit into them; and skills to assess, communicate, and advocate for all parts of themselves in all of their environments. By promoting access to and understanding of the many parts of their identity, a counselor supports clients' own choices and helps them to be able to negotiate their differences and inclusion in all of their environments. It is especially important that deaf children have the opportunity to develop their own awareness, knowledge, and skills in terms of multiple identities because of the language and communication issues associated with deafness and hearing loss and the tendency of many professionals and other significant people in their lives to promote either having deaf pride or being as hearing as possible. Deaf children, and often their parents, need opportunities to personally encounter many kinds of deaf people, to find natural and desired connections to deaf and hearing worlds.

Counselors also need to seek out exposure to many kinds of deaf people, to seek their own "cultural encounter" (Campinha-Bacote, 2002) with deaf people, to be proactive in this area, and to be able to affirm and celebrate many aspects of identity. Proposition 5 of Sue, Ivey, and Pedersen's (1996) theory of multicultural counseling and therapy encourages multiple helping roles. As counselor roles change in the direction of social justice, counselors working with deaf children need to look at the impact of a child's deafness on the family, group, school, and systemic levels as well as work with the child. Multicultural competencies respond to the need for counselors to fulfill multiple roles as advocates, social workers, case managers, and cultural bridges, helping them understand and negotiate the system in addition to developing clinical skills. Changing counselor roles emphasize relationship building, collaboration, cross-consultation, multiple roles, and multidisciplinary teaming (Ponterotto et al., 2006; Sue et al., 1996).

It is important to recognize dynamics between and among communities, too. Deaf people (i.e., individuals and groups whose language is ASL and who identify as culturally Deaf) may not trust hearing service providers or agencies. There are real differences to address, real disagreements about language development and its relationship to child development and about the impact of hearing technology and communication strategies.

Cross-cultural dialogue is critical in identifying, honoring, and working with these differences and conflicts. Such dialogue requires resources and skills related to simply making communication possible, such as skilled, fairly paid interpreters; quality real-time captioning (which requires equipment and captioners); and communication-friendly environments with good sight-lines, lighting, minimal background noise, accessible sound systems, and so on. Engaging in dialogue also requires expertise in both technical and people skills.

Deaf people have obtained access to equal rights through the disability rights movement and legislation such as Section 504 of the Rehabilitation Act of 1973, the Americans With Disabilities Act of 1990, the Individuals With Disabilities Education Act of 1990, and other education legislation. This legislation has shaped the deaf community's emphasis on advocacy. This often involves informing hearing people, public services, and organizations about a protected group that has rights to accessibility. There is often a focus on access to communication accomplished through qualified sign language interpreters. Advocacy is important and needed but can tend to emphasize accommodations per se, with less attention to building interpersonal and institutional relationships. Providing an interpreter or captioning may satisfy accessibility concerns around the equitable delivery of information, but it does not directly help deaf and hearing people to connect beyond exchanging information. Counselors need to look at being both an advocate for inclusion and equity and also an ally. Counselors need to be clear what and whom they are advocating for and against. They need to look at how advocacy relates to relationship building. These ideas are not mutually exclusive, and both are important.

For example, we worked on a child abuse case involving a teenage deaf Chinese girl. She had grown up in the San Francisco Bay Area and was fluent in ASL (her primary language). Her family spoke only Cantonese. Engaging all participants involved obtaining a referral for mental health counseling for the child with a deaf community-based agency and a local Chinese community-based family services agency to work with the family. Over time, with several other deaf community agencies, we provided periodic training to Child Protective Services staff. Our role was also to serve as case manager and liaison with all involved, to ensure that all cultural translations (deaf, Chinese, and American) were made, and to ensure that everyone understood and was engaged with the process. As a result of this collaboration, one Child Protective Services worker became interested in working with cases in the deaf community; additional training and consultation was focused on her. She in turn helped make linkages with local police and other services and resources.

Importance of Cultural Humility

It is helpful to start by helping parents explore their awareness and understanding what "deaf" means to them in relation to their child and themselves; what "hearing" means to them; and how the difference plays out in feelings and behaviors, skills, and creation of a family environment for their deaf child (or adult or elder, for that matter). The cultural humility (Juarez et al., 2006; Tervalon & Murray-Garcia, 1998) of really listening to the parent for understanding, without judging them, begins to create a realistic and respectful ground for providing other cultural perspectives about deafness and information about various resources and approaches.

Language is powerful. Counselors need to be aware of their own use of language related to deaf and hard of hearing people. Counselors need to clarify the client's way of describing his or her own deaf or hard of hearing identity. They also need to be aware and respectful of the language they use regarding parents. Terms such as *helicopter parents,* which describes parents who do everything for or overprotect their child, may reflect stereotypes about hearing parents and may not take into account the family's cultural values around parenting and deafness. This is in comparison to a deaf school's value of child autonomy, independence, and individual deaf identity. There is a common phrase: "Deaf CAN" (do anything except hear). The implication is that deaf individuals can do anything, and it is just a matter of access and advocacy for the right communication and accessibility. The phrase often does not consider talents, skills, relationships, collaboration, or interdependence. An emphasis on the development of the deaf individual is important but needs to synch with additional values and skills related to collective orientation, interdependence, and relationship building with deaf and hearing people. Counselors need to consider how to open a third space in which people (hearing parents and deaf professionals, or deaf parents and hearing professionals) can be genuine and really listen to one another for understanding.

For example, our students in a master's program in counseling, most of whom are themselves deaf, were invited to family night at a hearing elementary school with two classrooms for deaf students. One goal for the evening was for our deaf counseling students and parents of the school's deaf students to share their real-life experiences and questions about what it means to be deaf and what it means to parent a deaf child. Our guidelines were to "listen for understanding" and "speak from the heart." The parents had never met deaf college students and looked forward to hearing about their experience. The students all had strong opinions about parenting deaf children and assumptions about hearing parents; however, they also wanted to connect and build genuine relationships with these parents. What surprised and supported the students in sharing their stories was the genuineness and openness of the parents about the love, joys, and fears they felt about their deaf children; the students also felt the respect and appreciation of the parents. In this third space, real relationships began to develop; the students let go of their stereotypes about hearing parents to recognize some of their own countertransference related to being brought up by hearing parents. The parents really listened to the experiences shared by the deaf students, giving them some insight into what their own children might feel and face. They appreciated and enjoyed these deaf young adults as role models for themselves and their children. The evening was simply about building relationships and opening up a space in which disagreement or misunderstanding could be reflected on without judgment or blame. That third space does not exist if counselors start with an agenda to educate or inform. As a result of that evening, both the parents and the counseling students wanted to connect, work, and play with one another and the children who brought them together to build a community together.

Creating a third space in which dialogue can take place often requires access to communication supports, such as skilled sign language interpreters and a facilitator who can help to bridge cultural as well as language differences (Mindess, 1999). In situations in which hearing people do not speak English or deaf people do not use ASL, additional interpreters and the skillful use of space and time is critical (Hidalgo & Williams, 2010).

Creating a third space in which one can build a truly multicultural community allows for the possibility of mixing on multiple dimensions of diversity. It poses an even greater challenge or opportunity. The old image of the melting pot implies that the original ingredients are subsumed into some singular substance. The salad bowl image honors separateness, an unchanging character of the individual parts. A third space allows for something more like a blend: A change happens when individual people encounter other people with humility and kindness. The change is not necessarily full melting in the sense of being subsumed into a homogeneous whole but rather the creation of something new and different from the mutual contact. It is not the dimensions of deaf/hearing and/or people of color/White per se that are important but the intersections of these dimensions and how the different dimensions impact each other within the individual and the environment. Creating a third space, in which genuineness can emerge, people can listen for understanding and create relationships, not just reinforce everyone's right or pride or autonomy. There is a different kind of engagement that allows for disagreement *and* inclusion. Creating a third space requires structuring and preparing opportunities and allowing time for relationships to develop, for understanding to happen, and for change to occur. It actually promotes reflection and dialogue, which leads to equitable social action.

Four Primary Sociopolitical Systems That Affect Deaf People

Deaf and hard of hearing people (or their families) seek the help offered by sociopolitical systems. Some perceive their hearing status as a loss or impairment. Yet attempts to help or fix deaf people—to make them more hearing—are also perceived and experienced as oppression. This tension influences the deaf-versus-hearing polarization. Understanding deafness and associated helping systems can be confusing for families, especially those with little or no exposure to deaf people or culture.

Strong and often conflicting opinions, beliefs, and values are expressed by medical professionals, educators of deaf children, parent organizations, and deaf people themselves. The following four systems significantly influence how deaf people are perceived and treated both clinically and socially. Again, it is important for counselors to be aware of their individual and cultural beliefs, values, fears, and hopes about what it means to be deaf, hard of hearing, and hearing. Only then will he or she be able to think clearly and deeply about what is best for this individual child and workable for his or her family, school, and community.

1. *Medicine.* The medical model views disability

> as a medical problem that resides in the individual. It is a defect in or failure of a bodily system and as such is inherently abnormal and pathological. The goals of intervention are cure, amelioration of the physical condition to the greatest extent possible, and rehabilitation (i.e., the adjustment of the person with the disability to the condition and to the environment). (Olkin, 1999, p. 26)

Proponents of the medical model are likely to perceive and take action toward a deaf person as someone who is not hearing or whose hearing is broken and should be fixed. It tends to focus on the ears, not necessarily the whole person or the person-in-family-in-community. Medical practitioners, such as otolaryngologists, audiologists, and speech therapists, tend to focus on a particular area of expertise. The goal of the helping intervention is to improve hearing. The medical system also has practical structures of eligibility and access that include basic health care, quality assessments, hearing aids and other hearing technology, and surgery, among other things. Such interventions can be very helpful, particularly when the client desires them and is equipped to learn to use and maintain them. However, medical interventions do not cure deafness and often are not as effective as glasses can be for someone with poor vision. Perhaps the most sensitive and controversial area of medical technology concerns the use of cochlear implants in infants or children. It is important for counselors to ensure that parents understand all of the potential pros and cons and the practical reality of learning to use an implant, which only begins with the surgery. Cochlear implants do not work for all types of hearing loss. Once an implant is done, learning to utilize it requires extensive training and adjustments to the implant itself in order for the individual to learn to understand the meaning of all the sounds that are transmitted through the implant. Learning speech is an additional step. The equipment must be maintained (and replaced if broken). Thus, the surgery itself is only the beginning, and managing the rehabilitation and equipment can be costly and time consuming. Even a very successful cochlear implant does not cure deafness or replace normal hearing. If it is turned off, or not working correctly, the individual is still deaf (Leigh & Maxwell-McCaw, 2011; Paludneviciene & Harris, 2011). Marschark, Lang, and Albertini's (2002) book on cochlear implants is a helpful starting point for learning more about the use of cochlear implants in children.

The medical model stands in contrast to a Deaf cultural model that defines deafness as an identity to be honored and affirmed, not as a disability or something that needs to be fixed or changed. In the Deaf cultural model, being Deaf is an individual and collective identity to be celebrated and nurtured; access to deaf history and culture, a deaf community, role models, and early expert exposure to visual language (specifically ASL) are critical to positive Deaf identity development, and English is an important but second language (Lane, 2008).

Because of mandated newborn hearing screening, medical professionals usually are the first to communicate a child's deafness to the parents or family. Often it takes time for parents to gain a referral to the relatively small deaf community. Gaining awareness of and access to the deaf community can be especially difficult for culturally diverse families, especially those whose first language is not English and those who may not have access to transportation and other concrete resources. Parents have a tremendous amount to juggle: getting a diagnosis, understanding the etiology and potential treatment options, and gaining access to and an understanding of the deaf community and their child's potential supports and resources in that community (Marschark, 2007). Weighing these different factors through the lens of their own language and culture is a lot. Multiculturally competent counselors can be a major support here. If a child is a preemie or has medical complications, those factors may overshadow his or her deafness. Yet not recognizing and responding to a child's deafness can cause difficulties in language development and cognitive and psychosocial ramifications.

2. *Education.* The field of education for deaf children is full of differing approaches, generally along the spectrum of emphasis on English, speech, and residual hearing to emphasis on ASL as a first language. Deaf students may be isolated in a hearing school, attend

special day classes, or attend day and residential schools for deaf students (Marschark et al., 2002). Just as with any school, issues of access to a fair, equitable education are critical. Educators, like medical professionals, have their views about deaf children: Deaf children may be seen as simply culturally Deaf and in need of being taught with culturally competent strategies in appropriate environments, or they may be seen as disabled and in need of remediation. Whatever the educational context, families need to be involved in culturally meaningful ways, and it is important for Deaf children (including those with additional learning needs) to have access to Deaf culture and relationships (Christensen, 2010; Marschark, 2007; Williamson, 2007).

3. *Transition and rehabilitation.* Transition and rehabilitation services tend to focus on individual rather than environmental changes, and often families are not engaged in the process, especially if the client is older than 18. This can be appropriate for some clients. However, the family and cultural ties, roles, and experience of interdependence of multicultural deaf individuals may not be in line with such a value system. Multiply disabled deaf people in particular may continue to need the support of their families when service providers' offices are closed or when a shift has ended (Leung, 2003; Marshall, Leung, Johnson, & Busby, 2003).

4. *Communication technology.* Communication technology is rapidly becoming a new system. Changes in communication technology, such as the Internet, pagers and text messaging, telephone relay services, and videophones, have had a huge impact on the deaf community. Electronic media make possible a rich world of visual communication in which real-time text is easy, face-to-face real-time sign language communication is possible, and live sign language interpreting between deaf and hearing people is possible. Moreover, YouTube is available in sign language (and nonsigned postings may be captioned), and deaf-related websites can offer "vlogs" (video blogs) or articles delivered as signed video rather than text or voice. It has opened up access to information and interaction tremendously. It has the same potential for good and harm as any other form of social networking (e.g., Twitter, Facebook). Distance counseling via e-mail and videophone works well for some populations but not others: It is great for adults, for people who live in rural areas, for those who speak English, and for those with access to the technology. These communication technologies are not so great for developing direct relationships with children and families, communicating with people in multiple languages, and so on. There is a disproportionately negative impact on those who do not have access to technology.

A Social Justice Situation–Framing Approach to Cultural Encounters

Here we describe a six-part approach to multicultural assessment and intervention with culturally diverse deaf children and their families. It is a multicultural deaf/hard of hearing child/adolescent ecological model adapted from a number of theoretical models (Bay Area Network for Diversity Training in Early Childhood, 2003; Campinha-Bacote, 2002; Gorski, 2011; Root, 2003).

The model includes the counselor, the client or consumer, the family or community, and the structural systems that impact them all. The initial cultural encounter may be personally experienced, witnessed (on the street, in the classroom, even on television or video), or relayed (by a colleague, by a supervisee, by a teacher you are consulting with, or even through rumor).

Part 1: Reflection

In the initial situation, the counselor focuses on his or her own perceptions of what he or she saw; reflects on his or her own feelings, thoughts, judgments, and beliefs; and reflects on how these values shape his or her perceptions and formulation of the situation. The purpose of this step is for the counselor to become aware of where he or she is coming from and what positive and/or negative biases he or she may have.

Part 2: Dialogue

This part intentionally brings multiple perspectives to the situation. The counselor asks and engages others in considering questions such as the following: What do I know and not know? What do I need to find out, and how can I do so? Who are all the people involved or impacted by the encounter? What do they know, and how do they perceive the encounter? What potential conflicts exist? Who are potential allies or resources in the school, home, or larger community? This is a sort of brainstorming phase; it is important to widen perspectives before jumping into planning and action.

Part 3: Conceptualization

This part moves into shaping a more focused understanding of interdependent relationships. The counselor defines multiple contexts for the situation and understands the situation as a whole with multiple interlinked contexts. At this point the counselor revisits and redescribes the original encounter, with insights from the previous steps.

Part 4: Action Planning for Social Justice

In this part the counselor describes the desired changes or outcomes, with an emphasis on *equitable* approaches, interventions, and solutions that address *all levels* of engagement in the situation (individual, group, school, home, community, etc.). This includes identifying potential resources and allies for each approach, identifying which multicultural competencies (awareness, knowledge, skills, experience, and/or networks) are needed, and creating a plan that focuses on timeliness and accountability.

Part 5: Implementation, Experimentation, and Evaluation

In this part the counselor applies the action plan(s), consistently being mindful of cross-cultural competencies. It is important to explore the reactions and responses of individuals, groups, and systems and to evaluate outcomes to ensure social justice and equity. Enough flexibility should be built in to the action plan to maintain its integrity and be able to modify it as needed, and any changes should be effectively communicated to all involved. Measures should be structured in order to keep everyone accountable to themselves and one another. Process as well as specific content should be addressed: What worked? What did not work? How do we know? What needs to be done differently?

Part 6: A Recursive Process

People, environments, situations, counselors' competencies, and the resources counselors have on many levels change over time. The process of increasing awareness, knowledge, and skills is always changing; counselors revisit and cycle through all of these areas repeatedly, individually, and together.

The following case studies, based on real clients in our programs, demonstrate the social justice situation-framing approach to cross-cultural encounters.

Case Example: Delton

Delton was African American, about 6 years old, with a mild to moderate bilateral sensorineural hearing loss. He identified himself as hard of hearing or deaf depending on the situation. He had two hearing aids that he was constantly losing. He was being raised by his maternal grandmother (his legal guardian), who also cared for Delton's younger female cousin off and on. They lived in a low-income Black neighborhood. Delton's father was not present at all. His mother visited inconsistently, moved a lot, was not able to maintain a job; her own education was limited, and she had substance abuse issues. Following visits with his mother, Delton consistently expressed wild physical and emotional energy and had less control over his behavior.

Delton was very cute and social, had understandable speech, and was a skilled signer. He attended special day classes with deaf and hard of hearing peers at an inner-city public elementary school. He had a diagnosis of attention-deficit/hyperactivity disorder and presented oppositional behavior, lying, stealing, and tantrums. Delton's teacher, a young new teacher, was White and was frustrated at not having much contact with his grandmother. She was not able to handle Delton, and she blamed the grandmother (who worked) for not being available, interpreting that as not caring.

Part 1: Reflection

The school counselor helped school staff look more deeply at their views toward Delton and what he represented to them. Attitudes about Black people from Delton's area included low expectations and the idea that they were not educated and did not care about education, did not care about or have time for their kids, and did not have the capacity or motivation to deal with deafness. Delton fit the troublemaker image of a problem child, and thus low and negative expectations were set for him. School staff had already stereotyped him and the grandmother; the teacher took the grandmother's lack of contact very personally.

Hard of hearing Black boys were seen especially negatively and judged more harshly than deaf Black boys. Teachers had higher expectations of them because being hard of hearing gave them a presumed advantage over the deaf boys. These boys were seen as "all the same," as Black male special education problems, not so much as "deaf" (Corbett, 2010; Williamson, 2007). In our experience in both the deaf and hearing communities, hard of hearing Black boys are seen through a conflation of race, class, disability, and deafness.

At that time, our after-school program staff (all deaf) had little experience working with families and not much experience working with people who were hard of hearing. They also made assumptions about Delton's home life based on an absence of contact with his grandmother. We facilitated the reflection process with our own staff, intern, teachers, and other professionals.

Part 2: Dialogue

Engaging all of Delton's potential supports was the next step. His teacher would contact us when something happened, and our counselor did a lot of work trying to help her discern where his behaviors were coming from, what preceded or triggered the behaviors, and what strengths might be represented. The counselor also looked at what the teacher might be doing to reinforce the behavior. Delton was very curious, impulsive, and emotionally needy of attention; he was constantly testing and pushing the limits. Other kids found it easy to set him up to get into trouble—he would go for it and then try (unsuccessfully) to lie his way out. He got a lot of negative attention from adults and peers in this way.

Delton's teacher called his home frequently about his problematic behavior. His grandmother did not see the same kinds of behaviors at home. She felt they did not have the competence to contain him at school, and she did not perceive him as "bad" as they did. She asked our counselor during an evening home visit why they called only about bad things.

Our counselor's consultations engaged school staff in documenting Delton's incidents, including how the staff members' own behaviors might be triggering or reinforcing him. The school psychologist was brought in to observe and consider behavior plans. Our counselor coordinated services. At this point the school was not able to engage with the grandmother. She worked and was not available during school hours. They saw this as not caring enough, being uncooperative, and being unwilling to collaborate. Her behavior was interpreted negatively and negated her experience, responsibility, and nurturing.

Our counselor was able to engage the grandmother. Delton's grandmother was receptive to in-home services. We made an effort to report Delton's strengths as well as point out things that needed to be changed. She felt our staff really liked and appreciated Delton, which was true. She acknowledged that he could be manipulative and saw that we could relate to him similarly.

Our counselor saw Delton as having many strengths as well as special needs. He was bright, charming, cute, enthusiastic, resilient, and a survivor with street smarts. He had no communication limitations in settings like our after-school program; some limitations at school, where he was so stressed and always in trouble; and many limitations at home, where the family did not fully understand the impact of his hearing loss. A high-energy child, he talked constantly, always wanted to help, and often tried to be a bridge between his deaf classmates and hearing people. He could be manipulative, yet loving and appreciative. He seemed very needy, always with an emotional void that needed to be filled, which was the motivation for many of his behaviors.

Part 3: Conceptualization

It was important to see Delton in multiple environments, to see his behavior in the context of his overarching needs. His limited early relationship with his mother and her drug use impacted him early on, creating attachment issues. It seemed that he was always trying to make people love him, to fill that emotional void. He would steal things and then give them to his classmates and lie about where he had gotten them. Then he would fall apart when he could not maintain the lie or got caught stealing. He created a lot of stress and anxiety in this way. The dynamic between him and his teacher was problematic. Although he might have whined with our staff, at school he would have very physical tantrums, throwing desks and chairs at his teacher.

It was helpful for our staff to understand his behaviors in relation to his emotional loss and neediness. With a lot of scaffolding and support, Delton was able to maintain better self-awareness and more appropriate behavior. He needed containment and structure that provided him leadership roles at which he could succeed. With coaching, Delton could find his strengths and tap into them. We would anticipate him getting into trouble and engaged his peers not to set him up. Our after-school program was a well-structured place to work on these strategies. Delton occasionally used "but I didn't hear" as an excuse, and sometimes he really did not hear. However, because the after-school program staff were all deaf themselves, this did not work for him in that setting.

Our counselor had the advantage of getting to know Delton's family in a way the school could not. We could see that the life experiences of Delton's young White teacher were very different from those of his grandmother. The teacher's expectations and communication felt disrespectful to this older Black woman.

This conceptualization incorporated Delton's behaviors and where they came from, identifying the disconnect between the teacher and Delton and between the teacher and the grandmother. It also recognized Delton's strengths and fostered them in a contained and rewarding environment. Finally, it looked at his communication strengths and needs in different contexts.

Part 4: Action Planning for Social Justice

Our counselor worked with Delton individually to help him recognize and learn more appropriate ways to express his needs. She provided direct in-class behavioral interventions with him and modeled these for the teacher.

She worked with the teacher to show her how her behaviors triggered or reinforced Delton's behaviors. She also worked on repairing the damaged relationship with grandmother. For example, it was suggested that the teacher call the grandmother once a week to say something good about Delton. Providing home visits that offered family communication services, including sign language and nonverbal communication, helped the grandmother and cousin to understand Delton's hearing loss. The grandmother and cousin were used to his constant chattering and did not realize how much he was missing. The counselor worked with the grandmother on more consistent behavior management to parallel the strategies the teacher was using in school.

It was not possible to meet with Delton's mother. He was always upset and likely to get into trouble after he saw her. The grandmother would let us know when he would be with his mother, and our counselor would arrange to see him individually immediately afterward.

Part 5: Implementation, Experimentation, and Evaluation

Our counselor coordinated services. Delton was responsive to consistent supports: individual counseling at school, an after-school program, and weekend group activities. Curious, engaged, and high-energy but loving and fun, he enjoyed and did well with group activities. Adults learned to watch for potential temptations and utilize consistent and direct structures like time limits and warnings. We saw a gradual improvement in the teacher's relationship with Delton and his grandmother as her own self-awareness developed.

Part 6: A Recursive Process

Anticipating potential challenges and building on strengths developed individually and collectively was a big part of this case. Patterns had become predictable, so continual facilitation of home–school communication that worked on relationship building as well as problem solving was important. Delton's transition to middle school was something everyone anticipated as a potential challenge, and working collaboratively helped to start his middle school experience well.

Case Example: Lucia

Lucia, an 18-year-old deaf young woman from El Salvador, transferred to a large urban residential school for the deaf in the United States. She was the only deaf person in her family; her two siblings were much older than she was. Her family in El Salvador was upper middle class. Her father ran a small family business and had earned enough to provide Lucia with a daytime caregiver 5 days per week for most of her life. The caregiver served as an academic tutor, life skills coach, El Salvadoran sign language teacher and interpreter, and overall support person. There was no special school or program for deaf students near

Lucia's residence, so she attended a regular education program with her daytime caregiver, who would tutor and help interpret for Lucia. Eventually, however, Lucia's school felt that she could benefit from an American education where there was more accessibility and programs specifically for deaf students. The school felt she could do better academically, meet more people who were deaf, and be better prepared for her future. Lucia was a good student, was literate in Spanish, had friends, and participated in her church. There was a very small deaf community in her area, but few deaf people her age. Her parents knew minimal El Salvadoran sign language and used mostly gestures, home signs, and written and spoken Spanish to communicate with Lucia. Following the school's recommendation for her to access more meaningful education opportunities, Lucia's parents decided to bring Lucia to the United States to live with her mother's older sister, who lived within an hour-and-a-half drive of an urban residential school for the deaf.

The aunt had a daughter a couple years older than Lucia, and they had lived in the United States for 10 years. Although her aunt was a big support in concrete ways (providing housing, food, and transportation) and shared Lucia's culture and relationship with the family, she had minimal substantive communication with Lucia and the two communicated mostly through gesture and basic written Spanish. Lucia's cousin worked two jobs, and she and Lucia had minimal contact with each other. Lucia's parents were staying at another relative's home 4 to 5 hours away from the school. They did not speak English well but wanted to be involved with Lucia and her school.

On entering the school for the deaf, Lucia went through an initial battery of academic and developmental assessments and evaluations to identify any special learning needs, to evaluate her communication and language development, and to assess her social and emotional development. These initial assessments and evaluations revealed that at 18 years of age Lucia was too dependent on helpers and needed to be more independent, make her own decisions, practice independent living skills, and develop her own individual identity as a deaf person. In addition, her communication in ASL and English was minimal. These areas, therefore, were immediately identified as priority needs to be addressed. The recommendations did not address potential stressors or supports, particularly related to emotional separation from what was familiar and supportive or the process of acculturating both as a new immigrant and as a transfer student to her first significant deaf school and community. There was little or no dialogue with Lucia's aunt or parents, her former school, or the caregiver. Communication was oriented mostly toward logistics and getting the proper paperwork signed (e.g., individualized education program, individual transition plan, relevant consent forms).

For the first semester, the school provided a Spanish/English translator whose paraprofessional position was to help with communication in the classroom; she was a help at least as much to the teachers as to Lucia. It is not clear what training the paraprofessional had for this role. She did make a personal connection with Lucia as a mentor and something of a cultural bridge but then was suddenly removed in the second semester without discussion or advance notice to Lucia or her family. In addition, there was no transition process, closure, or explanation.

During the first semester, Lucia's family complied with school requests and suggestions. They were respectful and followed what they understood as the rules. The school directed most of its communications toward the aunt and had minimal contact with Lucia's parents.

During the first semester, Lucia was compliant and tried to do as asked. After the support person disappeared without explanation, Lucia experienced symptoms of depression and anxiety and academic difficulties in math and English. She was described by various school personnel as shy, increasingly socially isolated, and overly dependent. A month or so into the second semester, Lucia was reported to have expressed the desire to hurt herself to a classmate, who then reported this to a teacher. This eventually led to a counseling referral, and a contract counselor was brought into the situation in the middle of the semester.

The counselor assigned to Lucia was a White, deaf woman in her mid-20s. Lucia seemed comfortable with her, talked openly, and frequently asked for longer or additional sessions. In building a relationship with the counselor, Lucia was exploring getting to know someone. She was curious about the counselor's culture and experience and seemed to enjoy sharing her own culture and experience in return.

The school had strong American values of self-sufficiency and independence; had pride in deaf cultural identity and language; and, felt that, at 18, Lucia "needed to grow up." Their recommended strategy was for Lucia to acculturate and learn ASL through immersion as a student in a dormitory, where she would live on campus except for weekends, so she would not have any distractions or choice about language and culture. The family's desire and suggestions for personal supports and more mindful and gradual transitions were seen as in conflict with the school's value of individuality and independence, and so the family's values were ignored.

Lucia's family members increasingly felt that it was too hard to work with the school, which they felt was too demanding of them, would not negotiate, would not listen to their and Lucia's perspectives or goals, and could not meet Lucia's needs. They felt ignored and disrespected.

The one person who did develop a relationship with Lucia was the counselor. However, the school viewed counseling as limited in scope, focused on behavioral problem solving and on the development of independent living skills. When the counselor recommended bringing back the translator/mentor, she was told that there was no money for that, or for consultation with local Salvadoran cultural, mental health, or religious resources. The school was not willing to consider providing transportation so that Lucia might participate in after-school activities, as she had requested. These activities would not have had academic stressors; would have involved more collective activities like sports, which she was familiar; and would have been fun and provided natural opportunities for making friends.

The school was essentially looking for agreement from the family and the counselor for the school's agenda: the promotion of independence, the promotion of a deaf cultural identity (to the exclusion of Lucia's other identities), socialization with deaf people, and ASL (not Lucia's native sign language, which was viewed as less sophisticated than ASL). Any suggestion by the counselor or family of anything outside this agenda was met with "We don't have that" or "We don't have funding for that." As a contracted provider, the counselor had no power to address the systems changes that might open doors to addressing Lucia's needs to support her Salvadoreño identity, her native signed and written languages, or her continued engagement with her family and home culture. The family was seen as not understanding, as not valuing the deaf culture and language that was best for their daughter, as asking for too much that the school did not provide (and that the school saw as promoting dependency), and as interfering with what the school knew would help this young woman.

The family's way of finally resolving the conflict was to tell the school that the aunt was moving so that Lucia would have no place to go on weekends. They brought Lucia back to El Salvador.

The final outcome of the family removing their daughter from the school because they found it too difficult to deal with the school speaks strongly to the importance of educators and helping professionals working in culturally responsive ways with students and their families.

The use of the social justice situation-framing model could have broken through some of these barriers and built some bridges, strategies, and allies. Here are some thoughts about how the model could have been applied.

Part 1: Reflection

In this case, the school officials immediately made assumptions that this deaf young woman was like all other deaf young women; saw their client as only a young woman; and promoted their own agenda and culture rather exploring potential alignments and differences and potential conflicts in values, languages, cultures, and behaviors. Had they done this reflection step, it would have helped them to see what they knew and did not know. It would have helped them to see the disconnect between the report on how Lucia was doing at home (good academically, good grades and positive social relationships) and what was apparently happening at school. It would naturally have led them to see potential differences and identify what help they might need to better define and work with those differences as well as build on the strengths of all involved. Doing this reflection step they might also have identified ways the school itself might benefit from training, relationship building with local cultural community resources, professional development among school staff, and connections with communications experts for interpreting and translating resources. This step might also have enabled school officials to examine positions and policies that might have supported Lucia's social and academic inclusion more effectively by promoting effective acculturation to American deaf culture and sign language and greater well-being and achievement in the American deaf world. Perhaps Lucia and her family had some connections with the local hearing Salvadoreño community, such as a social worker or pastor. Those individuals and organizations did not reach out to the deaf community to see how they might better include Lucia and support her family through these changes; doing so could have led to more equitable inclusion of Lucia in the cultural community.

Part 2: Dialogue

A potential team of allies included the core circle of Lucia, the immediate service providers, and the family. These allies also included resources in El Salvador, like Lucia's schoolteachers and service providers, her caregiver, and others who could have helped frame a way to promote independence and autonomy that made sense in both cultures and built on cultural strengths rather than the school's insistence on immersion as the only alternative. This step would also have included nonjudgmental brainstorming on multiple levels of some strategies specific to Lucia's strengths and needs. This might have included exploring some systems-related strategies to increase the school's capacity and multicultural competency as well as cross-training between deaf and Salvadoreño cultural and mental health resources. It is important to document the brainstorming process. When dealing with people who speak multiple languages, and particularly with the deaf community, it is important to anticipate potential challenges to communication and conceptualization (Hernandez, 1999; Hidalgo & Williams, 2010). Strategies might include the use of interpreters of signed and spoken languages or the use of tools like ecomaps (McCormick, Stricklin, Nowak, & Rous, 2008) and genograms (Rigazio-DiGilio, Ivey, Kunkler-Peck, & Grady, 2005).

Other visual strategies might be considered to map the brainstorming and the ongoing process as well as the desired outcomes so that everyone on the team can see what is happening. By doing this visually, it is also easier to see what and who might be missing from the picture.

Part 3: Conceptualization

The counselor and/or someone from the school might have been designated to coordinate the conceptualization process. This would have involved reviewing and organizing the results of the brainstorming and collectively identifying immediate priorities. This should have led to an understanding of what was practical that could be worked on immediately and by whom and what additional resources would be required. In this case, there were likely priorities for Lucia herself, her aunt, her parents, and the rest of the family. Perhaps the counselor and a school representative could have engaged interpreting services to help make a connection between Lucia's previous school, the community, and her service providers. These connections could also have included her lifelong caregiver. Developing a relationship with a key person in the local Salvadoreño cultural community would have been important. This could have led to professional development initiatives and support to help Lucia's teachers and peers better understand her culture, values, and family and the deaf community in El Salvador. Helping school personnel see where Lucia was coming from could have helped stakeholders be more understanding, improved communication, and helped them be a more effective bridge to American deaf culture and sign language for Lucia and other deaf people from the Salvadoreño community. Choices about priorities and long- and short-term goals could have been identified at this point and communicated to all involved.

Part 4: Action Planning for Social Justice

Action planning should have addressed both immediate and long-term issues for Lucia, for her aunt and family in El Salvador, for the school, and for any other stakeholders. It would have been critical to document and communicate accessibly to all involved what could help Lucia to be more independent and actively engage in shaping her own situation.

Part 5: Implementation, Experimentation, and Evaluation

Informal as well as formal strategies could have been helpful. Leadership and other roles in the action plan should have been clear. As this part continued, longer term goals and objectives may have emerged.

Part 6: A Recursive Process

Working with Lucia's inclusion would have had an impact on her as an individual, on her family, on the school, and on the communities involved. These can be sources of conflict and difficulty and/or collaboration and enrichment. By considering, identifying, connecting, and working through the issues together, an environment can be developed that is more culturally competent. There are deaf people in every culture and country. Working together can lead to more equitable treatment of the multicultural deaf person in the deaf world, as well as more equitable treatment of deaf people in larger society. It can create supports for families and connect local cultural organizations and agencies with the deaf community. Collaboration with allies can generate opportunities for training, services, and inclusive program development. Training should address professional and paraprofessional development. Cross-training helps to build supportive relationships between deaf and hearing multicultural allies. Services might include interpreting and translation, including of relevant spoken, written, and signed languages. This should address cultural bridging for families as well as the deaf student, such as understanding what "deaf" means to people of different cultures and decoding the jargon of special education. Structured cultural encounters could be useful at the level of training service providers as well as developing multicultural competencies among students and even families. Program development could address relationship building and interpersonal connections as well as academic arenas: inclusive recreation, cultural arts, service-learning, and multicultural enrichment activities that engage and benefit all students. Working as allies offers opportunities for collective fund-raising and political action to help support such collective goals and initiatives.

Conclusion

Working with a deaf client requires recognizing and accommodating to his or her deafness and way of communicating and to his or her way of being deaf. This begins with recognizing your hearing identity, developing your intercultural skills, and providing the supports that make communication possible and your services and institution accessible and culturally competent. It requires seeing the individual in all of his or her identities, not only deafness. It requires not assuming that deafness per se is the focus of counseling, while at the same time recognizing the significance of deafness and others' responses to it.

Working with a deaf child engages the individual child, his or her family, and the social systems and institutions that affect their lives. There are deaf people in every community. As a counselor, do you know of deaf or hard of hearing members of your community? What cultural values and practices does your community hold toward deaf children, youth, adults, and seniors? What are culturally acceptable supports or interventions in your agency and in your community, and how might they apply to hearing families with deaf children? Do you know of, and have you connected with, local deaf community agencies or schools regarding the identification of mutual clients, cross-training, collaboration, shared celebrations, and the provision of services? Reflecting on these questions and developing these relationships can guide you toward honoring the intersections of diversity within deaf clients and providing ethical and effective services.

As a counselor, you can do a great deal to prevent the isolation of and enrich the lives of deaf children, their families, and even deaf communities that have limited access to ethnic or cultural information and supports because of long-standing communication and cultural barriers. The skills and roles of a counselor are powerful tools for identifying potential strengths and points of connection, pointing toward ways to build multicultural competency, and promoting engagement and inclusion across communities.

References

Bay Area Network for Diversity Training in Early Childhood. (2003). *Reaching for answers: A workbook on diversity in early childhood education.* Oakland, CA: Author.

Bauman, H-D. L. (Ed.). (2008). *Open your eyes: Deaf studies talking.* Minneapolis: University of Minnesota Press.

Campinha-Bacote, J. (2002). *The process of competence in the delivery of health care services: A culturally competent model of care* (4th ed.). Cincinnati, OH: Transcultural C.A.R.E. Associates.

Christensen, K. (Ed.). (2000). *Deaf plus: A multicultural perspective.* San Diego, CA: Dawn Sign Press.

Christensen, K. (Ed.). (2010). *Ethical considerations in educating children who are deaf or hard of hearing.* Washington, DC: Gallaudet University Press.

Corbett, C. A. (2002). Ethical issues when working with minority deaf populations. In V. Gutman (Ed.), *Ethics in mental health and deafness* (pp. 84–98). Washington, DC: Gallaudet University Press.

Corbett, C. A. (2010). Mental health issues for African American deaf people. In I. W. Leigh (Ed.), *Psychotherapy with deaf clients from diverse groups* (2nd ed., pp. 161–182). Washington, DC: Gallaudet University Press.

Edwards, L., & Crocker, S. (2008). *Psychological processes in deaf children with complex needs: An evidence-based practical guide.* Philadelphia, PA: Jessica Kingsley.

Gallaudet Research Institute. (2011, April). *Regional and national summary report of deaf from the 2009-2010 Annual Survey of Deaf and Hard of Hearing Children and Youth.* Washington, DC: Author.

Gorski, P. C. (2011). *Collaborative problem-solving for equity and justice: A 6-step model.* Retrieved from http://www.edchange.org/handouts/problem_solving_model.doc

Grushkin, D. A. (2003). The dilemma of the hard of hearing within the U.S. deaf community. In L. Monaghan, C. Schmaling, K. Nakamura, & G. H. Turner (Eds.), *Many ways to be deaf: International variation in deaf communities* (pp. 114–140). Washington, DC: Gallaudet University Press.

Hernandez, M. (1999). The role of therapeutic groups in working with Latino deaf adolescent immigrants. In I. W. Leigh (Ed.), *Psychotherapy with deaf clients from diverse groups* (pp. 227–252). Washington, DC: Gallaudet University Press.

Hidalgo, L., & Williams, S. (2010). Counseling issues for Latino deaf individuals and their families. In I. W. Leigh (Ed.), *Psychotherapy with deaf clients from diverse groups* (2nd ed., pp. 237–260). Washington, DC: Gallaudet University Press.

Holt, J., Hotto, S., & Cole, K. (1994). *Demographic aspects of hearing impairment: Questions and answers* (3rd ed.). Washington, DC: Gallaudet University, Center for Assessment and Demographic Studies.

Juarez, J. A., Marvel, K., Brezinski, K. L., Glazner, C., Towbin, M. M., & Lawton, S. (2006). Bridging the gap: A curriculum to teach residents cultural humility. *Family Medicine, 38,* 97–102.

Ladd, P. (2003). *Understanding deaf culture: In search of deafhood.* Tonawanda, NY: Multilingual Matters.

Lane, H. (2008). Do deaf people have a disability? In H-D. L. Bauman (Ed.), *Open your eyes: Deaf studies talking* (pp. 277–292). Minneapolis: University of Minnesota Press.

Leigh, I. W. (2009). *A lens on deaf identities.* New York, NY: Oxford University Press.

Leigh, I. W. (Ed.). (2010). *Psychotherapy with deaf clients from diverse groups* (2nd ed.). Washington, DC: Gallaudet University Press.

Leigh, I. W. (2012). Not just deaf: Multiple intersections. In R. Nettles & R. Balter (Eds.), *Multiple minority identities: Applications for practice, research, and training* (pp. 59–80). New York, NY: Springer.

Leigh, I. W., & Maxwell-McCaw, D. (2011). Cochlear implants: Implications for deaf identities. In R. Paludeneviciene & I. W. Leigh (Eds.), *Cohlear implants: Evolving perspectives* (pp. 95–110). Washington, DC: Gallaudet University Press.

Leung, P. (2003). Multicultural competencies and rehabilitation counseling/psychology. In D. B. Pope-Davis, H. L. K. Coleman, W. M. Liu, & R. L. Toporek (Eds.), *Handbook of multicultural competencies in counseling and psychology* (pp. 439–455). Thousand Oaks, CA: Sage.

Lucas, C., & Schatz, S. (2003). Sociolinguistic dynamics in the American deaf communities: Peer groups versus families. In L. Monaghan, C. Schmaling, K. Nakamura & G. H. Turner (Eds.), *Many ways to be deaf: International variation in deaf communities* (pp. 141–152). Washington, DC: Gallaudet University Press.

Lynch, E. W., & Hanson, M. J. (2004). *Developing cross-cultural competence: A guide for working with children and their families.* Baltimore, MD: Brookes.

Marschark, M. (2007). *Raising and educating a deaf child: A comprehensive guide to the choices, controversies, and decisions faced by parents and educators* (2nd ed.). New York, NY: Oxford University Press.

Marschark, M., Lang, H., & Albertini, J. A. (2002). *Educating deaf students: From research to practice.* New York, NY: Oxford University Press.

Marshall, C., Leung, P., Johnson, S. R., & Busby, H. (2003). Ethical practice and cultural factors in rehabilitation. *Rehabilitation Education, 17*(1), 55–65.

McCormick, K., Stricklin, S., Nowak, T., & Rous, B. (2008). Using eco-mapping to understand family strengths and resources. *Young Exceptional Children, 11*(2), 17–28.

Mindess, A. (1999). *Reading between the signs: Intercultural communication for sign language interpreters.* Yarmouth, ME: Intercultural Press.

Mitchell, R. E., & Karchmer, M. A. (2002). *Chasing the mythical ten percent: Parental hearing status of deaf and hard of hearing students in the United States.* Washington, DC: Gallaudet Research Institute.

Olkin, R. (1999). *What psychotherapists should know about disability.* New York, NY: Guilford Press.

Paludneviciene, R., & Harris, R. L. (2011). Impact of cochlear implants on the deaf community. In R. Paludneviciene & I. W. Leigh (Eds.), *Cochlear implants: Evolving perspectives* (pp. 3–19). Washington, DC: Gallaudet University Press.

Ponterotto, J. G., Utsey, S. O., & Pedersen, P. (2006). *Preventing prejudice: A guide for counselors, educators, and parents* (2nd ed.). Thousand Oaks, CA: Sage.

Portman, T. A. A. (2009). Faces of the future: School counselors as cultural mediators. *Journal of Counseling & Development, 87,* 21–27.

Rigazio-DiGilio, S. A., Ivey, A. E., Kunkler-Peck, K. P., & Grady, L. T. (2005). *Community genograms: Using individual, family, and cultural narratives with clients.* New York, NY: Teachers College Press.

Root, M. P. P. (2003). Racial identity development and persons on mixed race heritage. In M. P. P. Root & M. Kelley (Eds.), *Multiracial child resource book: Living complex identities* (pp. 34–41). Seattle, WA: Mavin Foundation.

Simms, L., Rusher, M., Andrews, J. F., & Coryell, J. (2008). Apartheid in deaf education: Examining workforce diversity. *American Annals of the Deaf, 153,* 384–395.

Sue, D. W. (2001). Multidimensional facets of cultural competence. *The Counseling Psychologist, 29,* 790–821.

Sue, D. W. (2003). *Overcoming our racism: The journey to liberation.* San Francisco, CA: Wiley.

Sue, D. W. (2006). The invisible Whiteness of being: Whiteness, White supremacy, White privilege, and racism. In M. G. Constantine & D. W. Sue (Eds.), *Addressing racism: Facilitating cultural competence in mental health and educational settings* (pp. 15–30). San Francisco, CA: Wiley.

Sue, D. W., Ivey, A. E., & Pedersen, P. B. (1996). *A theory of multicultural counseling and therapy.* Pacific Grove, CA: Brooks/Cole.

Sue, D. W., & Sue, D. (2008). White racial identity development: Therapeutic implications. In D. W. Sue & D. Sue, *Counseling the culturally diverse: Theory and practice* (5th ed., pp. 259–284). Hoboken, NJ: Wiley.

Tervalon, M., & Murry-Garcia, J. (1998). Cultural humility versus cultural competence: A critical distinction in defining physician training outcomes in multicultural education. *Journal of Health Care for the Poor and Underserved, 9*(2), 117–125.

Williamson, C. E. (2007). *Black deaf students: A model for educational success.* Washington, DC: Gallaudet University Press.

Additional Resources

The following websites provide a range of resources useful for counselors working with deaf or hard of hearing clients.

Deaf-Related Organizations With Resources for Counselors

American Deafness and Rehabilitation Association
www.adara.org
Double Pride
www.doublepride.com
Gallaudet Research Institute
http://www.gallaudet.edu/gallaudet_research_institute.html
National Counselors of the Deaf Association
www.ncdacounselors.org

Counselor Training Programs
(Counseling, Clinical Psychology, Rehabilitation)

Catalog of Projects Under the Rehabilitation Services Administration Training Program
    http://www2.ed.gov/students/college/aid/rehab/rsa-training-catalog-2011.pdf
    see "Rehabilitation of Individuals Who Are Deaf or Hard of Hearing" and "Training
    of Interpreters for Deaf Individuals"
Gallaudet University: Department of Counseling
    http://counseling.gallaudet.edu
Gallaudet University: Department of Psychology
    http://psychology.gallaudet.edu
Gallaudet University: Department of Social Work
    http://socialwork.gallaudet.edu
University of Rochester Medical Center: Deaf Wellness Center
    http://www.urmc.rochester.edu/deaf-wellness-center
Western Oregon University: Division of Special Education: Rehabilitation Counseling
    with Deaf and Hard of Hearing Individuals
    http://www.wou.edu/education/sped/rcdhha.php

Therapeutic Programs

Abused Deaf Women's Advocacy Services
    www.adwas.org
The Buckeye Ranch
    www.buckeyeranch.org
DeafHope
    www.deaf-hope.org
Desert Hills
    www.deserthills-nm.com
Five Acres
    www.5acres.org
Minnesota Chemical Dependency Program for Deaf and Hard of Hearing Individuals
    www.mncddeaf.org
National Deaf Academy
    www.nda.com
The Walden School/The Learning Center for the Deaf
    www.wsdeaf.org

Ethnic+Deaf Organizations

Deaf Aztlan
    http://www.deafvision.net/aztlan
Deaf Linx
    www.deaflinx.com
Deaf Women of Color
    www.deafwomenofcolor.com
National Asian Deaf Congress
    www.nadcongress.org

National Association of the Deaf
   www.nad.org
National Black Deaf Advocates
   www.nbda.org
National Council of Hispano Deaf and Hard of Hearing
   http://nchdhh.org
Rainbow Alliance of the Deaf
   www.rad.org
Sacred Circle
   www.deafnative.com

Culturally Deaf Organizations

Deaf Bilingual Coalition
   www.dbcusa.org
Deafhood Foundation
   www.deafhoodfoundation.org

Parent/Family Organizations

American Society for Deaf Children
   www.deafchildren.org

Auditory Programs for Deaf/Hard of Hearing

John Tracy Clinic
   www.Johntracyclinic.org
Option Schools, Inc.
   http://auditoryoralschools.org/default.aspx

Cochlear Implant Resources and Information

American Academy of Otolaryngology–Head and Neck Surgery: Cochlear Implants
   http://www.entnet.org/HealthInformation/cochlearImplants.cfm
Gallaudet University: Laurent Clerc National Deaf Education Center: Cochlear Implant Education Center
   http://www.gallaudet.edu/Clerc_Center/Information_and_Resources/Cochlear_Implant_Education_Center.html
The Listen-Up Web! Cochlear Implant Information and Resources
   http://www.listen-up.org/implant.htm
National Institute on Deafness and Other Communication Disorders: Cochlear Implants
   http://www.nidcd.nih.gov/health/hearing/coch.asp

Sign Language Interpreting

Registry of Interpreters for the Deaf
   www.rid.org

Chapter 16

Counseling and the Culture of Economic Disadvantage

William Ming Liu and Sherry K. Watt

As we wrote this chapter, the United States was part of a global economic collapse that started in 2007. Although there is some economic recovery and stability, most of the benefits of this recovery have been directed toward the wealthy (Goodman, 2010). Those in the lower social class groups, especially men and women of racial and ethnic minority backgrounds (e.g., African American, Asian American, Latino, Native American), are likely to persist in the unemployment and underemployment (i.e., part-time, underpaid) rolls for a long while. For individuals experiencing the most difficult economic circumstances, the recession did two things: First, it exposed the incredible chasm that exists between the super-wealthy (top 1%–10%) and the rest of Americans; and second, it exacerbated a long-simmering crisis of debt, low pay, and an overleveraged lifestyle for some. Economic disadvantage has been a long-term problem for some, and an intergenerational one for many, and the recession has only made their situations worse and their prospects for the future even more dim.

Counselors need to be especially aware of how economic and financial concerns affect the lives of clients. Often the topics of finances and money are taboo (Liu, 2011; Offer, 2006), and clients may be shy, reticent, and even coy about how their financial lives are impacting them. But given the ubiquity of social class issues in U.S. culture (Liu, 2011, 2012), it is almost impossible to escape the salience of money and economics in people's lives. Therefore, the purpose of this chapter is to present a rationale for why counselors need to address clients' economic and social class lives and to present a theory of social class and privilege that will allow counselors to work with clients. A case study is used to illustrate the approach, and the chapter ends with a list of useful online resources.

Why It Is So Difficult to Talk About Social Class and Classism

Social class and classism are intimately linked to economic disadvantage. Counselors interested in being multiculturally competent should inherently be interested in being knowledgeable of, aware of, and skilled with social class and classism concerns. But how are social class and classism relevant cultural constructs, and how can counselors be multiculturally competent in this area? Liu (2011) has suggested that multicultural competency comes from (a) knowing the social class and classism concerns relevant to the communities and populations one will likely serve; (b) exploring and understanding how values, beliefs, and cultural norms may be affected by social class; and (c) recognizing and celebrating the ways in which people and communities have survived and sometimes flourished. It is important to remember that social class does not demarcate a specific cultural group, but it does impact how communities enact, express, and perpetuate cultural values and mores.

For example, in Iowa, there are varied and diverse communities of White people; some have lived generations on farms whereas others have lived in the more affluent Iowa City. As a counselor, one cannot treat all of these White individuals similarly, especially with respect to social class and experiences with classism. For some clients, how the weather will impact their harvest is an important social class concern that is not salient for others. Other White individuals may value cultural norms and beliefs that are functional and supported in an agricultural community but not always endorsed by other Whites living in a more city-like environment. Finally, in some small and rural communities, residents have their own cultural celebrations that may seem odd to those uninitiated to them (e.g., Solon, Iowa's Meat Days). These examples represent different ways in which social class impacts, affects, and inflects itself onto a racially similar community and illustrate why counselors can be multiculturally competent around social class and classism.

An additional issue related to the difficulty counselors have working with social class and classism may be the terms used. The term *economic disadvantage* describes both situations, contexts, and processes. Poverty, for instance, is a situation, a context, and the outcome of economic disadvantage and inequality. Specifically, the U.S. Census describes a poverty threshold that demarcates a certain level of income in relation to an ability to provide minimum food for oneself and others under one's care (Liu, 2008). But *poverty* is often used as a generic term describing a situation or context wherein there is great economic disparity between social classes; those living and growing up in these situations will experience economic disadvantage. But regardless of the specificity of terms, *economic disadvantage* connotes a large number of hurdles and barriers that people face not just to upward mobility but to day-to-day living.

Economic disadvantage affects people's health and access to health care (Hopps & Liu, 2006), their educational experiences and opportunities (Liu & Hernandez, 2008), and even where they live. For example, people who are poor are likely to live in housing and neighborhoods that are the consequences of environmental classism (e.g., redlining as a means of cordoning off the poor into dilapidated neighborhoods; Liu, 2011). These neighborhoods often have few supermarkets, have an overabundance of liquor and tobacco stores, have few areas for recreation, and are marked by chaos and violence (Evans & Kim, 2007). Economic disadvantage also implies that upward social mobility is no small feat. As Liu (2011) has described it, growing up poor and growing up in poverty means that people who experience economic disadvantage have a drag on their upward mobility. Earning a college degree is no guarantee of upward mobility (Institute for Higher Education Policy, 2010), and neither is working hard at a minimum-wage job (Bernhardt et al., 2009; Center for Community and Economic Development, 2010; Sum & Khatiwada, 2010). Many people live in intergenerational patterns of economic crisis that are magnified by few jobs, poor schools, and exploitative financial institutions such as payday loans that only keep them in cycles of debt (Parrish & King, 2009). Liu (2010) likened living with these constraints as a form of drag, metaphorically similar to the gravitational drag that rockets must overcome in order to reach orbit. The drag is exponentially higher at the lower levels, and therefore most of the propulsion is used, and relatively absent at the highest levels. The speeds in orbit seem incomprehensible to those on earth. And like wealth and affluence, the millions and sometimes billions made by those in the upper echelon income ranks seem incomprehensible to those making a minimum wage; for those making a meager income, each dollar has an additive worth, but for those in the upper ranks of society, each dollar has an exponential worth. Economic disadvantage cannot be overcome by only addressing dispositional issues such as working harder or feeling efficacious; understanding the barriers means linking advocacy and social justice efforts to combat the sociopolitical (e.g., unequal distribution of power), sociohistorical (e.g., biased and inaccurate histories of peoples), and sociostructural (e.g., legal, education, and economic systems) forces that marginalize and oppress individuals (Liu & Ali, 2005). Given the enormity of issues related to working with people in economically disadvantaged situations, Liu (2011) has wondered whether this is one reason counselors have found it difficult to talk about and fully engage these people and communities.

In addition, Liu (2011) has posited that the difficulty in talking about social class and classism among counselors comes from two places. First, it is the difficulty of understanding and operationalizing a difficult, confusing, and nebulous concept such as social class. Second, he speculated that interpersonal and contextual issues are related to integrating dialogue on social class and classism into counseling. As Liu and his colleagues have suggested (Liu, 2001, 2002, 2006, 2008; Liu & Ali, 2008; Liu, Ali, et al., 2004; Liu, Soleck, Hopps, Dunston, & Pickett, 2004), social class and classism are often difficult concepts to understand because of helping professionals' tendency to rely on objective indexes such as income, education, and occupation to effect a particular social class category (e.g., middle class) even though there is no evidence to support these relationships (Liu & Ali, 2008). The limitations of a categorical approach to understanding a phenomenological and subjective experience such as social class and classism are (a) an assumption that everyone in that social class group sees and interacts with the world similarly; (b) an assumption that social class and classism concerns are related to those who possess these objective indexes of income, education, and occupation (i.e., working adults); (c) a failure to integrate the intersection of other salient identities such as race and gender (Liu, Fridman, & Hall, 2008; Liu & Hernandez, 2008; Liu, Hernandez, Mahmood, & Stinson, 2006); and (d) a failure to address fully the impact and relationship of classism as a cause and consequence of social class. Given these limitations, assumptions, and problems, it is no surprise that counselors have not fully integrated understanding social class and classism into their approaches with clients. Related to this problem is the overuse of these social class categories to discuss complex interpersonal relationships and intrapersonal worldviews and values. These relationships and worldviews are what Liu (2011, 2012) has referred to as the subjective understanding of social class and classism. He developed the Social Class Worldview Model (SCWM-R; Liu, 2011, 2012) as a means of conceptualizing and framing how an individual engages in his or her social class world.

Although counselor educators hope that counselors can set aside their biases when facilitating the counseling process, all communication is complicated by historical and structural dynamics of the relationship between the marginalized and dominant identities of those involved in the conversation. Interaction between two persons of the same race but different social classes is rarely completely without the historic memories that are associated with being raised in a society in which clear messages about one's social class role have been communicated through family, school, and friends (Liu, 2001, 2011, 2012). And if one were raised to identify with a lower social class, then one may consciously or unconsciously understand that those who are middle class and have higher education are more valued and considered the norm (Liu, 2011). Clients who come to counseling who are economically disadvantaged often meet with counselors who are perceived to be middle class, which comes with certain social and economic advantages (Liu & Arguello, 2006). When the client and the counselor view the world from different social class backgrounds, it often means that the therapeutic setting has the potential for difficult dialogues.

Essentially, a *difficult dialogue* "is a verbal or written exchange of ideas or opinions between citizens within a community that centers on an awakening of potentially conflicting views of beliefs or values about social justice issues (such as racism, sexism, classism)" (Watt, 2007, p. 116). Interacting with clients during a session can prove to be difficult because there is always the potential that in dialogue the counselor or the client might have an awakening to the different views that the client or the counselor might hold. It is likely that these differing views are rooted in the interrelationship of power, oppression, and privilege for marginalized and dominant groups in society.

How Is Dialogue in the Therapeutic Environment Shaped by Power, Oppression, and Privilege? Why Does It Matter?

The counselor and client relationship is situated within a larger cultural context. The interaction between the counselor and the client is shaped by the positioning of dominant and marginalized groups within the historical and structural context of power, oppression, and privilege in U.S. society (Reason & Davis, 2005; Spring, 2010). As Liu, Soleck, et al. (2004) pointed out, social class is a lens through which individuals view the world. Classism is manifested through individual and community interactions in which people are treated with prejudice and/or are discriminated against based on often negative perceptions of being a part of a lower social class. Thus, the interaction between a counselor and a client is likely complicated by multidirectional (upward, downward, and lateral) occurrences of classism in which power, privilege, and oppression work together in a way that affects the relationship (Liu, Soleck, et al., 2004).

In discussions of social class, classism, and privilege, *oppression* is still a very relevant and important term and construct; oppression still permeates how people understand inequality and disadvantage. *Oppression* is "an interlocking, multilevel system that consolidates social power to the benefit of members of privileged groups and is maintained and operationalized on three dimensions: (a) contextual dimensions, (b) conscious/unconscious dimension, and (c) applied dimension" (Hardiman, Jackson, & Griffin, 2007, p. 39). This interlocking system operates together to promote the "othering" of individuals and reinforces a proverbial norm (Pharr, 1997). The English language in referring to "the other" is often negative. For instance, terms used to refer to perceptions of lower social class status include *poor White trash* and *welfare queen*. This type of negative language fuels both conscious and unconscious perceptions of individuals' social class status, which can ultimately translate into how a person is treated. If a person is negatively stereotyped and perceived to fit in this marginalized group, then he or she can be discriminated against and treated violently on both the physical and psychological level. No one is immune to this socialization, and even counselors who have been trained to be aware of their biases are likely to have reactions that are based on the messages sent regularly in society through media and from their upbringing. This system of oppression permeates how individuals view and behave in the world and can invade the therapeutic relationship.

It is important that counselors are aware of the complexity social class and classism bring to their work with clients. If counselors are aware of the complexities, then it is more likely that they will be more effective in providing service to a client. Effective counselors are in a constant state of personal reflection in which they actively break down stereotypes and directly address the messages they have learned through socialization. Counselors need to be especially critical in their self-examination when they come from a background of social and economic privilege and must interrogate what it means to be in their particular social and economic position. As Watt (2009) described, counselors often display defensive behaviors when confronted with exploration of a privileged identity, such as a perceived higher social and economic status. However, it is important to note whether counselors and clients come from privileged or economically disadvantaged backgrounds, as perceptions of social class and classism are ever present in the counseling relationship. Counselors need to be keenly sensitized to how they have been conditioned by the general message sent through media and socialization that communicates a common negative perception of the economically disadvantaged juxtaposed with a collective value for the ambiguous middle-class social and economic position. It is necessary to understand that a person's worldviews impact the dialectic exchange during counseling sessions. Social class worldview not only impacts how counselors might interpret the client's experience but also shapes how counselors communicate with the client through artifacts such as language, facial expressions, appearance, and other nonverbal cues. Regardless of the social and economic position in which counselors perceive themselves sitting, they must acknowledge that their relationship with their clients is shaped by this often unconscious and unspoken worldview of classism. In general, counselors need to consciously attend to the subtle ways in which social class and classism are folded into communication between themselves and economically disadvantaged clients.

SCWM-R

One way to understand the social class and classism issues and perspectives of clients is through the SCWM-R. The SCWM-R posits that individuals live within multiple social class environments such that there is no one singular middle class but multiple middle classes that help shape a person's values, beliefs, and worldviews. These middle-class environments are the contexts within which the individual attempts to remain congruent so that he or she maintains his or her social class position. The worldview the individual develops helps him or her interpret these demands and expectations. This worldview is shaped by the individual's parents, his or her peers, and other influential persons and is also impacted by the level of awareness and consciousness the individual has about himself or herself as a social class being. This level of awareness and consciousness is described as the social class and classism consciousness (Liu, 2011, 2012). In terms of the social class and classism consciousness, individuals are described as not having any sense of how social class and classism function in their lives, having some conflicts and dissonance as they attempt to reconcile their worldview with classism experiences, or having an integrated awareness of self and other in relation to social class and classism.

The SCWM-R helps direct a person's behaviors through three lenses. The first lens is focused on materialism and refers to the individual's relationship to material objects, the second lens is focused on behaviors and refers to the individual's actions and behaviors that help him or her stay in a social class (e.g., etiquette, spoken accents), and the third lens is focused on lifestyle considerations or how the individual chooses to use his or her time (e.g., working, vacationing). These lenses vary with each individual, and the dominance of one lens over the others represents the dominant way in which the person interacts with others and sees himself or herself.

Finally, the last part of the SCWM-R refers to classisms. As Liu and his colleagues have suggested, there is more than one dominant form of classism, and this network of classisms works in concert to perpetuate inequalities and disadvantage. The operative word in terms of classism is *perceived* social class, as people conceptualize and interpret social class information from, for instance, a person's actions and material objects and then make an attribution toward or against the individual. One form of classism is what most people think of when considering classism. *Downward classism* occurs when someone from a perceived higher social class group marginalizes, oppresses, and exploits someone from a perceived lower social class group. Another form of classism is *upward classism,* which is prejudice and discrimination against someone perceived to be in a higher social class group. For instance, this may express itself when one refers to someone else as a "snob," "elitist," or "bougie" (a slang term for being too bourgeois or upper class). Another form of classism is *lateral classism,* which occurs when someone puts pressure on others (or experiences pressure from others) in a similar perceived social class group. The expression of lateral classism is a form of keeping up with the Joneses, wherein one feels compelled to buy objects or act in ways to remain congruent with a certain social class group. Finally, there is *internalized classism,* which involves feelings of anxiety, depression, frustration, and despondency that may arise from feeling incongruent with the expectations of one's social class group. This internalized anxiety is just noxious enough to motivate some to buy a new car, for instance, to remain on par with their neighbors. Yet for others, especially in a time of economic recession when there are no resources (e.g., income) to support a certain lifestyle, internalized classism may become overwhelming and demoralizing to the point of hopelessness.

When it comes to these different forms of classism, it is important to understand that individuals may enact one form of classism but also experience a different form. In addition, as Liu (2011, 2012) has noted, it cannot be said that by expressing upward classism a person in a lower social class has just as much power and privilege as an upper class individual. What is being considered in this form of upward classism is the interpersonal effect of classism such that any form of classism feeds into the network of power and oppression (Liu & Pope-Davis, 2003a, 2003b), and it is important that all individuals be aware of and sensitive to the ways in which they are biased.

Based on the SCWM-R, Liu (2012) developed a series of exemplar questions that counselors may use to help clients explore their social class worldview (see Appendix 16.1).

Focusing on Privilege

People express social class and classism in a great many ways. Social class and classism is virtually invisible except for the ways in which people choose to clothe themselves, the cars they drive, and the ways in which they spend their time, to name a few examples. Other ways in which social class is expressed and experienced by people is through classism, acts of entitlement, and of course privilege. *Privilege* is defined as unearned rights and benefits

(Liu, Pickett, & Ivey, 2007), and the term captures many forms of rights and benefits, such as Christian, heterosexual, White, and middle-class privilege (Liu et al., 2007).

Referring to Peggy McIntosh's well-known essay titled *White Privilege: Unpacking the Invisible Knapsack,* Robinson and Howard-Hamilton (2000) described privilege as "an invisible knapsack of assets an entitled group can refer to on a regular basis to negotiate their daily lives more effectively" (p. 60). For example, a counselor who works for an agency will probably share the cost of health insurance and other benefits with an employer. She will enjoy benefits such as paid sick leave and have access to myriad medical treatments for illness or injury that are covered by her insurance. In contrast, a client who is self-employed and cleans houses for a living has to shoulder the full burden of the cost of health care, which she may or may not be able to pay. If she becomes ill or injured and cannot work, she will lose money if she takes a sick day. The client might feel extreme pressure and fear about missing work, whereas for the counselor the need to take a sick day does not produce much anxiety because being at work is not directly hinged to her earnings for the day. A counselor's life circumstance informs how she hears what the client shares about her day-to-day life. The client may not feel heard if the counselor does not recognize the subtle aspects of the full extent of her situation. Because the counselor's life is not directly limited by a similar circumstance, it might unearth awakenings of power and privilege in interactions with the client. Although the counselor may intellectually understand and have empathy for the client's experience, her own privilege may desensitize her to aspects of the client's situation because her personal life is not limited by the same set of conditions.

Raising awareness surrounding privilege, power, and oppression involves examining on a personal and political level where one's own privileged identities are considered in relation to social phenomena such as racism, sexism, ableism, classism, and so on (Watt, 2007; Watt et al., 2009). To become sensitive beyond their own set of conditions and the unconscious socialization of a society in which oppression is all pervading counselors must reflect on central life questions such as the following: Who am I? How has my social upbringing shaped my worldview? and How might my biases affect how I hear my client? This type of intersected examination invites a complex exploration of feelings that requires a counselor to do a deep unearthing of what it means to have privilege and face this in relation to the counselor–client dynamic. Continuous reexamination of the complexities of privilege might necessitate a questioning of personal and familial relationships, and that process can be unsettling. To complicate matters, consideration of a privileged identity (e.g., higher social class) can be convoluted by the simultaneous empathy with having a marginalized identity (e.g., lesbian). The paradoxes inherent in reflecting on a mix of privileged and marginalized identities can be challenging and raise to the surface many complex feelings of shame, frustration, and sadness. Although it is necessary for a counselor to do this type of exploration in order to be in a meaningful relationship with a client, this type of self-reflection can be exhausting and can bring out defensive reactions. And yet counselors have to do this work; they cannot ignore the reality that their social class worldview and classism both subtlety and complexly influence the interactions they have with their clients during sessions.

Privileged Identity Exploration (PIE)

The PIE model identifies eight defenses that individuals often display when exploring their social or political position in society (Watt, 2007; Watt et al., 2009). This model can be helpful for counselors, as it provides a guide for self-reflection and a tool for raising awareness as it relates to potential reactions one might have in response to clients during a session.

Counselors who can recognize and explore when their defensive reactions to their own social and political positions might arise during a session will likely be able to decipher what might hinder their effectiveness and appropriately set it aside so that they might be a cleaner conduit for their client. This section suggests ways in which counselors can use the PIE model to reflect on how their perceptions of social class might interfere in their work with clients. Finally, strategies are given for ways in which counselors can be more effective at facilitating the counseling process.

Using the PIE Model: Application for Counselors

The Watt (2007) PIE model points to eight defensive behaviors individuals might display when engaging in difficult dialogue. The eight modes of defense are categorized by behaviors one exhibits when recognizing, contemplating, or addressing a privileged identity. *Recognizing privileged identity* describes reactions when one is first presented with anxiety-provoking stimuli surrounding a privileged identity, such as their feelings about social class status. Reactions are denial, deflection, and rationalization. *Contemplating privileged identity* explains counselors' reactions when they are beginning to think more carefully about provocative ideas, such as the impact of classism on a client's life. In making sense of these ideas, counselors might display intellectualization, principium, or false envy defenses. *Addressing privileged identity* portrays the behaviors of counselors who are attempting to face their dissonant feelings as they relate to classism and who are involved in some action to resolve to fight against social inequities. Reactions of benevolence or minimization may be displayed.

Six assumptions underlie the model, at least one of them particularly relevant to discussions regarding social class and classism: "Defense modes are normal human reactions to the uncertainty that one feels when exploring [one's] privileged identities in more depth" (Watt, 2007, p. 119). The PIE model assumes that responding defensively to feelings of discomfort is a normal and necessary part of gaining critical consciousness. In the process of working with a client, counselors should expect that their personal biases might be challenged directly or indirectly during the counseling process. Counselors should presume that a defensive reaction might arise in them, and they should embrace it as a normal part of the process and explore it as part of their professional preparation for working with a client.

A case is presented here with a specific focus on ways in which the PIE model might be used by a counselor to help him or her explore his or her reactions to a client from a different social class background.

The Case

Counselor: Jane is a 28-year-old White woman, holds a master's degree in counseling, and is working part time toward her PhD. Jane considers herself middle class. She owns her home, an older, small two-bedroom house with a fenced yard in which she has a small garden. She has lived there for 3 years. Jane is heterosexual and has been partnered with her long-time boyfriend for 7 years. Her boyfriend is a businessman who travels regularly. They would like to have children one day. She was raised in the southeastern part of the United States in a two-parent home. Both her mother and father were college educated and owned their home. She has two siblings. Her siblings both received college degrees and live nearby. Her hobbies include walking her dog in the local dog park. She is also a staunch environmental advocate. Jane considers herself an advocate for social justice, particularly for race and social class. She took courses beyond the ones required for her master's degree to raise her awareness of racism and classism. Part of the reason Jane became a counselor was to help those less fortunate. In addition to her full-time counselor position at the hospital, she volunteers two evenings a week and every other weekend at the Women's Center and provides both individual and group counseling to women who are destitute.

Client: Cindy is a 35-year-old White woman; she has her bachelor's degree in business administration. Cindy attended college part time. Her education was funded in part by Pell grants. Cindy considers herself to be of a lower social and economic status, though she is proud to say that she has never "lived on the system." She started her education at a community college before transferring to the local university. It took her 7 years to complete her degree. She is from the Midwest. Cindy is a single parent with two children (7- and 9-year-old boys) who have different fathers. They live in a two-bedroom apartment. Cindy was raised by her grandparents because her mom could not provide her and her two brothers with a stable home environment. Cindy's grandparents owned and lived on a small farm. When Cindy was growing up, her mother was not able to find steady work and was often in and out of abusive relationships with men. Cindy wanted to be different from her mother but often states that she "has fallen into some of the same traps." Although she is not in a regular relationship with either of her boys' fathers, she is in an on-again/off-again cycle with the father of the youngest boy. Cindy works as an administrative assistant for a packing and shipping warehouse. She works 12- to 15-hour days.

Scenario: Cindy comes to the Women's Center to receive support services after a fire in her apartment. The fire did not burn down the entire apartment but caused damage to the kitchen and living room area. There was water and smoke damage to the clothes, furniture, and most of her family's possessions. The landlord's insurance will fix the structural damage, and Cindy will be able to return to the apartment. Cindy and her children can stay temporarily at the Women's Center shelter. However, as stipulated in her rental contract, she has to continue paying rent on the apartment for the 6 months she will be displaced. Cindy is unable to end the lease and move to another apartment because she cannot afford the rent in any other apartment on the bus route. Cindy did not have renter's insurance, and neither her family nor the fathers of her children have the resources to help her. Cindy has to turn to Social Services and other agencies for help. Cindy and her children are given clothing and other needed items that have been donated to the Women's Center. She is also eligible to receive food stamps from Social Services, but she is ashamed to use them in the store. Cindy has mentioned that her family is eating even more fast food because it is cheap and easy to access. Jane has been counseling Cindy for the past 2 months and having a session with her once a week. Jane feels pulled to help Cindy. Each week Jane brings some vegetables from her garden for Cindy's family. The first time Cindy is very appreciative, but Jane notices that the third time she brings vegetables to Cindy her client's affective response seems to be dampened initially and even throughout the session. Toward the end of their session, Jane shares with Cindy her observation of what she perceives as a dampened affective response. Cindy says, "I know the fresh vegetables you bring are good for us, but I am just not able to use them right now. I do not want to offend you, but I just feel bad about wasting them." Cindy's response comes as a surprise to Jane, though Jane responds appropriately to Cindy by saying that she understands. As they finish up the session, Jane notices that Cindy's affect seems to be a bit livelier. After some time to reflect, Jane notices that she is having some feelings about Cindy's refusal to receive more vegetables and embraces this as an opportunity to explore her reaction.

Using the PIE Model to Explore Responses

This section presents brief descriptions of three of the eight defenses and how Jane might use the PIE model to explore her feelings. The principium, false envy, and benevolence defenses are likely to appear surrounding social class and classism. Suggestions are given for ways in which Jane might use the model on her own or in consultation with a colleague to explore her potential defensive reactions as she prepares to provide effective counseling to Cindy. Once Jane cues in to her dissonance related to Cindy's refusal to receive more vegetables, she could respond to it as an invitation to do some more in-depth self-exploration using the PIE model to prompt her questioning. Jane might journal about her feelings and/ or discuss them in consultation with a colleague.

Principium Potential Responses
A principium response is a defensive reaction driven by a personal or political belief. As Jane furthers her reaction to Cindy's refusal to receive any more vegetables, she might become aware of her values for eating whole foods. She might recall that she personally has not eaten fast food in more than 6 months. As she reflects on her reaction, she may want to examine more closely how what she believes impacted her decision to bring the vegetables to Cindy. To explore the issue thoroughly Jane might want to reflect on different angles of the issue. For instance, she may need to acknowledge that her life includes a stable home and routine and that her existence aligns with the luxury of being able to grow her own vegetables and choose more carefully what she eats. She might notice the personal principle she holds in thinking that preparing fresh food is actually simpler. Yet she may not be sensitized to what it is like to have her life disheveled or to have a long-term disruption in routine, and she might not understand what it is like to use great effort to manage daily life tasks such as preparing food. Jane might acknowledge that she looks down on Cindy not valuing what she values and that it connects to her perceptions of those of what she perceives as lower social class status. She might actually think, "I do not understand why 'they' don't want to eat healthier. You just do it." She might defend why she thinks it is necessary and just good common sense to eat well and take care of one's body. She might notice that is why she is defensive. As she comes to terms with how she has judged Cindy, she might want to sit with those feelings of discomfort before she starts to dissect more her thoughts, values, or beliefs. She might want to set aside her value of eating well and explore in more depth her feelings of being upset or disregarded by talking with a family member or friend who does not share her same values regarding food.

False Envy Potential Responses
A false envy defense is signified by a display of affection for a person or a feature of a person in an effort to deny the complexity of the social and political context. Another reaction Jane might have to Cindy's refusal to receive her offer of the vegetables is a shift toward reinforcing and admiring Cindy's strength in this difficult situation and applauding her for being direct. In feeling this admiration, Jane might focus on the strength that Cindy is displaying in managing all that is on her plate and excuse Cindy for not accepting the gift she is giving because she can see why Cindy is overwhelmed, but is so strong. Jane might not immediately acknowledge her complex feelings and therefore might want to be affirming to Cindy. Cindy's reaction can be viewed as condescending or patronizing. It also can serve to deny Cindy's humanity. If this reaction arises in Jane, she might want to reflect on where her admiration emerges and how that admiration might be veiling the way she really feels about Cindy's food choices. Jane might also consider wrestling with the power position in which

she sits and explores her social position in relation to Cindy's and explores what it means to pity or admire a person in a lower social position while she herself sits in the higher position or more privileged circumstance.

Benevolence Potential Responses

A benevolence defensive response is based on displaying an overly sensitive attitude toward a social and political issue based on an attitude of charity. In consultation with a colleague, Jane might be asked how she feels about not recognizing how her offer to help Cindy might be rooted in her social class worldview. Her colleague might point out that Jane assumes that Cindy would be grateful for the vegetables. Another reaction Jane might have to Cindy's not accepting her offer of help might be a defensive response in which she avoids exploring the complex feelings that arose by shifting the focus to how she has helped so many people. Jane might respond by saying to her colleague, "I volunteer at the Women's Center regularly. I really feel like I know these women and can relate to their experience. I also do so many other things in the community and participate in research on those less fortunate than I."

Jane's colleague might encourage her to begin her reflection by acknowledging her commitment to help her clients, then invite her to delve deeper and explore the dynamics of power and privilege that are in acts of charity. If Jane is open, her colleague might point out to her that the underlying message in her statement is that she knows best what her client needs. The colleague could invite Jane to explore the power relationship implied when she feels she knows best over someone who has less power and who is actually living in the situation. Even further, she might be asked to consider how acts of charity are centered on both the power of the giver and the powerlessness of the receiver. She could be asked to grapple with how reaching down to help those of a lower social status than herself contributes to maintaining the current dominant society structure. Another aspect for reflection could come from this question: Jane might ask herself, "What am I getting from this interaction?" This question might guide her to explore emotionally intense feelings about the intersections of her service to her clients and her own social position. Sitting with these feelings of discomfort and reflection on why she feels defensive about her acts of goodwill would be productive self-exploration.

In sum, the PIE model suggests that responses such as the ones discussed previously are primal responses that emerge out of feelings of fear or entitlement or both. Counselors who authentically examine their primal responses to interactions with their clients will be more aware of when their biases are interfering with their ability to provide meaningful interactions when in a helping relationship with clients.

Conclusion

The focus of this chapter has been to provide a rationale for why it is imperative for counselors to integrate social class and classism into their work with clients. Social class and classism are nebulous, often vague, and not very discreet concepts and terms. We have attempted to address some of these issues as a way to provide some clarity to the issues of economic disadvantage. We also encourage counselors to consider that their perceptions of social class, classism, economics, and a person's finances are always relevant to the client. In addition, counselors need to remember that their life circumstance influences their worldview and how they are in relationship with the client. The client may not necessarily talk about money as a concern, but these issues are always inflected in the client's life. The role and responsibility of the counselor is to be sensitive to and aware of how these issues are expressed and to help frame these concerns in a way that is useful and helpful for the client. To this end, this chapter has provided counselors with a framework for addressing social class and classism through the lens of privilege. Using the SCWM-R and the PIE model, we have attempted to illustrate and explain a social class interaction between a client and a counselor.

References

Bernhardt, A., Milkman, R., Theodore, N., Heckathorn, D., Auer, M., DeFilippis, J., . . . Spiller, M. (2009). *Broken laws, unprotected workers: Violations of employment and labor laws in America's cities.* Retrieved from http://nelp.3cdn.net/1797b93dd1ccdf9e7d_sd-m6bc50n.pdf

Center for Community Economic Development. (2010, Spring). *Lifting as we climb: Women of color, wealth, and America's future.* Retrieved from http://www.insightcced.org/uploads/CRWG/LiftingAsWeClimb-InsightCenter-Spring2010.pdf

Evans, G. W., & Kim, P. (2007). Childhood poverty and health: Cumulative risk exposure and stress dysregulation. *Psychological Science, 18,* 953–957.

Goodman, P. S. (2010, February 20). *Millions of unemployed face years without jobs.* Retrieved from http://www.nytimes.com/2010/02/21/business/economy/21unemployed.html

Hardiman, R., Jackson, B., & Griffin, P. (2007). Conceptual foundations. In M. Adams, L. A. Bell, & P. Griffin (Eds.), *Teaching for diversity and social justice* (2nd ed., pp. 36–66). New York, NY: Routledge.

Hopps, J. A., & Liu, W. M. (2006). Working for social justice from within the health care system. In R. L. Toporek, L. H. Gerstein, N. A. Fouad, G. Roysricar, & T. Israel (Eds.), *Handbook for social justice in counseling psychology: Leadership, vision, and action* (pp. 318–337). Thousand Oaks, CA: Sage.

Institute for Higher Education Policy. (2010, June). *A portrait of low-income young adults in education.* Retrieved from http://www.ihep.org/assets/files/publications/m-r/(Brief)_A_Portrait_of_Low-Income_Young_Adults_in_Education.pdf

Liu, W. M. (2001). Expanding our understanding of multiculturalism: Developing a social class worldview model. In D. B. Pope-Davis & H. L. K. Coleman (Eds.), *The intersection of race, class, and gender in counseling psychology* (pp. 127–170). Thousand Oaks, CA: Sage.

Liu, W. M. (2002). The social class-related experiences of men: Integrating theory and practice. *Professional Psychology: Research and Practice, 33,* 355–360.

Liu, W. M. (2006). Classism is much more complex. *American Psychologist, 61,* 337–338.

Liu, W. M. (2008). Poverty. In F. T. L. Leong (Ed.), *Encyclopedia of counseling* (Vol. 3, pp. 1264–1269). Thousand Oaks, CA: Sage.

Liu, W. M. (2010, April). *If you're not the breadwinner, what are you? Economic distress and masculinity.* Presentation at the Counseling Men in Difficult Times: Strategies for the Mental Health Needs of Men conference, California State University, Fullerton.

Liu, W. M. (2011). *Social class and classism in the helping professions: Research, theory, and practice.* Thousand Oaks, CA: Sage.

Liu, W. M. (2012). Developing a social class and classism consciousness: Implications for research and practice. In E. Altmaier & J. I. Hansen (Eds.), *Handbook of counseling psychology* (pp. 326–345). New York, NY: Oxford University Press.

Liu, W. M., & Ali, S. R. (2005). Addressing social class and classism in vocational theory and practice: Extending the emancipatory communitarian approach. *The Counseling Psychologist, 33,* 189–196.

Liu, W. M., & Ali, S. R. (2008). Social class and classism: Understanding the impact of poverty and inequality. In S. D. Brown & R. W. Lent (Eds.), *Handbook of counseling psychology* (4th ed., pp. 159–175). New York, NY: Wiley.

Liu, W. M., Ali, S. R., Soleck, G., Hopps, J., Dunston, K., & Pickett, T., Jr. (2004). Using social class in counseling psychology research. *Journal of Counseling Psychology, 51*, 3–18.

Liu, W. M., & Arguello, J. (2006). Social class and classism in counseling. *Counseling and Human Development, 39*(3), 1–12.

Liu, W. M., Fridman, A., & Hall, T. (2008). Social class and school counseling. In H. L. K. Coleman & C. Yeh (Eds.), *Handbook of school counseling* (pp. 145–156). New York, NY: Erlbaum.

Liu, W. M., & Hernandez, J. (2008). Social class and educational psychology. In N. J. Salkind (Ed.), *Encyclopedia of educational psychology* (pp. 908–912). Thousand Oaks, CA: Sage.

Liu, W. M., Hernandez, J., Mahmood, A., & Stinson, R. (2006). The link between poverty, classism, and racism in mental health. In D. W. Sue & M. G. Constantine (Eds.), *Racism as a barrier to cultural competence in mental health and educational settings* (pp. 65–86). Hoboken, NJ: Wiley.

Liu, W. M., Pickett, T., Jr., & Ivey, A. E. (2007). White middle-class privilege: Social class bias and implications for training and practice. *Journal of Multicultural Counseling and Development, 35*, 194–207.

Liu, W. M., & Pope-Davis, D. B. (2003a). Moving from diversity to multiculturalism: Exploring power and the implications for psychology. In D. B. Pope-Davis, H. L. K. Coleman, W. M. Liu, & R. L. Toporek (Eds.), *The handbook of multicultural competencies in counseling and psychology* (pp. 90–102). Thousand Oaks, CA: Sage.

Liu, W. M., & Pope-Davis, D. B. (2003b). Understanding classism to effect personal change. In T. B. Smith (Ed.), *Practicing multiculturalism: Internalizing and affirming diversity in counseling and psychology* (pp. 294–310). New York, NY: Allyn & Bacon.

Liu, W. M., Soleck, G., Hopps, J., Dunston, K., & Pickett, T. (2004). A new framework to understand social class in counseling: The social class worldview and modern classism theory. *Journal of Multicultural Counseling and Development, 32*, 95–122.

Offer, A. (2006). *The challenge of affluence: Self-control and well-being in the United States and Britain since 1950.* New York, NY: Oxford University Press.

Parrish, L., & King, U. (2009, July). *Phantom demand: Short-term due date generates need for repeat payday loans, accounting for 76% of total volume.* Washington, DC: Center for Responsible Lending.

Pharr, S. (1997). *Homophobia: A weapon of sexism.* Berkeley, CA: Chardon Press.

Reason, R. D., & Davis, T. L. (2005). Antecedents, precursors, and concurrent concepts in the development of social justice attitudes and actions. *New Directions for Student Services, 2005*(110), 5–15.

Robinson, T. L., & Howard-Hamilton, M. (2000). *The convergence of race, ethnicity, and gender: Multiple identities in counseling.* Columbus, OH: Merrill Prentice Hall.

Spring, J. (2010). *Deculturalization and the struggle for equality: A brief history of the education of dominated cultures in the United States.* New York, NY: McGraw-Hill.

Sum, A., & Khatiwada, I. (2010, February). *Labor underutilization problems of U.S. workers across household income groups at the end of the Great Recession: A truly great depression among the nation's low income workers amidst full employment among the most affluent.* Retrieved from http://www.clms.neu.edu/publication/documents/Labor_Underutilization_Problems_of_U.pdf

Watt, S. K. (2007). Difficult dialogues, privilege and social justice: Uses of the privileged identity exploration (PIE) model in student affairs practice. *College Student Affairs Journal, 26*(2), 114–126.

Watt, S. K. (2009). Facilitating difficult dialogues at the intersections of religious privilege. *New Directions for Student Services, 2009*(125), 65–73.

Watt, S. K., Curtiss, G., Drummond, J., Kellogg, A., Lozano, A., Tagliapietra Nicoli, G., & Rosas, M. (2009). Privileged identity exploration: Examining White female counselor trainees' reactions to difficult dialogue in the classroom. *Counselor Education and Supervision, 49,* 86–105.

Additional Resources

The following websites provide additional information related to economic disadvantage.

American Psychological Association: Socioeconomic Status Office
http://www.apa.org/pi/ses/index.aspx
This website provides resources, highlights concerns related to socioeconomic status, and has free reports for download.

MacArthur Research Network on Socioeconomic Status and Health
www.macses.ucsf.edu
This website provides the largest compendium of resources related to social class and its relationship to a number of health factors. Included here are some resources for measuring social class in research. Most important, for counselors interested in the specific relationships of social class and physical health, this website provides a good starting point for exploration.

The following social class interventions are targeted toward the client's experiences of classism. Upward, downward, lateral, and internalized classisms are the focus of the therapist. Through collaboration, the client is helped to gain the following:

- Insight about his or her experiences of classism, his or her worldview, and the pressures he or she experiences as a part of an economic culture
- Empathy from the therapist toward his or her classism experiences
- Challenge from the therapist regarding irrational cognitions about social status and what he or she needs to do to maintain or achieve a social status
- Help integrating his or her history with his or her current situation
- Encouragement to develop self-efficacy in coping with and managing his or her situation
- Assistance in identifying situations in which certain feelings are tied to classism experiences

Step 1—Help the client identify and understand his or her economic culture.

Sample query:
- Tell me what kind of pressure you feel/experience as you try to keep up with your friends.
- *Identify* answers that touch on cultural, social, and human capital pressures/expectations.

Step 2—Help the client identify the social class messages he or she receive(d).

Sample queries:
- What would your parent(s)/peers say about your current situation?
- How would your parent(s)/peers help you resolve your current situation?
- List the ways you are acting to live out messages given to you by your parent(s)/peers.
- Tell me about your peer group. Your support network.
- *Identify* answers that focus on strong/salient cultural socialization messages still running in the client's mind that drive the client's behavior and attitudes.

Step 2a—Help the client identify social class behaviors, lifestyles, and material possessions that are salient to the client in his or her current situation.

Sample queries:
- Tell me how you imagine your life.
- How would you ideally be spending your time?
- What do others have that you want?
- What do you notice about how other people act/behave that you like?
- *Identify* answers that pinpoint the client's materialism values, how he has changed his or her lifestyle to fit into a new group, and how he or she has changed his or her behavior to belong in a new group.

Step 3—Identify the client's experiences with classism and move toward developing an adaptive, realistic, and healthy expectation about himself or herself.

Sample queries:
- Do people look down on you?
- Do you look down on others who are not like you?
- What do your peers expect from you to maintain your status with them?

(Continued)

Appendix 16.1 • Social Class Interventions Using the Social Class Worldview Model
(Continued)

- What does it feel like for you when you can't keep up with your peers? What do you do?
- *Identify* answers that express high social class expectations and negative consequences related to not meeting specific demands. In addition, in what ways is the client participating in classism to maintain his or her social class standing?

Step 4—Help the client integrate his or her experiences of classism.

Sample queries:
- Now that we've started talking about all these aspects of your social class experience, tell me what it means to you.
- What are you aware of about yourself that you didn't know before we started?
- *Identify* an ability to understand and integrate the social class discussions into other aspects of the client's life.

Step 4a—Help the client take action and make changes in his or her life.

Sample query:
- What is the one thing you could do to change your awareness, situation, or perception?
- *Identify* an ability to make personal changes in the client's life.

Note. Reprinted with permission from "Developing a Social Class and Classism Consciousness: Implications for Research and Practice," by W. M. Liu, in *Handbook of Counseling Psychology,* E. Altmaier and J. I. Hansen (Eds.), 2012, New York, NY: Oxford University Press.

Counseling Military Clients: Multicultural Competence, Challenges, and Opportunities

Marvin Westwood, David Kuhl, and Duncan Shields

A man's chief quality is courage. —Cicero

• • •

This chapter is written with the goal of taking you inside individual and group work with military clients so that you can see the interventions and approaches that relate specifically to counseling active military members, veterans, and their families. Counselors who work with military personnel know the burden that these clients carry from their military service. These clients rarely share their experiences with others. The toll that personal difficulties take on careers and relationships with spouses or partners, parents, children, and siblings is often very evident. Although counselors hold the men and women who serve in the military in high regard and wish to use their best skills to help them come to terms with difficult military experiences, many clinicians find that their theoretical approaches fit poorly with this population. Soldiers challenge the therapeutic status quo. If counselors can get them through the door at all, it may be difficult to keep them engaged or prevent them from dropping out.

Because the military is a unique culture, members are best served by counselors who are prepared to use multicultural perspectives (Fennell, 2008). It is essential to have a strong understanding of this particular culture and the dominant influence of traditional masculine gender roles within it. To optimize their effectiveness, counselors need to understand the important issues, concepts, and approaches that impact their work with clients who are part of the military culture. Counselors need to enhance multicultural competence by developing alternative models or modifications to the existing helping approaches in order to better engage and serve this particular client group.

This chapter describes the prevailing military culture and obstacles to help seeking based on an adherence to this culture. An effective model for overcoming these challenges is identified, and the therapeutic implications for working with military clients are discussed. In addition, we show how to integrate a multicultural competence approach with military clients in both an individual and group counseling context.

Why a Gender and Cultural Lens?

Traditional male socialization underpins the foundation of military culture. It is important to differentiate between gender and biological sex, as they are two of the most central components of many peoples' identities and are frequently confused (Brown, 2008). *Sex* is a term that describes the biological makeup of the body, whereas *gender* is a series of schemata and roles that are both internalized and enacted. These schemata and roles begin to be imposed on children from the moment the sex of the fetus is determined (Brown, 2008).

Both women and men are capable of conforming to masculine norms, and these are particularly relevant when one is seeking to understand the learned values and norms of military identity. In order to work effectively with military clients, it is important to understand how these learned cultural norms impact help-seeking behaviors and expectations. In turn, these learned cultural norms influence the effectiveness of counseling interventions. It is also important for counselors to be aware of their own gender schemata and norms that they might impose on the gender expressions of others (Brown, 2008).

There are seven scripts or gender roles that men adopt and frequently present in counseling (Fennell, 2008). Characteristics of these scripts include projecting an image that (a) males are stoic and in control of themselves; (b) males are able to manage emotions, especially those associated (or deemed associated) with being vulnerable; (c) males are fearless and indestructible; (d) the only acceptable male emotion is anger; (e) males are competitive, achievement oriented, and successful; (f) males are strong and independent; and finally (g) to be male is to be the opposite of any of the characteristics associated with either femininity or homosexuality.

Numerous studies and surveys have shown that clients with high conformity to masculine gender norms are less likely to seek counseling and/or drop out early. Some researchers have suggested that this is in part due to a conflict between masculine and therapeutic norms (Addis & Mahalik, 2003; Brooks, 2001; Englar-Carlson, 2006). For instance, Brooks (2001) argued that traditional male socialization predisposes these clients to hide private experiences, maintain personal control, appear stoic, present the self as invincible, and value action over introspection. In contrast, traditional counseling approaches tend to favor clients who self-disclose, relinquish control, recognize and express emotion, introspect, experience vulnerability, and admit failure and/or ignorance.

Engaging the Military Client: A Culture of Hypermasculinity

"Culture is a shared, acquired pattern of values, attitudes, beliefs and schemata that consciously and unconsciously shape peoples' identities and behaviors" (Brown, 2008, p. 53). For military personnel, traditional masculine gender roles are extended or emphasized in a hypermasculine cultural norm that includes a high standard of self-discipline and control; a professional ethos of loyalty and self-sacrifice; an emphasis on group identity; and a strong warrior persona that is aggressive, dominant, and risk taking. This precludes the experience or expression of weakness.

These qualities, which are highly valued within the military context, may exacerbate and exaggerate emotional, behavioral, and relational difficulties. The need to maintain the appearance of stoic competence makes it more difficult for these clients to admit that they have problems, seek professional help, or have faith in the efficacy of treatment. The resulting code of silent stoicism isolates military personnel during times of distress and perpetuates a myth that real warriors neither ask for nor need help. For military personnel who conform to these cultural norms, seeking help may initially be seen as an admission of weakness and thus may be a source of shame and identity loss.

Brooks (2010) postulated that although the creation and the development of the psychotherapy establishment has historically been dominated by men, it has "largely failed to develop models of counseling that are more harmonious with men's unique ways of experiencing emotional pain and coping with their psychological distress" (p. 34). Traditional methods of counseling have failed to attract or interest these clients, and therefore caution needs to be exercised to ensure that the client is not blamed in any way for his failure to engage in the counseling process (Brooks, 2001; Englar-Carlson, 2006). There is a stigma associated with seeking psychological care, and therefore military personnel rarely seek care. The fear of stigmatization in regard to help seeking is always present, particularly in the early stages of contact with the mental health system (Hoge et al., 2004).

Multicultural theories and approaches can be helpful for reducing the client's fear of stigmatization and fostering trust. Making counseling culturally safe for military clients calls for clinicians to become culturally competent. It is important to acknowledge, respect, and value differences that arise from traditional masculine gender roles and military cultural norms. Furthermore, careful attention needs to be paid to the attitudes and therapeutic structural barriers that can make it difficult for this population to begin counseling and to benefit from it.

In order to reconceptualize how they work with military clients it is necessary for counselors to identify and challenge their own values, prejudices, and biases. Do they recognize and have respect for the strengths inherent in traditional masculine roles? Can they retool their therapeutic approaches to leverage the strengths inherent in these roles?

Essential to any satisfactory therapeutic outcome is the helping alliance, which begins with meeting the client where he or she is. This way of looking at counseling encourages clinicians, regardless of their own cultural background and gender roles, to communicate and practice in ways that respect and take into account the cultural, political, linguistic, and spiritual realities of the people with whom they are working. It also behooves counselors not only to meet the military client on his (or her) own terms but also to be sensitive to frame the work to be done together within the context of the client's existing value and belief systems.

The most important first step is to make a connection with the client. This is referred to as *establishing the therapeutic alliance* that is essential for the process of helping to begin. Without a successful interpersonal connection the client will feel lost. This stance bypasses the question of whether counseling should strive to bring balance to clients by teaching alternative strategies (e.g., emotional expression) not previously learned or internalized through gender socialization or whether it should be adapted to match and support clients' coping styles on the basis of their gender norms (i.e. complimentary vs. reinforcing approaches) (Owen, Wong, & Rodolfa, 2010). Instead, counseling should pursue both approaches by helping clients consolidate existing skills and resources and clarify their motivation to make positive changes within their existing values and cultural and gender socialization. It must also equip them with added skills and awareness to increase versatility and flexibility in coping and problem solving.

Without some agreement about the nature of the issues at stake, agreement about how to address those concerns, or an understanding of how change occurs, it is difficult for the counselor and client to agree on an approach. In military terms this could be conceptualized as defining objectives of a plan of attack that is acceptable to both. Regardless of the cultural and gender lens of the counselor, he or she must provide explanations and interventions that are consistent with the client's perspective and point of view. In short, the counselor must work collaboratively with the client to establish safety and trust so the client is willing to come along for the ride and is able to move out of his or her current comfort zone and into foreign territory.

Effective Approaches for Helping to Initiate Client Contact and Engagement

A change in counseling work with military clients is required in three primary areas: (a) a new language for the process, (b) an adjusted port of entry for engagement, and (c) the use of culturally appropriate interventions.

Language

The language of counseling leaves many clients cold and estranged from the process. It is important to use words that are familiar to the military client and not associated with giving up control or being in a one-down position. Replace terms such as *psychotherapy, treatment,* or *sessions* with words like *meetings, consultations,* or *conversations.* Frame the work of counseling in terms of examining goals, making plans, and doing experiments (e.g., "How about trying something new or different?") rather than creating treatment goals or planning interventions. Familiar language such as *dropping baggage* that references experiences in their lives where they feel competent is more acceptable to clients. Emphasize *skills* and *picking up tools.* With respect to the process of counseling, use words like *expressing* versus *feeling, letting it go* versus *crying, experiencing* versus *feeling,* and *I've got your back* versus *I will support you.*

Port of Entry

In order to bring military clients through the door and into the counseling space, individually or in a group, it is necessary to create a trajectory of counseling that moves from creating a "safe zone" to creating a process for "dropping baggage" and ends with consolidating gains and planning for the future or "moving up and out." This requires a very different approach to forming the alliance, establishing trust, and fulfilling objectives. Without a buy-in it is difficult to fully engage the client. The following are key starting points for establishing a productive and relevant environment with this client population:

1. *Listen.* Engaging in culturally safe practice does not mean applying a stereotype to every military client who walks in the door. Some military clients are perfectly comfortable in counseling. What is required is to assess whether clients are open to the conventional counseling process or whether they require an approach more in line with military cultural values. Are they defensive and having trouble admitting to any distress, or do they seem suspicious of the process? Are they having difficulty talking about their issues or their emotional experience? Determine their readiness and motivation and acknowledge any concerns about the process right away. Listen carefully and without judgment to their language, their attitudes, their experience, and their beliefs.

2. *Normalize.* These clients benefit from an understanding that their experiences are normal within the military population. Reframing an admission of problems as evidence of strength and character helps them to own their experiences. It is valuable to inform those who have experienced trauma-related injuries that what they are experiencing is a normal reaction to an abnormal event.

3. *Keep clients informed.* Discuss confidentiality. Provide information about process norms and rules. In a group context, norms and rules might include a discussion of rights to equal air time, nonjudgmental listening, timeliness, respectful communication, or rules of engagement. Group members might be educated about their opportunity to drop some baggage and about the importance of their role in assisting others. Whether in an individual or group context, make the process predictable and assure clients that they will be able to maintain personal control at all times.

4. *Be transparent and egalitarian.* Invite questions, as some group members will keep silent as a measure of respect, caution, or fear. Although this population is used to hierarchies and taking orders, do not assume you outrank your client. Answer all questions and challenges frankly and openly to earn and maintain trust. These clients may see counselor self-disclosure, and the therapeutic alliance may be disrupted if you are seen as holding back. Soldiers appreciate signs that you are willing to get down in the trenches with them and do the work. They are more likely to trust you if you can talk frankly about your own struggles and model your own successful outcomes. An aloof clinical stance that conveys superiority will almost certainly destroy trust and limit client self-disclosure. This challenges you to strike a careful balance that maintains professionalism and yet also transmits a degree of transparency and equality.

5. *Convey competence.* You need to convey in a believable and convincing manner that your competencies will help the client achieve his (or her) goals. Tentativeness on your part can signal weakness or uncertainty. This undermines the client's confidence that working together will be of benefit. Too often counselors are overly cautious of being more assertive and direct, as they want to be seen as unconditionally accepting. This may be confusing and may weaken the trust for someone seeking the kind of clear direction that is the way of helping so common in military culture.

6. *Start where clients are at.* Begin with whatever the client wants to work on or discuss, including small talk such as sports, the daily news, or a television program. Many of these clients are living behind a mask of competence and are isolated as a result. Once they discover that they can talk freely and without being judged, they will come to value the meetings. However, they need to discover that sense of safety and cannot be pushed too quickly. Counselors are generally well trained in listening and in seeking clarity. Eliciting the client's stories at the beginning creates a sense of being in control at the outset and helps him (or her) adapt to the positive features of group membership or the therapeutic alliance with you as the counselor. In listening carefully you become aware of information and client strengths that can be leveraged later in your work together. Storytelling is a familiar activity for military personnel, as it is a large part of interpersonal contact among comrades while on duty and while socializing.

7. *Hold clients accountable.* Be understanding without coddling clients. Expressed sympathy may be perceived as caregiving and may turn clients away. Although it is important that clients not feel judged or put down, it is equally important that you are able to point out the role that clients play in destructive patterns of behavior and help them to be accountable for creating change. Clearly distinguish *responsibility for behavior* from *blame and shame about behavior.* A strong value for members of the

military is to be responsible in and for their work, and it is an equally important value to reinforce in counseling.

Appropriate Interventions Consistent With Military Culture

What social norms and values within the military culture can be readily leveraged as assets to enhance engagement and propel the process of change? Soldiers are explicitly taught particular values in their training and are expected to live them in everything they do. Counseling can be consciously retooled to leverage these values. Some of these explicit values adapted from military training include the following:

- *Courage.* Military personnel must face fear, danger, or adversity. This is a matter of enduring physical and emotional duress and at times risking personal safety. This may also be called on in the long, slow process of continuing to do the right thing, even if taking those actions is not popular with others. (Sample questions: Have you ever been in harm's way? When were you expected to complete a task that seemed to ask more of you than you were able to give? When in your service did you experience fear, danger, or adversity?)
- *Commitment.* Military personnel fulfill their obligations and take pride in tackling the hard challenge and doing the tough work. They must resist the temptation to take the easy way or shortcuts that might undermine the integrity of the final product. (Sample questions: What is one thing you did that makes you proud of being in the military? What is the toughest thing you had to do while serving in the military? How did that affect you then? How does it affect you today?)
- *Loyalty and selfless service.* Military personnel put the welfare of others, the nation, the military, and their team before their own. They commit to going a little further, enduring a little longer, and looking a little closer to see how they can add to the effort. Loyalty and service to others requires that these clients consider the impact of their behavior not only on themselves but also on their family, their team, and their community. (Sample questions: When were you expected to work for the good of the whole group regardless of the cost to you? Could you tell me about that please?)
- *Integrity.* Integrity calls on clients to assume accountability for their behavior and to take steps to enhance or recover their personal fitness and well-being. Assist clients to identify what part they have played in the events that led them to counseling and what part belongs to others or the military. (Sample questions: What helped you in your decision to come here today? Is there one thing that happened recently that brings you here today? How did that happen?)

In order to demonstrate that counseling is relevant and helpful to military clients, the process can be recast so that it capitalizes on these military values and is seen as a relevant means of helping clients become all that they can be. It can be beneficial to help clients see that their personal courage will be tested—counseling is not for the faint of heart! Commitment is required in the face of setbacks, and they will be called on to give 110% because counseling will not be an easy way. They will be held accountable for their behavior and called on to do and give their very best. As one military client observed, "Sitting in the bar is a lot easier than being in here."

These core values can be honored and integrated into specific approaches to counseling. The following specific considerations will allow counselors to tailor their work to capitalize on, rather than work against, the dominant military culture:

1. *Be goal oriented and hit the ground running.* Initially, these clients are often uncomfortable with introspective discussions and may prefer focusing on approaches that emphasize relevance and action. It is frequently of great benefit to apply cognitively oriented approaches in the early stages of the work. (Sample questions: Take me through a challenging day when you were proud of how you handled yourself. What were you saying to yourself? How did you carry yourself physically? What did you do?) It is also beneficial to explore values and strengths. (Sample questions: What does it mean to you to be in military service? What were the reasons you signed up? What is one of the things you most enjoyed, most valued, most disliked?)

2. *Educate.* Action-focused skills training or activities tap into a familiar learning style reinforced in military training and service. You can provide specific information on such relevant areas of concern, such as the psychobiology of trauma, effective communication skills, specific self-regulation techniques, and other skill-based or problem-solving tools.

3. *Use a strengths-based approach.* When you actively seek out and acknowledge the client's strengths, the client feels respected and recognized for his (or her) competence. Clients need to be given the space to inform you about themselves and about what competencies underpin who they are or were. Be aware that clients may worry or feel anxious that they will be judged or that counseling may uncover all of their weaknesses. For that reason they may work to correct this perception or may have difficulty dropping the shield of competence they have assembled to compensate for feeling out of control. (Sample questions: What is one thing you do or did that went really well? Tell me about a time that you made a positive difference to your buddies. What did you do for fun while in the military?)

4. *Ensure safety by augmenting clients' control.* One military client who came for counseling was quickly reduced to tears when he started telling his story. When the counselor interrupted his storytelling and taught him a self-regulation technique, he learned immediately and first hand that the consultation would give him reliable tools for staying in control. This is important, as early disclosure can be overwhelming and, if it occurs before the establishment of trust, can result in embarrassment for the client and precipitate early termination. It's important to teach clients how to disclose while being grounded at the same time, in order to keep them from becoming hyperaroused.

5. *Explore clients' issues within a structure and with pacing in mind.* Utilizing structured storytelling assignments is one example of giving clients a sense of personal control, as they can choose what they do and do not want to talk about. Adhering to masculine gender roles may result in a client feeling uncomfortable or incompetent in the area of emotional self-disclosure and self-reflection normally expected by the counselor. It becomes easier to focus attention on feelings and the expression of inner states once the client has first established himself or herself in a place of strength. It is important to create safety first, build rapport, and then facilitate introspection and self-examination. Note that this is in contrast to how counselors are normally taught to use relationship-building skills, emphasizing insight, emotion, and self-reflection in the initial stage. Be mindful that for many traditional men, all emotions are funneled toward anger until they learn to expand their vocabulary of emotion and acquire the skills for expressing them.

6. *Use somatic awareness and physical sensation as a way to begin emotion identification and expression.* Despite the fact that many clients with high masculine gender conformity may not be able to access and describe their emotions, they still experience the

physiological effects of those emotions in their bodies. When these clients are unable to identify and express these emotions, the emotions may be experienced as a general feeling of frustration or anger. You can assist clients in expanding their awareness and insight by helping them identify emotional themes in their stories and begin to focus on and label bodily sensations. Focusing on sensations in the body helps clients identify internal states and yet does not maroon them in the unfamiliar territory of emotion, where they may lack language to describe their experience.

Individual Case Demonstration: Dan

The suggested approaches for applying these multicultural competencies in the practice of counseling can be demonstrated in the following opening sequence between Dan and his counselor. Dan is an infantry specialist in his late 20s. He is also training to be a mechanic. He served one tour in Afghanistan, where he was exposed to civilian casualties due to land mine explosions on several occasions. Since Dan has returned from duty his Commanding Officer (CO) and others have noticed a change in his behavior. He is experiencing increasing conflict with his girlfriend, and they are now taking a break from the relationship. He has been irritable and is apt to express high levels of anger at minor annoyances. There have been several incidents of public inebriation that have caused problems for him with family, friends, military superiors, and civilian police. Dan is also avoiding training exercises. Dan attended several counseling sessions after his return and also attended a standard military group stress debriefing at the end of his tour. He has set up a consultation at the urging of his CO, but reluctantly.

Initial Meeting Task

Dan's counselor should first greet Dan and make him comfortable in the counseling office. The counselor should explore Dan's reticence about receiving counseling, as he terminated sessions with his previous counselor. He or she should also explore with Dan some of the reasons he has now returned for counseling. The counselor should establish a goal and explore ways in which he or she can be an ally in helping Dan achieve any objectives he may have set for himself.

Counselor: Hi Dan, come on in. [*The therapist's voice is strong and low, handshake is firm, and eye contact is brief but direct. Posture is square-on and open.*] Sit wherever you like . . . and the choice of chair doesn't tell me anything.
[*Dan laughs and takes a seat facing the door*]
(*Many military clients appreciate being able to face the door because of having become hypervigilant for threat of attack. Giving them a choice of seating in a flexible arrangement sets the tone of collaboration from the first instant of interaction. Mindful use of humor relieves tension and helps restore perspective. For example, the counselor can make a light-hearted comment about secretly assessing the client, even through the choice of the chair. This brings any anxiety into the room and begins to demonstrate counselor transparency. The use of humor early lets the client know that humor is allowed and is a normal part of the processing experience.*)
Counselor: Alright Dan—so I understand you have consulted a counselor before. That right?
Dan: Yeah, I went for a few, a few times when I got back home.

Counselor: So, you know then that everything starts with the paperwork . . .

[*Issues of confidentiality and consent are addressed, emphasizing clear expectations and Dan's right to terminate the session at any time.*]

Counselor: So Dan, going to see the counselor before—I was wondering whether you found that helpful.

Dan: Actually, it was a bit of a waste of time, frankly. No offense. I mean, sure, some people must find it useful, but it didn't do much for me. My CO suggested I come in or I probably wouldn't have come. He keeps asking me if I'm okay ever since I got back.

Counselor: No offense taken, I appreciate your honesty. What was missing from those consults for you do you think?

Dan: Well, we just talked about the same stuff every time, and I didn't see the point. I think ultimately you've got to deal with your own crap, and nobody else can really change that.

Counselor: There is some truth to that Dan.

Dan: And no one who hasn't been down range can really understand what it's like anyway.

Counselor: No, I think you're right about that. I've walked along this road with enough guys who have been "down range," as you say, so I do know what has helped them, but it's totally different than being there. So what is your CO seeing that has him concerned about you?

Dan: I guess I've been avoiding going on training, and I got in trouble for being drunk a couple of times.

Counselor: And that's different behavior for you, is it? He's paying attention because he's noticed a change?

Dan: Yeah, I was pretty stellar before. They kept asking me to go officer, but nobody is asking me to now! [*Dan laughs, but there is bitterness and an angry edge to his laugh.*] (*At this point, a counselor could go deeper into the emotion—or, in military parlance, could "drill down"—and Dan might access and reveal the extent of pain that is there. However, Dan has already expressed the opinion that his baggage is for him to deal with alone, and further inquiry might just as easily close Dan down or propel him away from counseling. Self-disclosing emotional material before trust is established might be embarrassing for Dan and might cause him to terminate counseling.*)

Counselor: Pretty stellar . . . Tell me some more about yourself from before. What was it about you that officers saw? You must have had some military and personal successes . . .

(*There has been a quick transition from the acknowledgement of a problem to an exploration of resources and strengths. Counselors steeped in the tradition of focus on diagnosis, disorder, disease, and deficit will need to be watchful for negative bias and a tendency to focus on problems early. The emphasis of early counseling is on helping the military client remain in control and creating a safe zone in the meeting.*)

[*Dan starts to tell stories that highlight a reputation for dependability and stoic toughness. As he tells these stories, his posture lifts and he becomes somewhat more animated. The counselor keeps the stories going, eliciting as much information as possible about Dan's resources, aptitudes, interests, and strengths so that he can acknowledge Dan's strengths and resilience.*]

Counselor: So, Dan, it seems like you've been a pretty dependable guy, and from your stories I get that you're pretty strong and used to solving your own problems. I also get that you also set pretty high standards for yourself—you drive yourself. I'm struck by the difference between how you have been in the past and what your CO is seeing now and figuring that you're probably not proud of how you're handling things—

you're not living up to your own standards of what it means to be strong and be a soldier right now. Does that sound right? *(The counselor is exploring whether Dan has a desire to change based on his own values vs. being pushed to change by the people around him.)*

Dan: Yeah, that's pretty much it.

Counselor: Dan, you're a bright guy, and you have a history of successfully tackling whatever challenge you've had thrown at you. What is working and what isn't working for you in tackling this challenge? I mean, I'm wondering what would be different for you if you were to handle this as you would ideally like to.

Dan: I don't know. I think it's just time I need. *[Dan looks down, his posture has slumped, and he sounds defeated again as the conversation shifts into a focus on the problem. Dan appears uncomfortable talking at this point.]*

(Now the task of the counselor is to identify how change occurs for this client and start to establish how the alliance can help him achieve his own objectives. A useful shift of frame at this point can help the client use his or her own experience and understanding of how problems are solved to transfer that skill back into the new problem area. This allows the client to see the problem from a position of experience and strength rather than as a new problem that his or her prior experience has no bearing on. In this case, Dan is training to be a mechanic, so mechanical troubleshooting provides a useful metaphor for change and a port of entry into framing how to view the process.)

Reframing the Process—Establishing Buy-In

Counselor: Dan, if you were to go out in the morning and try to start your truck and nothing happened, you could spend a lot of time pulling the engine and replacing it. It would be hard work, cost a lot, and you might do that really well—but it wouldn't do you much good if it was really the battery that was dead. So really, we can work hard at a problem, but if you don't know where to put the effort in, you may or may not get the desired result. Does that make sense?

Dan: Yeah. Anybody can pull wrenches; it's the troubleshooting that's the key.

Counselor: Right. So that's where I might be able to speed things up for you. I think you'll solve this problem on your own in time, actually. But where we might be able to get this done faster together is if we coordinate your courage, work ethic, and high standards with my ability to point you to the right places to apply the effort. I've walked this road a few times, Dan, and although I can't and won't pull the wrenches for you, I think I can troubleshoot to help you get yourself from A to B without spending a lot of time in the ditch.

Dan: Okay, so what do you think I need to do?

(The client is offering to hand over control here, but the counselor should resist the temptation to direct until Dan has articulated clear outcomes for himself. Otherwise, he may successfully fail proposed solution after solution. Goals and directives need to be identified collaboratively at every step.)

Establishing Goals

Counselor: Well, first I would say let's define what success looks like. If we were to work together, 1 hour per week for X number of weeks, how would you know that you were making progress down the road? I mean, if the mechanical troubleshooter was directing you to the wrong places, you'd fire him . . . so how would you know whether to fire me? What would be different, what would you be doing more of, or less of, if you were to drop some of this baggage?

Dan: Well, I think I'd have better control of my anger.

Counselor: Okay, let's look at the kinds of situations you'd like to react differently in, look forward at the next week to identify some situations that are likely to ambush you, and look for some specific warning signs and tools you can put in your tool kit. Let's hit the ground running on this.

Once Dan identified specific objectives, the counselor was able to help him define the desired change in observable behaviors. No judgment of the prior behavior occurred, but the counselor helped Dan compare his behavior with his own goals and values. Once Dan identified that a change was important to him, it was time to go to work. The counselor used a very matter-of-fact approach that communicated that he believed that Dan was strong and capable enough to change.

Over the course of several sessions, Dan gradually came to acknowledge that his drinking was interfering with his ability to be the kind of man he wanted to be and that he was using alcohol as a way of numbing himself and escaping. He was also quite clear that his drinking was not an effective solution for him and that it did not make him "proud." He expressed concern, guilt, and shame around the negative effects his drinking had had on his career and relationships. At this point he shifted his goals to include a specific focus on his emerging addiction.

Dan learned about the physiology of stress and trauma. He came to understand that what he was experiencing was a predictable and normal reaction and that warriors throughout history have recorded similar experiences. Initially he identified a "kind of physical pressure" in his head and chest that built throughout the day and made him feel ready to "explode." Later, as he learned to watch for these signs in his body, label them as stress, and start to take early preventive action to address these feelings, he learned to better manage his anger and reduce his drinking. Physical exercise and specific behavioral self-regulation skills helped him feel more in control of his body and behavior. Problem-solving and communication skills helped him reduce his frustration and start to repair his relationships.

After discovering the effectiveness of the skills that he had learned in counseling, Dan became very committed to his meetings with the counselor and began to speak very openly about some of his more painful memories and experiences. The work of repairing the trauma could only begin by building on a firm relationship that Dan had tested and found trustworthy.

Group Counseling Study:
The Veterans Transition Program (VTP)

Not all counseling with military clients occurs in a one-to-one setting. There are opportunities and advantages for utilizing group-based counseling approaches with this particular population. The next case study, which describes working in groups, incorporates many of the cross-cultural competencies and perspectives presented in the previous case study.

The group approach presented here draws on the inherent capabilities present in any military group. When we ask soldiers what got them through their most difficult experiences in the service, they typically say that they trust and rely on (a) their equipment and technology, (b) their training, and (c) the soldier beside them. Counselors need to prepare them the same way by giving them the tools, the training, and the support they need. Bringing soldiers together in a group offers an efficient mechanism for teaching skills but also presents a unique opportunity for soldiers to obtain support from the social group for which they have the most respect and with which they share the most cohesion. Validation received from a group of fellow soldiers has far more credibility than validation from a counselor—even one in the military.

The group approach is a culturally appropriate intervention for working with soldiers for all of the reasons outlined previously. Most soldiers are group trained, group experienced, and group ready, as this is the context of their daily work and has been since day one of their military experience.

A Case for the Group: Soldiers Helping Soldiers

A number of researchers have recommended approaching the treatment of traumatized combat veterans with group approaches, as the benefits are considerable (Coalson, 1995; Greene et al., 2004; Ruzek et al., 2001; Shea, McDevitt-Murphy, Ready, & Schnurr, 2009; van der Kolk, 1987). Van der Kolk, McFarlane, and Weisaeth (1996) suggested that veteran groups include built-in peer input, the potential for interpersonal support, and the benefits of social regulation. He stressed the value of the group for trauma work with veterans. Group counseling is an effective first-line treatment for many clients with posttraumatic stress disorder. An encouraging, mutually supportive environment is commonly experienced as empowering for the participants (van der Kolk, 1987). Group-based therapeutic approaches offer additional therapeutic support beyond what is possible in individually oriented clinical therapies. The advantages of group-based therapies have been summarized by Coalson (1995), Foa, Keane, and Friedman (2009), Ford and Stewart (1999), Rozynko and Dondershine (1991), and Ruzek et al. (2001). In particular, the group setting serves to counteract and confront the socially avoidant and self-isolating tendencies of traumatized individuals (Fontana & Rosenheck, 2001; Greene et al., 2004). Carefully planned and facilitated groups can provide a structured and safe environment for promoting self-awareness, emotional expression, and cognitive reframing to aid coping and symptom reduction.

Setting Up and Conducting the Group

The VTP program focuses on (a) creating a safe, cohesive environment wherein soldiers can experience mutual support, receive understanding from others who have been there, and process their reactions; (b) normalizing soldiers' military experiences overseas and their difficulties with reentry back to civilian life; (c) offering critical knowledge to help soldiers understand trauma and its origins, symptoms, and impact on the self and others along with provision of specific relational and self-regulation strategies for trauma symptom management; (d) reducing the symptoms of the stress-related issues that arise from soldiers' military experiences; (e) teaching interpersonal communication skills to help military personnel manage difficult interactions or enhance relationships with others (e.g., spouses, friends, coworkers); (f) helping soldiers generate life goals and learn how to initiate career exploration; and (g) involving spouses and other family members in family awareness evenings.

These components of the VTP are conducted in a structured fashion in order to reduce reactivation; promote increased trust formation; and permit greater self-awareness, self-disclosure, emotional expression, and cognitive reframing. The group involves veterans only, unlike many trauma recovery groups in which veterans are expected to join with civilians.

The group facilitation team typically consists of three professional clinicians (i.e., a combination of psychologists, counselors, and a physician with doctoral-level training in psychology) assisted by two soldiers paraprofessionally trained in basic interaction, communication, and group skills. They model caring and supportive behavior and engage in the expected behavioral outcomes of the program (Alcock, Carment, & Sadava, 2001). Veterans report that they trust others who have had similar experiences. Witnessing and validation from other soldiers is an essential component in the repair of war-related traumas.

Six to eight veterans meet for approximately 80 hours in a residential program occurring over an 8- to 12-week period. Consistent with military nomenclature, participants refer to the program as a "course" rather than a counseling group. The terms *counseling* or *psychotherapy* are seen as stigmatizing to the veterans and discourage others from joining the group. Research has demonstrated that military personnel are cautious about revealing information to others regarding a possible weakness, such as a psychologically based injury (Rosebush, 1998).

Following the first phase of establishing a solid working group, the counselors begin to assist individuals in addressing symptoms and beginning the work of trauma repair. This is accomplished by having members share life narratives through a group-based life review process (Birren & Birren, 1996; Birren & Deutchman, 1991). In this process participants write short autobiographical accounts on preselected themes in both civilian and military life. These stories are read aloud to the group. After each story has been read, others respond to what they have heard without making any judgment, making any interpretation, or giving advice. Rather, they speak about how the story affected them. The goal of this work is to simply and clearly let the speaker know that his or her story was heard and understood (Birren & Birren, 1996; Birren & Deutchman, 1991).

Participants practice identifying and disclosing the personal impact of listening to another person's story. By coaching participants not to give advice, the facilitators ensure that the soldiers have the opportunity to practice identifying and verbalizing personal impact and the storytellers experience being heard by their peers. The facilitators are very active in this stage of the group process, modeling the communication skills and checking how feedback is received by the storyteller.

It is important to give the implicit and explicit message that the disclosure of difficult personal information is respected as a sign of strength and is not seen as a sign of weakness or as a need for advice and assistance. An example of this occurs when a member is able to disclose feelings of threat or fear when under attack and hears from others that they were afraid to disclose similar feelings until they witnessed another soldier being courageous enough to do so. Hearing the reactions of others to one's story can help normalize difficult feelings such as anger, guilt, and shame. Sharing common military experiences in particular promotes trust and greater group cohesiveness (Corey, 1990).

The use of a life review is a relatively low risk way to initiate self-disclosure, as it allows individuals to engage and disclose at their own pace. "An autobiography is a story of a life, the explanation or interpretation of this life by the individual who has lived it" (de Vries, Birren, & Deutchman, 1995, p. 166). This narrative method is a semistructured, topical, group approach to the life review. Participants receive selected themes with guided-response questions so that they can write up a 1.5-page story on the theme. The first one used is the "Branching Points of One's Life," which asks participants to identify critical events across their life span from childhood to the present that have helped shape who they are today. This narrative process helps to highlight strengths and capabilities that have been shown to decrease depressive symptoms (Birren & Birren, 1996; Birren & Deutchman, 1991; Rife, 1998).

Once the group members have told their individual narratives, they are ready to enact critical life events through the therapeutic enactment (TE) process. TE is a group intervention in which individuals begin to integrate the traumatic event into their lives. TE is a highly structured intervention in which participants are able to externalize internal processes of trauma by enacting specific trauma narratives. The soldiers refer to this process as "dropping baggage." Through the enactment process group members are able to learn about their triggers; stressors; and patterns of activation, relapse, and regression. They begin to understand that their reactions of numbing, shame, and helplessness are normal responses to abnormal events that prevent emotional release (Herman, 1997). They come to recognize that the experience of letting baggage go through TE in a structured, safe environment is highly therapeutic as trauma symptoms begin to lessen. To maintain a feeling of safety and in order to remain grounded through the enactment process, group members are taught emotional self-regulation skills. This prevents them from moving into hyperactivation (i.e., heightened anxiety response) or hypoactivation (i.e., decreased sympathetic nervous system responding). By attending to ways of regulating clients' psychological responses, the counselors are able to facilitate the integration of the trauma memory without triggering clients into a hyper- or hypoarousal response, thus stopping the integrating process. Ogden referred to this as staying within the "window of tolerance" (Ogden & Minton, 2000, p. 7). Through actively expressing emotion (verbally, emotionally, and somatically) while describing the event for the group, the person doing the enactment integrates the trauma reactions into the narrative. This enables the individual to make sense of what occurred and promotes cognitive reintegration. Participants are able to successfully integrate their reactions at a thinking, feeling, and experiencing level, thereby helping to develop a story of coherence versus confusion and reactivity.

The process follows a distinct number of steps: (a) In the planning phase, the counselor and the soldier work together to plan a critical event to be enacted. (b) In the enactment itself, group members are asked to take on the key roles of significant others who were part of the event or to act as witnesses to the enacted event. Techniques such as doubling and role reversal are used to help the soldier access and express the buried feelings and the negative cognitions attached to the problematic event. (c) The enactment phase is completed by having the members who took roles and the witnesses tell what they experienced, what they observed, and how the enactment affected them personally. Completing this process deepens trust among members and further strengthens group cohesiveness and support.

Group Case Demonstration

Greg, a 24-year-old sapper (combat engineer), begins to read a story to the group that outlines a critical incident related to his combat experience. He explains that he has been having a lot of bad dreams and intrusive thoughts related to the death of his buddy Don, which occurred during his last tour in Afghanistan. He reports that he cannot sleep, as he sees Don's face come to focus in his nightmare, after which he wakes up. It is clear to the team leaders that Greg's symptoms of trauma are tied to this incident, as Greg has stated that it really should have been him who died, not Don. Greg had asked Don to drive that day because Greg had been drinking the night before and was hungover. Don had said that he would be glad to cover for his buddy and drive that day. They drove over an explosive device that struck the driver's side of the vehicle. Don was severely injured and unable to get out of the driver's seat. Within minutes his side of the vehicle was engulfed by flames. Greg tried to pull him out but could not because of the heat. He had to get out himself to save his life.

Greg recalls that when the shell took out his buddy, he was unsure whether Don was still alive. He feels he does not deserve to survive and feels tremendous guilt in setting up the death of his mate by asking him to drive. He has carried this guilt and shame for 2 years. In the group he wants to reexperience the explosion, to slow the events down so he can show and explain to the group what happened and how he had tried to save Don. Following the steps of reenactment, Greg and the leader begin to show the group what happened by selecting someone to take the role of Don and someone else to play Greg (a technique known as *doubling*). The rest of the group witnessed what occurred that day.

After the group reenacts the scene, the leaders bring Don back into the group so Greg can tell him directly what he wishes he could have said at the time of attack. Most important, Greg wants Don to know how much he misses him, how guilty he feels asking him to drive, and how it really should have been him that died. Greg adds that life is hardly worth living with the knowledge that Don would still be alive if Greg had not asked him to drive.

Participating in the reenactment permits Greg to do all of this so he can grieve and release the pain he has carried for 2 years. In addition, the reenactment ends with Greg being placed in the role of Don (a technique known as a *role reversal*) so he can speak to the person in the role of Greg. Hence, Greg is able to forgive himself by hearing himself as Don say, "I knew what I was doing when I agreed to drive. I would have done the same thing as you did if the roles had been reversed. It's just the luck of the draw, and that's what we signed up for." Following this re-creation and the release of his grief through bringing back his mate and saying goodbye, the other soldiers each take turns telling Greg that what he did was not his fault but something each of them would have done to back up a buddy when asked.

Hearing the others' input and reactions, which convey understanding and validation of what he feels and what he did, allows Greg to let go of the regret and shame that has troubled him for the past months. In addition, the other guys remind Greg that he did the right thing by not going back into the vehicle to try to pull Don out, as Greg himself would have died also.

In the end, Greg is invited to say goodbye to Don. He tells Don what he valued most about him and what he will carry with him in his memory. After he has said all there is to say, Greg bends down to cover Don's body with a sheet. This registers an end and closure as he stands up and walks away. This completes an unfinished grief reaction that has contributed to Greg's symptoms of posttraumatic stress.

As part of the follow-up several months later, Greg reports that he feels lighter and that his nightmares of Don's face have stopped completely. He is pleased to add that he is sleeping through the night.

TE is well suited to the treatment of combat-related traumas because it is action oriented, requires low verbal expression, involves the support of many others, provides validation and normalization from peers, and has an established support group base for follow-up treatment (Black, 2003; Cave, 2003; Coalson, 1995; Ragsdale, Cox, Finn, & Eisler, 1996; Westwood, Black, & McLean, 2002).

Once they release much of the trauma stored within, participants begin to shift their focus to their future goals and plans (family, school, work, etc.). Consolidating new learning and creating clear achievable goals and objectives for the future is part of the final phase of the VTP. This phase could be referred to as a type of posttraumatic growth phase as described by Tedeschi and Calhoun (2004). Participants are encouraged to discuss and generate life goals, including initiating possible career paths not previously considered. The group ends with members setting up a postgroup network of communication with one another.

Research has demonstrated that there are significant gains for members who have completed the VTP, including a reduction in trauma symptoms, decreased depression, and higher levels of self-esteem (Westwood, McLean, Cave, Borgen, & Slakov, 2010). Once trauma-related symptoms are reduced, there is less life interference and an increased ability to respond to and plan for future life tasks within the family and at work (Westwood et al., 2010). Qualitative outcome studies reinforce the value of the group as a place where clients can be validated by others who have been there. Member-to-member support strengthens clients' sense of confidence to move forward. Having increased skills and knowledge about how to navigate in the civilian world allows them to be better prepared and more effective in the work world. Finally, there are considerable benefits for relationships with spouses and children (McLean, 2005). For further information on how to set up and conduct such a group, please see Westwood et al. (2010).

Conclusion

Viewing military clients through a cross-cultural lens permits counselors to better understand how this client group can become engaged and benefit directly from counseling. Although traditional approaches to counseling have sometimes devalued or been critical of clients with high masculine gender conformity, counseling can be retooled to take advantage of unique masculine language, values, and ways of experiencing emotional pain and coping with distress. Change is required in three primary areas: (a) a new language for the process, (b) an adjusted port of entry for engagement, and (c) the use of culturally appropriate interventions. However, the foundation for effective work with this population, just as with any other cultural group, is built on the existence of high regard and profound respect for the other.

The need to maintain an appearance of stoic competence may make it more difficult for military clients to enter counseling, but once engaged they bring a formidable work ethic and energy to the challenge. Making counseling culturally safe for military clients calls for clinicians to embrace the strengths inherent in traditional masculine gender roles and military cultural norms while helping clients break free of the code of silent stoicism that isolates them when they are in pain.

The benefits of group work for all client groups have been addressed by a number of researchers (e.g., Yalom, 1995). Bringing military clients together to drop baggage is particularly appropriate given that their lives are typically lived in groups and they are very accustomed to the value of helping others in their group. We invite counselors to embrace a different approach to entering the process. We advocate adapting language and interventions so as to mirror the values that already exist in this clientele. These can be integrated into existing helping models to promote change for the military client.

When military clients are able to access therapeutic modalities that allow them to heal from a position of strength, they emerge with dedication and a drive to contribute back to their communities. Empowered and equipped to escape the long tradition of masculine silence and take personal responsibility for their lives, they do not fail to engage in the work they need to do. Rather, as Hollis (1994) observed, they approach their therapeutic work as "the report of a soldier to his general: This is what I did today, this is how I fought the battle in my own sector, these are the obstacles I found, this is how I plan to fight tomorrow" (p. 135).

References

Addis, M., & Mahalik, J. (2003). Men, masculinity, and the contexts of help seeking. *American Psychologist, 58*, 5–14.

Alcock, J. E., Carment, D. W., & Sadava, S. W. (2001). *A textbook of social psychology* (5th ed.). Toronto, Ontario, Canada: Prentice Hall.

Birren, J. E., & Birren, B. E. (1996). Autobiography: Exploring the self and encouraging development. In J. E. Birren, G. M. Kenyon, J. E. Ruth, J. J. F. Schroots, & T. Svensson (Eds.), *Aging and biography: Explorations in adult development* (pp. 283–301). New York, NY: Springer.

Birren, J. E., & Deutchman, D. (1991). *Guiding autobiography groups for older adults.* Baltimore, MD: Johns Hopkins University Press.

Black, T. (2003). *Individual narratives of change in therapeutic enactment.* Unpublished doctoral dissertation, University of British Columbia, Vancouver.

Brooks, G. (2001). Masculinity and men's mental health. *Journal of American College Health, 49,* 285–297.

Brooks, G. R. (2010). *Beyond the crisis of masculinity: A transtheoretical model for male-friendly therapy.* Washington, DC: American Psychological Association.

Brown, L. S. (2008). *Cultural competence in trauma therapy.* Washington, DC: American Psychological Association.

Cave, D. G. (2003). *Enacting change: A therapeutic group-based program for traumatized soldiers.* Unpublished doctoral dissertation, University of British Columbia, Vancouver.

Coalson, B. (1995). Nightmare help: Treatment of trauma survivors with PTSD. *Psychotherapy, 32,* 381–388.

Corey, G. (1990). *Theory and practice of group counseling.* Pacific Grove, CA: Brooks/Cole.

de Vries, B., Birren, J. E., & Deutchman, D. E. (1995). Method and uses of guided autobiography. In B. K. Haight & J. D. Webster (Eds.), *The art and science of reminiscing: Theory, research methods and applications* (pp. 165–178). London, England: Taylor & Francis.

Englar-Carlson, M. (2006). Masculine norms and the counseling process. In M. Englar-Carlson & M. A. Stevens (Eds.), *In the room with men: A casebook of therapeutic change* (pp. 13–47). Washington, DC: American Psychological Association.

Fennell, D. L. (2008, June). Towards recovery and well-being. *Counseling Today Online.* Available from http://ct.counseling.org/2008/06/a-distinct-culture/

Foa, E. B., Keane, T. M., & Friedman, M. J. (2009). *Effective treatments for PTSD: Practice guidelines from the International Society for Traumatic Stress Studies.* New York, NY: Guilford Press.

Fontana, A., & Rosenheck, R. (2001). A model of patients' satisfaction with treatment for posttraumatic stress disorder. *Journal of Administration and Policy in Mental Health and Mental Health Services Research, 28,* 475–489.

Ford, J. D., & Stewart, J. (1999). Group psychotherapy for war-related PTSD with military veterans. In B. H. Young & D. D. Blake (Eds.), *Group treatments for post-traumatic stress disorder* (pp. 75–100). London, England: Taylor & Francis.

Greene, L. R., Meisler, A. W., Pilkey, D., Alexander, G., Cardella, L. A., Sirois, B. C., & Burg, M. M. (2004). Psychological work with groups in the Veterans Administration. In J. L. DeLucia-Waack, D. A. Gerrity, C. R. Kalodner, & M. T. Riva (Eds.), *Handbook of group counseling and psychotherapy* (pp. 322–337). Thousand Oaks, CA. Sage.

Herman, J. (1997). *Trauma and recovery.* New York, NY: Basic Books.

Hoge, C. W., Castro, C. A., Messer, S. C., McGurk, D., Cotting, D. I., & Koffman, R. L. (2004). Combat duty in Iraq and Afghanistan, mental health problems, and barriers to care. *New England Journal of Medicine, 351,* 13–22.

Hollis, J. (1994). *Under Saturn's shadow: The wounding and healing of men.* Toronto, Ontario, Canada: Inner City Books.

McLean, H. (2005). *A narrative study of the spouses of traumatized Canadian soldiers.* Unpublished doctoral dissertation, University of British Columbia, Vancouver.

Ogden, P., & Minton, K. (2000). Sensor motor psychotherapy: One method for processing traumatic memory. *Traumatology, 6,* 3–8.

Owen, J., Wong, J. Y., & Rodolfa, E. R. (2010). The relationship between clients' conformity to masculine norms and their perceptions of helpful therapist actions. *Journal of Counseling Psychology, 57,* 68–78.

Ragsdale, K. G., Cox, R. D., Finn, P., & Eisler, R. M. (1996). Effectiveness of short-term specialized in-patient treatment for war-related posttraumatic stress disorder: A role for adventure-based counseling and psychodrama. *Journal of Traumatic Stress, 9,* 269–283.

Rife, J. (1998). Use of life review techniques to assist older workers coping with job loss and depression. *Clinical Gerontologist, 20,* 75–79.

Rosebush, P. A. (1998). Psychological intervention with military personnel in Rwanda. *Military Medicine, 163,* 559–563.

Rozynko, V., & Dondershine, H. E. (1991). Trauma focus group counseling for Vietnam veterans with PTSD. *Psychotherapy, 28,* 157–161.

Ruzek, J. I., Riney, S. J., Leskin, G., Drescher, K. D., Foy, D. W., & Gusman, F. D. (2001). Do post-traumatic stress disorder symptoms worsen during trauma focus group treatment? *Military Medicine, 166,* 898–902.

Shea, M. T., McDevitt-Murphy, M., Ready, D. J., & Schnurr, P. P. (2009). Group therapy. In E. B. Foa, T. M. Keane, M. J. Friedman, & J. A. Cohen (Eds.), *Effective treatments for PTSD* (pp. 306–326). New York, NY: Guilford Press.

Tedeschi, R. G., & Calhoun, L. G. (2004). Post-traumatic growth: Conceptual foundations and empirical evidence. *Psychological Inquiry, 15,* 1–18.

van der Kolk, B. A. (1987). The role of group in the origin and resolution of the trauma response. In B. A. van der Kolk (Ed.), *Psychological trauma* (pp. 153–172). Washington, DC: American Psychiatric Press.

van der Kolk, B. A., McFarlane, A. C., & Weisaeth, L. (1996). *Traumatic stress: The effects of overwhelming experience on mind, body, and society.* New York, NY: Guilford Press.

Westwood, M. J., Black, T. G., & McLean, H. B. (2002). A re-entry program for peacekeeping soldiers: Promoting personal and career transition. *Canadian Journal of Counseling, 36,* 221–232.

Westwood, M. J., McLean, H. B., Cave, D., Borgen, W., & Slakov, P. (2010). Coming home: A group based approach for assisting military veterans in transition. *Journal for Specialists in Group Work, 35,* 44–68.

Yalom, I. D. (1995). *The theory and practice of group psychotherapy* (4th ed.). New York, NY: Basic Books.

Part
III

The Counselor as
Human Being:
Professional and Personal
Issues in Counseling
Across Cultures

Ethical Issues in Multicultural Counseling

Beth A. Durodoye

In the United States, ethical considerations in counseling have reached a cultural turning point. Society's continually changing demographics have mandated that the profession and its attending ethical processes and procedures be expanded to consider people and situations in broad and intersecting contexts. Hays (2008) guided practitioners to do this with her ADDRESSING model. The name of the model is an acronym for the cultural distinctions of age, developmental and acquired disabilities, religion and spirituality, ethnicity, socioeconomic status, sexual orientation, indigenous heritage, national origin, and gender (Hays, 2008). Although the model does not encompass every identity, counselors are challenged to mind the significance of expanded viewpoints in their work with clients. This chapter captures this philosophy to examine issues, frameworks, and strategies relevant to ethical practice with diverse client populations.

The Nature of Ethics: Principle and Virtue Ethics

Ethics refers to the philosophy of morals and moral choices made by an individual within the context of his or her interactions with others. Issues involving behavior that is good or bad, or right or wrong, play a part in how ethics are viewed (Remley & Herlihy, 2010). In relating this philosophy to the counseling arena, Remley and Herlihy (2010) framed it as those postures judged as good or correct that guide members of the counseling profession. Ethics in the counseling context, then, speaks to one's professional conduct and interactions.

Two important principles are believed to be fundamental to the moral philosophy. First, counseling as a profession has generally aligned itself with principle ethics, which is the model of ethics emphasized in medicine and bioethics (Cottone & Tarvydas, 1998; Urofsky, Engels, & Engebretson, 2008). Principle ethics focuses on the application of the rules and directives that guide one's acts and choices in a given situation (Freeman, 2000). Five duties associated with principle ethics were identified by Kitchener (1984) in her eminent work:

1. *Autonomy.* This principle addresses one's right to self-determination. This right is also accorded to others. Counselors encourage clients to direct their own beliefs and personal courses of action.
2. *Nonmaleficence.* This concept entails doing no harm to others. Counselors shun behaviors that intentionally hurt clients. Counselors also avoid behaviors that risk inflicting harm on others.
3. *Beneficence.* Beneficence refers to the quality of charitableness. Counselors are obligated to contribute to the well-being of clients through good and helpful service.
4. *Justice.* Justice is associated with the idea of fairness. Counselors treat clients in an appropriate manner, all the while weighing equal versus fair versus different treatment.
5. *Fidelity.* Fidelity involves ideas surrounding faithfulness, commitment, and loyalty. Counselors respect their therapeutic obligations and fulfill these obligations in a trustworthy manner.

Remley and Herlihy (2001) added a sixth moral principle that has also been commonly cited in the professional counseling literature, *veracity,* which refers to the quality of truthfulness. Counselors are expected to interface with clients in an honest and factual capacity.

The second moral principle, virtue ethics, incorporates a more global view in its vision. Virtue ethics promotes the idea that ethics are more than just the sum of moral actions. Emphasis is placed on the examination of those personal qualities that will lead one to become a better individual and a productive citizen. A virtue ethics stance is complementary to, albeit totally different from, a principle ethics stance (Meara, Schmidt, & Day, 1996; Urofsky et al., 2008). Virtue ethics considers counselor characteristics integral to responsible practice, whereas principle ethics emphasizes the tangible, concrete, and cognitive aspects of the counseling process (Tarvydas, 1998); virtue ethics embraces the ideals to which counselors aspire, whereas principle ethics are bound by prima facie obligations (Meara et al., 1996); virtue ethics ponders the Aristotelian question "Who shall I be?" rather than the question "What shall I do?" (Vasquez, 1996).

Meara et al. (1996) delineated five characteristics of virtuous agents as well as virtues considered germane to mental health professionals. A virtuous individual (a) is motivated to do good; (b) is clear-sighted; (c) understands how affect influences the assessment of appropriate conduct; (d) is highly self-aware; and (e) is involved in the community and understands the interface between the community and political, economic, and social forces.

The following four virtues are based on those believed by Meara et al. (1996) to contribute to the betterment of ethical decisions and policies and to the improvement of the character of mental health professionals:

1. *Prudence.* This is a multidimensional concept that encompasses planfulness, cautiousness, foresight, and good judgment. Counselors are motivated to do what is good on the basis of sound goals and the deliberate planning it takes to accomplish them.
2. *Integrity.* This virtue involves upholding one's beliefs and integrating them into judgment and action. Counselors have the ability to articulate to others their views of and adherence to moral values.

3. *Respectfulness.* This virtue addresses the respect accorded to another individual on the shared basis of humanness. Counselors believe in the worthiness of others yet are receptive to others' personal views on the meaning of respect and how others might wish to be respected.

4. *Benevolence.* Benevolence means wanting to do good. Counselors protect the welfare of others and contribute to the common good of society.

Meara et al. (1996) contended that an increased focus on virtues may be a reaction to what some consider the extremes of individual rights. As far as multicultural contributions are concerned, Meara et al. believed that a virtue ethics approach emphasizes self- and other awareness, focuses on similarities and differences of cultural groups, promotes the evaluation and development of virtues appropriate to the profession, and considers the inclusion of ideals to ensure that ethical behaviors take place in professional multicultural interactions. Kitchener (1996) stated that too much reliance on community-specific virtues promotes ethnocentrism. She wisely cautioned that "neither principles nor virtues are absolute guarantees of ethical responses to others" (p. 95).

There is room to include both principle and virtue ethics in the philosophical debate concerning the appropriateness of one or the other of these perspectives (Urofsky et al., 2008). A complementary rather than a dichotomous view of these approaches "provides concrete direction to virtuous traits and prudence to principles and rules" (Freeman, 2000, p. 97).

Ethical Guidelines and Multicultural Counseling

A code of ethics is a written document of ethical standards and guidelines meant for particular professionals. The code of ethics used by professional counselors is the *ACA Code of Ethics* (American Counseling Association [ACA], 2005). These guidelines encompass measures of protection, education, accountability, motivation, regulation, and stabilization for professional counselors and the public they serve (Remley & Herlihy, 2010).

The historical path toward multiculturally sensitive ACA ethical guidelines has been circuitous. Watson, Herlihy, and Pierce (2006) described this journey as beginning in 1961 with the publication of the first American Personnel and Guidance Association (now ACA) code of ethics. This code contained no references to cultural awareness. However, the 1974 revision of the American Personnel and Guidance Association code of ethics referred twice to diverse clients in its Measurement and Evaluation section. In addition to these two references, a third reference was included in the third revision of the code in 1981. This additional standard urged counselors to be aware of the ways in which discrimination and stereotyping can impact the counseling dynamic.

The 1995 ACA *Code of Ethics and Standards of Practice* was the fourth revision of this code and the first to directly address multicultural issues (Watson et al., 2006). The *Code's* preamble stated, "Association members recognize diversity in our society and embrace a cross-cultural approach in support of the worth, dignity, potential, and uniqueness of each individual" (ACA, 1995, p. 1). Threaded throughout this code were 13 standards that highlighted cultural diversity (Welfel, as cited in Watson et al., 2006).

Despite these efforts, the 1995 *Code* continued to be criticized for its lack of cultural foresight (Watson et al., 2006; Wiggins Frame & Braun Williams, 2005). The Western views that permeate principalism were in some cases antithetical to non-Western views. For example, ethnic minority groups traditionally stress group cooperativeness rather than individual feats. Intuitiveness may be valued over rationality. Religion and spirituality may not be considered distinct from the self but an everyday and holistic part of the self. Meara et al. (1996) related that principalism emphasizes autonomy and self-determinism over communal issues. Its rational framework deemphasizes emotionalism. Secularism competes with spiritual wisdom. In essence, it promotes myopic ethical objectives. Given these and like points, the 10-year revision of the 1995 *Code* portended a redress of such criticisms.

During his tenure as ACA President in 2002, David Kaplan created a 10-member ACA Ethics Code Revision Task Force that was specifically charged with attending to issues of multiculturalism, diversity, and social justice (Kaplan et al., 2009; Kocet, 2006; Watson et al., 2006). Task Force member Courtland Lee stated that the work of the committee was guided by two questions that encompassed (a) a need to consider the impact of demographics on multicultural considerations and (b) an examination of any missing code components that would add cultural inclusiveness (Kaplan et al., 2009).

New or revised standards oriented toward diversity can be found throughout the *ACA Code of Ethics* (ACA, 2005). Examples include Standard A.1.d., which has been revised to emphasize "Support Network Involvement" rather than "Family Involvement," particularly because a client's source of personal support may encompass more than his or her biological family (Glosoff & Kocet, 2006). New to the 2005 *Code* is Standard F.11.c ("Multicultural/Diversity Competence"). This standard directs counselor educators to incorporate multicultural and diversity competencies into their work with students in the classroom, in supervision, and in any other teaching capacities (Kaplan et al., 2009). Standard A.6.a. ("Advocacy") is also new to the 2005 *Code* (Kocet, 2009). Though multicultural counseling and advocacy are separate entities, they are intertwined. When issues of power, privilege, and the "isms" (e.g., ableism, classism, sexism, racism) arise, counselors may be called on to address client issues at successively broader levels. This standard allows the counselor to focus on the systemic as well as individual contexts that may inhibit client growth.

A Dilemma to Contemplate

Dr. Taft began his career as a counselor educator 32 years ago. He has seen many changes take place in the field over that period of time. He believes that some of those changes have been creeping into the way he runs his class, which he is not too happy about. Just last week a student came to him during his office hours to talk about accommodations because of her learning disability. Dr. Taft told the student that no accommodations were necessary because he taught class in a way that everyone could understand. Apparently the student did not like that answer and reported him to his chair and to the Disability Office. First the chair and then a Disability Office representative contacted Dr. Taft to discuss the matter and offer suggestions about how to promote a more sensitive classroom style. Following these conversations, Dr. Taft thought, "I've been teaching this long to all kinds of students, and now someone has to tell me how to do things the correct way? I'm a counselor—now I have to be a social worker, too?" Dr. Taft has summarily dismissed the conversation because "someone has to take a stand." He is tired of all the treatment "those disabled students get anyway" and believes that most of them are just trying to cheat the system. He goes on to think, "When will all the social politics in the classroom end?"

Multicultural Analysis and Synthesis

Dr. Taft brings decades of experience to his job as a counselor educator. Unfortunately, he is willing to be neither understanding nor flexible in addressing multicultural issues in the classroom. Rather than speak to the needs of his student, he has chosen to take the situation personally. Dr. Taft has dismissed the student's request and taken those of his chair and the Disability Office representative as affronts rather than as constructive criticism. It appears that he is also questioning issues of professional identity as well as what role advocacy plays in his classroom. Ethically speaking, it would behoove Dr. Taft to review two particular sections of the *ACA Code of Ethics*. Section F.11.b. ("Student Diversity") includes the statements that "counselor educators demonstrate commitment to multicultural/diversity competence by recognizing and valuing diverse cultures and types of abilities students bring to the training experience. Counselor educators provide appropriate accommodations that enhance and support diverse student well-being and academic performance" (ACA, 2005, p. 16). Dr. Taft also needs to review Section A.6.a. ("Advocacy"), given the importance of addressing the individual-level barriers that he has enacted that prevent his student from accessing learning opportunities. In addition, Dr. Taft's language is biased. In his musings about the student, he defines her by her disability, rather than by her individuality (Sue & Sue, 2008). The use of people-first language (i.e., "person with a disability" instead of "disabled person") is most appropriate. Hopefully, Dr. Taft will take the time to consider what is being asked of him by his student, chair, and university representative. Failing to do so would be an ethical breach. Moreover, his stand may prove to be a legal breach as well.

Selected Practice Issues in Multicultural Counseling

The Counseling Relationship

The counseling profession struggles with questions, concerns, and inquiries regarding counseling relationships (Glosoff & Freeman, 2007; Herlihy & Watson, 2003). From a multicultural perspective, differences between individualist and collectivist perspectives have been a source of tension (Herlihy & Watson, 2003). Helms and Cook (1999) confronted the issue of dual relationships as related to considerations of race, culture, and multiple relationships at a time when counselors were ethically bound to avoid such relationships if at all possible. The authors stated that although they adamantly endorsed the principle of doing no harm to clients, they did believe that "relationships outside of the therapy room per se need not harm the client. Rather, we view such interactions, when handled properly, as extensions of the therapeutic relationship" (p. 196).

After years of contemplation, significant ethical changes have now taken place with regard to this issue. One such change, located in Section A of the *ACA Code of Ethics* (ACA, 2005), is the use of the descriptive terms "potentially beneficial interactions" or "roles and relationships" versus the more questionable term "dual relationships" (Kaplan et al., 2009, p. 244).

This change of events validates examples of multiple role considerations that may be found in the African American community (Parham, 1997). Ideas of collectiveness and interconnectedness are central to the African worldview. The ethics that guide this thinking are concerned with proper ways of being rather than with Western principles that seek to control behavior. The traditional expectation for African Americans is that they will help others. This might involve them assuming multiple roles, such as supporter adviser, protector, and instructor. As persons interact with one another in these capacities, the positive intent of the helper is stressed over the possibility of exploitation. There is the likelihood, then, that a counselor would be expected to participate in multiple roles, especially if both the counselor and the client believed the relationship to be in the best interest of the client.

Evaluation, Assessment, and Interpretation

Because of biases in mental health treatment, diverse populations have been psychiatrically mislabeled and treated on the basis of mainstream definitions of what is normal. A Mexican

American woman who resides at home with her parents until she marries is not necessarily displaying enmeshed tendencies. Her living situation may be a result of a gender-role expectation in her family, of which she approves. Symptoms of major depression in a 76-year-old adult male should not be ignored or simply attributed to the aging process. Assessment and treatment may be warranted, as these symptoms are not a natural part of getting older. For some individuals who hail from the southern United States, hearing the voice of very close but recently deceased relative does not necessarily denote schizophrenia. This may be a self-expressive state that is condoned in the respective culture during trying life events. All traditional Sioux folk healers should not be dismissed as charlatans. These professionals may be part of a client's support system and act as a point of therapeutic intervention in conjunction with the work of the therapist.

Sue and Sue (2008) noted that in addition to differential diagnoses, ethnic minorities have tended to receive less favored treatment modalities. Section E.5.b. ("Cultural Sensitivity") of the *ACA Code of Ethics* asks counselors to be cognizant of how culture impacts a client's perceptions of his or her problems. Moreover, Section E.5.c. ("Historical and Social Prejudices in the Diagnosis of Pathology") reminds counselors that there are "historical and social prejudices in the misdiagnosis and pathologizing of certain individuals and groups and the role of mental health professionals in perpetuating these prejudices through diagnosis and treatment" (ACA, 2005, p. 12).

In 1979, a decision was rendered in California in the case of *Larry P v. Wilson Riles*. Litigation was focused on the disproportionate representation of minority children in educably mentally retarded special education classes (Lambert, 1981). The use of IQ tests to place children in these classes was ruled unconstitutional if the use of the tests resulted in the disproportionate placement of African American children in these classes. This case is a classic example of how sectors of ethnic minority populations can be tested and subsequently labeled on the basis of mainstream normative measures. Section E.6.c. ("Culturally Diverse Populations") of the *ACA Code of Ethics* states, "Counselors are cautious when selecting assessments for culturally diverse populations to avoid the use of instruments that lack appropriate psychometric properties for the client population" (ACA, 2005, p. 12). Section E.8. ("Multicultural Issues/Diversity in Assessment") addresses diversity in assessment and states the following:

> Counselors use with caution assessment techniques that were normed on populations other than that of the client. Counselors recognize the effects of age, color, culture, disability, ethnic group, gender, race, language preference, religion, spirituality, sexual orientation and socioeconomic status on test administration and interpretation, and place test results in proper perspective with other relevant factors. (ACA, 2005, p. 13)

Counselors also need to understand that the idea of counseling may vary depending on one's background. Some clients may not be familiar with the process of counseling as it is traditionally known and practiced in the United States. For example, the Babalawo is a traditional Yoruba healer in Nigeria, West Africa. This individual works from a holistic perspective and is perceived to have powers that can be used to call on the client's ancestors to facilitate the wellness process for that individual. In this instance, the expectations of a counselor that a traditional Yoruba client residing in the United States and a traditionally trained U.S. counselor would have would diverge. Thus, the counselor cannot assume that the client has been informed about his or her qualifications to work with diverse populations, the goals and procedures of the process, or treatment outcomes.

Supervision, Training, and Teaching

Counselors' roles and responsibilities may be quite varied in their work with counselors-in-training. These professional relationships are often manifested in the form of supervisor, educator, trainer, and advocate. In focusing on the supervisory relationship, Section F.2.a. ("Supervisor Preparation") of the *ACA Code of Ethics* states, "Prior to offering clinical supervision services, counselors are trained in supervision methods and techniques. Counselors who offer clinical supervision services regularly pursue continuing education activities including both counseling and supervision topics and skills" (ACA, 2005, p. 14). This section does not stand alone, however, as Section F.2.b. ("Multicultural Issues/Diversity in Supervision") goes on to state, "Counseling supervisors are aware of and address the role of multiculturalism/diversity in the supervisory relationship" (p. 14). Clearly, an integral part of ethical supervisor training involves paying attention to multicultural competence.

It is ironic that little attention has been given specifically to the counselor educator's awareness of her or his own prejudices (Brown & Landrum-Brown, 1995; Midgette & Meggert, 1991), as much of the literature in this area is tilted toward counselor training. This situation is changing for counseling professionals, though, as new multicultural competency literature, research, and ensuing conversations are put forth (Holcomb-McCoy, 2004; Utsey, Ponterotto, & Porter, 2008).

Henderson (2009) provided one such conversation with her comprehensive look at the culturally skilled supervisor. Culturally astute supervision includes three main ideas, each with related areas of concentration. The first involves the manifestation of *cultural responsiveness*. This refers to an awareness that supervisors, supervisees, and clients are all part of a larger multicultural context. It is necessary to acknowledge this broader environment while at the same time understanding that clients are unique in their individual experiences. Counselors risk alienating clients if they ignore, downplay, or minimize the salience of their clients' identities.

Second is the importance of supervisors accepting responsibility for their supervisees' cultural competencies (Henderson, 2009). This involves providing ethical and multicultural competency resources. Supervisors must also assist their supervisees in appropriately communicating with diverse populations in verbal and nonverbal capacities. Supervisees must then take this information into consideration as they continue to gather knowledge and understanding about the various cultural facets of specific populations.

Third is a focus on the strategies that undergird a culturally responsive supervisor, supervisee, and client support system (Henderson, 2009). Henderson promotes departmental commitment to the affirmation of diversity by way of philosophical stance, belief system, and modeling. Supervisors are also encouraged to continuously self-examine through professional development opportunities. Recruiting, employing, and retaining departmental staff that are representative of the client base also demonstrates cultural commitment. This extends as well to an assessment of culturally relevant service delivery systems that interface with the department.

There is no question that the field of multicultural counseling is now an established discipline. This means that serious and deliberate training in this area involves more than topical attention. A counselor who chooses to work behind a facade of multicultural competency is committing academic fraud. Sue and Sue (2008) reminded counseling professionals that the courage to acknowledge one's own multicultural liabilities is a strength and an ethical responsibility.

A Dilemma to Contemplate

Tanis Johnson is a 42-year-old counseling student who is near the end of her master's program. She is currently enrolled in a practicum course. For the past 3 months she has been working with a 24-year-old man who has struggled to overcome personal and financial hardships at home that have affected his performance at work. Since coming to counseling, the client has made excellent progress, and now he is even being promoted on the job. The client believes he is ready to terminate his counseling sessions, as does Ms. Johnson, and a final session is scheduled. When they meet for the final time, Ms. Johnson would like to give him a gift, which is not unheard of in her Native American culture. She has the perfect one in mind—an inexpensive plaque that says "I Did It." As she was driving to the mall to purchase the gift she cringed and thought that giving a client a gift might not be such a good idea. She also remembered that the *ACA Code of Ethics* says something about gift giving. Ms. Johnson immediately turned around, drove home, and called her supervisor to set up an appointment to talk about her sudden quandary.

Multicultural Analysis and Synthesis

Ms. Johnson is to be commended for her attentiveness to ethical issues and the role they play in her practicum experience. It appears that she and her client have been working closely together to help him achieve his goals. She would like to commemorate his efforts on the last day they will be meeting. At the same time, she is feeling enough discomfort to check in with her practicum supervisor about her idea.

At their meeting, Ms. Johnson's supervisor informs her that although there is no specific section in the *ACA Code of Ethics* about counselors giving gifts, they could be guided by Section A.10.e. ("Receiving Gifts"), which highlights the acceptance of gifts from clients. The supervisor helps Ms. Johnson to see that there are times when accepting or even giving a gift to a client may be appropriate. To help Ms. Johnson decide whether to give a gift, her supervisor asks her to further explore her relationship with her client, how much the gift will cost, and the reason Ms. Johnson believes it is important to give the gift. Her supervisor also tells her that she will need to document this interaction in her notes. After some thought, Ms. Johnson comes to the conclusion that in this case maybe the gift giving was more about her own personal expectations than something that was therapeutically necessary. With the help of her supervisor, Ms. Johnson looks at how she can structure her termination session to more appropriately focus on the needs of her client.

Research and Publication

The amount of research encompassing mental health and diverse populations has seen a significant increase in the past 40 years (Trimble, 2010). Concomitant to this development is unease among diverse groups about the nature of this research and the researchers themselves (Trimble, 2010). This unease is not unfounded. Examples of the negative treatment of various cultural groups by researchers abound, as do examples of research that ranges from questionable to nefarious. For example, the Tuskegee syphilis experiment was conducted over a period of 40 years (beginning in 1932) on approximately 600 African American men who had contracted syphilis (Sue & Sue, 2008), and the 1970 Tearoom Trade study examined 100 male sexual encounters in public restrooms (Humphreys, 1970). Finally, renowned anesthetist Henry Beechler wrote an article in 1966 that exposed the use of unethical medical practices with unsuspecting patients, many of them adults and children with intellectual disabilities and older persons (Harkness, Lederer, & Wikler, 2001).

The introduction of Section G ("Research and Publication") of the *ACA Code of Ethics* stresses, in part, that "counselors minimize bias and respect diversity in designing and implementing research programs" (ACA, 2005, p. 16). Moreover, Section G.1.g. ("Multicultural/Diversity Considerations in Research") states that "when appropriate to research goals, counselors are sensitive to incorporating research procedures that take into account cultural considerations. They seek consultation when appropriate" (p. 17). This stance leads the way to responsible scholarly inquiry. Sue and Sue (2008) aptly pointed out that research is a powerful and useful tool that can be used to inform, rather than misinform, the literature.

Ethical Decision Making

In the face of an ethical breach, ethical codes can seem daunting. Cottone, Tarvydas, and Claus (2007) reframed this situation by stating that "ethical dilemmas are not so much a failure of ethical codes as a natural and appropriate juncture of recognizing the importance of professional judgment" (p. 86). The juncture that Cottone et al. mentioned comprises the process of ethical decision making. It is a process that links the use of teaching and learning skills to the counselor's own intuitive inferences.

Numerous counseling and psychology models are available to guide counselors in their determination of appropriate courses of action in the wake of ethical dilemmas (Cottone & Claus, 2000). These models represent theoretical, practice-based, and specialty practice conceptualizations (Cottone & Claus, 2000; Cottone et al., 2007). In their look toward future directions for multicultural ethics, LaFromboise, Foster, and James (1996) called for the resolution of ethical problems through new or different approaches that consider culturally astute moral reasoning within social environments such as the workplace, professional organizations, and the broader community.

One answer to this call seems to lie in the area of postmodernism in counseling. One psychological construct borne out of this trend is social constructivism. This idea contends that reality is construed from the conversations of people (Nystul, 1999). Nystul (1999) noted that the theory suggests that "human experience is a highly individualized process based contextually on the interactions of cognition, social-cultural forces, language, and narratives. Knowledge and the concept of 'truth' are therefore subjective and generate the possibility of multiple realities" (p. 69). The counseling process in this context focuses on an exploration of personal narratives to elicit insights that generate new personal perspectives. The ready acknowledgment of culture and language as components to this conceptual rubric is a powerful fit for the multicultural counseling discipline.

A Postmodern Ethical Decision-Making Approach

Postmodernist thinking is central to Cottone's (2001) proposal of a social constructivist approach to the ethical decision-making process. Several decision-making models have been construed as autonomous (Cottone, 2001; Sperry, 2007), with an abundance of attention paid to individual, intrapsychic, and intuitive processes, thereby deemphasizing an interpersonal process. This is a reflection of the Western worldview that permeates the counseling process and that is, in some cases, antithetical to non-Western views.

The social constructivist position to ethical decision making stresses group and cooperative work values. This position maintains that there is no absolute reality; there are several ways in which the world can be understood. Reality is considered to be the outcome of the interaction and construction of a people's understanding of the world. Social constructivism also asserts that certain understandings prevail in a given field because they serve a function. Lastly, social constructivism dictates that one's understanding of the world has direct implications for one's perceptions of and responses to the environment. Following this mode of thought, Cottone and Claus (2000) indicated that "the social constructivism perspective of the ethical decision making takes the decision out of the 'head,' so to speak, and places it in the interactive process between people" (p. 277). Exemplifying this philosophical concept is Cottone's Social Constructivism Model of Ethical Decision Making (Cottone, 2001; Cottone et al., 2007).

Cottone's (2001) model incorporates multicultural elements into the definition of good ethical procedure. Cottone et al. (2007) underlined the model's connection to relational theory, infusion of diversity, and acknowledgement of multicultural limitations. The model is composed of five steps: (a) gathering information from each party, (b) assessing the nature of current relationships, (c) consulting professional peers and experts (this includes ethical standards and other pertinent literature), (d) negotiating when disagreement exists, and (e) responding in a consensual fashion about continued negotiation (Cottone, 2001). A lack of consensus entails continued negotiation, consensus, or possible arbitration (Cottone, 2001). These steps are illuminated in the next section.

A Postmodern Ethical Decision-Making Model in Action

Case Study

Mrs. Anita McKee is a high school counselor who has worked in the field for 11 years. She is the assigned counselor for Khaleem Jackson, a ninth grader who is new to the district. Khaleem came to her office the first week in November to tell her that a girl in one of his classes was bothering him. On further questioning, Khaleem stated that the student, who happened to be White, was calling him "monkeyish" and making remarks that Black people were no good. Mrs. McKee told Khaleem that she would look into the situation. The next week, Khaleem came back to her office to tell her that the girl would not stop with the comments. Now she was saying that he was a "Black ass" and that he had "big Black people lips three times bigger" than hers. Mrs. McKee appeared worried and said that she would think about what needed to be done. In the meantime, Khaleem's mother called Mrs. McKee and said that her son had told her he was being called derogatory names by a certain female student. Mrs. McKee acknowledged that Khaleem had notified her of the incidents and expressed her concerns to the mother. She told the mother that she was a little torn about what to do, as "it's probably just a situation where the young woman is attracted to Khaleem and doesn't know how to express herself appropriately. You know how kids are at that age." Mrs. McKee went on to say that she sure hoped it was not anything more serious than that. Khaleem's mother became upset and demanded that something be done, as she believed her son was being harassed. When Mrs. McKee was again contacted by Khaleem's mother early the following week, Mrs. McKee stated that she had decided to call the young woman into her office and tell her "in no uncertain terms" that she was bothering Khaleem. Unfortunately, the young woman became angry at Khaleem for telling on her and enlisted the help of some of her friends to make fun of Khaleem, throw things at him, and continue with the name calling when their teacher was not around. When Khaleem and his mother reported this, Mrs. McKee stated that she planned to bring Khaleem and the young woman in for a mediation session. At that point, Khaleem's mother told Mrs. McKee that she was going to report her unethical behavior to her supervisor and then the school board.

Multicultural Analysis and Synthesis

This is a case in which ignoring or downplaying racial issues has caused a situation to spiral out of control. Rather than immediately confronting the harassment that Khaleem was experiencing, the counselor chose to ignore his complaints over a period of weeks. Mrs. McKee tentatively committed to taking action only after a second visit from the student and a call from his mother. It appears that on some level Mrs. McKee was aware of the racial elements of the case but chose to provide a less threatening reason for the young woman's behavior—a teenage crush. The counselor's solutions to the harassment only became more tenuous as the situation became more problematic and, consequently, more insulting to Khaleem and his mother. Mrs. McKee worked to keep the situation quiet and contained, thereby limiting the number of effective options for all concerned.

In contrast, handling this case from a social constructivist decision model perspective involves understanding that steps need to be actively taken to resolve the situation in a collective and culturally sensitive manner. This would involve a supervisor meeting separately with Mrs. McKee, Khaleem and his mother, and the young woman in Khaleem's class to get their interpretation of events (gathering information from those involved). If Mrs. McKee and the student do not deny the charges made by Khaleem and his mother (assessing the nature of the relationship), the supervisor would proceed to the next phase. In Mrs. McKee's situation, the supervisor can seek the opinion of colleagues regarding the case, which should be presented anonymously (consulting colleagues). It would also be important for the supervisor to be familiar with the *ACA Code of Ethics* (consulting the ethical standards), particularly Sections A.1.a. ("Primary Responsibility"), A.4.b. ("Personal Values"), and C.2.a. ("Boundaries of Competence"). Should the supervisor conclude that the counselor did not behave in an ethical manner, he or she would meet with Mrs. McKee to discuss this as well as the issue of the appropriate handling of racial harassment complaints. The supervisor would point out that Mrs. McKee's ethical actions, or lack thereof, around these blatantly racial incidents served as a barrier to a student's safety and equitable access to learning. These actions include Mrs. McKee's inappropriate suggestion that Khaleem meet with the young woman in question for mediation in this type of case instead of a solid reprimand to the young woman and parental notification. Mrs. McKee would also be reprimanded for her lack of school protocol in harassment situations.

The supervisor would also need to meet with Khaleem and his mother to inform them of how the school will handle the process from this point forward (negotiation). It would be important to acknowledge Khaleem and his mother for bringing the racial harassment incident to the school's attention as they sought to rectify the situation. The supervisor would also inform Khaleem and his mother that this situation is now being actively addressed with his counselor, the young woman, and her parents. Should both Khaleem and his mother be satisfied with this intervention, the case would close, although follow-up with both parties would be encouraged. If at any point in the process there is disagreement with those involved, continued negotiation and even arbitration would be warranted (negotiation, consentualization).

Clearly, this episode and others like it do not have to be swept under the rug or the participants placated or dealt with intrapsychically. This case was resolved in a private and consensual manner, all in the midst of a highly social, interactive, and culturally astute process.

Conclusion

Ethics in multicultural counseling is an ever-changing enterprise. Nested within the considerations for diverse cultural elements may be issues of power, privilege, and oppression to which counselors must attend. Responsible ethical practice, then, demands responsible multicultural and advocacy sensibilities. These process and procedural efforts require a deliberate and focused use of the counselor's time, effort, and skills. Counselors who are versed in these fundamentals prepare themselves to take on ethical issues in a multicultural context, regardless of what form they take. This stance serves to uphold the spirit and practice of the *ACA Code of Ethics* (ACA, 2005) to more fully address the well being of clients and society.

References

American Counseling Association. (1995). *Code of ethics and standards of practice.* Alexandria, VA: Author.

American Counseling Association. (2005). *ACA code of ethics.* Alexandria, VA: Author.

Brown, M. T., & Landrum-Brown, J. (1995). Counselor supervision. In J. G. Ponterotto, J. M. Casas, L. A. Suzuki, & C. M. Alexander (Eds.), *Handbook of multicultural counseling* (pp. 263–285). Thousand Oaks, CA: Sage.

Cottone, R. R. (2001). A social constructivism model of ethical and professional issues in counseling. *Journal of Counseling & Development, 79,* 39–45.

Cottone, R. R., & Claus, R. E. (2000). Ethical decision-making models: A review of the literature. *Journal of Counseling & Development, 78,* 275–283.

Cottone, R. R., & Tarvydas, V. M. (Eds.). (1998). *Ethical and professional issues in counseling.* Upper Saddle River, NJ: Prentice Hall.

Cottone, R. R., Tarvydas, V., & Claus, R. E. (2007). Ethical decision-making processes. In R. R. Cottone & V. M. Tarvydas (Eds.), *Ethical and professional issues in counseling* (3rd ed., pp. 85–113). Upper Saddle River, NJ: Pearson Education.

Freeman, S. J. (2000). *Ethics: An introduction to philosophy and practice.* Belmont, CA: Wadsworth.

Glosoff, H. L., & Freeman, L. T. (2007). Report of the ACA Ethics Committee: 2005–2006. *Journal of Counseling & Development, 85,* 251–254.

Glosoff, H. L., & Kocet, M. M. (2006). Highlights of the 2005 *ACA Code of Ethics.* In G. R. Walz, J. C. Bleuer, & R. K. Yep (Eds.), *Vistas: Compelling perspectives on counseling, 2006* (pp. 5–10). Alexandria, VA: American Counseling Association.

Harkness, T., Lederer, S. E., & Wikler, D. (2001). Laying ethical foundations for clinical research. *Bulletin of the World Health Organization, 79,* 365–372.

Hays, P. A. (2008). *Addressing cultural complexities in practice* (2nd ed.). Washington, DC: American Psychological Association.

Helms, J. E., & Cook, D. A. (1999). *Using race and culture in counseling and psychotherapy: Theory and process.* Boston, MA: Allyn & Bacon.

Henderson, P. G. (2009). *The new handbook of administrative supervision in counseling.* New York, NY: Routledge.

Herlihy, B., & Watson, Z. E. (2003). Ethical issues and multicultural competence in counseling. In F. D. Harper & J. McFadden (Eds.), *Culture and counseling: New approaches* (pp. 363–378). Boston, MA: Pearson Education.

Holcomb-McCoy, C. (2004). Assessing the multicultural competence of school counselors: A checklist. *Professional School Counseling, 7,* 178–183.

Humphreys, L. (1970). *Tearoom trade: Impersonal sex in public places.* Chicago, IL: Aldine.

Kaplan, D. M., Kocet, M. M., Cottone, R. R., Glosoff, H. L., Miranti, J. G., Moll, E. C., . . . Tarvydas, V. M. (2009). New mandates and imperatives in the revised *ACA Code of Ethics. Journal of Counseling & Development, 87,* 241–256.

Kitchener, K. S. (1984). Intuition, critical evaluation, and ethical principles: The foundation for ethical decisions in counseling psychology. *The Counseling Psychologist, 12,* 43–55. doi:10.1177/0011000084123005

Kitchener, K. S. (1996). There is more to ethics than principles. *The Counseling Psychologist, 24,* 92–97. doi:10.1177/0011000096241005

Kocet, M. M. (2006). Ethical challenges in a complex world: Highlights of the 2005 *ACA Code of Ethics. Journal of Counseling & Development, 84,* 228–234.

Kocet, M. M. (2009). Multicultural ethical perspectives. In C. C. Lee, D. A. Burnhill, A. L. Butler, C. P. Hippolito-Delgado, J. Humphrey, O. Munoz, & J. Shin (Eds.), *Elements of culture in counseling* (pp. 193–210). Upper Saddle River, NJ: Pearson Education.

LaFromboise, T. D., Foster, S., & James, A. (1996). Ethics in multicultural counseling. In P. B. Pedersen, J. G. Draguns, W. J. Lonner, & J. E. Trimble (Eds.), *Counseling across cultures* (4th ed., pp. 47–72). Thousand Oaks, CA: Sage.

Lambert, N. M. (1981). Psychological evidence in *Larry P v. Wilson Riles:* An evaluation by a witness for the defense. *American Psychologist, 36,* 937–952. doi:10.1037/0003-066X.36.9.937

Meara, N. M., Schmidt, L. D., & Day, J. K. (1996). Principles and virtues: A foundation for ethical decisions, policies, and character. *The Counseling Psychologist, 24,* 4–77. doi:10.1177/0011000096241002

Midgette, T. E., & Meggert, S. S. (1991). Multicultural counseling instructions: A challenge for faculties in the 21st century. *Journal of Counseling & Development, 70,* 136–141.

Nystul, M. S. (1999). *Introduction to counseling: An art and science perspective.* New York, NY: Allyn & Bacon.

Parham, T. A. (1997). An African-centered view of dual relationships. In B. Herlihy & G. Corey (Eds.), *Boundary issues in counseling* (pp. 109–112). Alexandria, VA: American Counseling Association.

Remley, T. P., & Herlihy, B. (2001). *Ethical, legal, and professional issues in counseling* (1st ed.). Upper Saddle River, NJ: Prentice Hall.

Remley, T. P., Jr., & Herlihy, B. (2010). *Ethical, legal, and professional issues in counseling* (3rd ed.). Upper Saddle River, NJ: Pearson Education.

Sperry, L. (2007). Multicultural, relational, and spiritual issues in ethics. In L. Sperry (Ed.), *The ethical and professional practice of counseling and psychotherapy* (pp. 37–52). Boston, MA: Pearson Education.

Sue, D. W., & Sue, D. (2008). *Counseling the culturally diverse: Theory and practice* (5th ed.). New York, NY: Wiley.

Tarvydas, V. M. (1998). Ethical decision-making processes. In R. R. Cottone & V. M. Tarvydas (Eds.), *Ethical and professional issues in counseling* (pp. 144–155). Upper Saddle River, NJ: Prentice Hall.

Trimble, J. E. (2010). The principled conduct of counseling research with ethnocultural populations: The influence of moral judgments on scientific reasoning. In J. G. Ponterotto, J. M. Casas, L. A. Suzuki, & C. M. Alexander (Eds.), *Handbook of multicultural counseling* (3rd ed., pp. 147–161). Thousand Oaks, CA: Sage.

Urofsky, R. I., Engels, D. W., & Engebretson, K. (2008). Kitchener's principle ethics: Implications for counseling practice and research. *Counseling and Values, 53,* 67–78.

Utsey, S. O., Ponterotto, J. G., & Porter, J. S. (2008). Prejudice and racism, year 2008—Still going strong: Research on reducing prejudice with recommended methodological advances. *Journal of Counseling & Development, 86,* 339–347.

Vasquez, M. J. T. (1996). Will virtue ethics improve ethical conduct in multicultural settings and interactions? *The Counseling Psychologist, 24,* 98–104 doi:10.1177/0011000096241006

Watson, Z. E. P., Herlihy, B. R., & Pierce, L. A. (2006). Forging the link between multicultural competence and ethical counseling practice: A historical perspective. *Counseling and Values, 2,* 99–107.

Wiggins Frame, M., & Braun Williams, C. (2005). A model of ethical decision making from a multicultural perspective. *Counseling and Values, 3,* 165–179.

Additional Resources

The following websites provide additional information related to ethics and multicultural counseling.

ACA Code of Ethics
http://www.counseling.org/Resources/CodeOfEthics/TP/Home/CT2.aspx

Association for Multicultural Counseling and Development
http://www.amcdaca.org/amcd/default.cfm

Counselors for Social Justice
http://counselorsforsocialjustice.com/

Ethics Updates
http://ethics.sandiego.edu

Multicultural Pavilion
http://www.edchange.org/multicultural/

National Institute of Mental Health
www.nimh.nih.gov

National Institute for Multicultural Competence
http://www.coedu.usf.edu/zalaquett/nimc/nimc.html

Southern Poverty Law Center
www.splcenter.org

Global Literacy:
The Foundation of
Culturally Competent Counseling

Courtland C. Lee

If you were playing Trivial Pursuit, the popular game that tests a player's ability to answer general knowledge and popular culture questions, would you know the answers to the following questions?[1]

- Who is August Wilson?
- What happened at the Stonewall Inn in New York City on June 28, 1969?
- What is Public Law 94-142?
- What is *Sábado Gigante?*
- What is a burka?
- Who is Jim Thorpe?
- Who is Jaime Escalante?
- What is the major theme of the play *Angels in America?*

You might ask, "What does knowing the answers to these questions have to do with being a culturally competent counselor?" The answer is—everything. Knowing the answers to questions such as these underscores the entire concept of multicultural competency, as it suggests an awareness of important cultural and historical figures as well as events that impact the realities of people from a number of diverse groups. It is impossible to be a culturally competent counselor in a globally interconnected world without having a passing knowledge of the historical, sociological, political, and economic dynamics that form the foundation of diverse cultural contexts.

---

[1] The answers to these questions can be found in Appendix 19.1 (pp. 313–314).

Ideally, therefore, in order to be truly multiculturally competent as a professional counselor, one should spend years studying history, anthropology, sociology, economics, religion, politics, and any number of other social science disciplines in an attempt to develop the knowledge base to truly understand the cultural dynamics of diverse groups of people. Or one could commit oneself to living a life that is truly open to experiencing cultural diversity in all of its many facets. The purpose of this chapter is to examine the nature of such commitment. This chapter introduces the concept of global literacy and explores its role as a foundational aspect of not only multicultural counseling competency but a way of life consistent with the diverse realities of the 21st century.

Global Literacy Defined

Global literacy is the breadth of information that extends over the major domains of human diversity. It consists of the basic information that a person needs to know in order to successfully navigate life in the technologically sophisticated, globally interconnected world of the 21st century, a world in which people from diverse cultural backgrounds interact in ways that were inconceivable in previous centuries. The concept of global literacy can be seen as a logical progression of the ideas first advanced by E. D. Hirsch (1987) in his controversial book *Cultural Literacy: What Every American Needs to Know*. Hirsch conducted a critical analysis of American education and concluded that educational failure among youth in the United States could be attributable to large gaps in the youths' basic knowledge of geography, history, literature, politics, and democratic principles. Hirsch advocated for the development of a core knowledge base that could be taught across schools in the United States. Hirsch stated that this knowledge base would promote the development of cultural literacy among students. The major thrust of Hirsch's argument was underscored by a list he developed with hundreds of names, dates, places, and events that he stated represented the core body of knowledge for a culturally literate individual.

A review of Hirsch's list would suggest that it is very heavily weighted with items that promote a core knowledge base that is strongly Eurocentric in nature and generally does not reflect many of the contemporary issues so important for life in the 21st century. Therefore, any revisions of such a list should reflect the global nature of contemporary U.S. society and the impact that people from increasingly diverse backgrounds from all over the world are having on its present status and future direction. Therefore, the concept of cultural literacy is reframed here as global literacy.

Global literacy implies an understanding of the contemporary world and how it has evolved over time. It encompasses important knowledge of cultural variations in areas such as geography, history, literature, politics, economics, and principles of government. Global literacy is the core body of knowledge that an individual gains over a lifetime about the world in which he or she lives. The driving force behind the development of global literacy is the commitment one makes to ensure that openness to cultural diversity is the cornerstone of his or her life. Although multicultural competency is the goal for professional counseling practice, global literacy is the goal for a life lived in a culturally competent manner. It logically follows, therefore, that one cannot be a culturally competent counselor if one is not a globally literate person.

Importance of Global Literacy to Culturally Competent Counseling

In early 2011 the people of Egypt sparked a revolution that ultimately led to the end of the 30-year regime of President Hosni Mubarak. The Egyptian people's brave strike for an end to tyranny and call for human rights and democracy resonated throughout the world. In the United States scores of Egyptian Americans, many with strong family ties back in Egypt, became caught up in the euphoria of the possibility of significant change in their country of origin. Along with this euphoria, however, came a great deal of stress, as many Egyptian Americans worried about the fate of relatives caught up in the struggle back home. Imagine, therefore, an Egyptian American client coming into a counseling session and saying to a counselor, "I really can't focus on my issues with career indecision today; I am too anxious thinking about my grandmother in Cairo." Continue to imagine this as the counselor's response: "What issue is your grandmother dealing with?" Finally, imagine the client standing up and shouting, "What is she dealing with? Where have you been for the last 2 weeks? Egypt is falling apart and you ask what issue my grandmother is facing?"

Despite any progress that might have been made to this point, it can be speculated that the working alliance between this counselor and client could be in serious jeopardy given the counselor's lack of awareness about the current situation in Egypt. This counselor may have wonderful counseling skills, he or she may even be knowledgeable about the multicultural counseling literature, but because this counselor has obviously not watched television news or read a newspaper, he or she has placed this counseling relationship in jeopardy.

Although one could argue that it would seem impossible for the counselor in this case to have been completely oblivious of the events happening in Egypt, the point remains that the success of counseling cannot be predicated on cultural competency and globally illiteracy, as the two are mutually exclusive. If a counselor expects to be effective with a client from a different culture yet ignorant of the historical and contemporary context that shapes that client's worldview, he or she is entering into a counseling relationship that is bound to fail.

Becoming a Globally Literate Person

The development of global literacy is a lifelong process that is rooted in a commitment to living one's life in a manner that makes cultural diversity a core principle. A globally literate person exhibits ongoing cultural curiosity that is characterized by openness to engaging in new cultural experiences whenever possible. He or she embraces and celebrates cultural difference as opposed to fearing the fundamental distinctions in worldviews that underlie human diversity. A globally literate individual approaches diverse lifestyles from a position that transcends tolerance and promotes mutual respect and understanding. Embracing a globally literate lifestyle also involves a commitment to social justice and social responsibility.

Although there are many ways to develop global literacy, the following are concrete action strategies for promoting an awareness of the world that transcends one's own cultural boundaries:

- *Experience cultural diversity firsthand.* There is a limit to how much can actually be learned about people who are culturally different from oneself from textbooks, classes, and workshops. The best way to learn about culturally diversity is to experience it firsthand. Therefore, attending and participating in diverse cultural activities or traveling (both domestically and internationally) on an ongoing basis becomes critical to gaining the knowledge that reflects global literacy.
- *Experience diverse cultural aesthetic traditions.* When planning a night at the movies or theater, one should consider attending a film or play that depicts the realities of a cultural group with which one is not familiar. Similarly, when looking for books to read one should consider works from culturally diverse literary traditions. Likewise,

one should frequent art galleries and concerts that showcase diverse graphic and musical styles and traditions.

- *Stay abreast of current events.* In a world of 24/7 news, there is no excuse for not knowing what is going on in the world. A major aspect of global literacy is having a working knowledge of current world events. It is important, therefore, to read at least one newspaper (either in print or online) on a daily basis. In addition to news headlines, a globally literate person also reads editorials and opinion articles in order to better assess the news in a critical fashion. In addition to daily newspapers, reading weekly news magazines (e.g., *Time* or *Newsweek*) should enhance one's knowledge of current events. Knowledge of world events should also be gained through watching television news programs, watching news webcasts, or following informational social networks or blogs on a consistent basis. In addition to the so-called mainstream media, globally literate individuals also make an attempt to read newspapers and periodicals as well as view programming and Web-based news from diverse cultural groups to gain different perspectives on local, national, and world events.

Conclusion

The questions that begin this chapter, although seemingly trivial, underscore the true nature of the process by which one develops multicultural counseling competency. Successfully completing a multicultural counseling class, attending a diversity workshop, or reading this book are not endpoints in one's development as a culturally competent counselor. Indeed, although these are important aspects of ongoing professional development, they should be seen as small components of a lifelong personal journey. It has been suggested that being a professional counselor is a way of life (Gladding, 2008). If this is true, then one's life should be lived in a manner that reflects a commitment to continually expanding one's cultural comfort zone to include knowledge of and active interaction with people from diverse cultural backgrounds. It also means that one is constantly aware of how events, both past and current, impact on people's well-being. Global literacy, therefore, cannot be learned in a classroom; rather, it is the result of one's attempt to become a lifelong student of cultural diversity and a true citizen of the world.

References

Gladding, S. T. (2008). *Counseling: A comprehensive profession* (6th ed.). Upper Saddle River, NJ: Prentice Hall.

Hirsch, E. D. (1987). *Cultural literacy: What every American needs to know.* Boston, MA: Houghton Mifflin.

Appendix 19.1 • Answers to the Trivia Questions in This Chapter

- **Who is August Wilson?**

  August Wilson was a Pulitzer Prize–winning African American playwright most noted for his 10-play collection known as the "Century Cycle," which portrays aspects of the African American experience in each decade of the 20th century. Shortly after his death in 2005 a Broadway theater was named in his honor.

- **What happened at the Stonewall Inn in New York City on June 28, 1969?**

  On Friday June 28, 1969, a raid by New York City police took place at the Stonewall Inn, a homosexual social gathering spot in Greenwich Village. This raid sparked a series of violent demonstrations against the ongoing persecution of sexual minorities by police. These demonstrations, which took place during the weekend of June 28–30, 1969, are widely considered to be the start of the gay rights movement in the United States.

- **What is Public Law 94-142?**

  Public Law 94-142, the Education for All Handicapped Children Act of 1975, is a federal law that requires states to provide public education for every child between the ages of 3 and 21 regardless of how seriously disabled he or she may be. Public Law 94-142 was the first law to clearly define the rights of disabled children to free appropriate public education. This law also ensures that students with disabilities are given nondiscriminatory tests that take into consideration their native language and the effects of their disability and that due process procedures are in place to protect parents and students.

- **What is *Sábado Gigante*?**

  Sábado Gigante ("Giant Saturday") is the longest running television variety show in the world. This eclectic Spanish-language show includes contests, human interest stories, and live entertainment. It is hosted by Chilean television star Don Francisco.

- **What is a burka?**

  A burka is an outer garment worn in public places by women in some Islamic traditions to cover their bodies. It consists of a loose body covering, a head covering, and a face veil.

- **Who is Jim Thorpe?**

  Jim Thorpe was an American Indian from the Sac and Fox nation in Oklahoma. He was one the greatest athletes in American history. He won Olympic gold medals in 1912 for the pentathlon and decathlon. He also played both collegiate and professional football as well as professional baseball and basketball. He lost his Olympic medals after it was discovered that he had been paid for playing two seasons of semi-professional baseball before competing in the Olympics. In 1983, 30 years after his death, the International Olympic Committee restored his Olympic medals.

- **Who is Jaime Escalante?**

  Jaime Escalante was a Bolivian American educator well known for teaching students calculus from 1974 to 1991 at a high school in East Los Angeles. Instead of gearing classes to poorly performing students, Escalante offered advanced placement calculus and set high standards. In 1982, 18 of his students passed the Advanced Placement calculus exam. The Educational Testing Service found these scores to be suspicious, because all of the students made exactly the same math error. Those students who were allowed to retake the test subsequently passed. In 1983, the number of Escalante's students taking and passing the Advanced Placement calculus test more than doubled. Escalante's story was told in the movie *Stand and Deliver*.

  (Continued)

Appendix 19.1 • Answers to the Trivia Questions in This Chapter
(Continued)

- **What is the major theme of the play *Angels in America?***
  Angels in America: A Gay Fantasia on National Themes was written by playwright Tony Kushner and won the Pulitzer Prize in 1991. Its major theme revolves around issues of homosexuality in the era of AIDS.

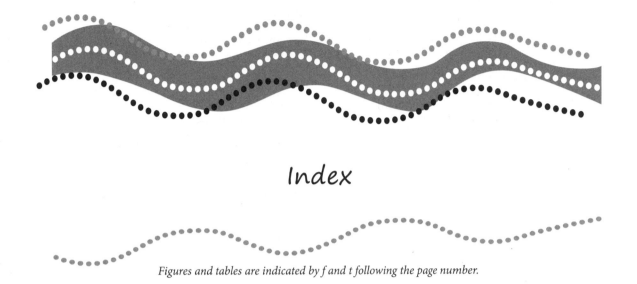

Index

Figures and tables are indicated by f and t following the page number.

D

(Continued)

M

(Continued)